SPICE & WOLF

Lawrence

A clever young merchant. Traveling in search of Holo's homeland of Yoitsu.

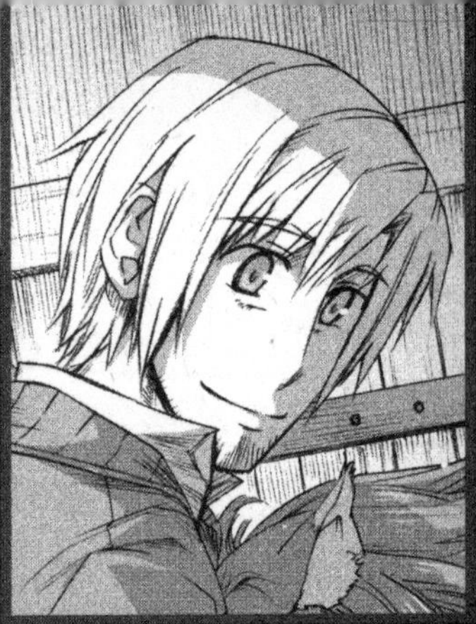

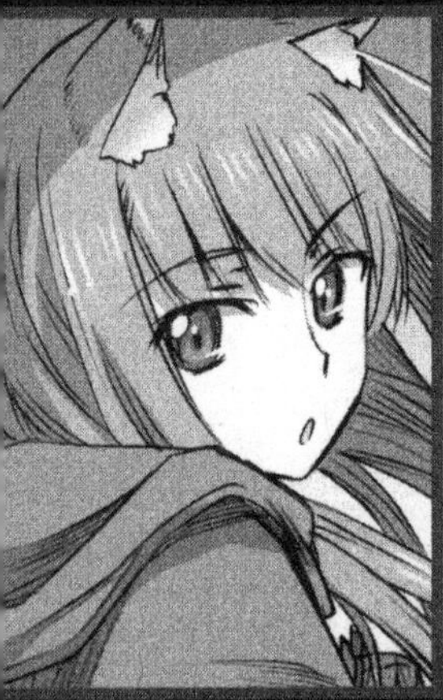

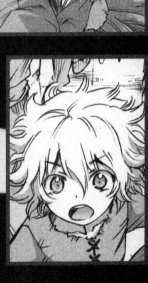

Holo

Lawrence's traveling companion, a beautiful girl. Her true form is that of the wolf-god of the harvest.

Col

A boy saved by Lawrence at the river checkpoint. A naive but clever lad.

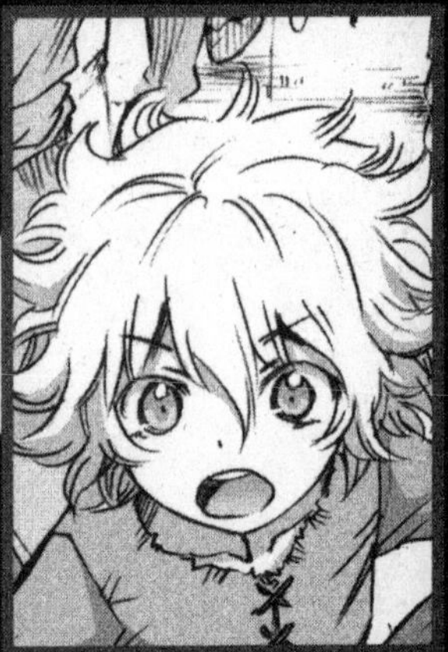

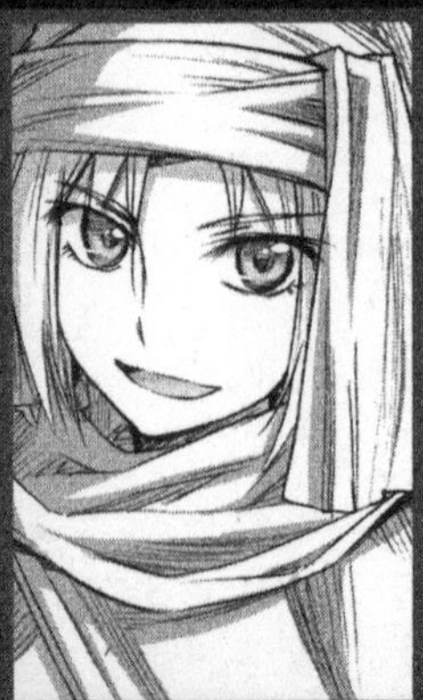

Eve

A mysterious merchant woman. Normally hides her face and dresses like a man.

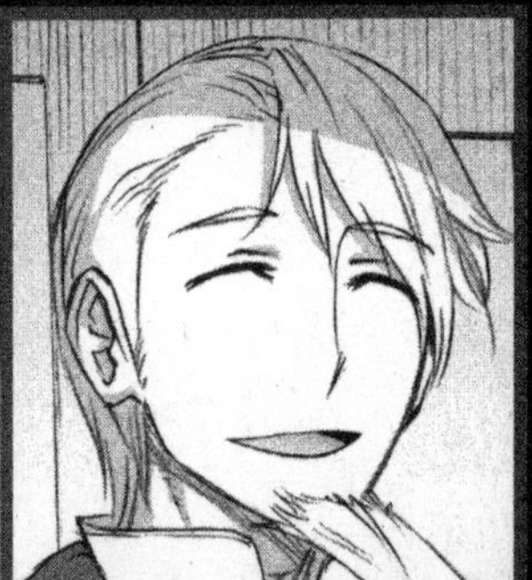

Kieman

The Kerube branch chief of the trade guild that counts Lawrence as one of its members. A cool-headed, canny businessman.

Introduction

In search of the forest of Yoitsu, Holo's homeland, Lawrence and Holo continue their travels. Avoiding an unstable situation in the town of Lenos, they proceed downriver toward the port town of Kerube. Along the way, they hear from a boatman about a forbidden book that tells of how to strip-mine a mountain bare. Lawrence and Holo decide to seek out the text to protect Yoitsu. Setting out to gather information in Kerube, Lawrence is approached by a certain merchant at the inn, and......?

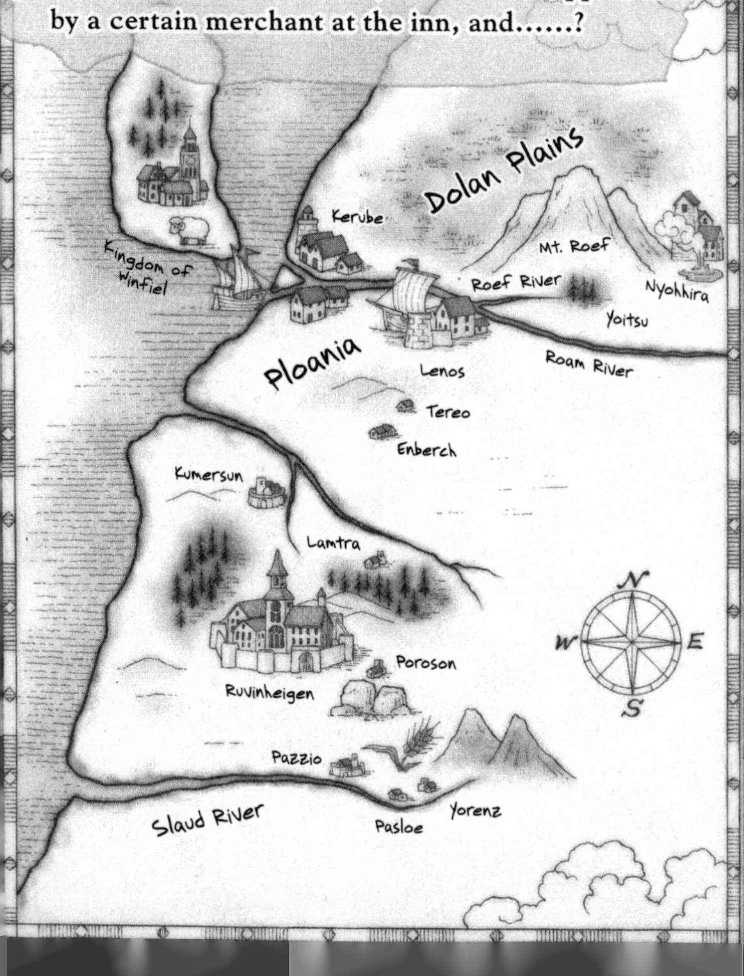

Dolan Plains
Kerube
Kingdom of Winfiel
Mt. Roef
Roef River
Nyohhira
Yoitsu
Roam River
Ploania
Lenos
Tereo
Enberch
Kumersun
Lamtra
N
W
E
S
Poroson
Ruvinheigen
Pazzio
Slaud River
Yorenz
Pasloe

SPICE&WOLF
CONTENTS

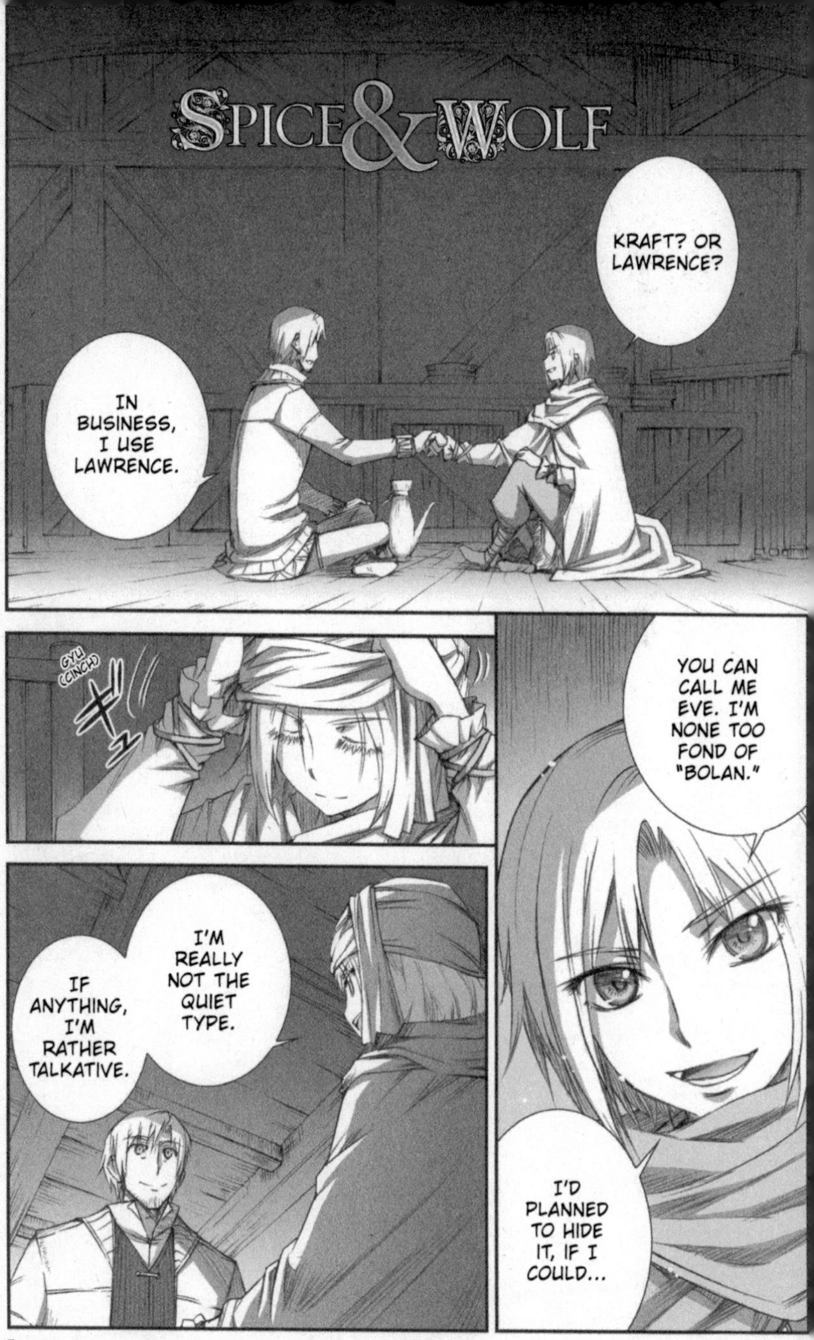
SPICE & WOLF
KRAFT? OR LAWRENCE?
IN BUSINESS, I USE LAWRENCE.
YOU CAN CALL ME EVE. I'M NONE TOO FOND OF "BOLAN."
I'D PLANNED TO HIDE IT, IF I COULD...
GYU (CINCH)
I'M REALLY NOT THE QUIET TYPE.
IF ANYTHING, I'M RATHER TALKATIVE.

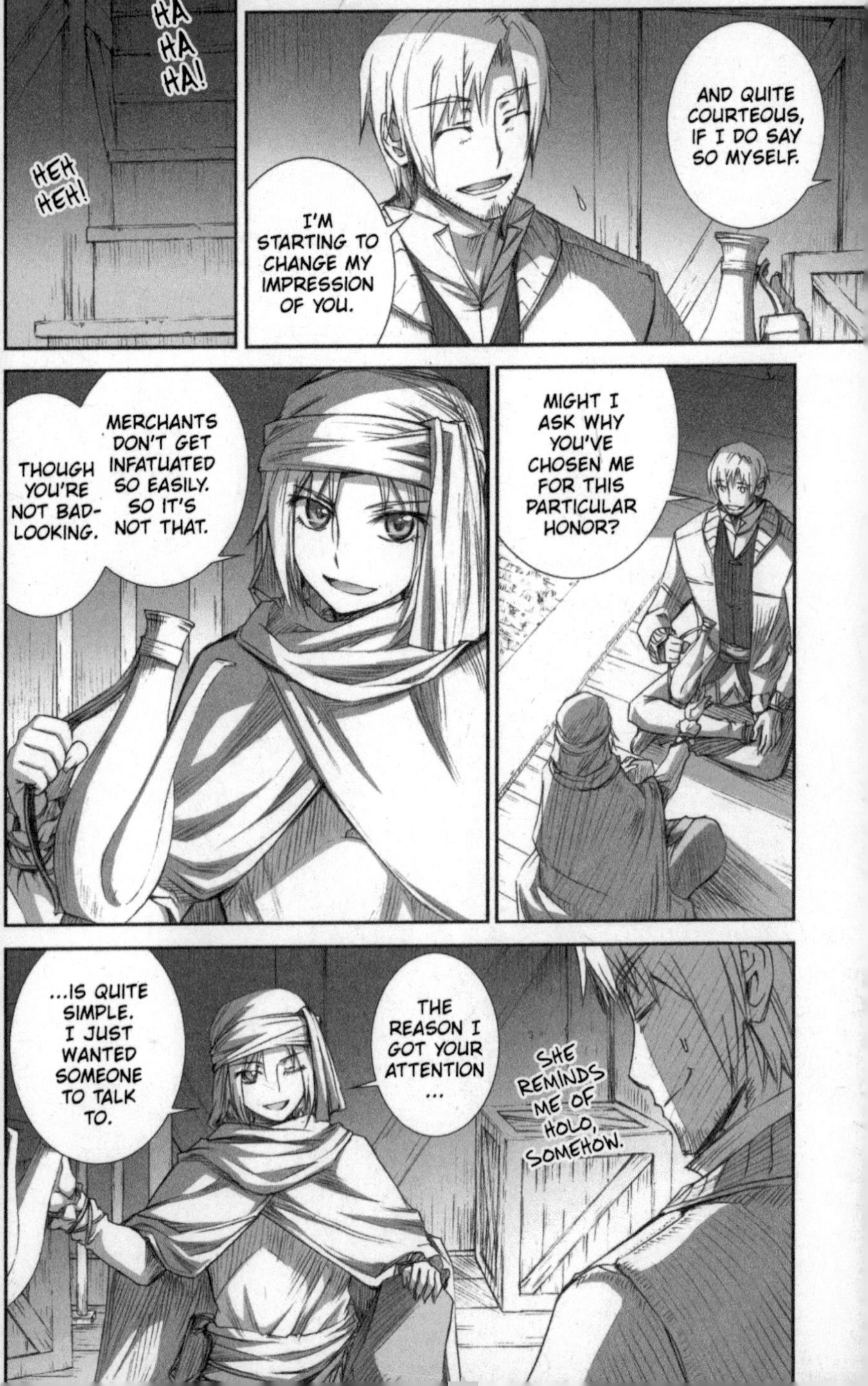
AND QUITE COURTEOUS, IF I DO SAY SO MYSELF.
I'M STARTING TO CHANGE MY IMPRESSION OF YOU.
HA HA HA!
HEH HEH!
MIGHT I ASK WHY YOU'VE CHOSEN ME FOR THIS PARTICULAR HONOR?
MERCHANTS DON'T GET INFATUATED SO EASILY. SO IT'S NOT THAT.
THOUGH YOU'RE NOT BAD-LOOKING.
SHE REMINDS ME OF HOLO, SOMEHOW.
THE REASON I GOT YOUR ATTENTION...
...IS QUITE SIMPLE. I JUST WANTED SOMEONE TO TALK TO.

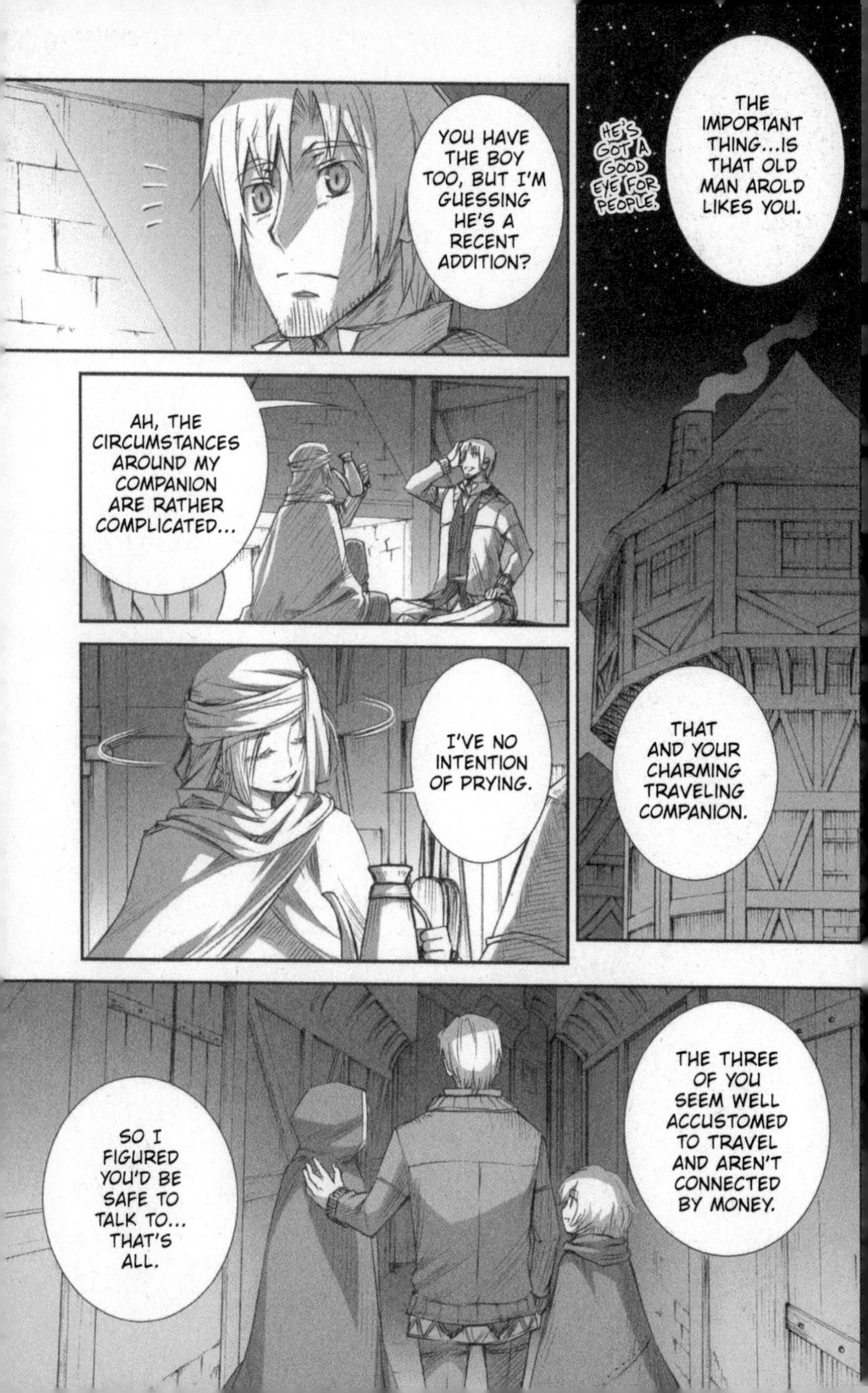
THE IMPORTANT THING...IS THAT OLD MAN AROLD LIKES YOU.
HE'S GOT A GOOD EYE FOR PEOPLE.
THAT AND YOUR CHARMING TRAVELING COMPANION.
YOU HAVE THE BOY TOO, BUT I'M GUESSING HE'S A RECENT ADDITION?
AH, THE CIRCUMSTANCES AROUND MY COMPANION ARE RATHER COMPLICATED...
I'VE NO INTENTION OF PRYING.
THE THREE OF YOU SEEM WELL ACCUSTOMED TO TRAVEL AND AREN'T CONNECTED BY MONEY.
SO I FIGURED YOU'D BE SAFE TO TALK TO... THAT'S ALL.

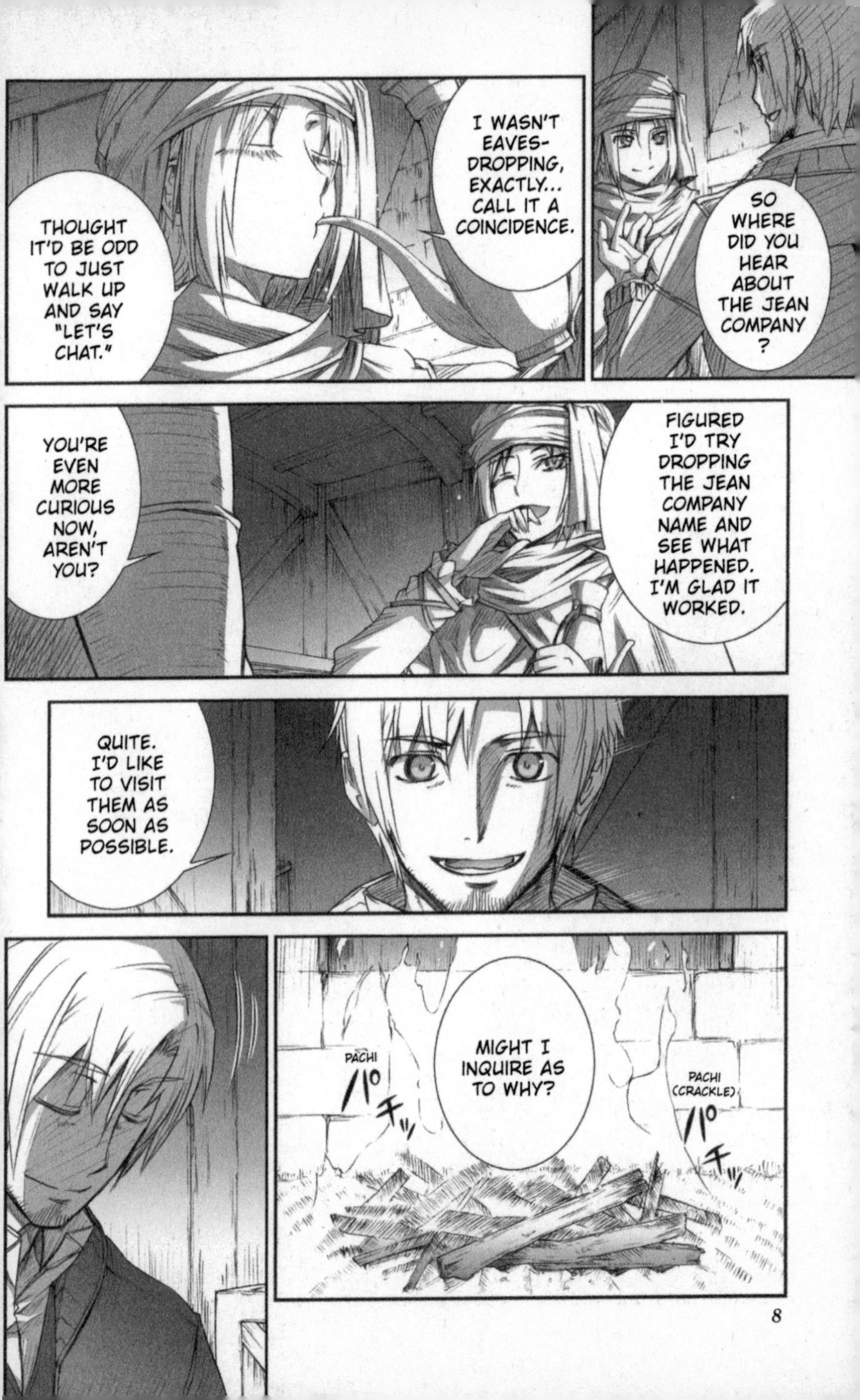
SO WHERE DID YOU HEAR ABOUT THE JEAN COMPANY?
I WASN'T EAVES-DROPPING, EXACTLY... CALL IT A COINCIDENCE.
THOUGHT IT'D BE ODD TO JUST WALK UP AND SAY "LET'S CHAT."
FIGURED I'D TRY DROPPING THE JEAN COMPANY NAME AND SEE WHAT HAPPENED. I'M GLAD IT WORKED.
YOU'RE EVEN MORE CURIOUS NOW, AREN'T YOU?
QUITE. I'D LIKE TO VISIT THEM AS SOON AS POSSIBLE.
PACHI (CRACKLE)
パチッ
MIGHT I INQUIRE AS TO WHY?
PACHI
パチッ

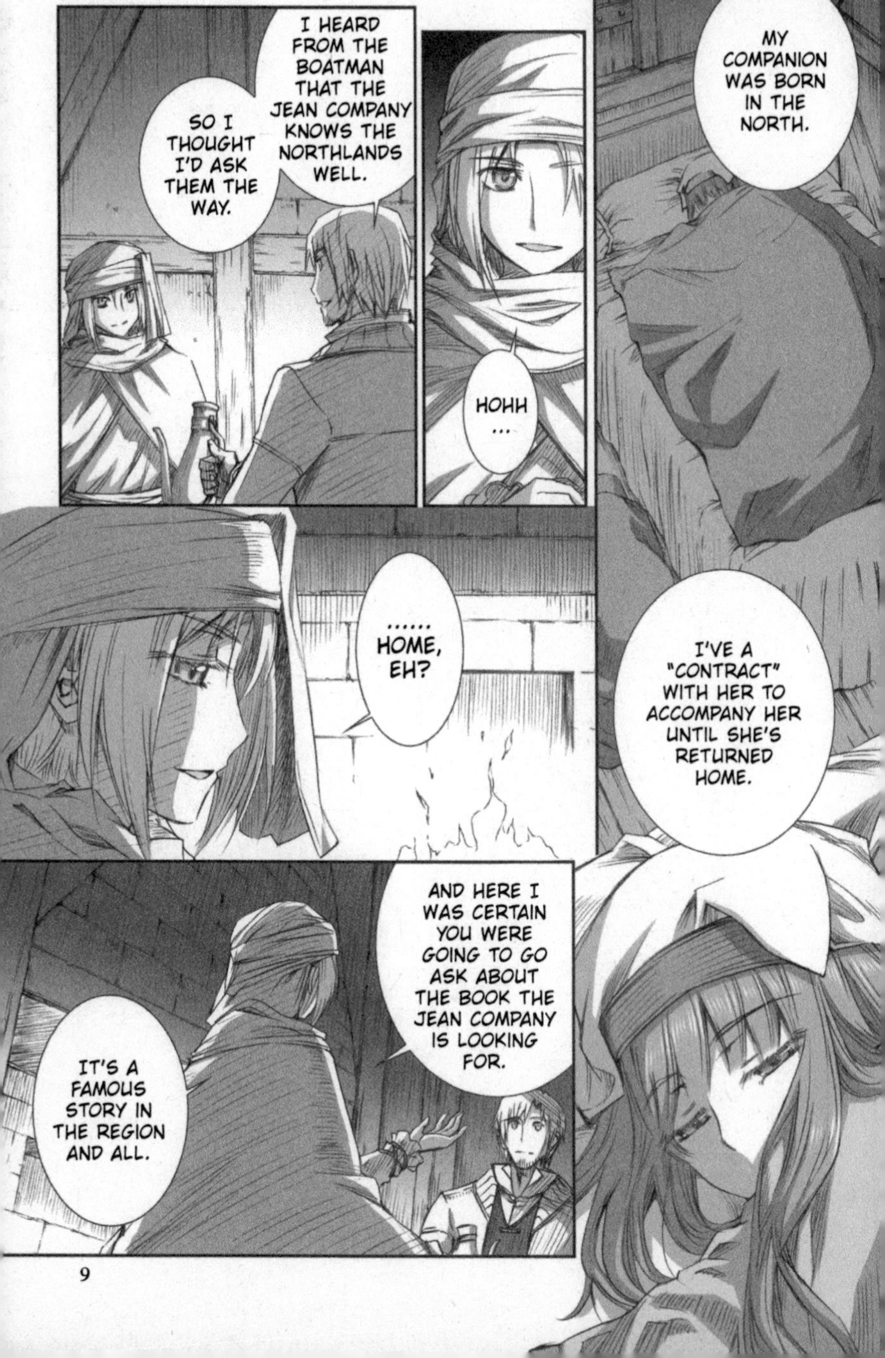
MY COMPANION WAS BORN IN THE NORTH.
HOHH ...
I HEARD FROM THE BOATMAN THAT THE JEAN COMPANY KNOWS THE NORTHLANDS WELL.
SO I THOUGHT I'D ASK THEM THE WAY.
I'VE A "CONTRACT" WITH HER TO ACCOMPANY HER UNTIL SHE'S RETURNED HOME.
...... HOME, EH?
AND HERE I WAS CERTAIN YOU WERE GOING TO GO ASK ABOUT THE BOOK THE JEAN COMPANY IS LOOKING FOR.
IT'S A FAMOUS STORY IN THE REGION AND ALL.

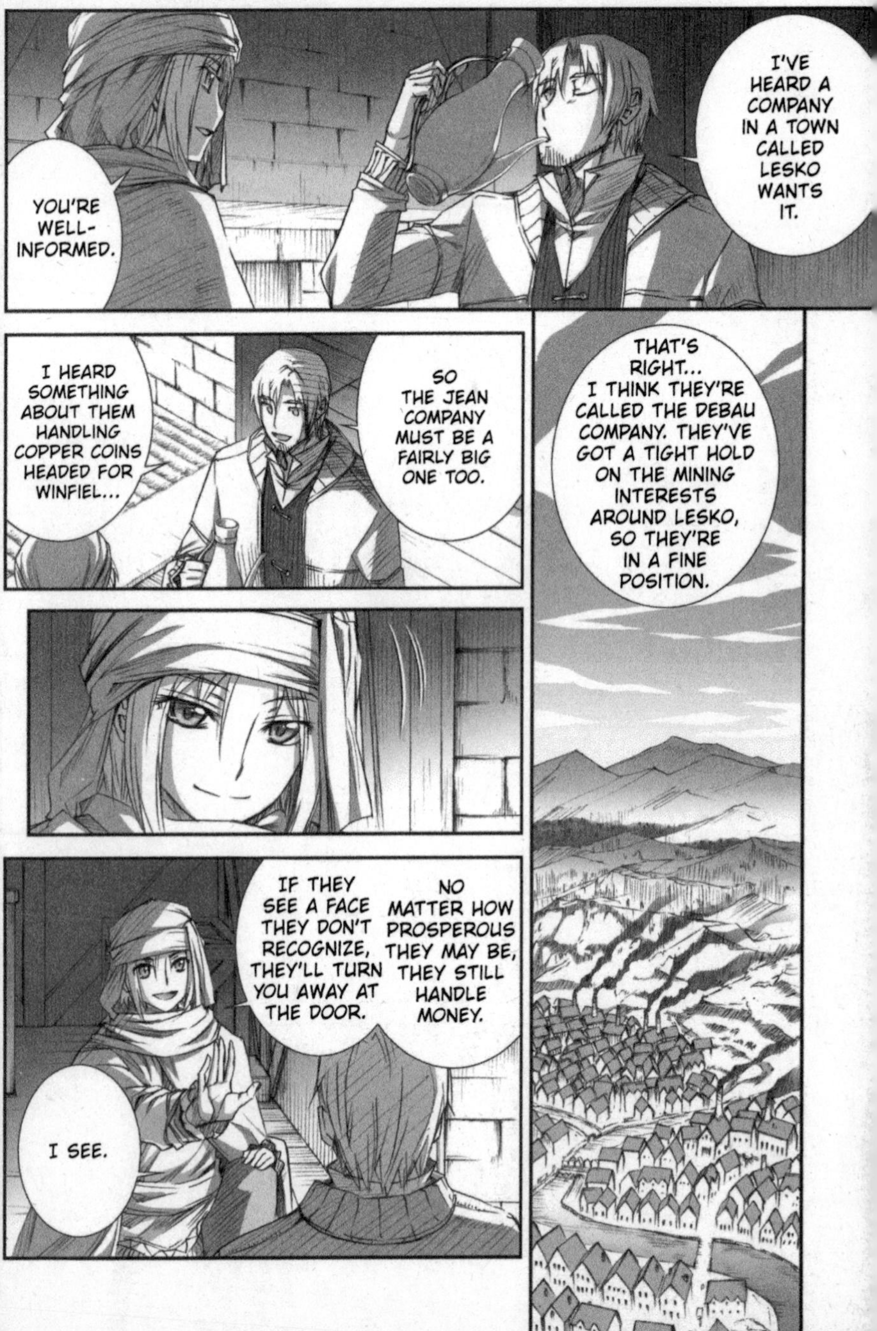
I'VE HEARD A COMPANY IN A TOWN CALLED LESKO WANTS IT.
YOU'RE WELL-INFORMED.
THAT'S RIGHT... I THINK THEY'RE CALLED THE DEBAU COMPANY. THEY'VE GOT A TIGHT HOLD ON THE MINING INTERESTS AROUND LESKO, SO THEY'RE IN A FINE POSITION.
SO THE JEAN COMPANY MUST BE A FAIRLY BIG ONE TOO.
I HEARD SOMETHING ABOUT THEM HANDLING COPPER COINS HEADED FOR WINFIEL...
NO MATTER HOW PROSPEROUS THEY MAY BE, THEY STILL HANDLE MONEY.
IF THEY SEE A FACE THEY DON'T RECOGNIZE, THEY'LL TURN YOU AWAY AT THE DOOR.
I SEE.

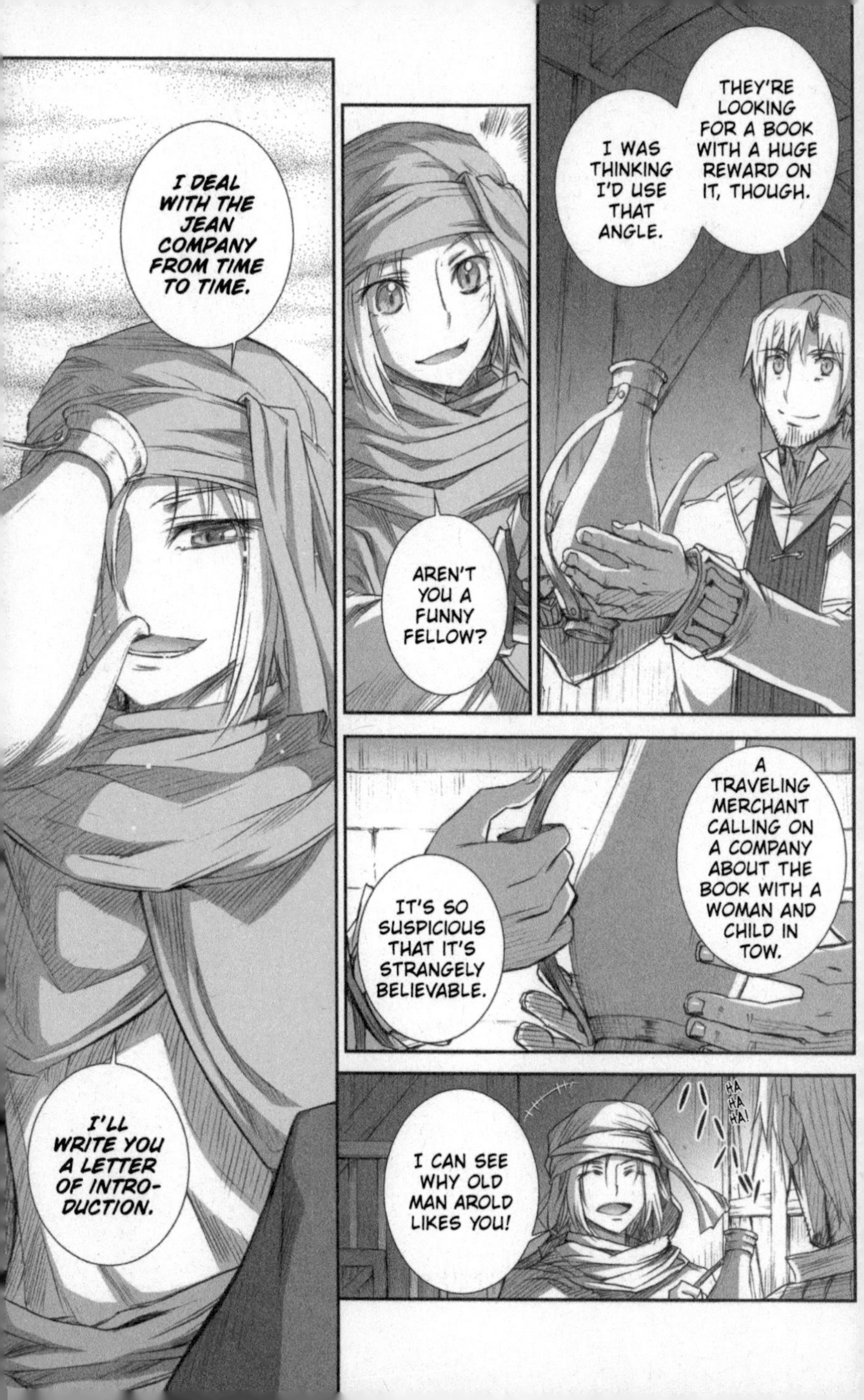
THEY'RE LOOKING FOR A BOOK WITH A HUGE REWARD ON IT, THOUGH.
I WAS THINKING I'D USE THAT ANGLE.
AREN'T YOU A FUNNY FELLOW?
A TRAVELING MERCHANT CALLING ON A COMPANY ABOUT THE BOOK WITH A WOMAN AND CHILD IN TOW.
IT'S SO SUSPICIOUS THAT IT'S STRANGELY BELIEVABLE.
HA HA HA!
I CAN SEE WHY OLD MAN AROLD LIKES YOU!
I DEAL WITH THE JEAN COMPANY FROM TIME TO TIME.
I'LL WRITE YOU A LETTER OF INTRO-DUCTION.

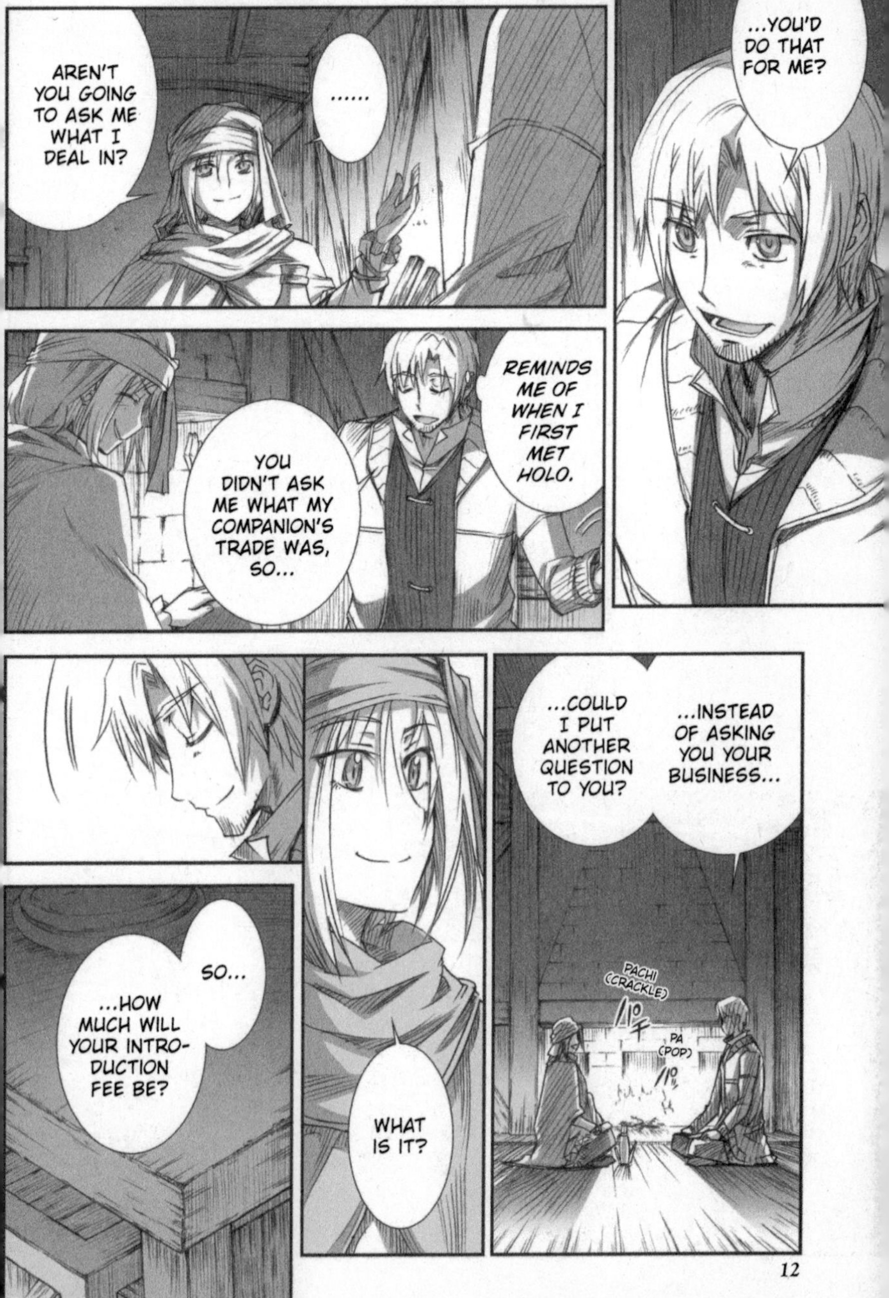
...YOU'D DO THAT FOR ME?
......
AREN'T YOU GOING TO ASK ME WHAT I DEAL IN?
REMINDS ME OF WHEN I FIRST MET HOLO.
YOU DIDN'T ASK ME WHAT MY COMPANION'S TRADE WAS, SO...
...INSTEAD OF ASKING YOU YOUR BUSINESS...
...COULD I PUT ANOTHER QUESTION TO YOU?
PACHI (CRACKLE)
PA (POP)
WHAT IS IT?
SO...
...HOW MUCH WILL YOUR INTRO-DUCTION FEE BE?

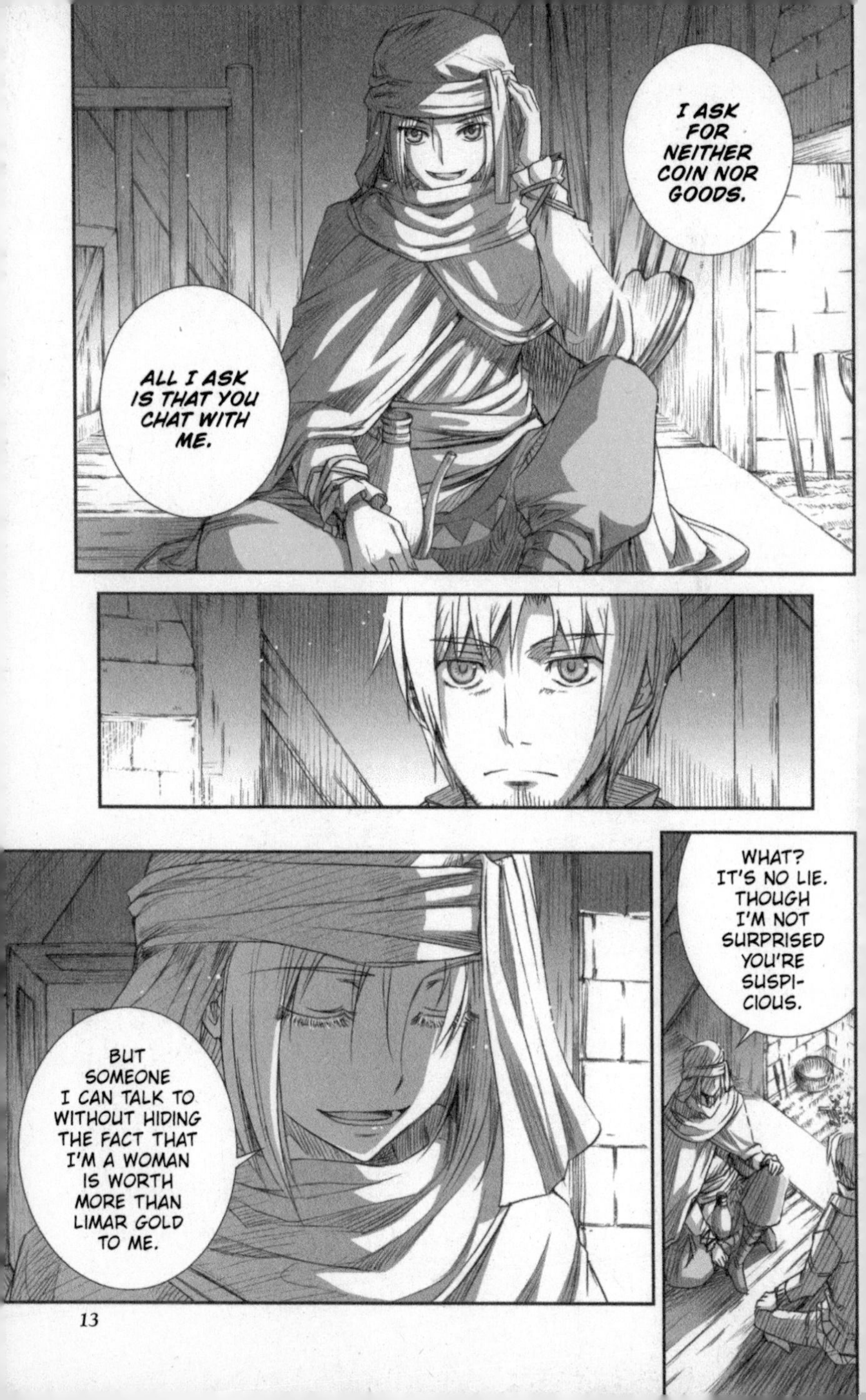
I ASK FOR NEITHER COIN NOR GOODS.
ALL I ASK IS THAT YOU CHAT WITH ME.
WHAT? IT'S NO LIE. THOUGH I'M NOT SURPRISED YOU'RE SUSPI-CIOUS.
BUT SOMEONE I CAN TALK TO WITHOUT HIDING THE FACT THAT I'M A WOMAN IS WORTH MORE THAN LIMAR GOLD TO ME.

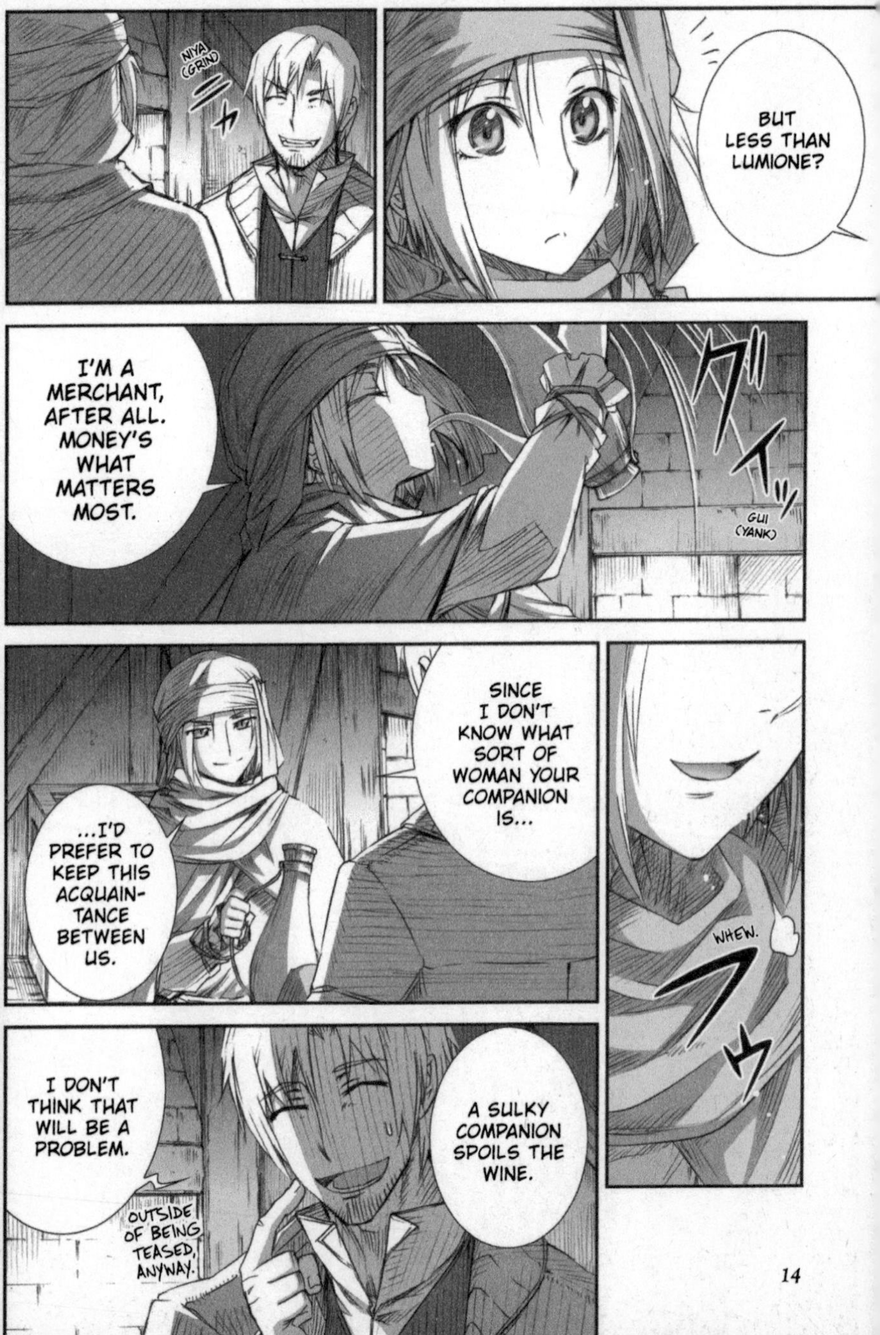
BUT LESS THAN LUMIONE?
NIYA (GRIN)
I'M A MERCHANT, AFTER ALL. MONEY'S WHAT MATTERS MOST.
GUI (YANK)
WHEW.
SINCE I DON'T KNOW WHAT SORT OF WOMAN YOUR COMPANION IS...
...I'D PREFER TO KEEP THIS ACQUAIN-TANCE BETWEEN US.
A SULKY COMPANION SPOILS THE WINE.
I DON'T THINK THAT WILL BE A PROBLEM.
OUTSIDE OF BEING TEASED, ANYWAY.

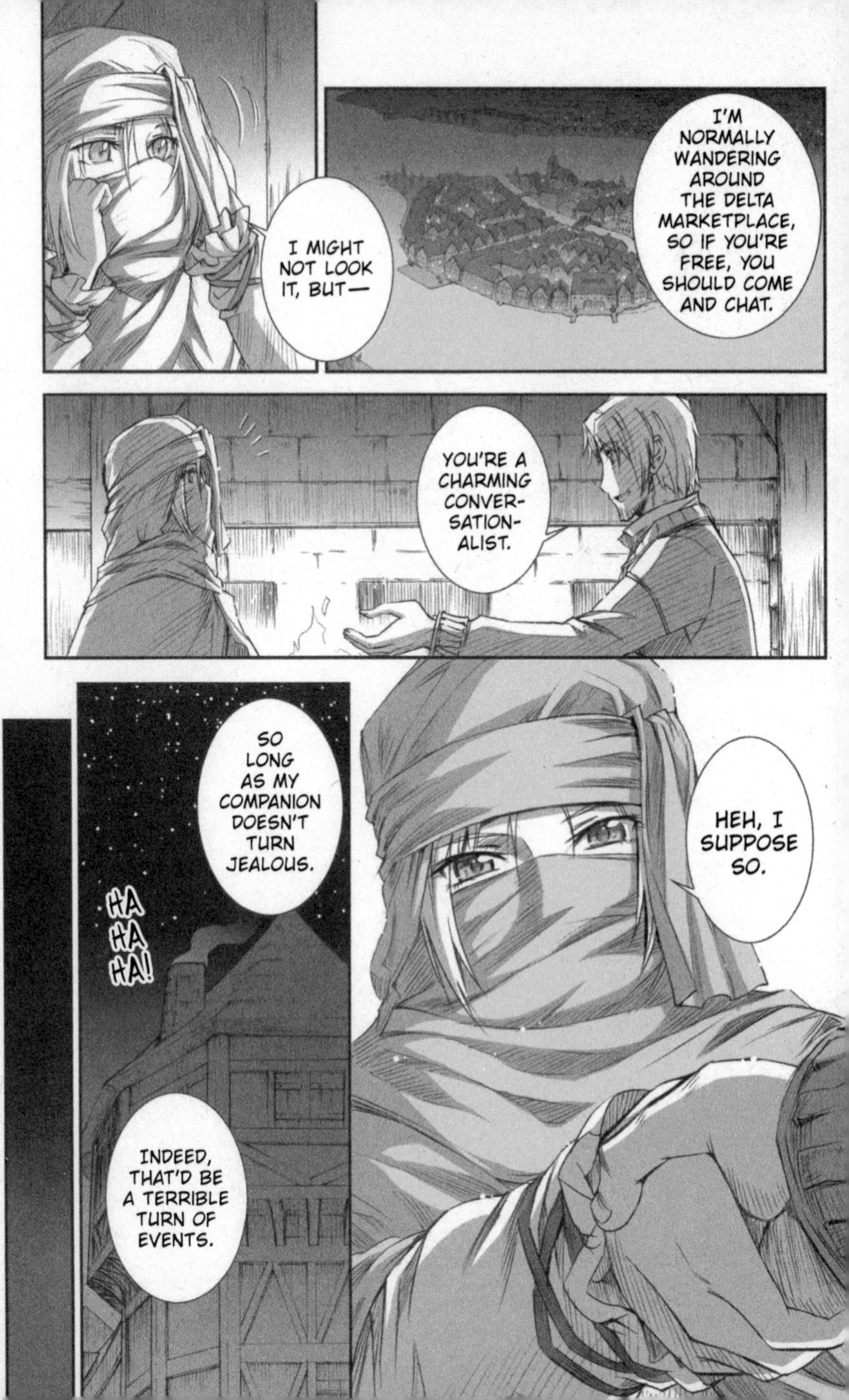
I'M NORMALLY WANDERING AROUND THE DELTA MARKETPLACE, SO IF YOU'RE FREE, YOU SHOULD COME AND CHAT.
I MIGHT NOT LOOK IT, BUT—
YOU'RE A CHARMING CONVER-SATION-ALIST.
HEH, I SUPPOSE SO.
SO LONG AS MY COMPANION DOESN'T TURN JEALOUS.
HA HA HA!
INDEED, THAT'D BE A TERRIBLE TURN OF EVENTS.

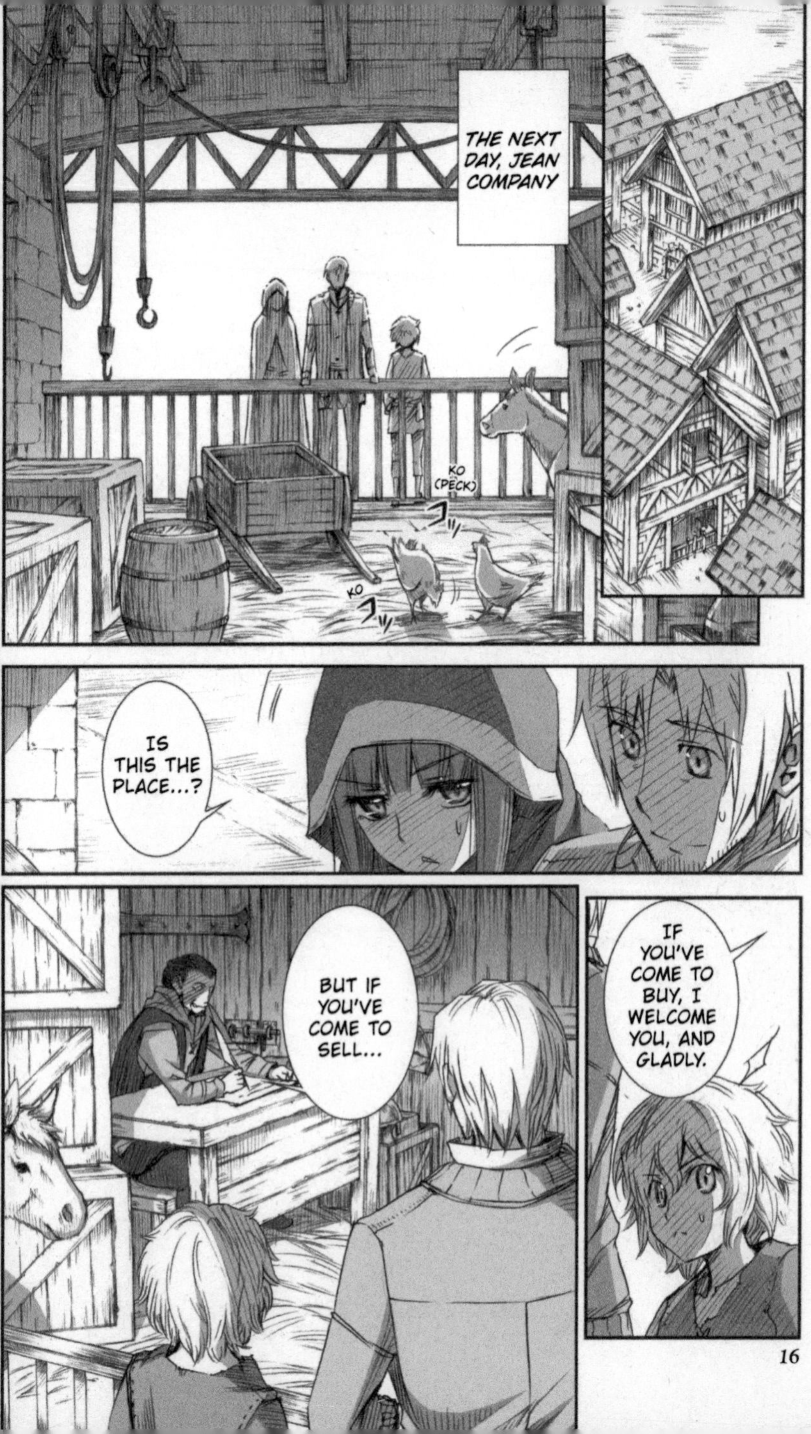
THE NEXT DAY, JEAN COMPANY
KO (PECK)
KO
IS THIS THE PLACE...?
IF YOU'VE COME TO BUY, I WELCOME YOU, AND GLADLY.
BUT IF YOU'VE COME TO SELL...

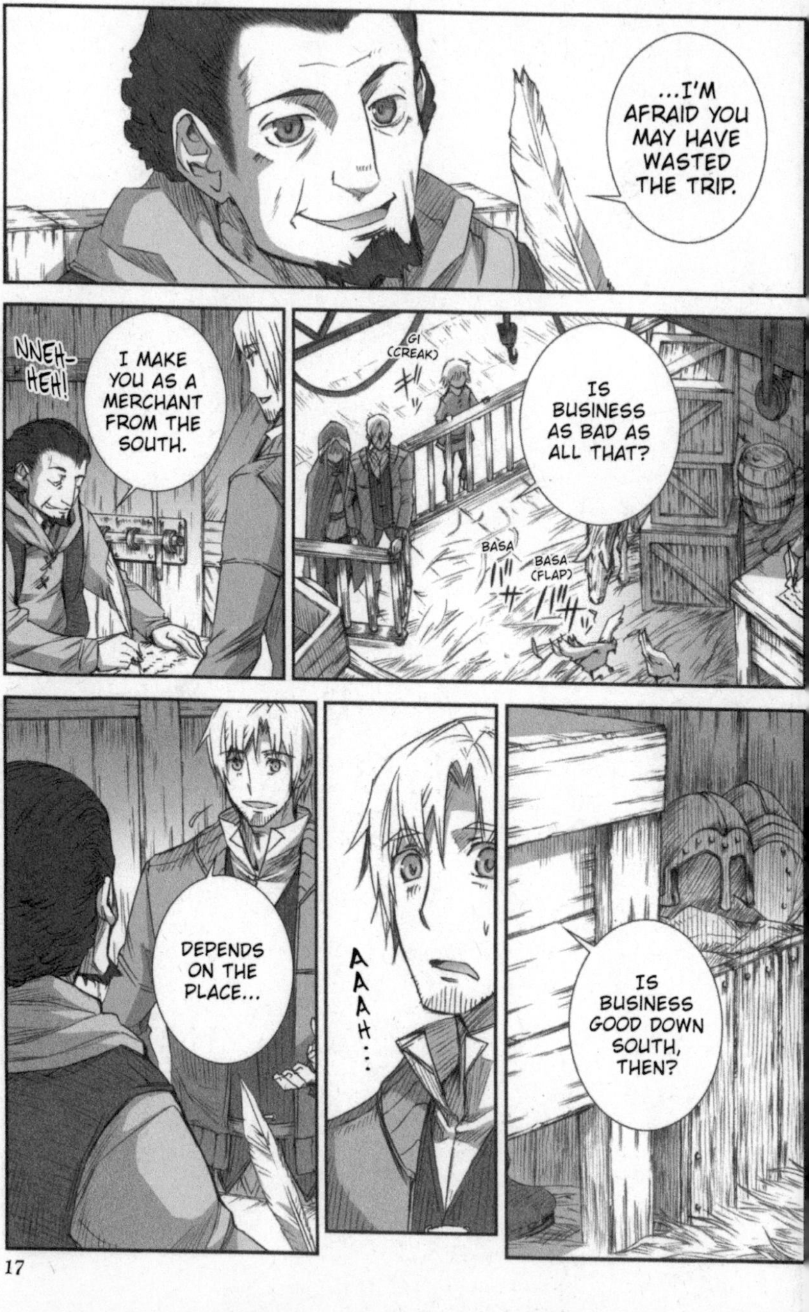

...I'M AFRAID YOU MAY HAVE WASTED THE TRIP.
GI (CREAK)
IS BUSINESS AS BAD AS ALL THAT?
BASA
BASA (FLAP)
I MAKE YOU AS A MERCHANT FROM THE SOUTH.
NNEH-HEH!
IS BUSINESS GOOD DOWN SOUTH, THEN?
AAAH...
DEPENDS ON THE PLACE...

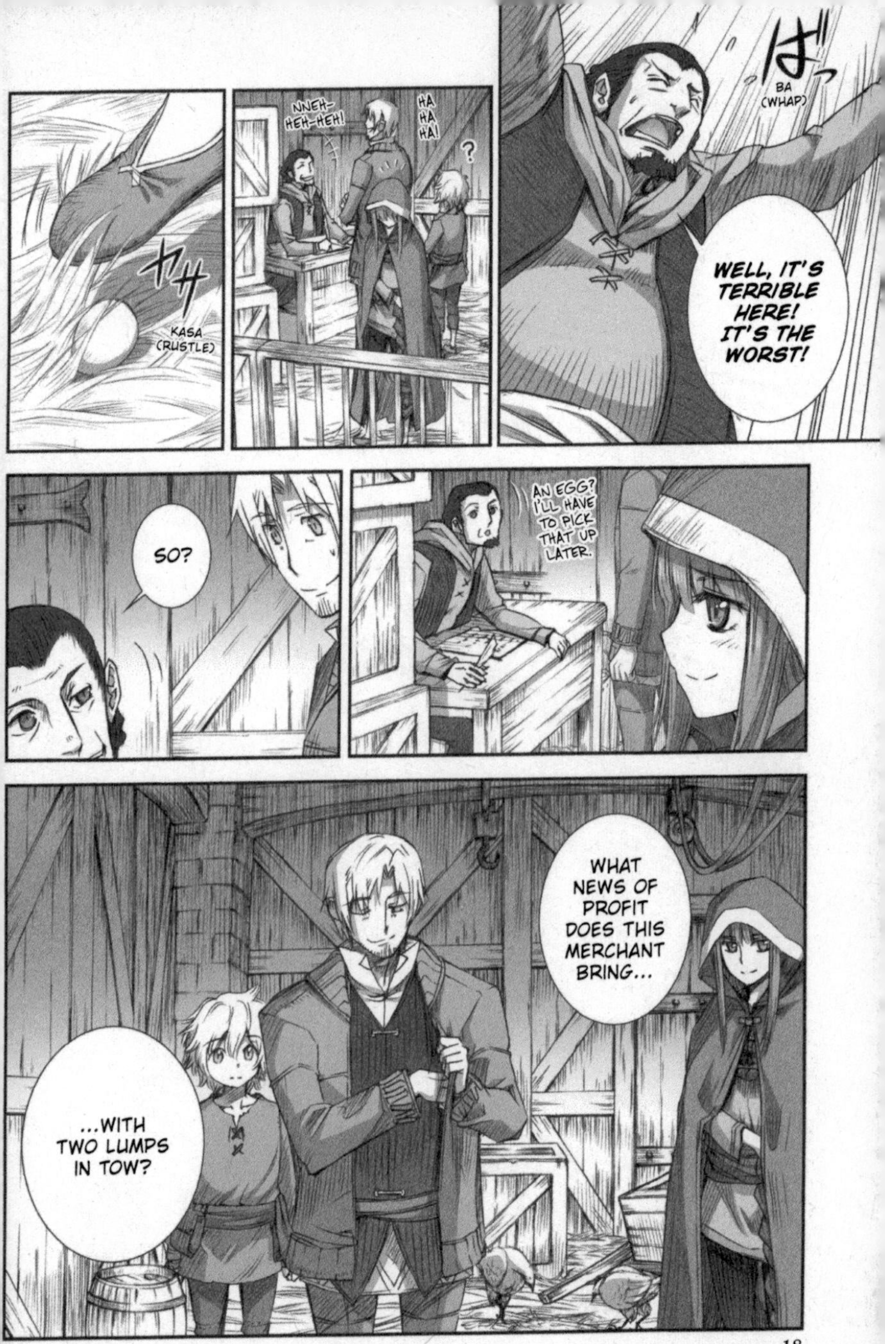
ばっ
BA (WHAP)
WELL, IT'S TERRIBLE HERE! IT'S THE WORST!
HA HA HA!
NNEH-HEH-HEH!
?
カサ
KASA (RUSTLE)
AN EGG? I'LL HAVE TO PICK THAT UP LATER.
SO?
WHAT NEWS OF PROFIT DOES THIS MERCHANT BRING...
...WITH TWO LUMPS IN TOW?

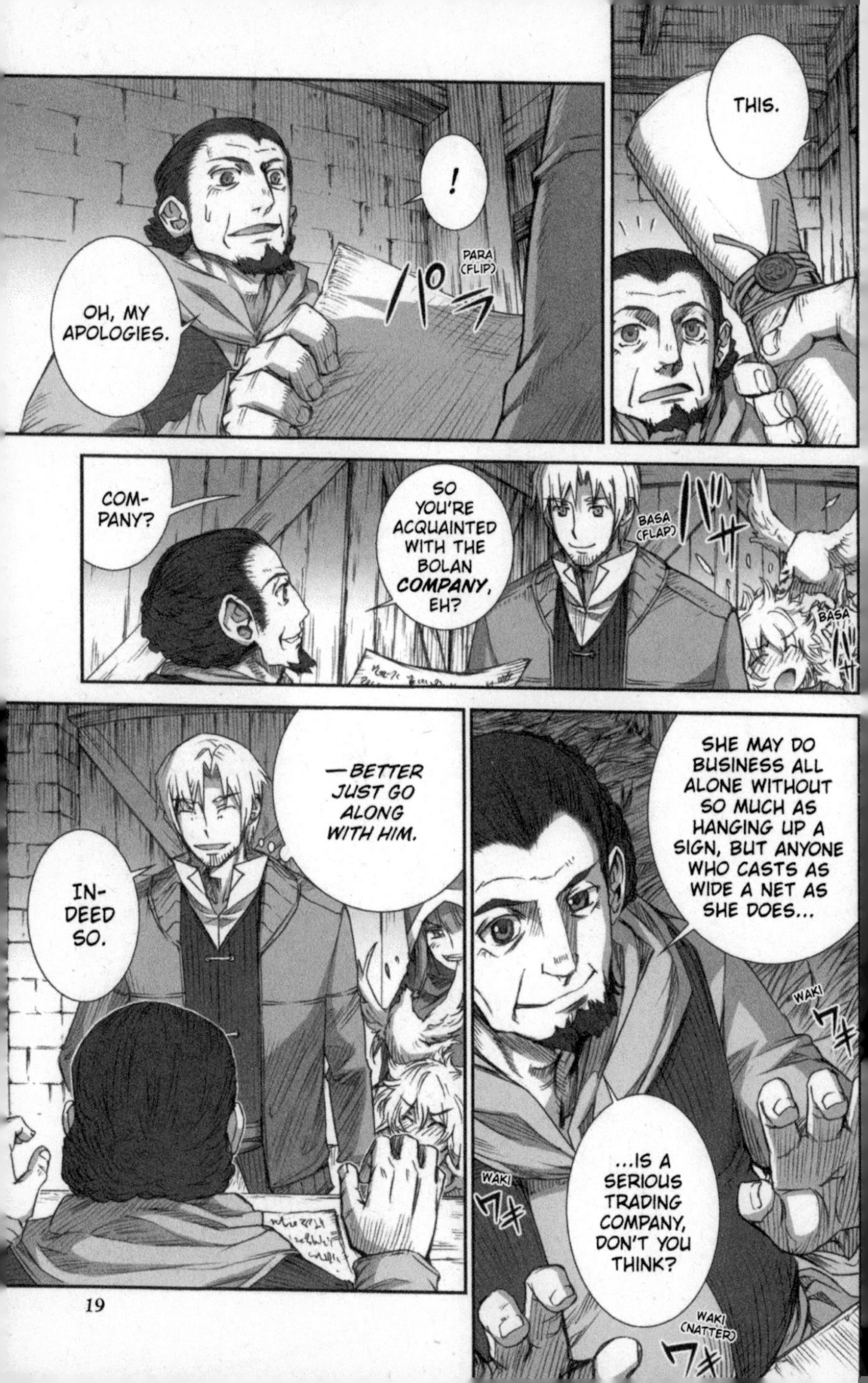
THIS.
!
PARA (FLIP)
OH, MY APOLOGIES.
BASA (FLAP)
BASA
SO YOU'RE ACQUAINTED WITH THE BOLAN COMPANY, EH?
COM-PANY?
SHE MAY DO BUSINESS ALL ALONE WITHOUT SO MUCH AS HANGING UP A SIGN, BUT ANYONE WHO CASTS AS WIDE A NET AS SHE DOES...
WAKI
...IS A SERIOUS TRADING COMPANY, DON'T YOU THINK?
WAKI
WAKI (NATTER)
—BETTER JUST GO ALONG WITH HIM.
IN-DEED SO.

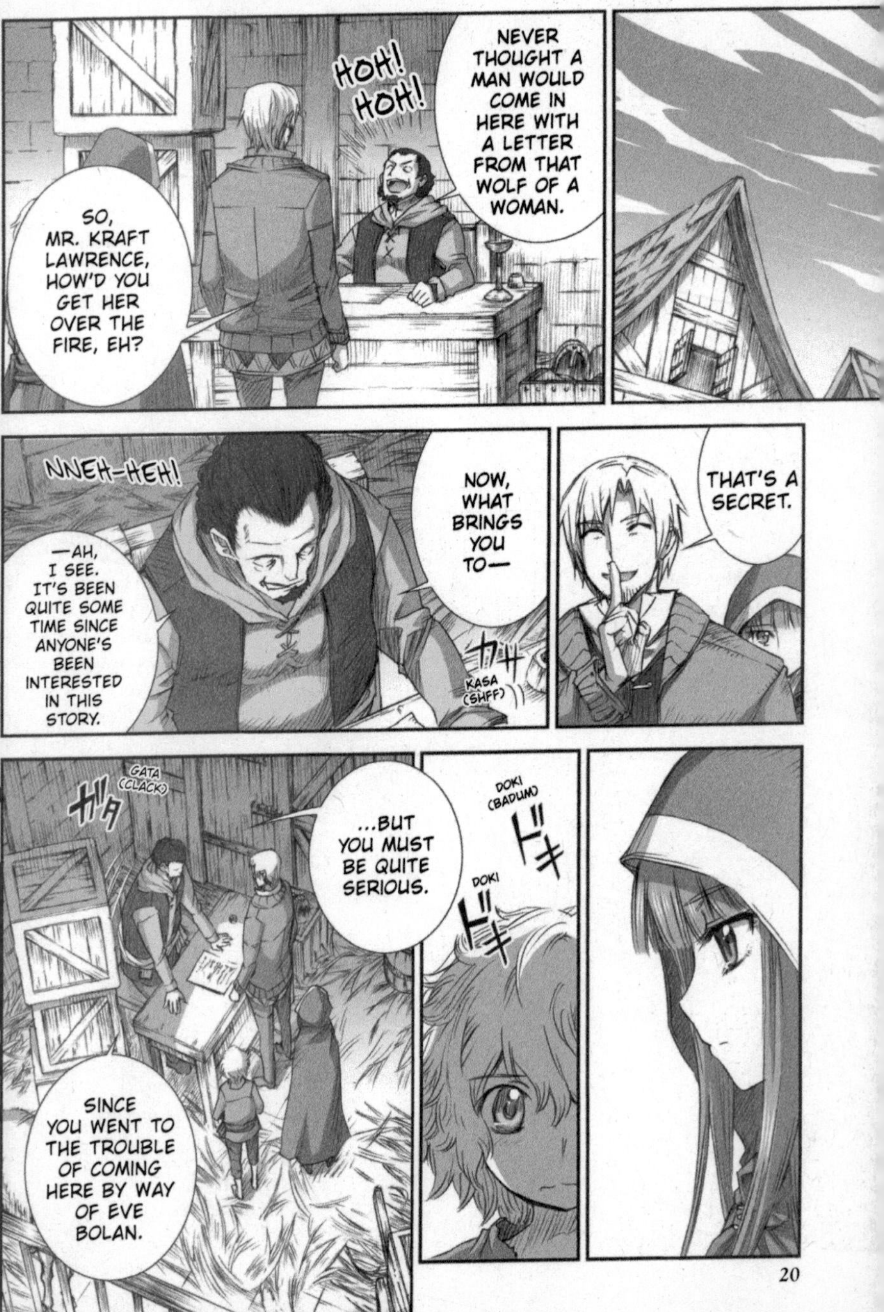
NEVER THOUGHT A MAN WOULD COME IN HERE WITH A LETTER FROM THAT WOLF OF A WOMAN.
HOH! HOH!
SO, MR. KRAFT LAWRENCE, HOW'D YOU GET HER OVER THE FIRE, EH?
THAT'S A SECRET.
NOW, WHAT BRINGS YOU TO—
NNEH-HEH!
—AH, I SEE. IT'S BEEN QUITE SOME TIME SINCE ANYONE'S BEEN INTERESTED IN THIS STORY.
ガサ
KASA (SHFF)
ドキ
DOKI (BADUM)
ドキ
DOKI
ガタ
GATA (CLACK)
...BUT YOU MUST BE QUITE SERIOUS.
SINCE YOU WENT TO THE TROUBLE OF COMING HERE BY WAY OF EVE BOLAN.

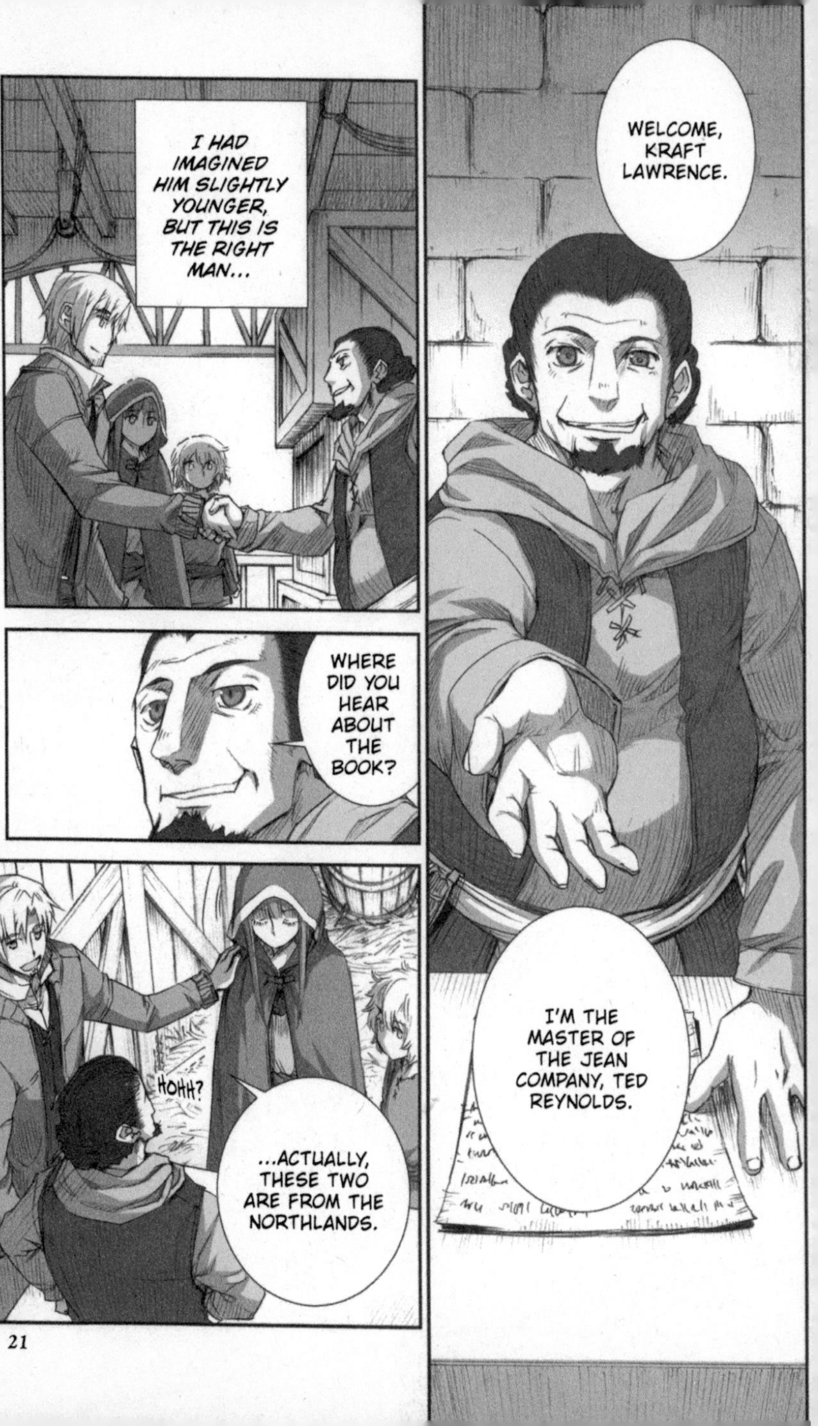
WELCOME, KRAFT LAWRENCE.
I'M THE MASTER OF THE JEAN COMPANY, TED REYNOLDS.
I HAD IMAGINED HIM SLIGHTLY YOUNGER, BUT THIS IS THE RIGHT MAN...
WHERE DID YOU HEAR ABOUT THE BOOK?
HOHH?
...ACTUALLY, THESE TWO ARE FROM THE NORTHLANDS.

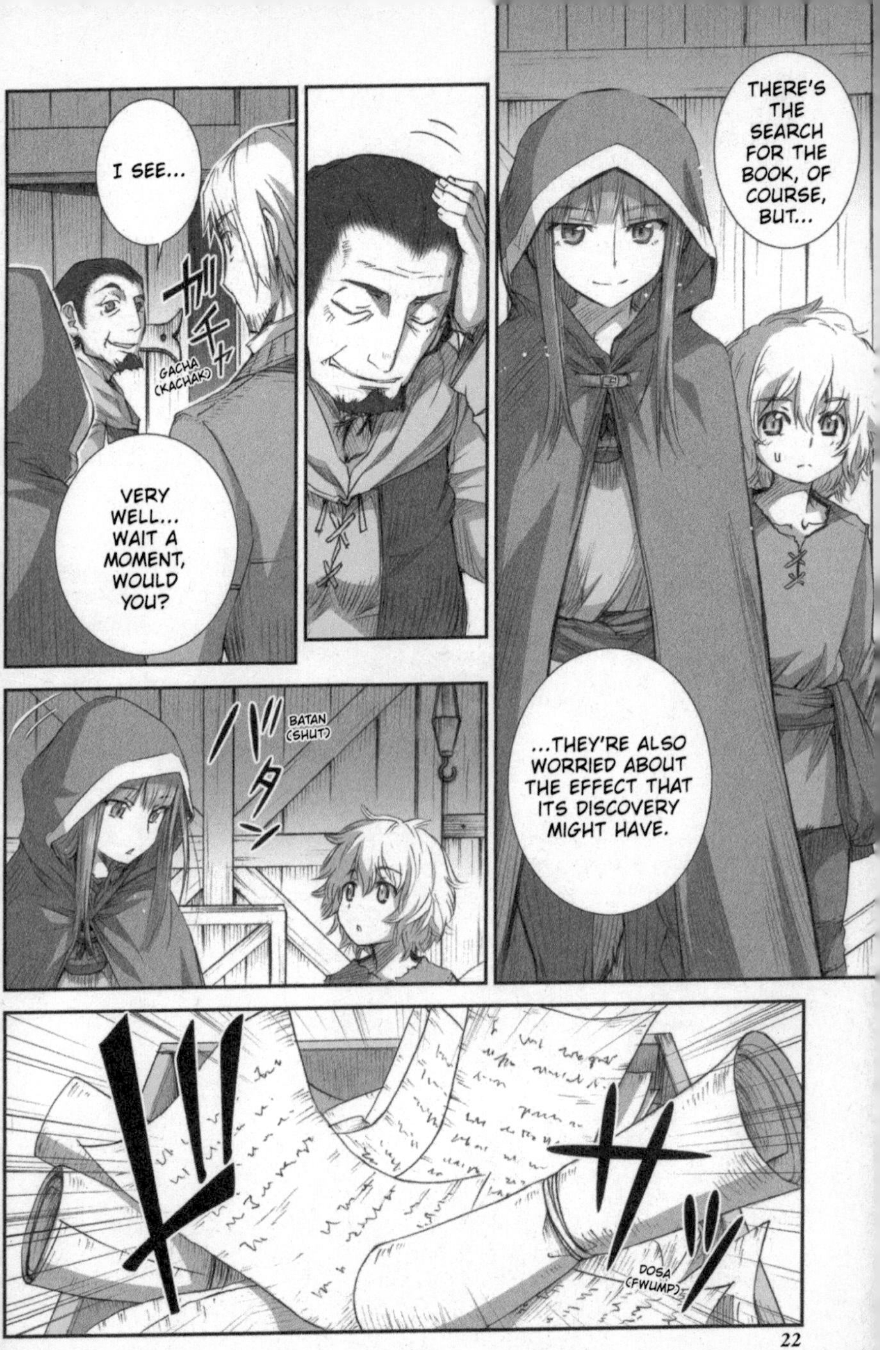
THERE'S THE SEARCH FOR THE BOOK, OF COURSE, BUT...
...THEY'RE ALSO WORRIED ABOUT THE EFFECT THAT ITS DISCOVERY MIGHT HAVE.
I SEE...
GACHA (KACHAK)
VERY WELL... WAIT A MOMENT, WOULD YOU?
BATAN (SHUT)
DOSA (FWUMP)

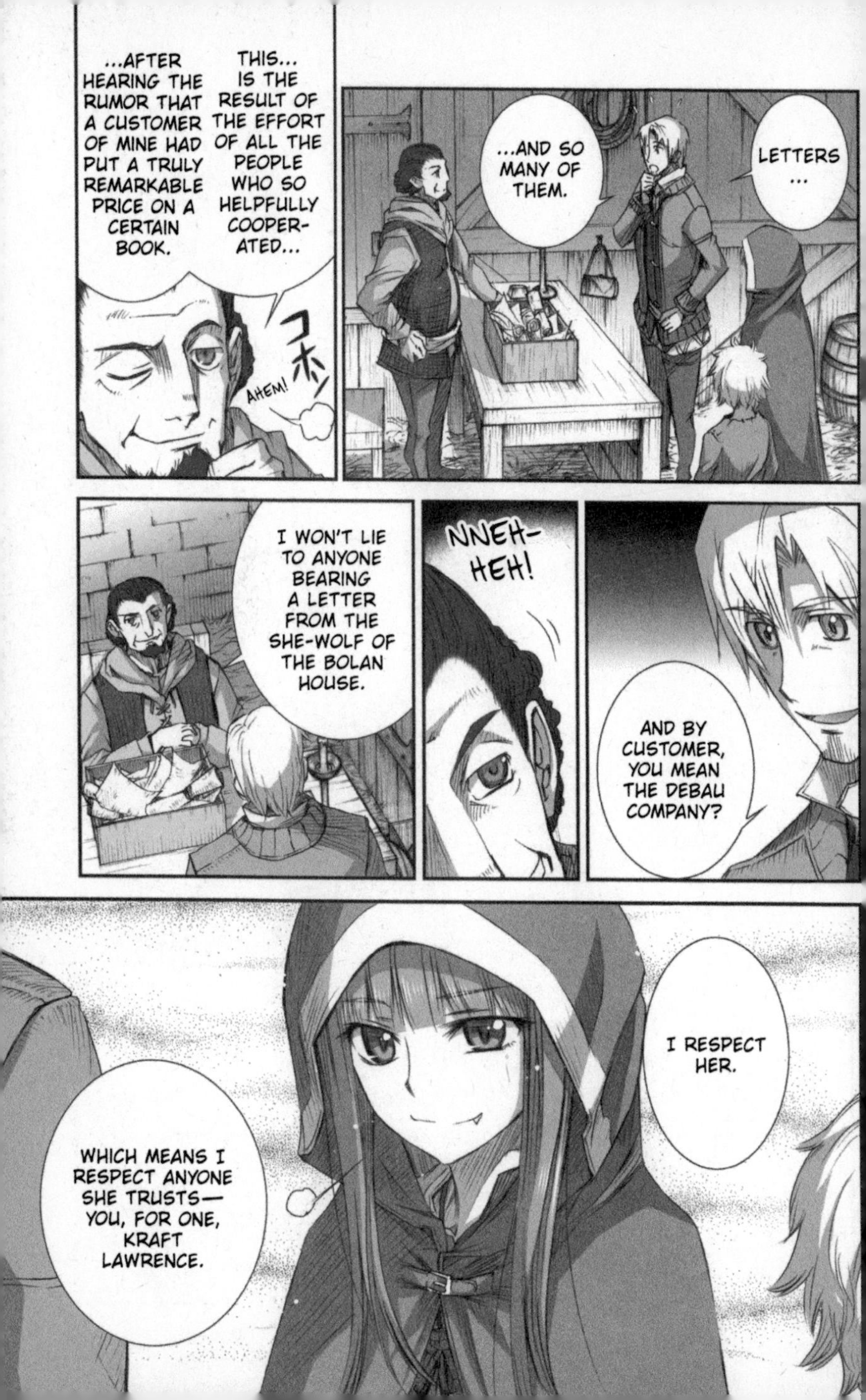
LETTERS...
...AND SO MANY OF THEM.
THIS... IS THE RESULT OF THE EFFORT OF ALL THE PEOPLE WHO SO HELPFULLY COOPERATED...
...AFTER HEARING THE RUMOR THAT A CUSTOMER OF MINE HAD PUT A TRULY REMARKABLE PRICE ON A CERTAIN BOOK.
コホン
AHEM!
AND BY CUSTOMER, YOU MEAN THE DEBAU COMPANY?
NNEH-HEH!
I WON'T LIE TO ANYONE BEARING A LETTER FROM THE SHE-WOLF OF THE BOLAN HOUSE.
I RESPECT HER.
WHICH MEANS I RESPECT ANYONE SHE TRUSTS—YOU, FOR ONE, KRAFT LAWRENCE.

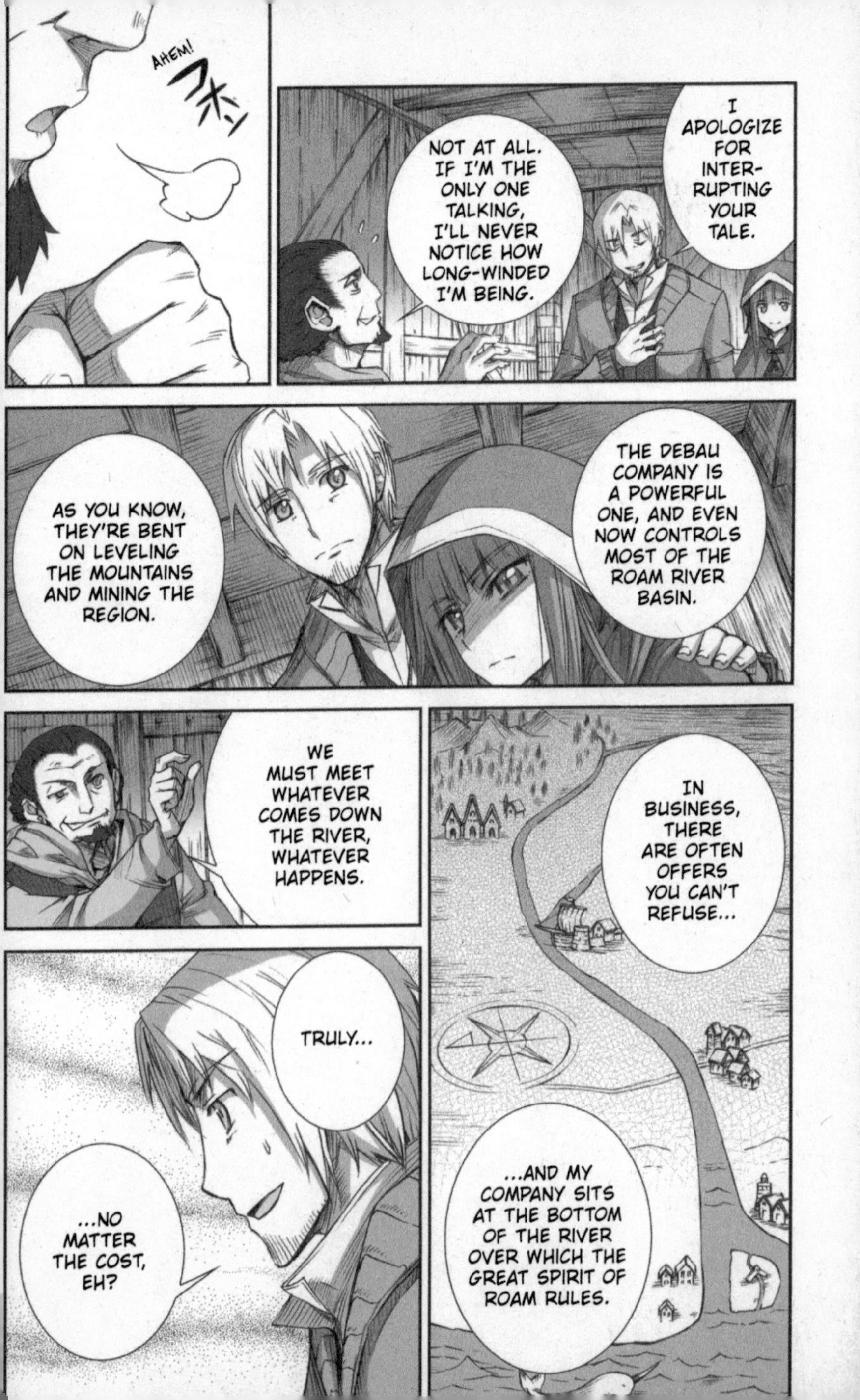
I APOLOGIZE FOR INTER-RUPTING YOUR TALE.
NOT AT ALL. IF I'M THE ONLY ONE TALKING, I'LL NEVER NOTICE HOW LONG-WINDED I'M BEING.
AHEM!
THE DEBAU COMPANY IS A POWERFUL ONE, AND EVEN NOW CONTROLS MOST OF THE ROAM RIVER BASIN.
AS YOU KNOW, THEY'RE BENT ON LEVELING THE MOUNTAINS AND MINING THE REGION.
IN BUSINESS, THERE ARE OFTEN OFFERS YOU CAN'T REFUSE...
...AND MY COMPANY SITS AT THE BOTTOM OF THE RIVER OVER WHICH THE GREAT SPIRIT OF ROAM RULES.
WE MUST MEET WHATEVER COMES DOWN THE RIVER, WHATEVER HAPPENS.
TRULY...
...NO MATTER THE COST, EH?

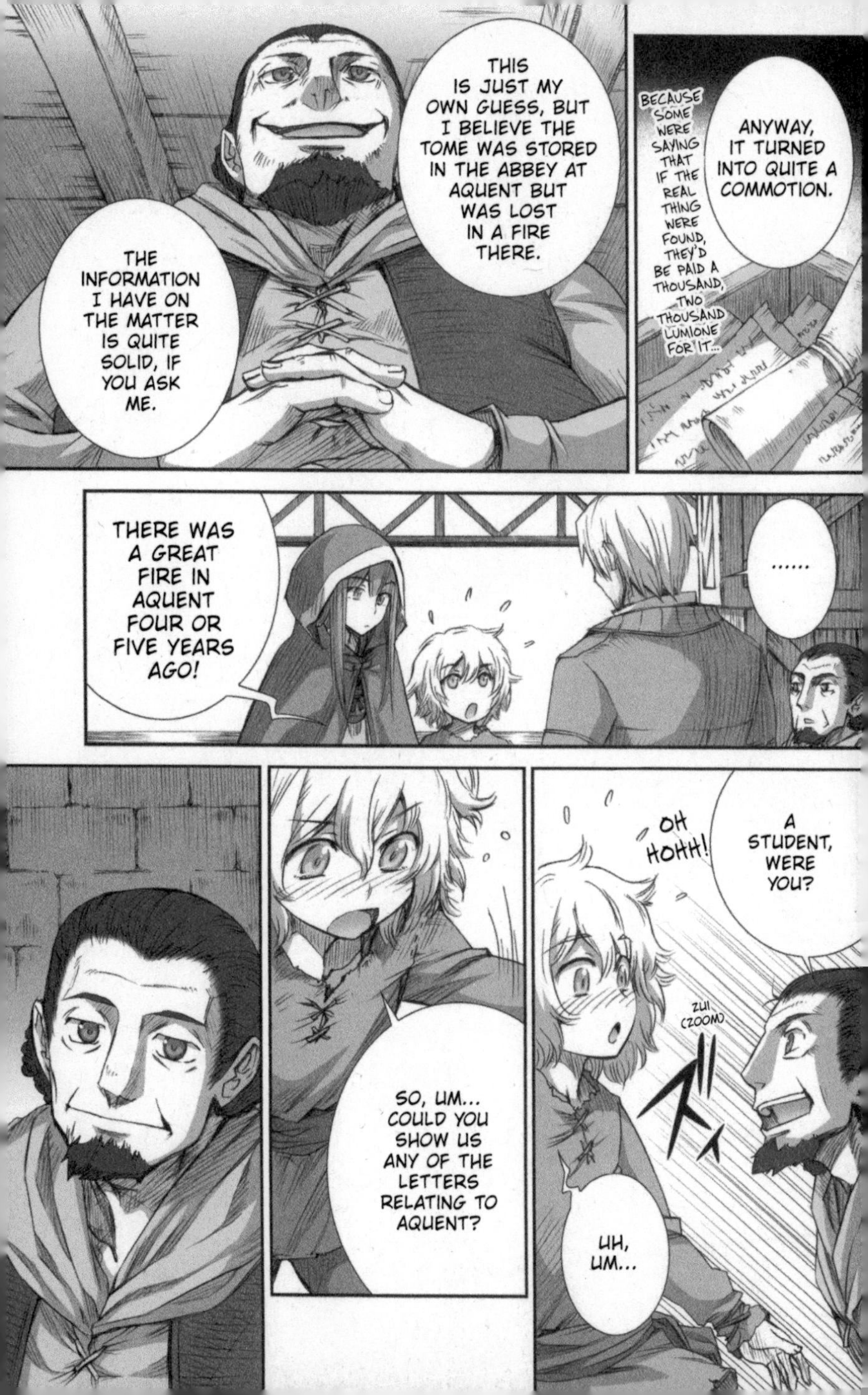
ANYWAY, IT TURNED INTO QUITE A COMMOTION.
BECAUSE SOME WERE SAYING THAT IF THE REAL THING WERE FOUND, THEY'D BE PAID A THOUSAND, TWO THOUSAND LUMIONE FOR IT...
THIS IS JUST MY OWN GUESS, BUT I BELIEVE THE TOME WAS STORED IN THE ABBEY AT AQUENT BUT WAS LOST IN A FIRE THERE.
THE INFORMATION I HAVE ON THE MATTER IS QUITE SOLID, IF YOU ASK ME.
......
THERE WAS A GREAT FIRE IN AQUENT FOUR OR FIVE YEARS AGO!
A STUDENT, WERE YOU?
OH HOHH!
ZUI (ZOOM)
UH, UM...
SO, UM... COULD YOU SHOW US ANY OF THE LETTERS RELATING TO AQUENT?

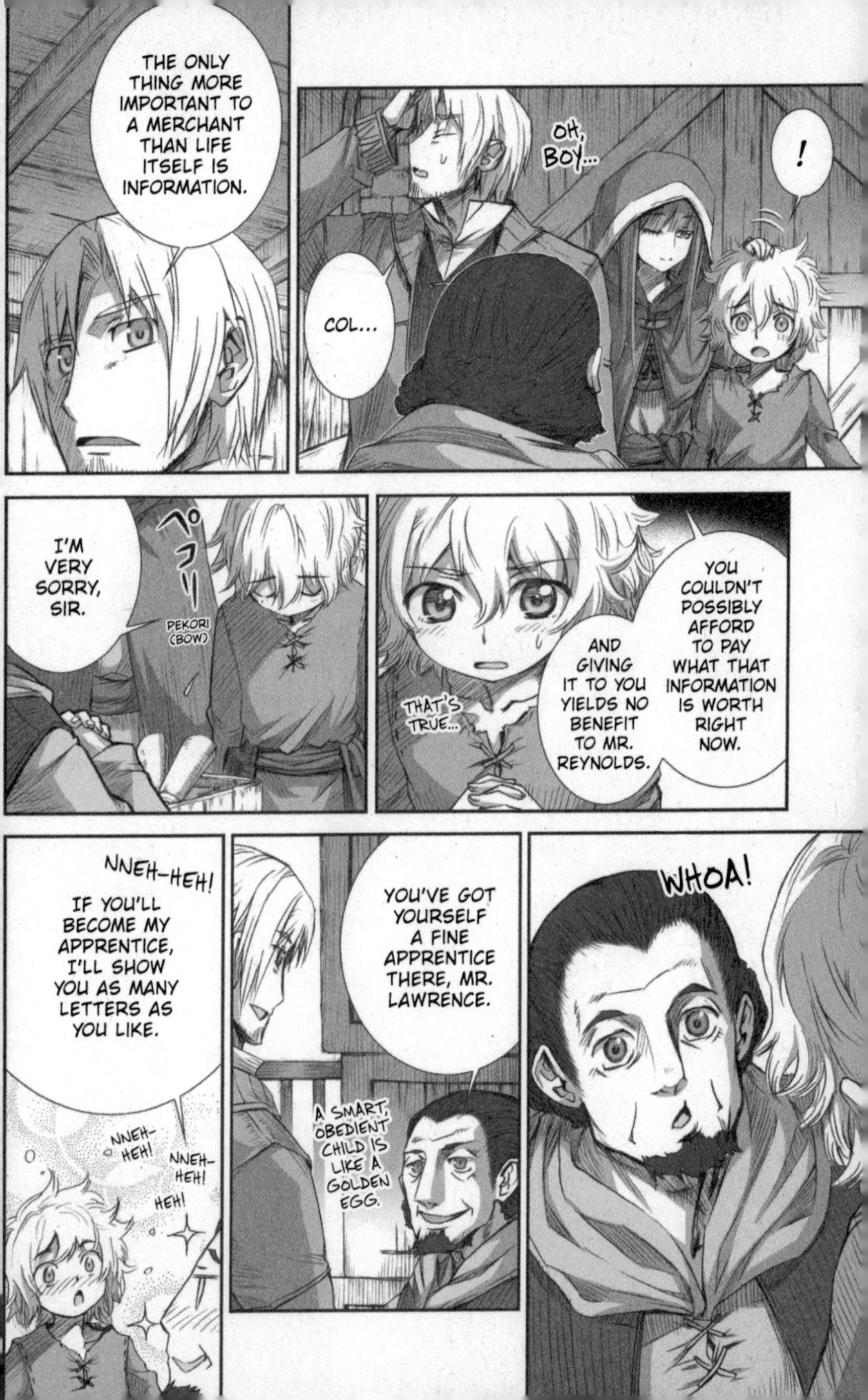
!
OH, BOY...
COL...
THE ONLY THING MORE IMPORTANT TO A MERCHANT THAN LIFE ITSELF IS INFORMATION.
YOU COULDN'T POSSIBLY AFFORD TO PAY WHAT THAT INFORMATION IS WORTH RIGHT NOW.
AND GIVING IT TO YOU YIELDS NO BENEFIT TO MR. REYNOLDS.
THAT'S TRUE...
ペコリ
PEKORI (BOW)
I'M VERY SORRY, SIR.
WHOA!
YOU'VE GOT YOURSELF A FINE APPRENTICE THERE, MR. LAWRENCE.
A SMART, OBEDIENT CHILD IS LIKE A GOLDEN EGG.
NNEH-HEH!
IF YOU'LL BECOME MY APPRENTICE, I'LL SHOW YOU AS MANY LETTERS AS YOU LIKE.
NNEH-HEH! NNEH-HEH! HEH!

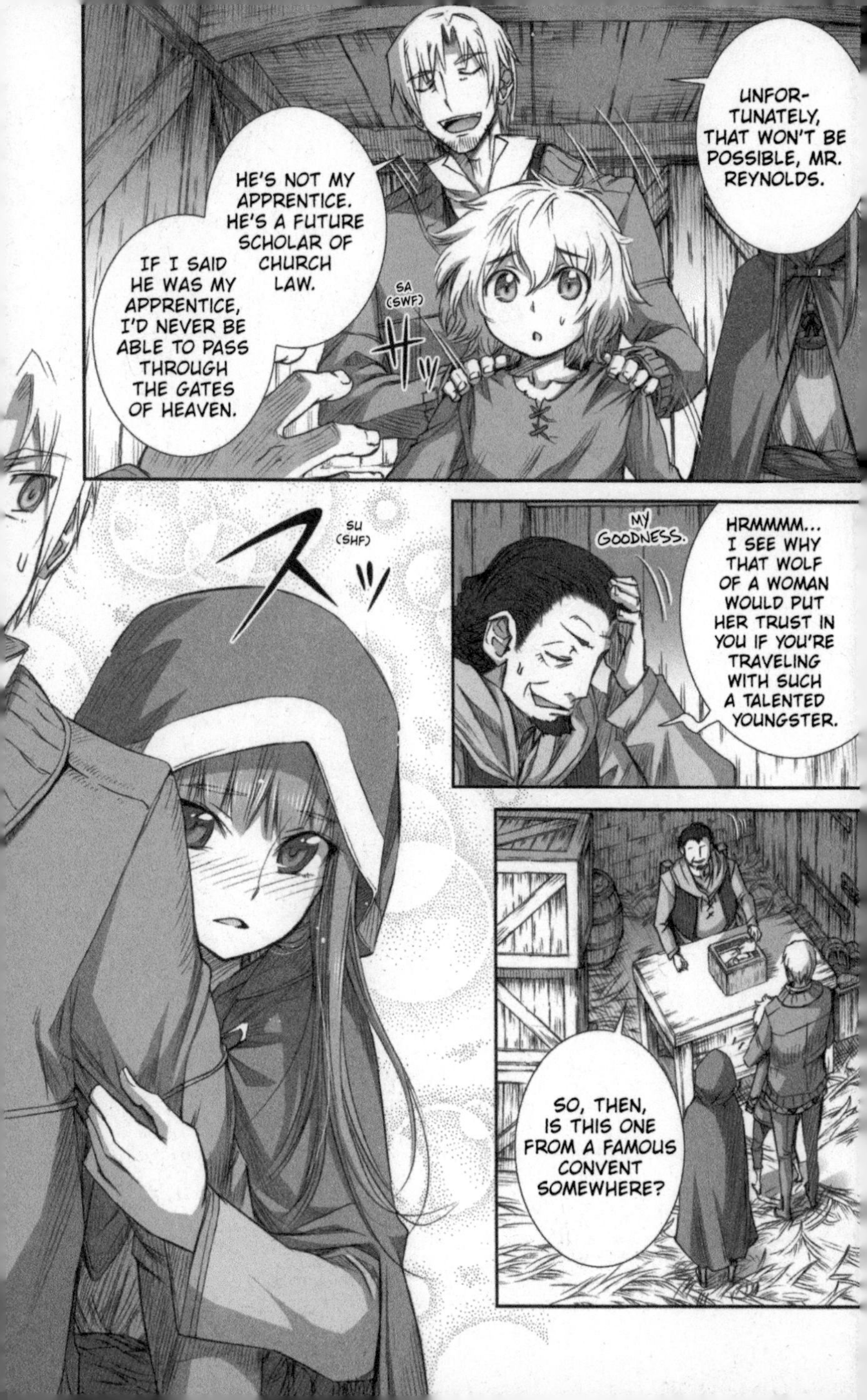
UNFOR-TUNATELY, THAT WON'T BE POSSIBLE, MR. REYNOLDS.
HE'S NOT MY APPRENTICE. HE'S A FUTURE SCHOLAR OF CHURCH LAW.
SA (SWF)
IF I SAID HE WAS MY APPRENTICE, I'D NEVER BE ABLE TO PASS THROUGH THE GATES OF HEAVEN.
HRMMMM... I SEE WHY THAT WOLF OF A WOMAN WOULD PUT HER TRUST IN YOU IF YOU'RE TRAVELING WITH SUCH A TALENTED YOUNGSTER.
MY GOODNESS.
SO, THEN, IS THIS ONE FROM A FAMOUS CONVENT SOMEWHERE?
SU (SHF)

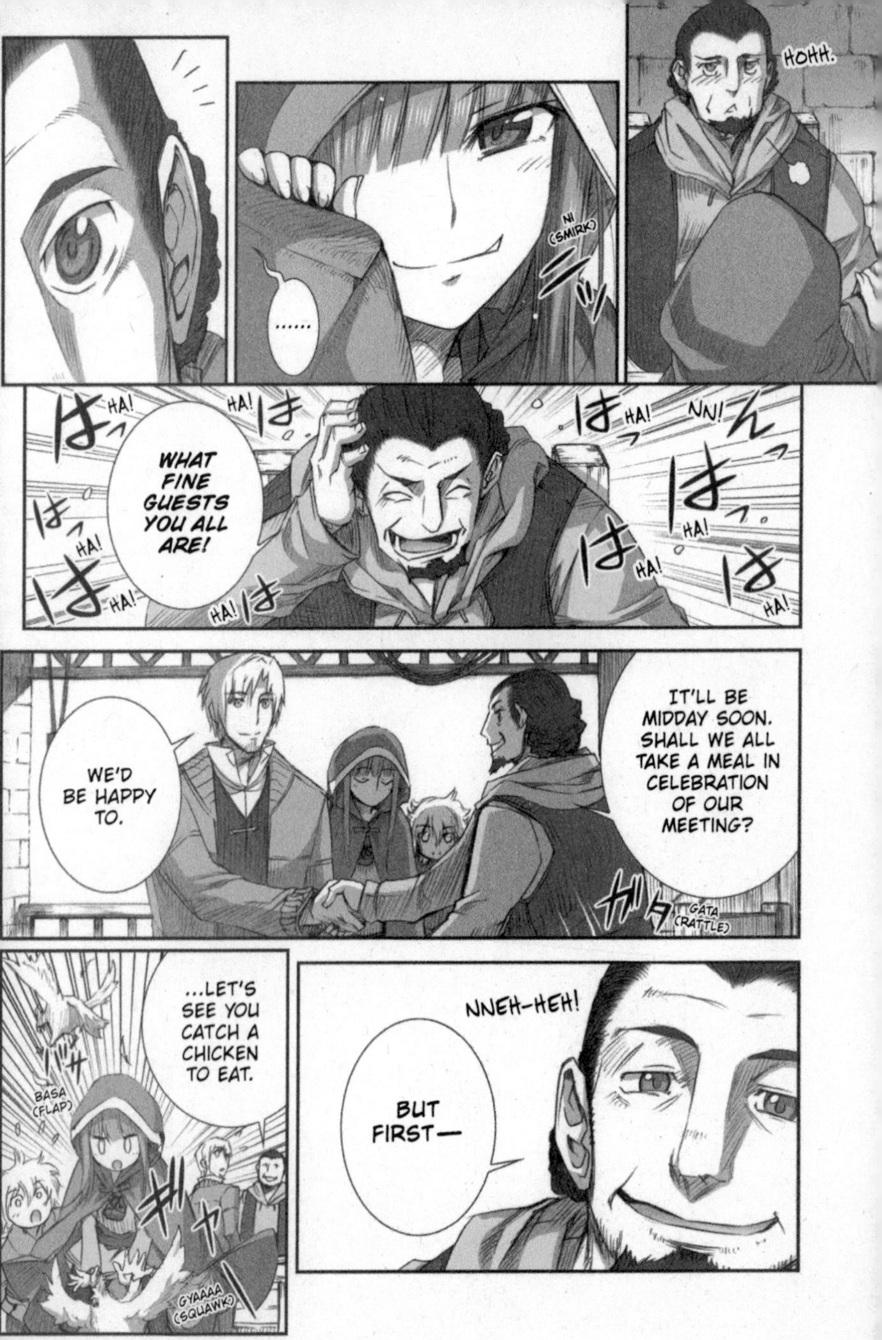
HOHH.
NI (SMIRK)
......
NN! HA!
HA! HA!
WHAT FINE GUESTS YOU ALL ARE!
HA! HA! HA! HA! HA! HA!
IT'LL BE MIDDAY SOON. SHALL WE ALL TAKE A MEAL IN CELEBRATION OF OUR MEETING?
GATA (RATTLE)
WE'D BE HAPPY TO.
NNEH-HEH!
BUT FIRST—
...LET'S SEE YOU CATCH A CHICKEN TO EAT.
BASA (FLAP)
GYAAAA (SQUAWK)

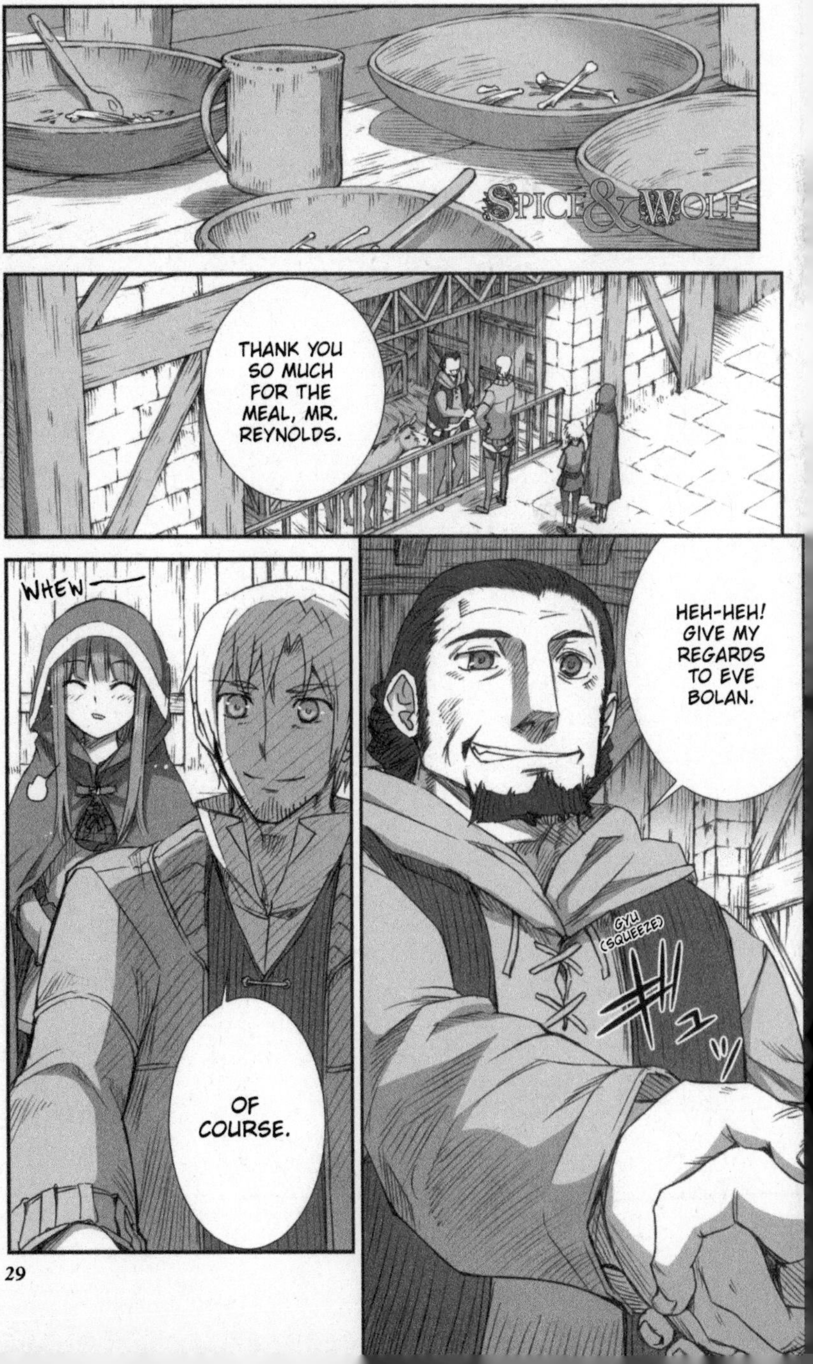
SPICE & WOLF
THANK YOU SO MUCH FOR THE MEAL, MR. REYNOLDS.
HEH-HEH! GIVE MY REGARDS TO EVE BOLAN.
GYU (SQUEEZE)
WHEW—
OF COURSE.

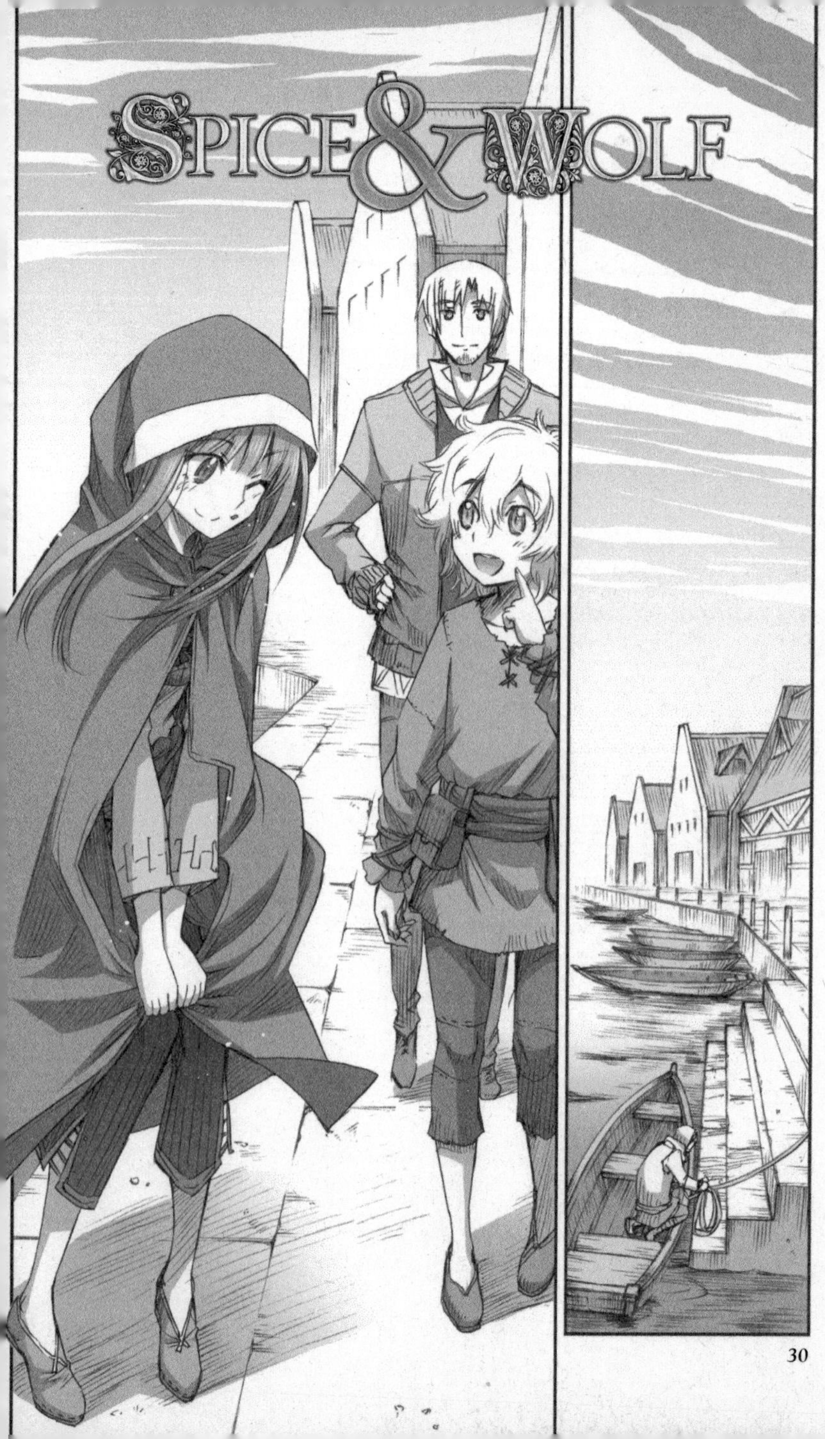
SPICE & WOLF

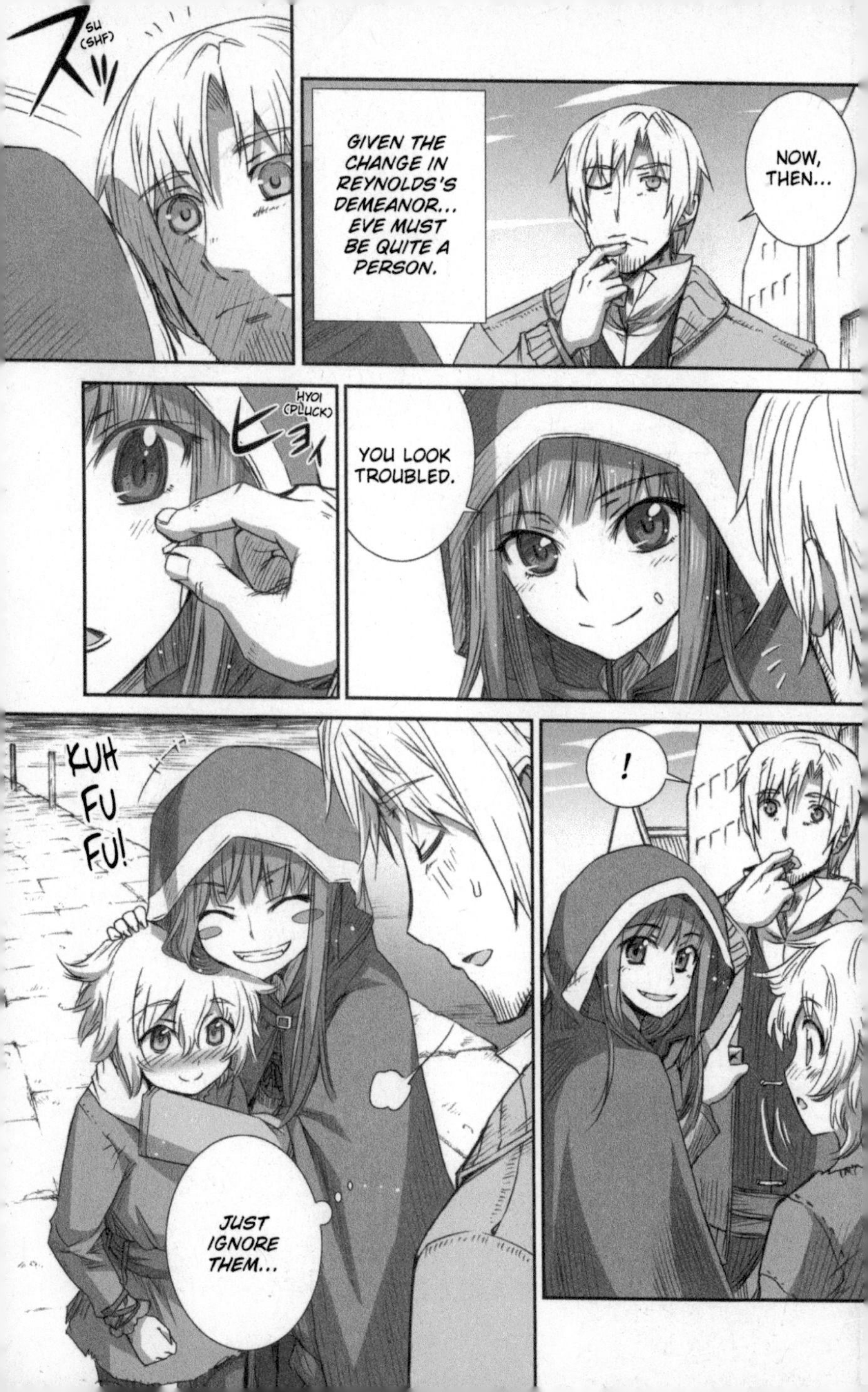
NOW, THEN...
GIVEN THE CHANGE IN REYNOLDS'S DEMEANOR... EVE MUST BE QUITE A PERSON.
ス
SU (SHF)
YOU LOOK TROUBLED.
ヒョイ
HYOI (PLUCK)
!
KUH FU FU!
JUST IGNORE THEM...

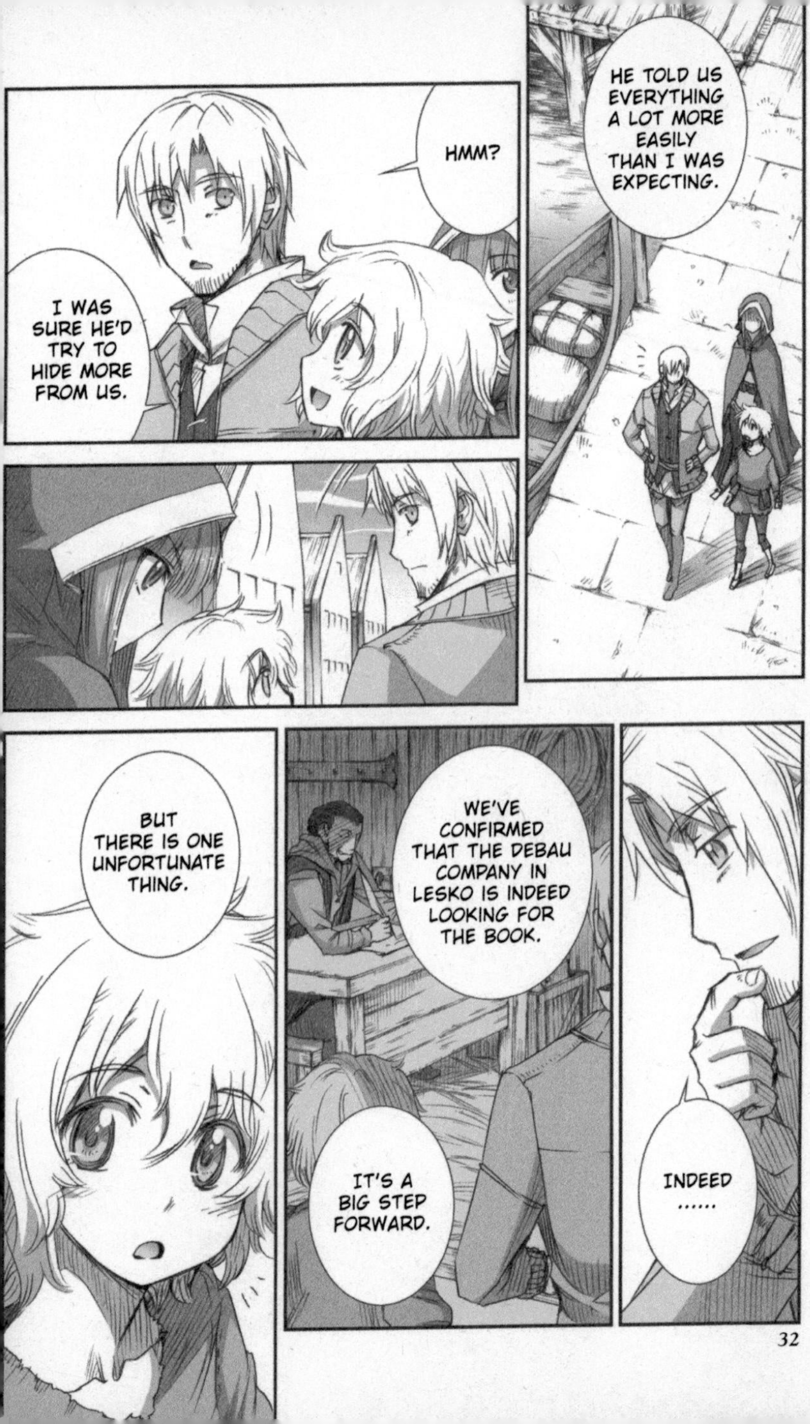
HE TOLD US EVERYTHING A LOT MORE EASILY THAN I WAS EXPECTING.
HMM?
I WAS SURE HE'D TRY TO HIDE MORE FROM US.
INDEED ......
WE'VE CONFIRMED THAT THE DEBAU COMPANY IN LESKO IS INDEED LOOKING FOR THE BOOK.
IT'S A BIG STEP FORWARD.
BUT THERE IS ONE UNFORTUNATE THING.

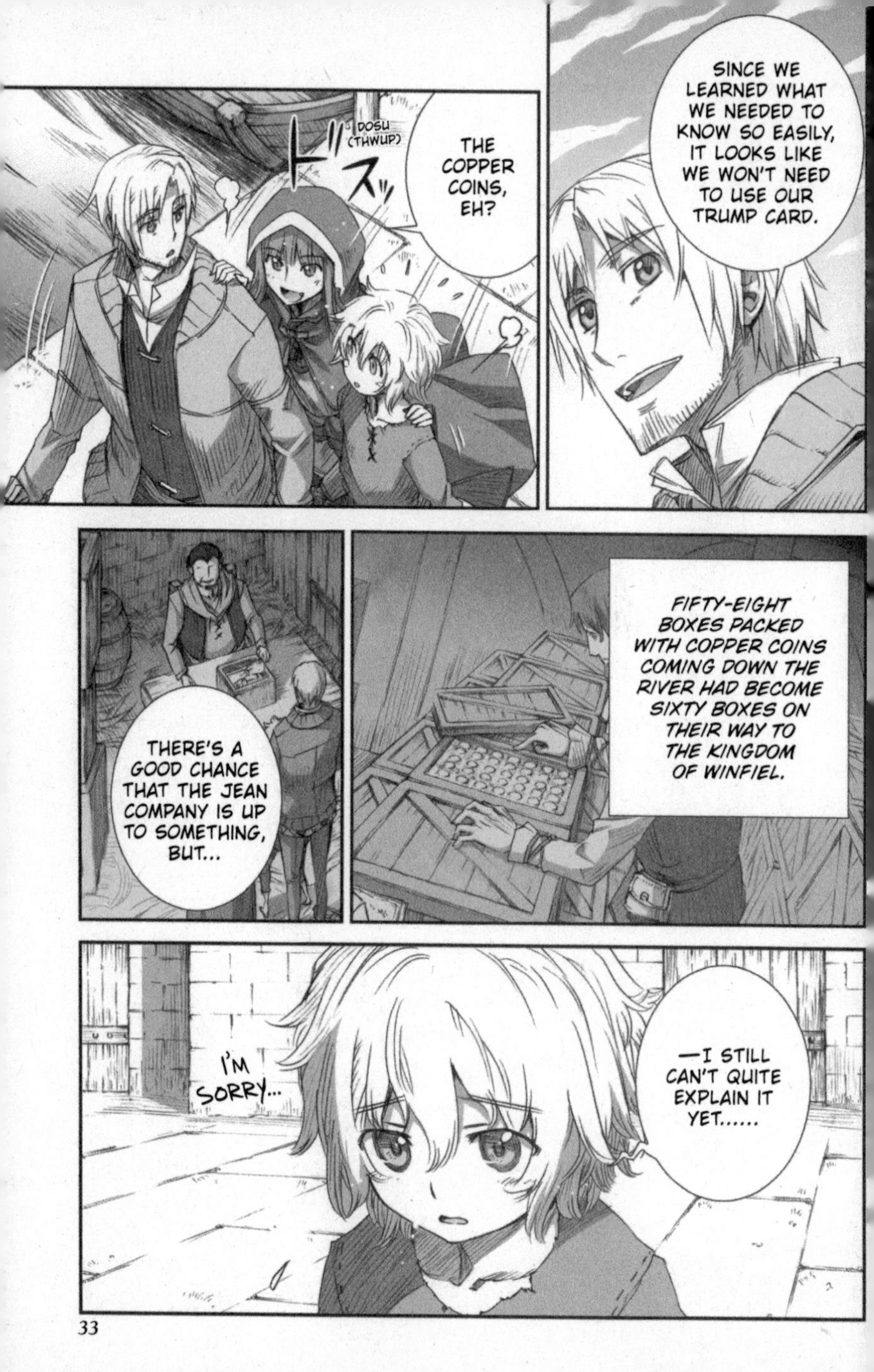
SINCE WE LEARNED WHAT WE NEEDED TO KNOW SO EASILY, IT LOOKS LIKE WE WON'T NEED TO USE OUR TRUMP CARD.
THE COPPER COINS, EH?
DOSU (THWUP)
FIFTY-EIGHT BOXES PACKED WITH COPPER COINS COMING DOWN THE RIVER HAD BECOME SIXTY BOXES ON THEIR WAY TO THE KINGDOM OF WINFIEL.
THERE'S A GOOD CHANCE THAT THE JEAN COMPANY IS UP TO SOMETHING, BUT...
—I STILL CAN'T QUITE EXPLAIN IT YET......
I'M SORRY...

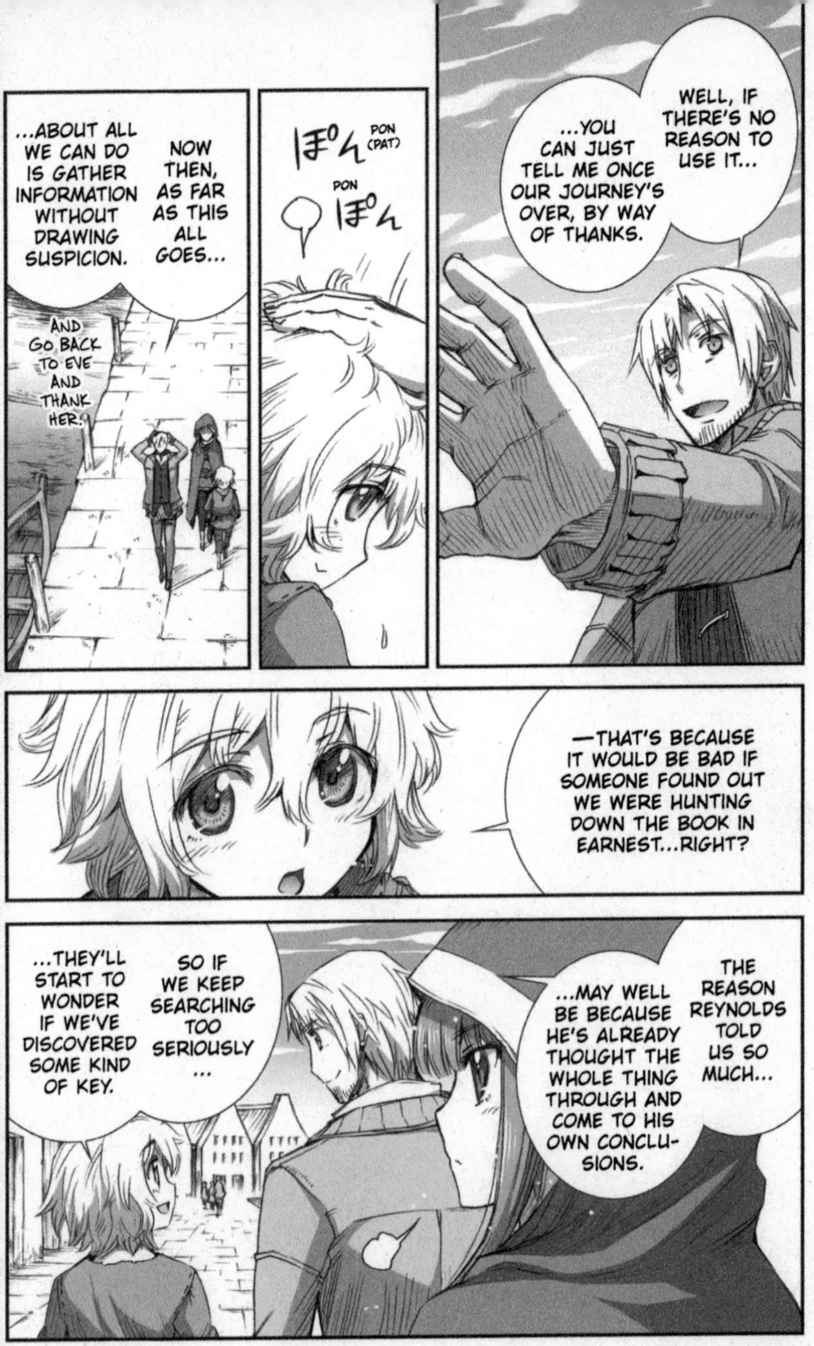
WELL, IF THERE'S NO REASON TO USE IT...
...YOU CAN JUST TELL ME ONCE OUR JOURNEY'S OVER, BY WAY OF THANKS.
ぽん PON (PAT)
PON ぽん
NOW THEN, AS FAR AS THIS ALL GOES...
...ABOUT ALL WE CAN DO IS GATHER INFORMATION WITHOUT DRAWING SUSPICION.
AND GO BACK TO EVE AND THANK HER.
—THAT'S BECAUSE IT WOULD BE BAD IF SOMEONE FOUND OUT WE WERE HUNTING DOWN THE BOOK IN EARNEST...RIGHT?
THE REASON REYNOLDS TOLD US SO MUCH...
...MAY WELL BE BECAUSE HE'S ALREADY THOUGHT THE WHOLE THING THROUGH AND COME TO HIS OWN CONCLU-SIONS.
SO IF WE KEEP SEARCHING TOO SERIOUSLY...
...THEY'LL START TO WONDER IF WE'VE DISCOVERED SOME KIND OF KEY.

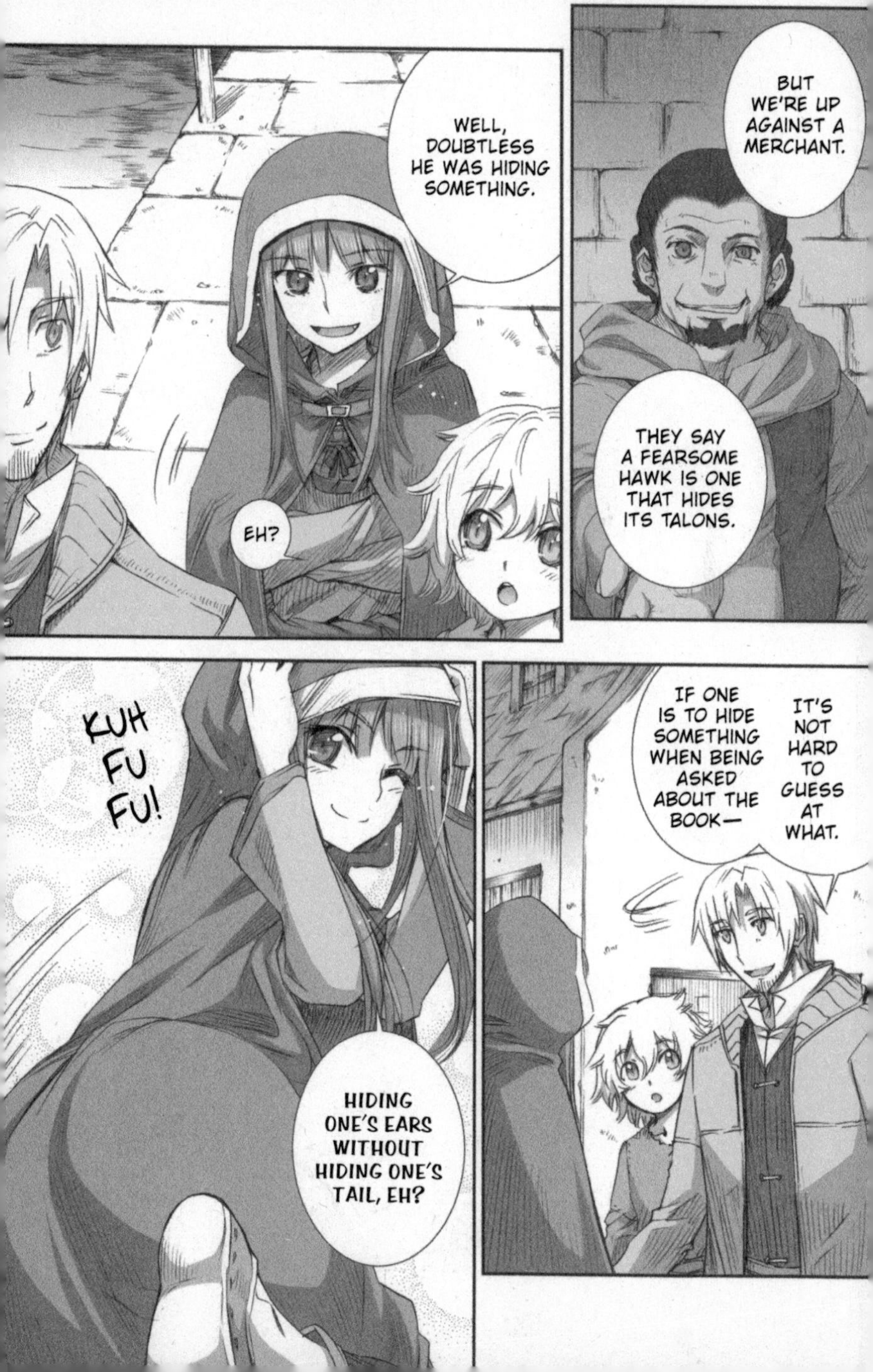
BUT WE'RE UP AGAINST A MERCHANT.
THEY SAY A FEARSOME HAWK IS ONE THAT HIDES ITS TALONS.
WELL, DOUBTLESS HE WAS HIDING SOMETHING.
EH?
IF ONE IS TO HIDE SOMETHING WHEN BEING ASKED ABOUT THE BOOK— IT'S NOT HARD TO GUESS AT WHAT.
KUH FU FU!
HIDING ONE'S EARS WITHOUT HIDING ONE'S TAIL, EH?

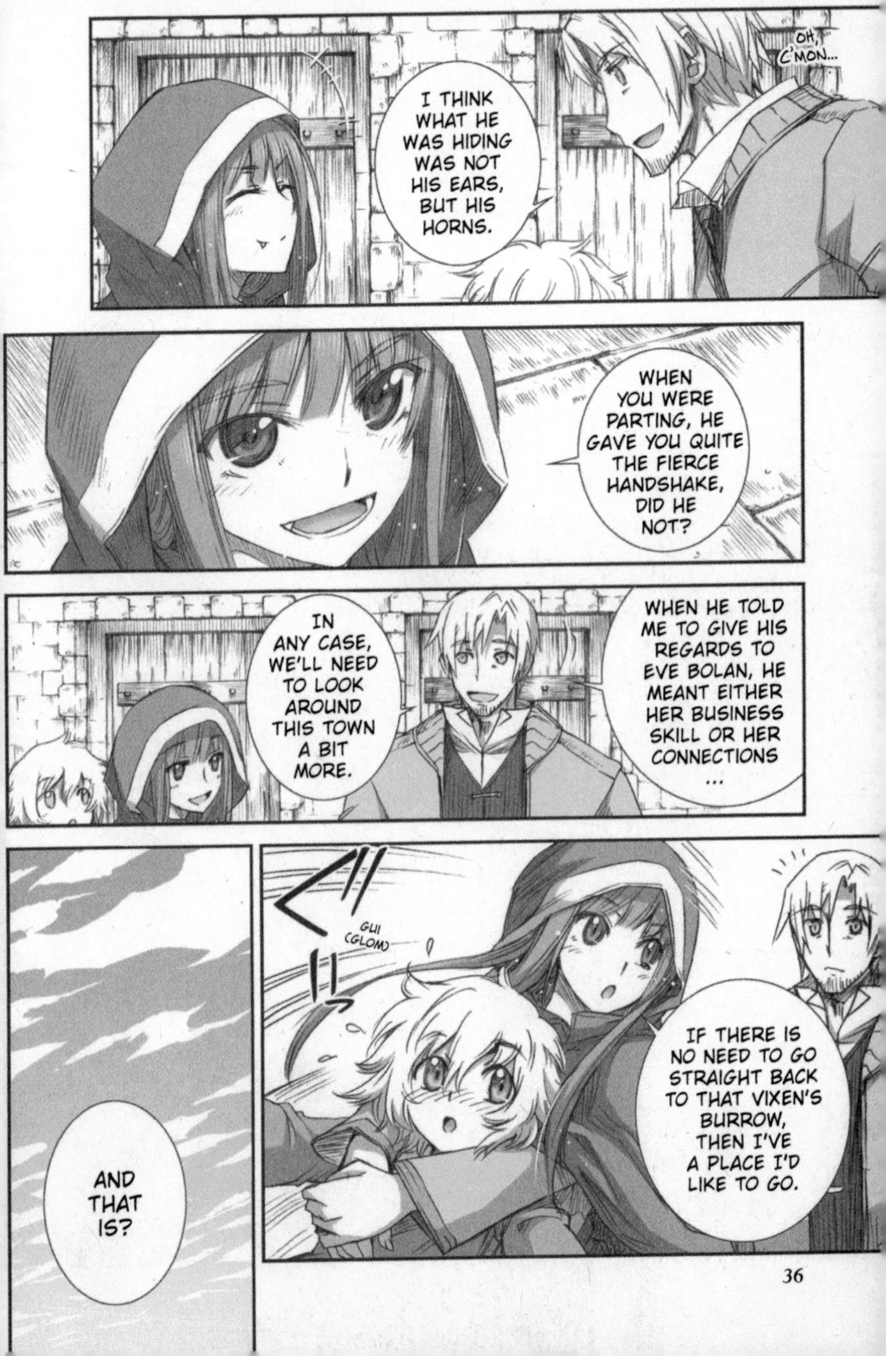
OH, C'MON...
I THINK WHAT HE WAS HIDING WAS NOT HIS EARS, BUT HIS HORNS.
WHEN YOU WERE PARTING, HE GAVE YOU QUITE THE FIERCE HANDSHAKE, DID HE NOT?
WHEN HE TOLD ME TO GIVE HIS REGARDS TO EVE BOLAN, HE MEANT EITHER HER BUSINESS SKILL OR HER CONNECTIONS ...
IN ANY CASE, WE'LL NEED TO LOOK AROUND THIS TOWN A BIT MORE.
GUI (GLOM)
IF THERE IS NO NEED TO GO STRAIGHT BACK TO THAT VIXEN'S BURROW, THEN I'VE A PLACE I'D LIKE TO GO.
AND THAT IS?

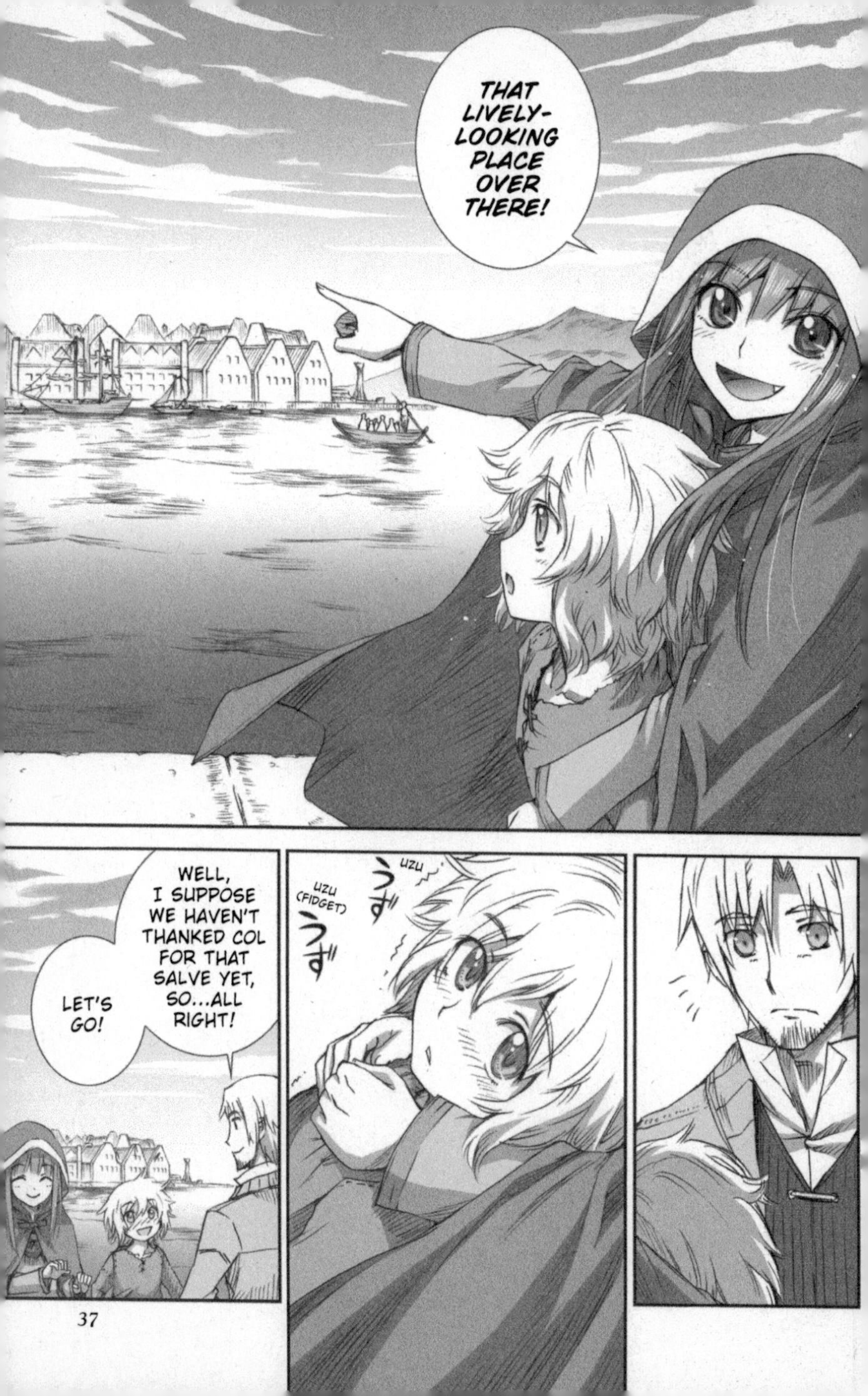
THAT LIVELY-LOOKING PLACE OVER THERE!
うず
UZU
うず
UZU (FIDGET)
WELL, I SUPPOSE WE HAVEN'T THANKED COL FOR THAT SALVE YET, SO...ALL RIGHT!
LET'S GO!

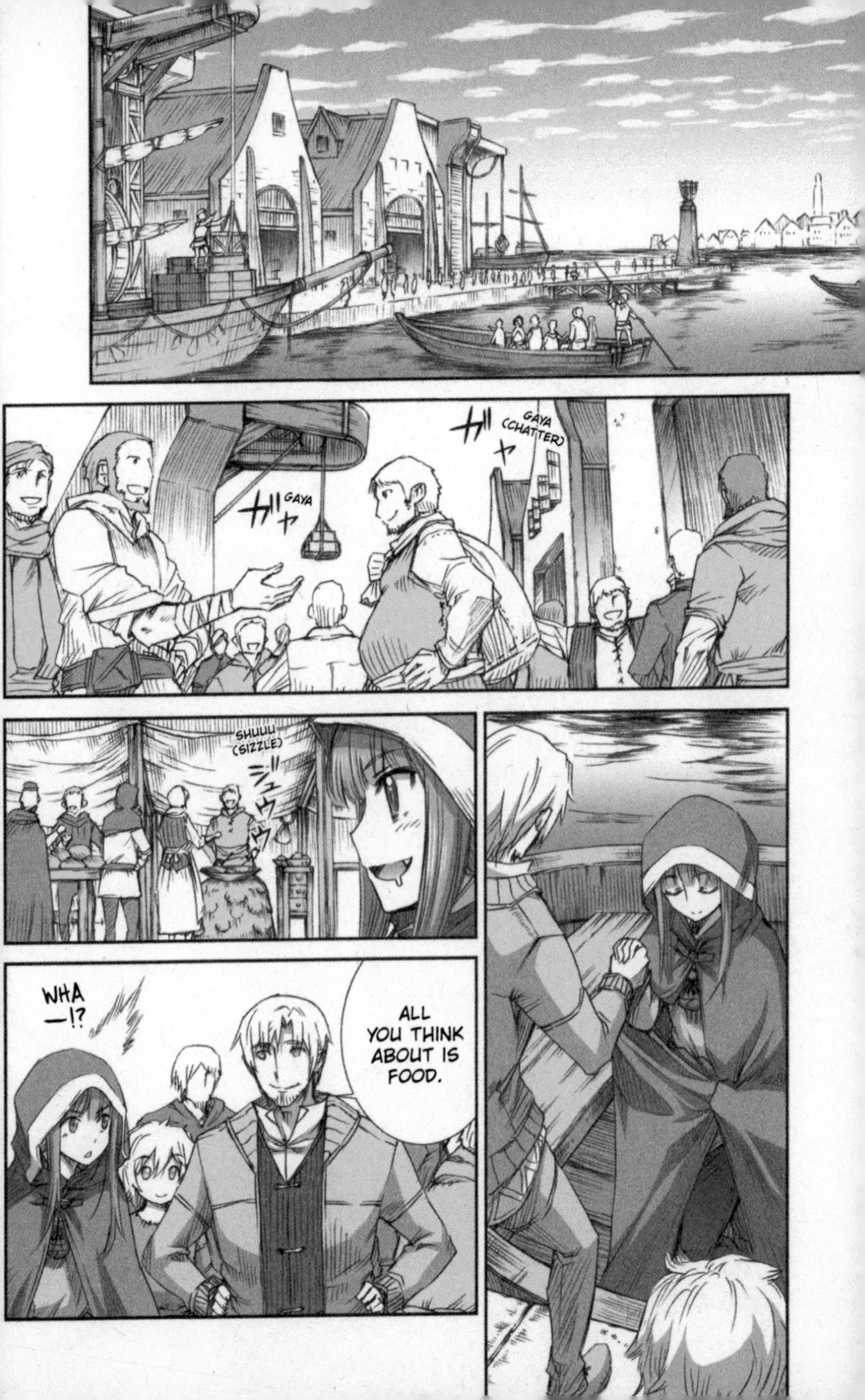

ガヤ
GAYA (CHATTER)
ガヤ
GAYA
ジュウウ
SHUUU (SIZZLE)
ALL YOU THINK ABOUT IS FOOD.
WHA—!?

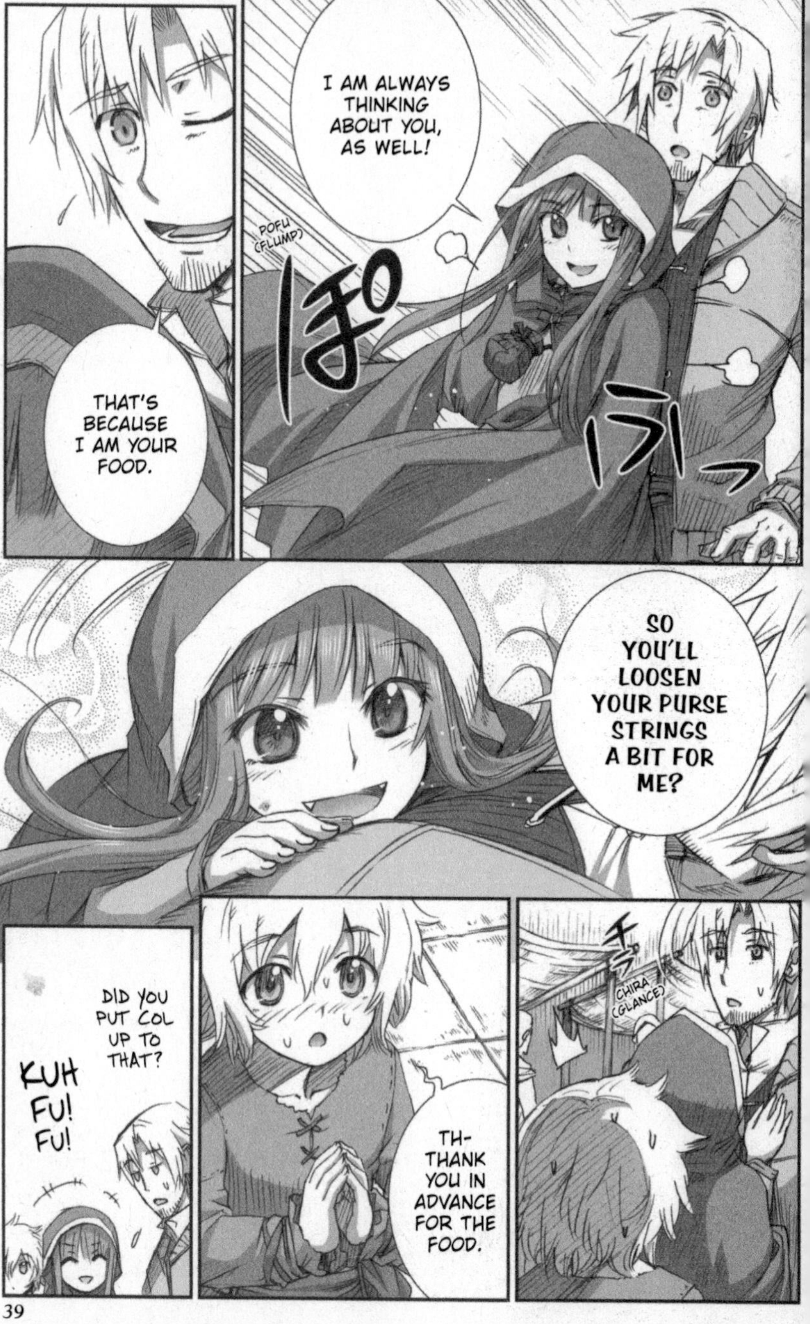
I AM ALWAYS THINKING ABOUT YOU, AS WELL!
POFU (FLUMP)
ぽ
THAT'S BECAUSE I AM YOUR FOOD.
SO YOU'LL LOOSEN YOUR PURSE STRINGS A BIT FOR ME?
チラ
CHIRA (GLANCE)
TH- THANK YOU IN ADVANCE FOR THE FOOD.
DID YOU PUT COL UP TO THAT?
KUH FU! FU!

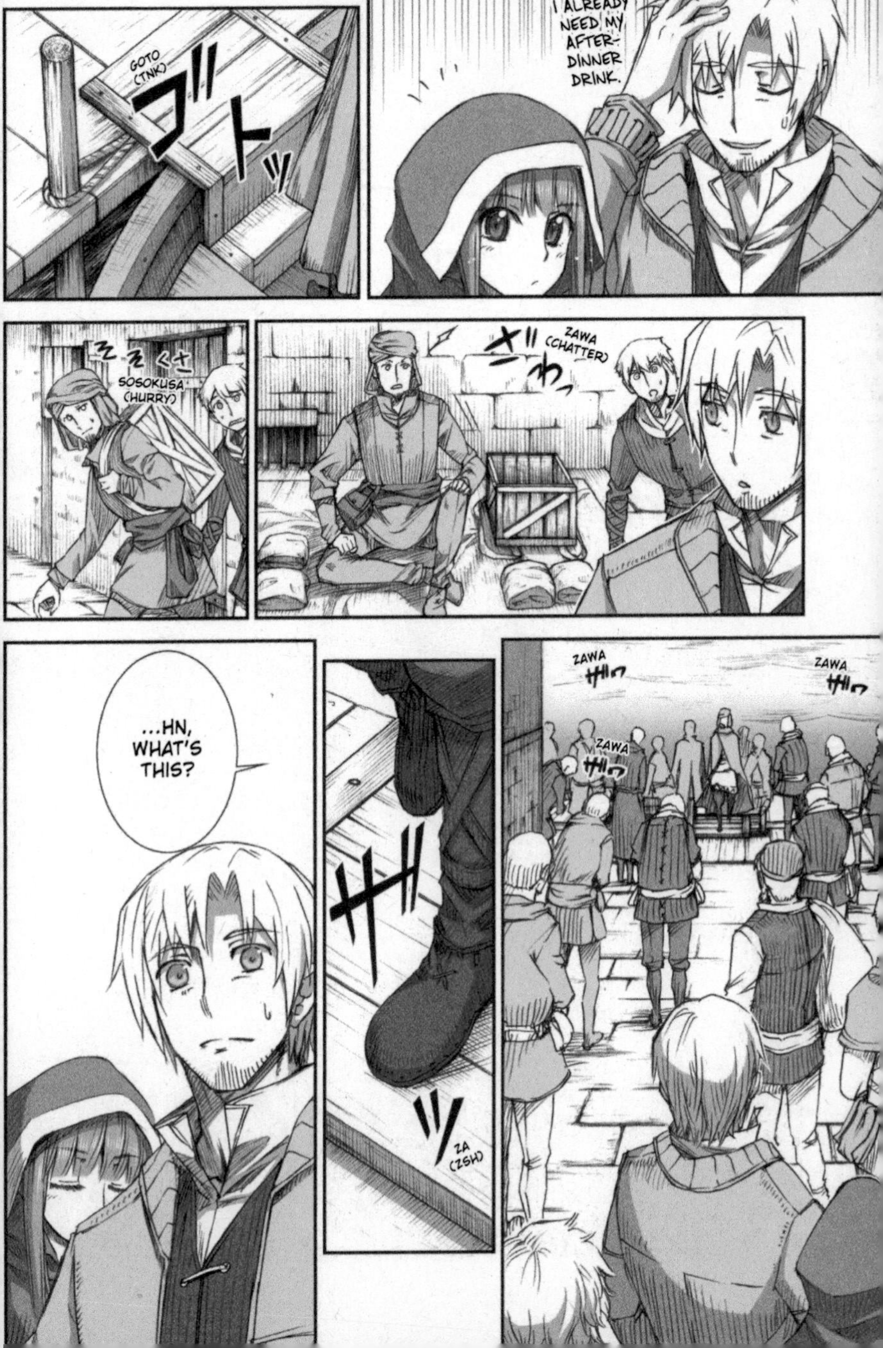
BROTHER... I FEEL LIKE I ALREADY NEED MY AFTER-DINNER DRINK.
GOTO (TNK)
ZAWA (CHATTER)
SOSOKUSA (HURRY)
ZAWA
ZAWA
ZAWA
ZA (ZSH)
...HN, WHAT'S THIS?

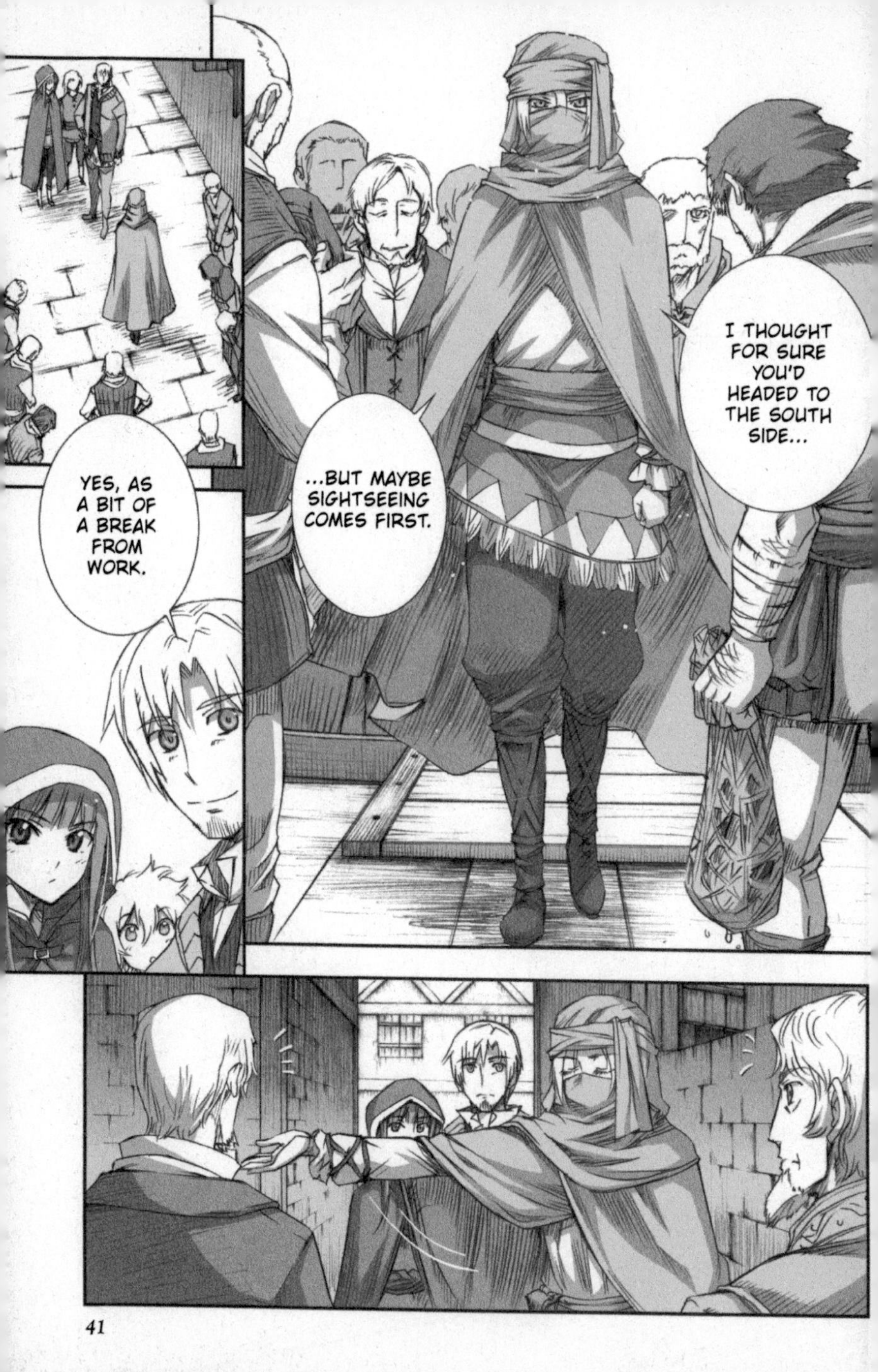
I THOUGHT FOR SURE YOU'D HEADED TO THE SOUTH SIDE...
...BUT MAYBE SIGHTSEEING COMES FIRST.
YES, AS A BIT OF A BREAK FROM WORK.

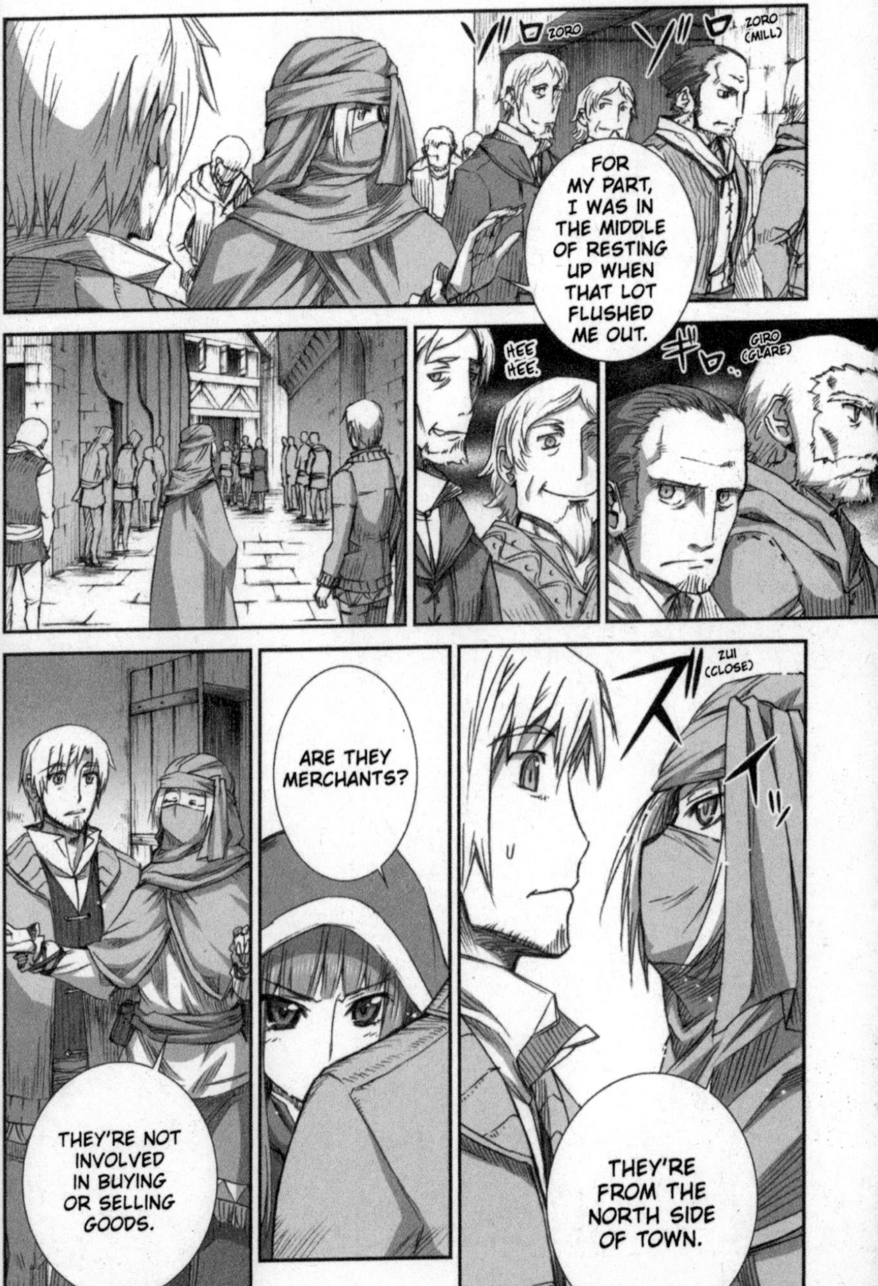
ZORO (MILL)
ZORO
FOR MY PART, I WAS IN THE MIDDLE OF RESTING UP WHEN THAT LOT FLUSHED ME OUT.
GIRO (GLARE)
HEE HEE.
ZUI (CLOSE)
THEY'RE FROM THE NORTH SIDE OF TOWN.
ARE THEY MERCHANTS?
THEY'RE NOT INVOLVED IN BUYING OR SELLING GOODS.

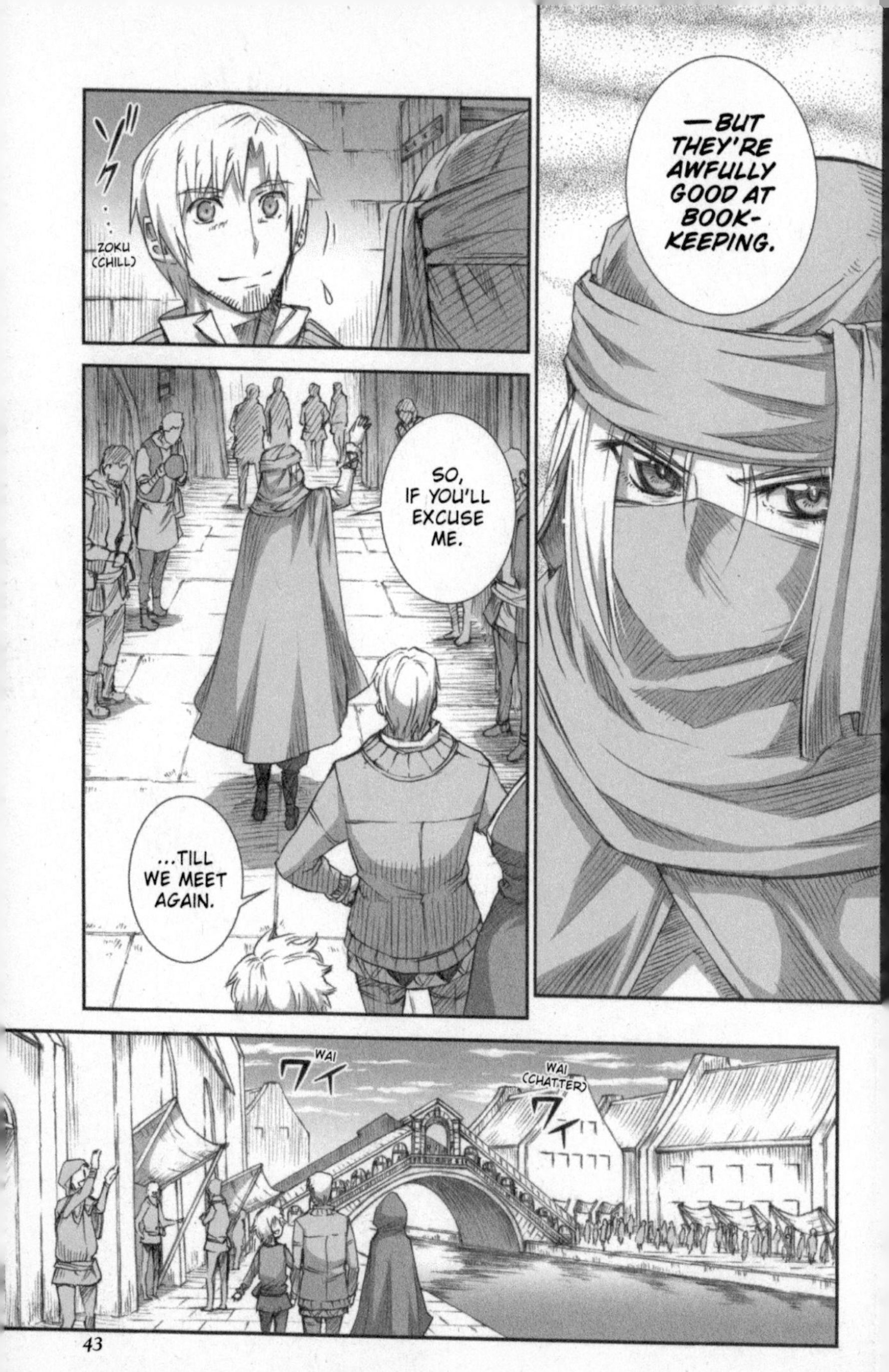
—BUT THEY'RE AWFULLY GOOD AT BOOK-KEEPING.
ZOKU (CHILL)
SO, IF YOU'LL EXCUSE ME.
...TILL WE MEET AGAIN.
WAI
WAI (CHATTER)

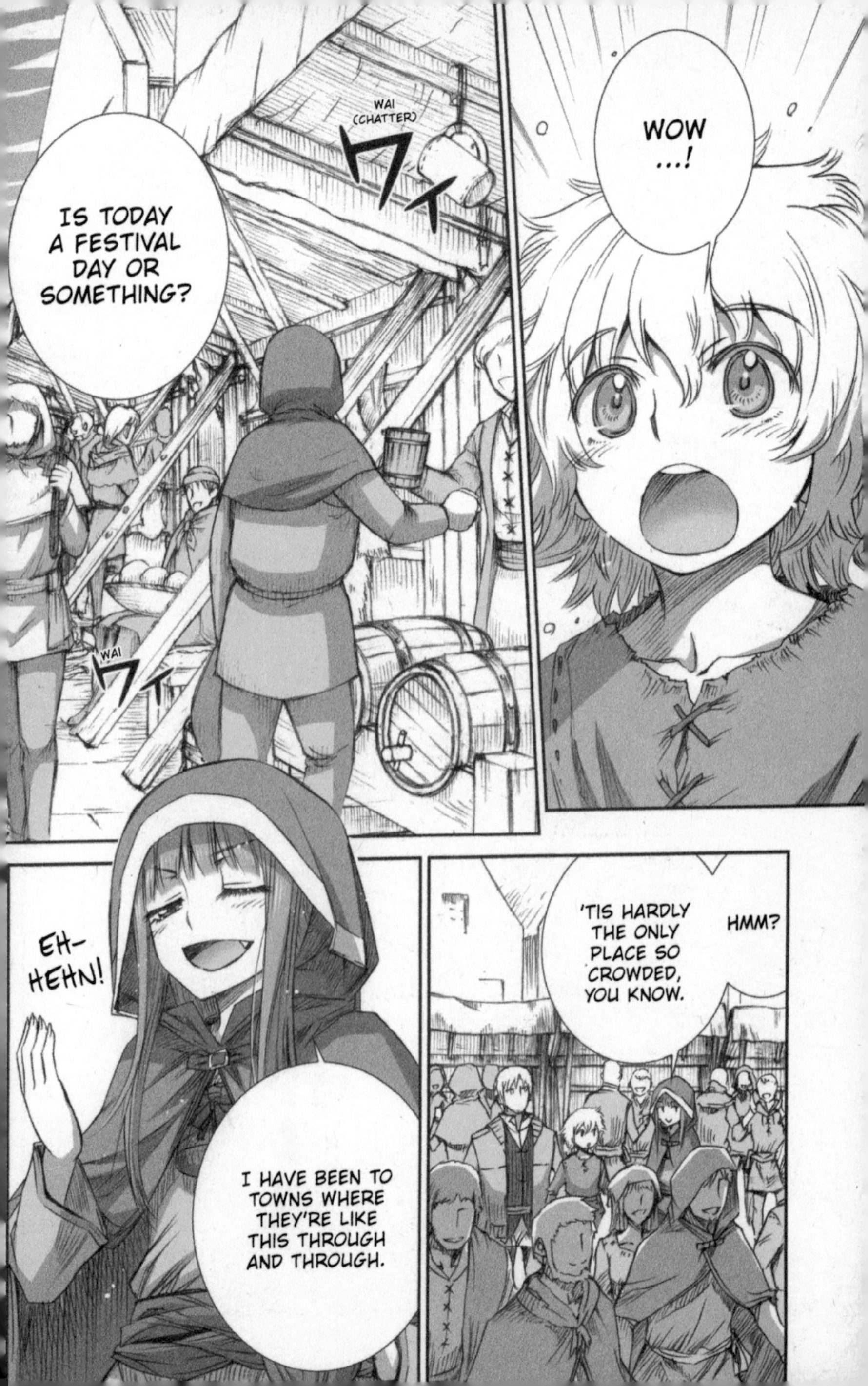
WOW ...!
WAI (CHATTER)
IS TODAY A FESTIVAL DAY OR SOMETHING?
WAI
HMM?
'TIS HARDLY THE ONLY PLACE SO CROWDED, YOU KNOW.
EH-HEHN!
I HAVE BEEN TO TOWNS WHERE THEY'RE LIKE THIS THROUGH AND THROUGH.

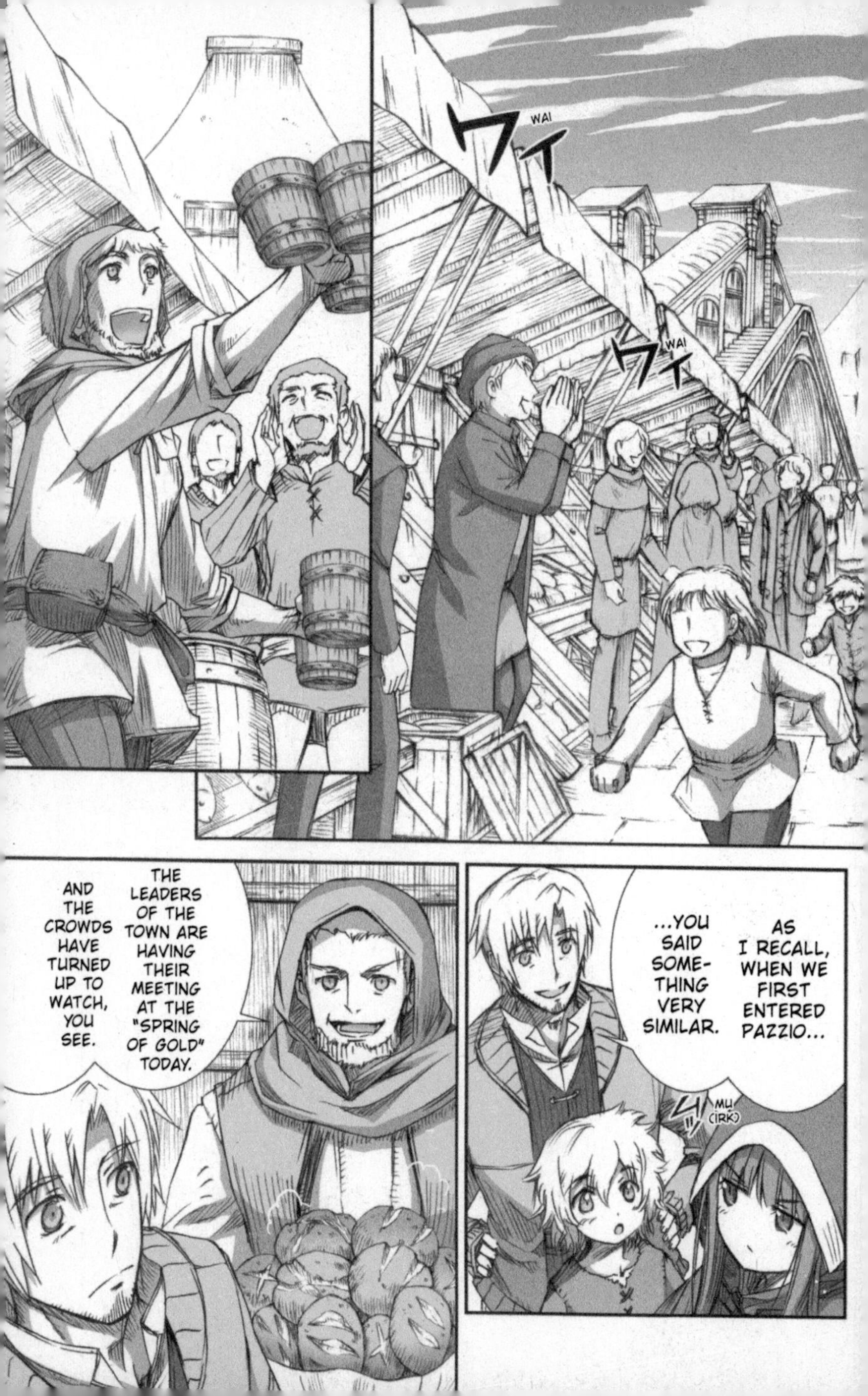
ワイ WAI
ワイ WAI
AS I RECALL, WHEN WE FIRST ENTERED PAZZIO...
...YOU SAID SOMETHING VERY SIMILAR.
MU (IRK)
THE LEADERS OF THE TOWN ARE HAVING THEIR MEETING AT THE "SPRING OF GOLD" TODAY.
AND THE CROWDS HAVE TURNED UP TO WATCH, YOU SEE.

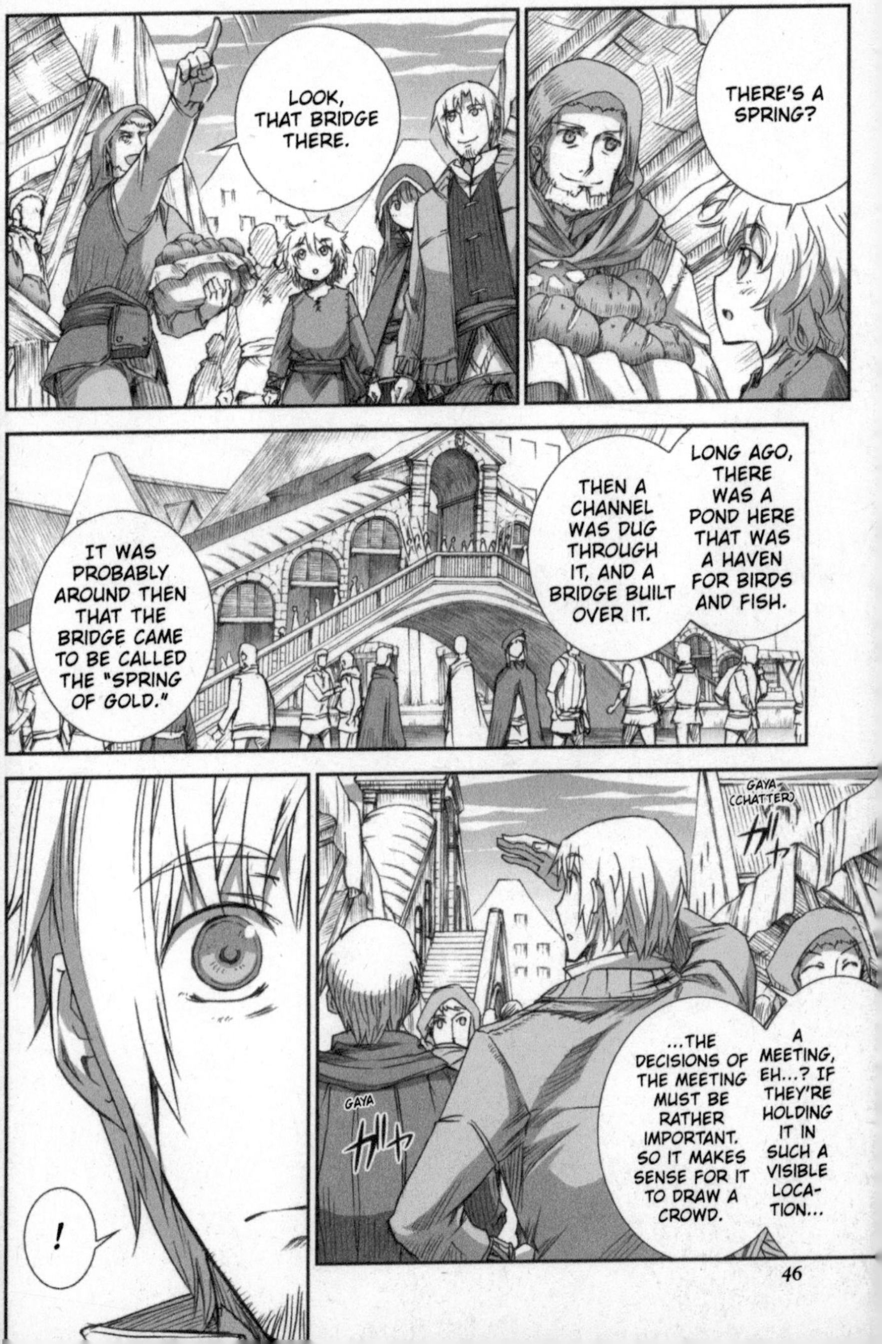
THERE'S A SPRING?
LOOK, THAT BRIDGE THERE.
LONG AGO, THERE WAS A POND HERE THAT WAS A HAVEN FOR BIRDS AND FISH.
THEN A CHANNEL WAS DUG THROUGH IT, AND A BRIDGE BUILT OVER IT.
IT WAS PROBABLY AROUND THEN THAT THE BRIDGE CAME TO BE CALLED THE "SPRING OF GOLD."
GAYA (CHATTER)
A MEETING, EH...? IF THEY'RE HOLDING IT IN SUCH A VISIBLE LOCA-TION...
...THE DECISIONS OF THE MEETING MUST BE RATHER IMPORTANT. SO IT MAKES SENSE FOR IT TO DRAW A CROWD.
GAYA
!

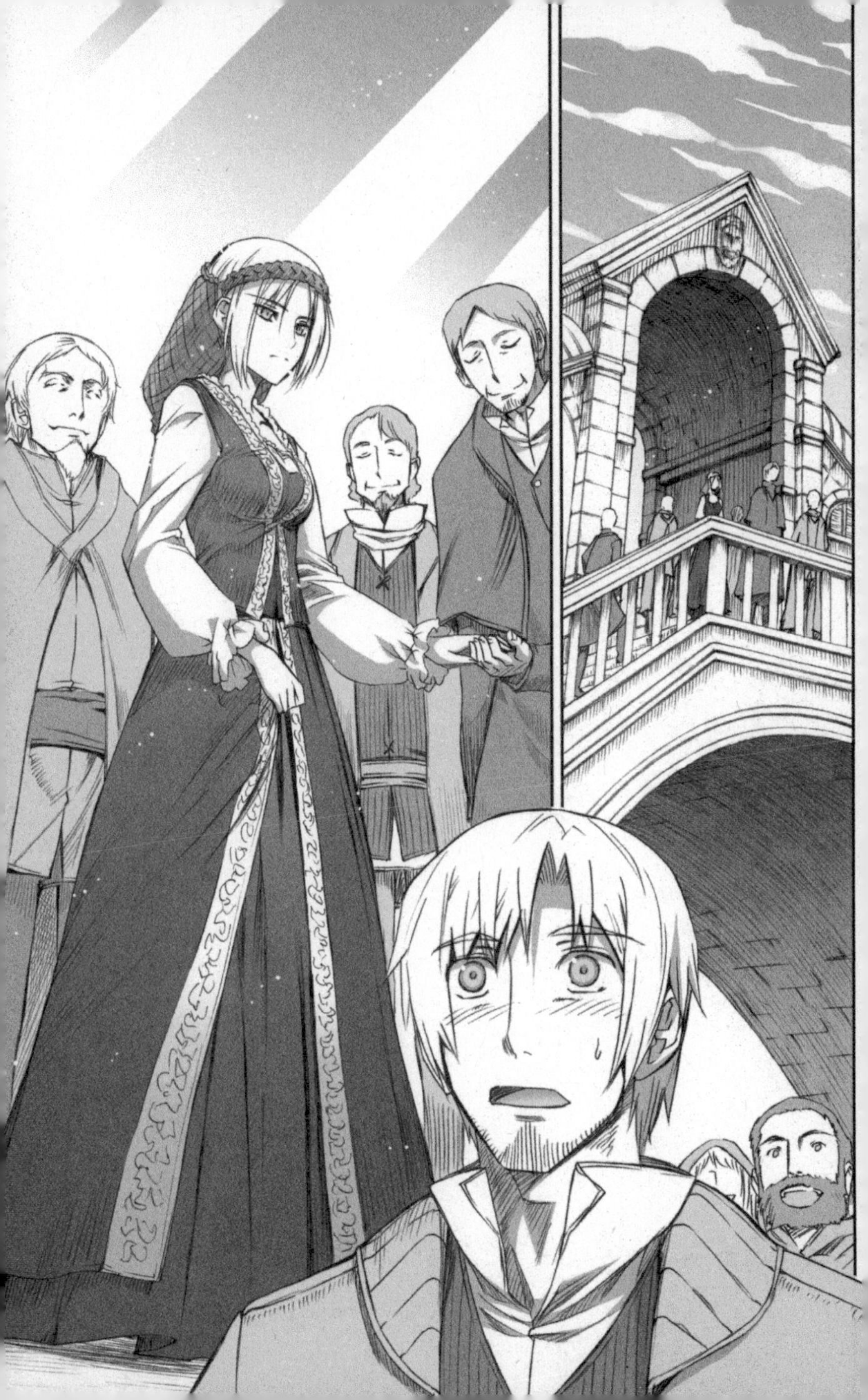

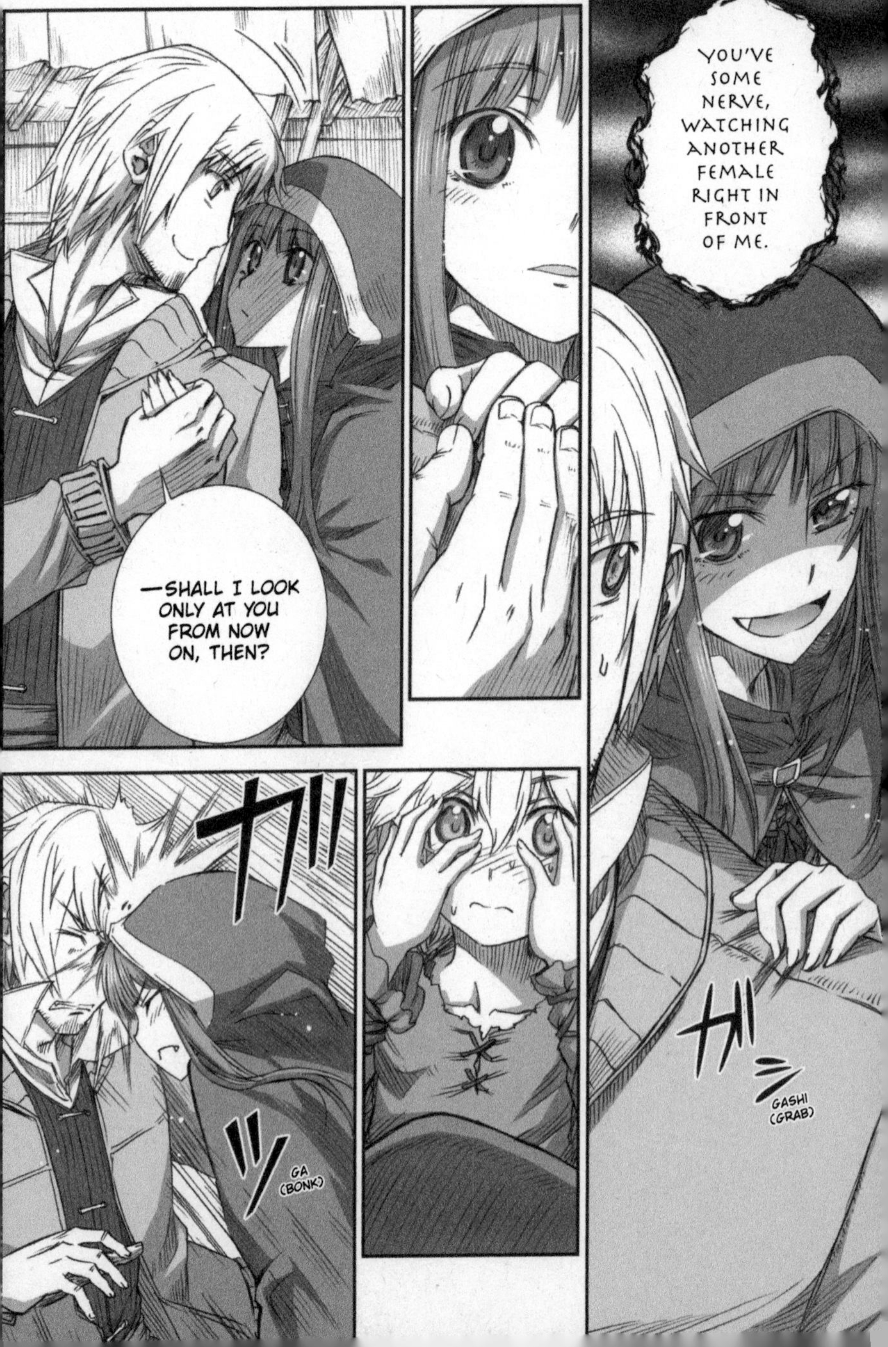
YOU'VE SOME NERVE, WATCHING ANOTHER FEMALE RIGHT IN FRONT OF ME.
GASHI (GRAB)
—SHALL I LOOK ONLY AT YOU FROM NOW ON, THEN?
GA (BONK)

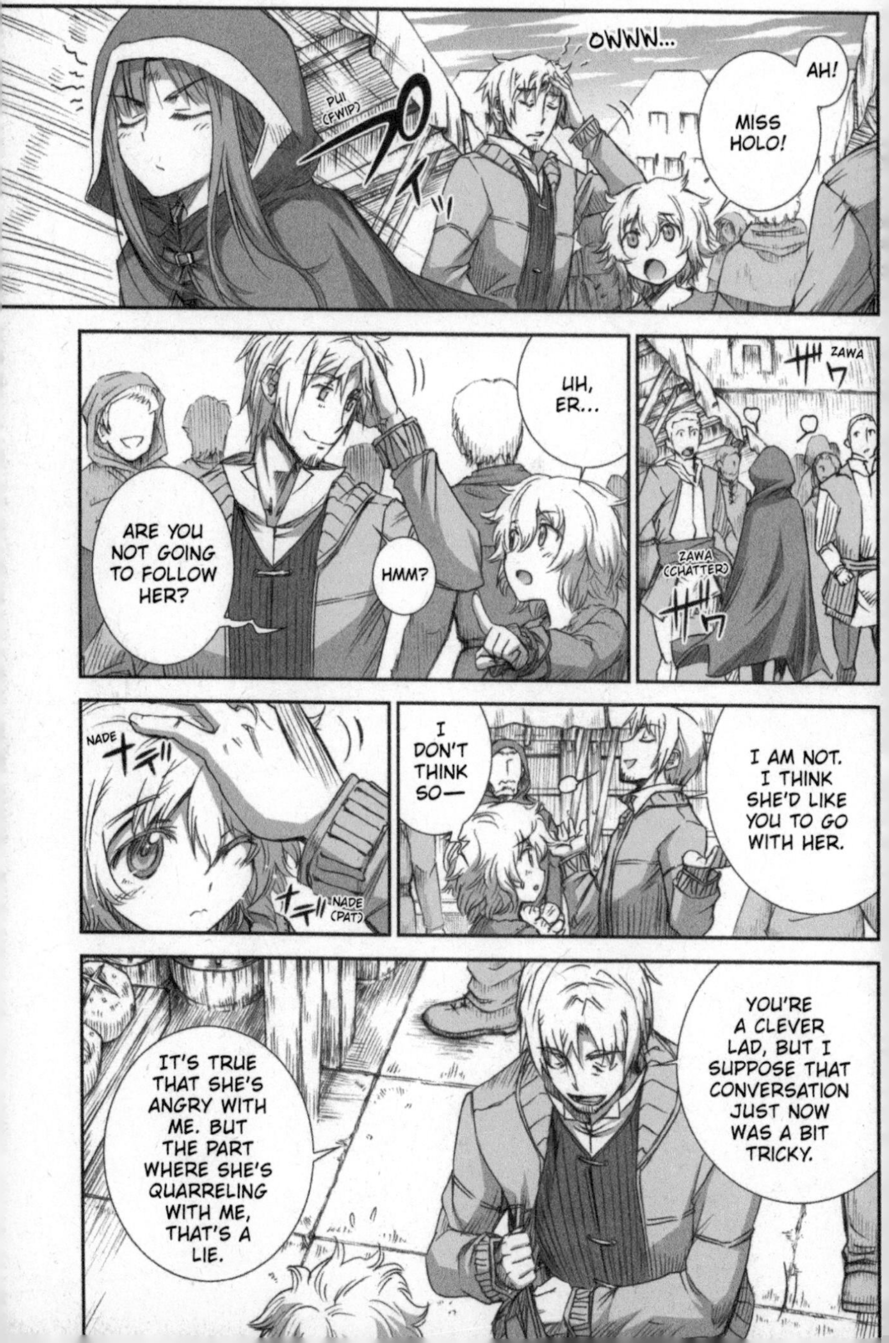
AH! MISS HOLO!
OWWW...
PUI (FWIP)
ZAWA
ZAWA (CHATTER)
UH, ER...
HMM?
ARE YOU NOT GOING TO FOLLOW HER?
I AM NOT. I THINK SHE'D LIKE YOU TO GO WITH HER.
I DON'T THINK SO—
NADE
NADE (PAT)
YOU'RE A CLEVER LAD, BUT I SUPPOSE THAT CONVERSATION JUST NOW WAS A BIT TRICKY.
IT'S TRUE THAT SHE'S ANGRY WITH ME. BUT THE PART WHERE SHE'S QUARRELING WITH ME, THAT'S A LIE.

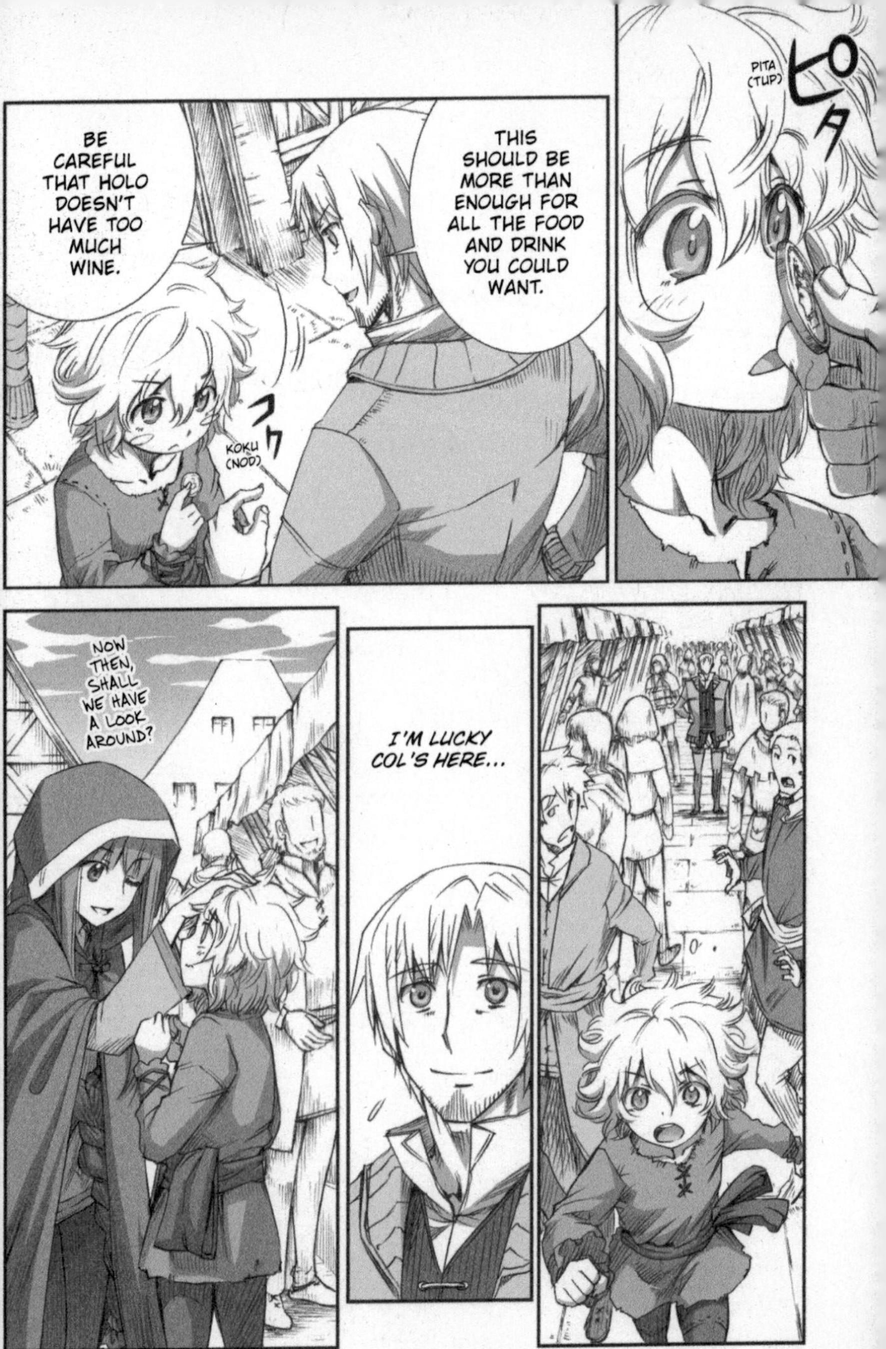
ピタ
PITA (TUP)
THIS SHOULD BE MORE THAN ENOUGH FOR ALL THE FOOD AND DRINK YOU COULD WANT.
BE CAREFUL THAT HOLO DOESN'T HAVE TOO MUCH WINE.
コク
KOKU (NOD)
I'M LUCKY COL'S HERE...
NOW THEN, SHALL WE HAVE A LOOK AROUND?

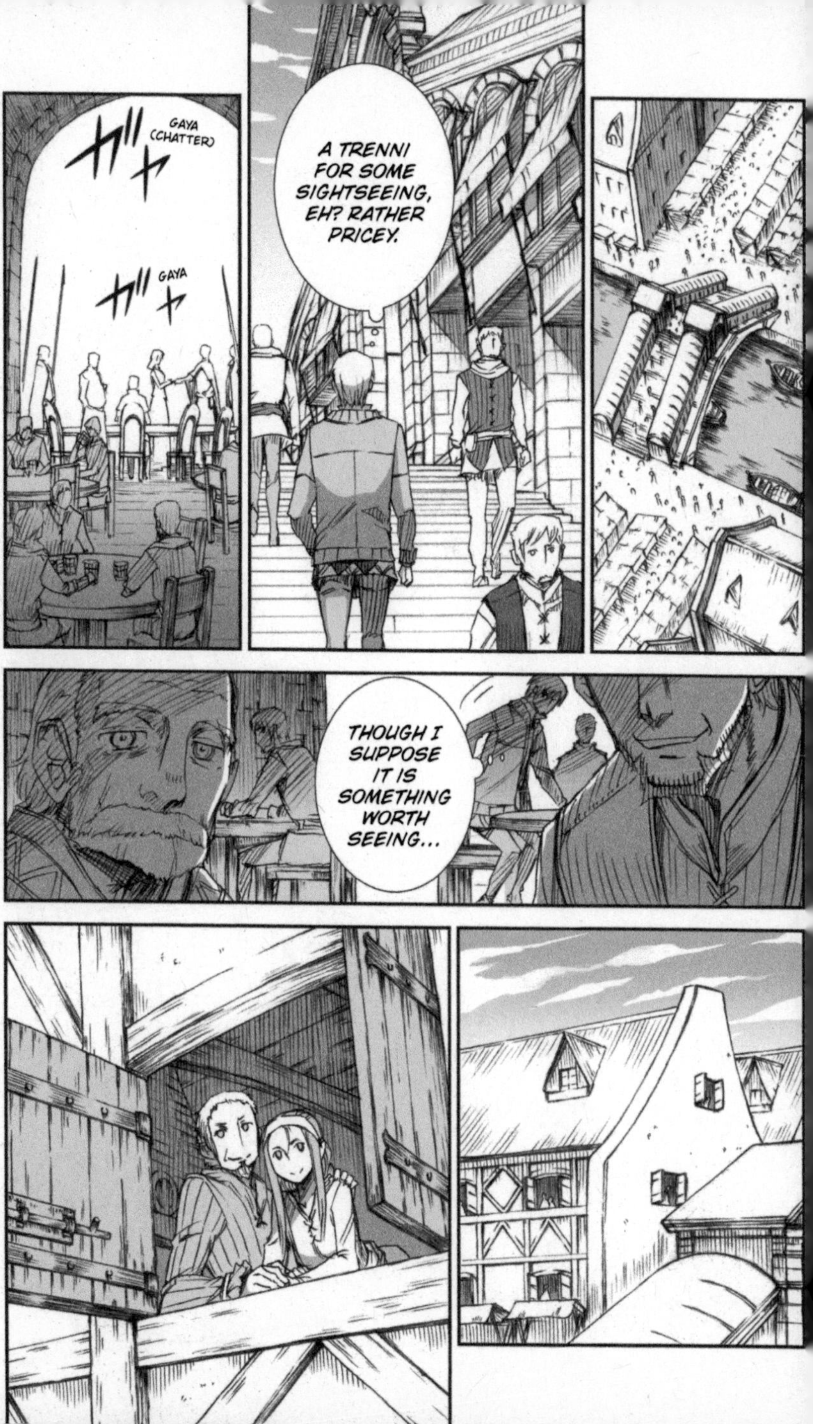
A TRENNI FOR SOME SIGHTSEEING, EH? RATHER PRICEY.
ガヤ
GAYA (CHATTER)
ガヤ
GAYA
THOUGH I SUPPOSE IT IS SOMETHING WORTH SEEING...

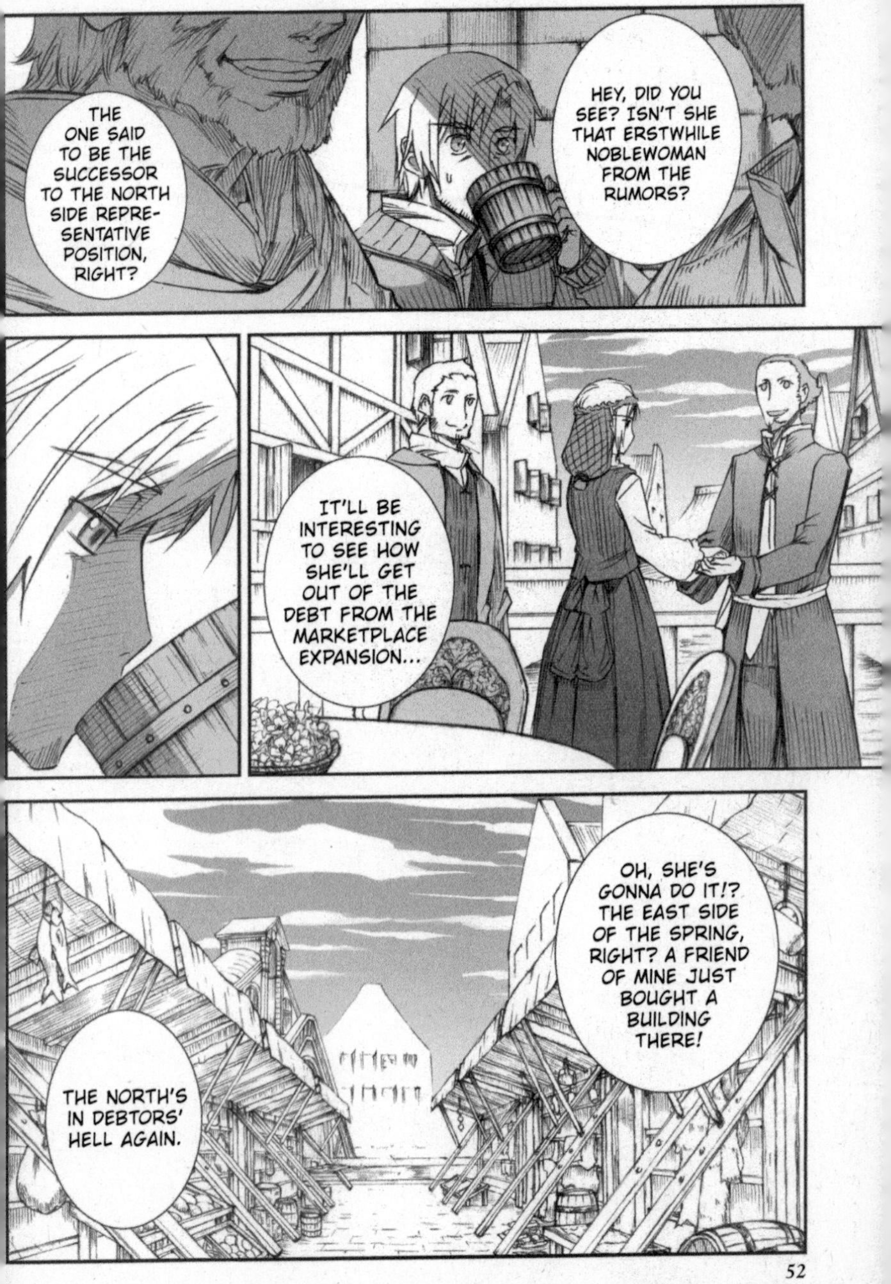
HEY, DID YOU SEE? ISN'T SHE THAT ERSTWHILE NOBLEWOMAN FROM THE RUMORS?
THE ONE SAID TO BE THE SUCCESSOR TO THE NORTH SIDE REPRE-SENTATIVE POSITION, RIGHT?
IT'LL BE INTERESTING TO SEE HOW SHE'LL GET OUT OF THE DEBT FROM THE MARKETPLACE EXPANSION...
OH, SHE'S GONNA DO IT!? THE EAST SIDE OF THE SPRING, RIGHT? A FRIEND OF MINE JUST BOUGHT A BUILDING THERE!
THE NORTH'S IN DEBTORS' HELL AGAIN.

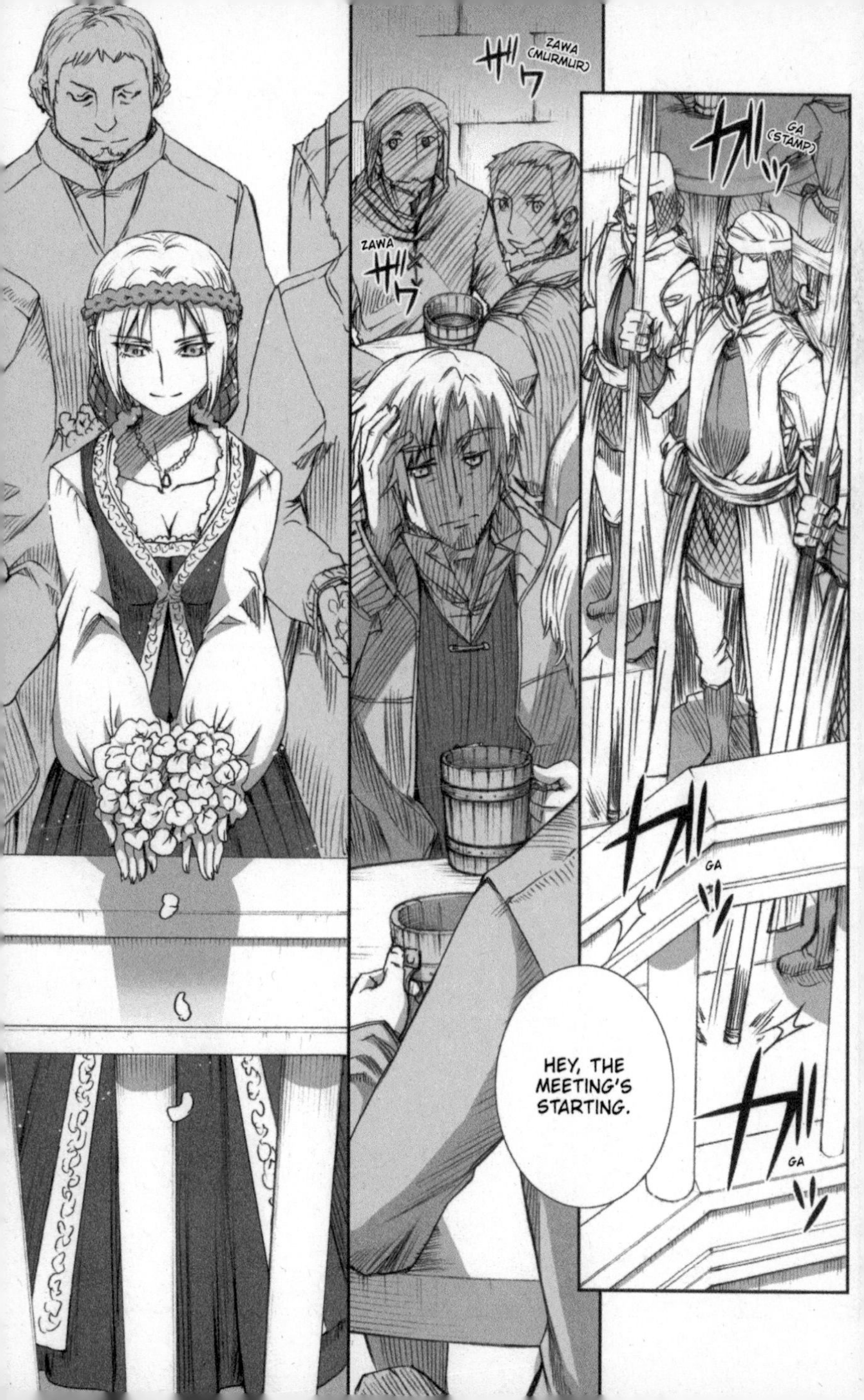
GA (STAMP)
GA
GA
ZAWA (MURMUR)
ZAWA
HEY, THE MEETING'S STARTING.

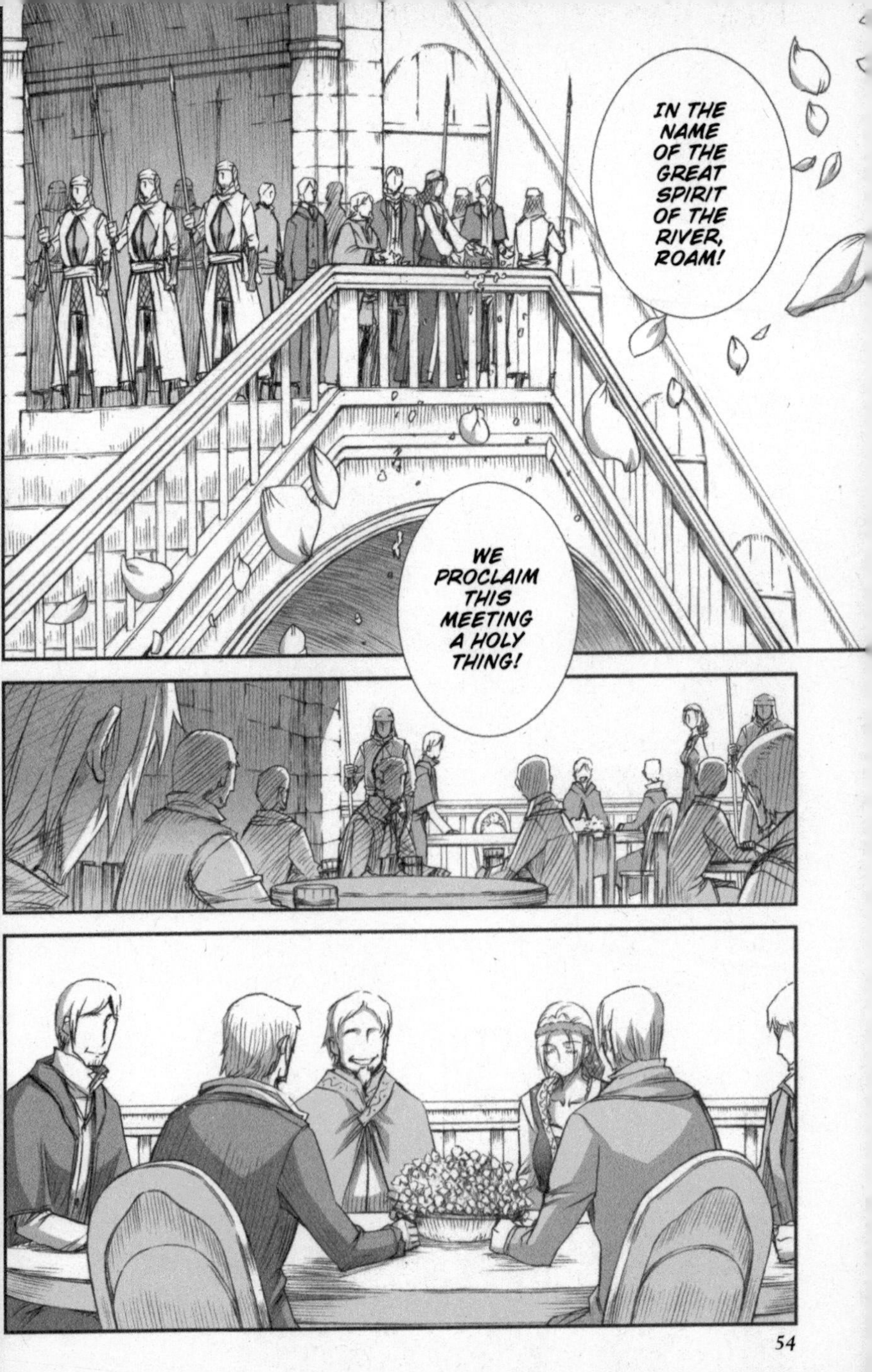
IN THE NAME OF THE GREAT SPIRIT OF THE RIVER, ROAM!
WE PROCLAIM THIS MEETING A HOLY THING!

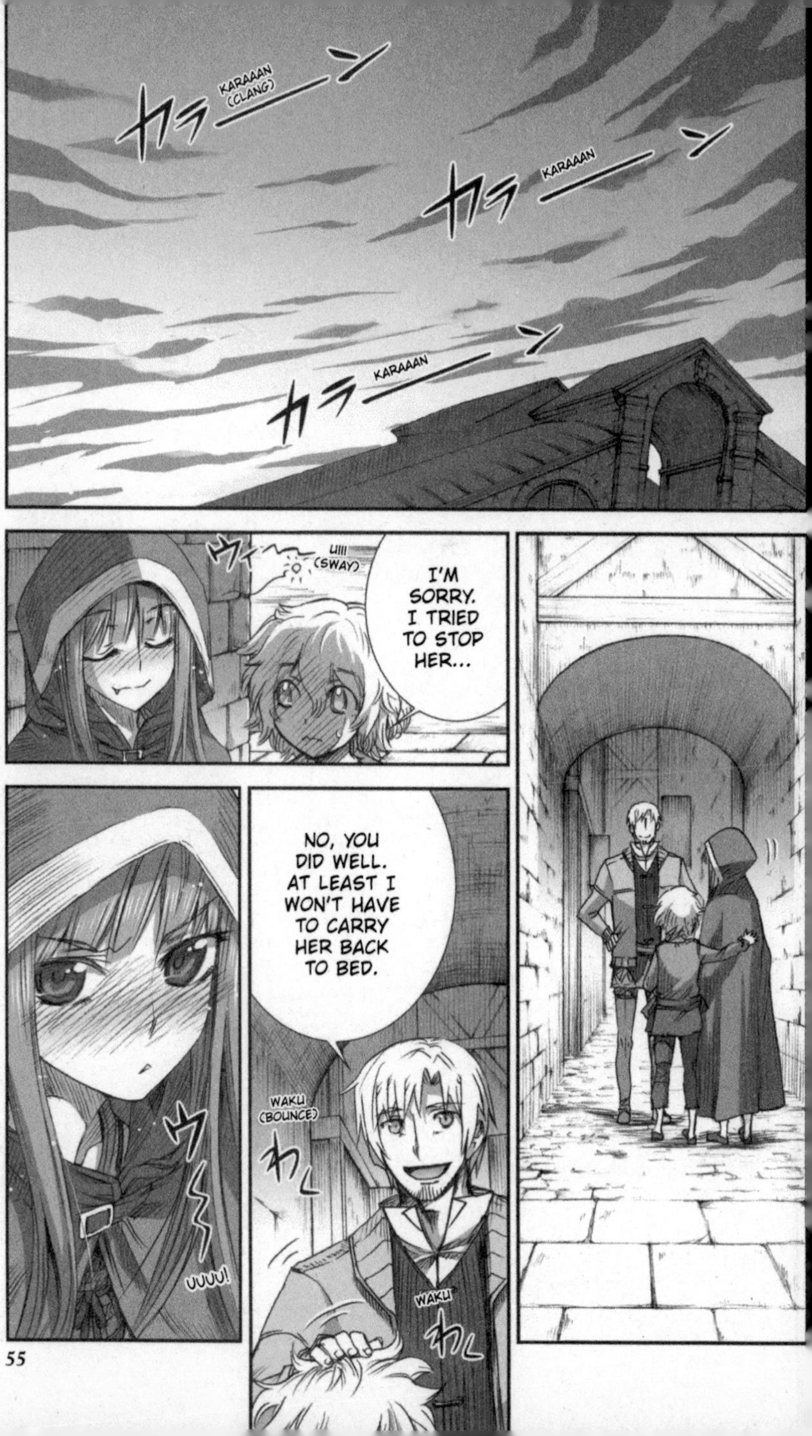
KARAAAN (CLANG)
KARAAAN
KARAAAN
UIII (SWAY)
I'M SORRY. I TRIED TO STOP HER...
NO, YOU DID WELL. AT LEAST I WON'T HAVE TO CARRY HER BACK TO BED.
WAKU (BOUNCE)
WAKU
UUUU!

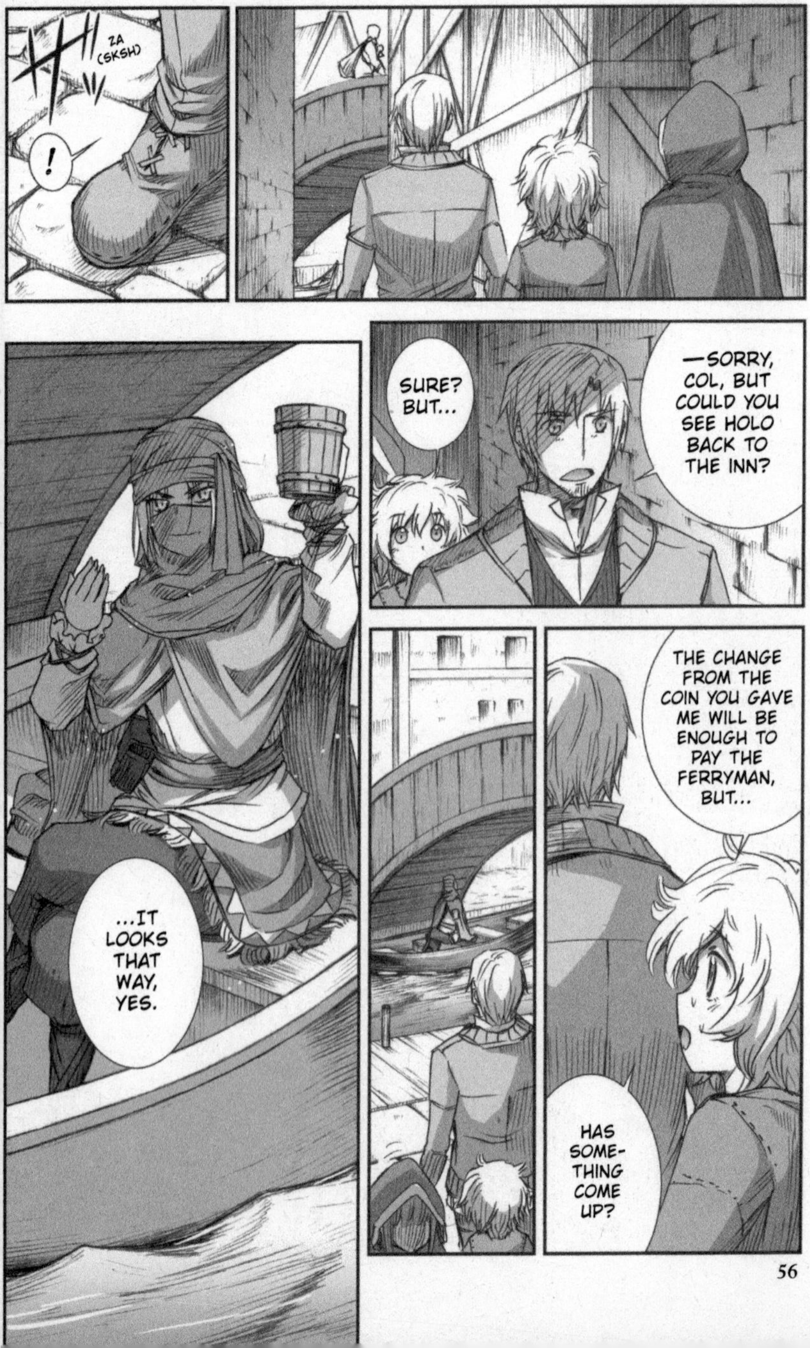
ZA (SKSH)
!
—SORRY, COL, BUT COULD YOU SEE HOLO BACK TO THE INN?
SURE? BUT...
THE CHANGE FROM THE COIN YOU GAVE ME WILL BE ENOUGH TO PAY THE FERRYMAN, BUT...
HAS SOME-THING COME UP?
...IT LOOKS THAT WAY, YES.

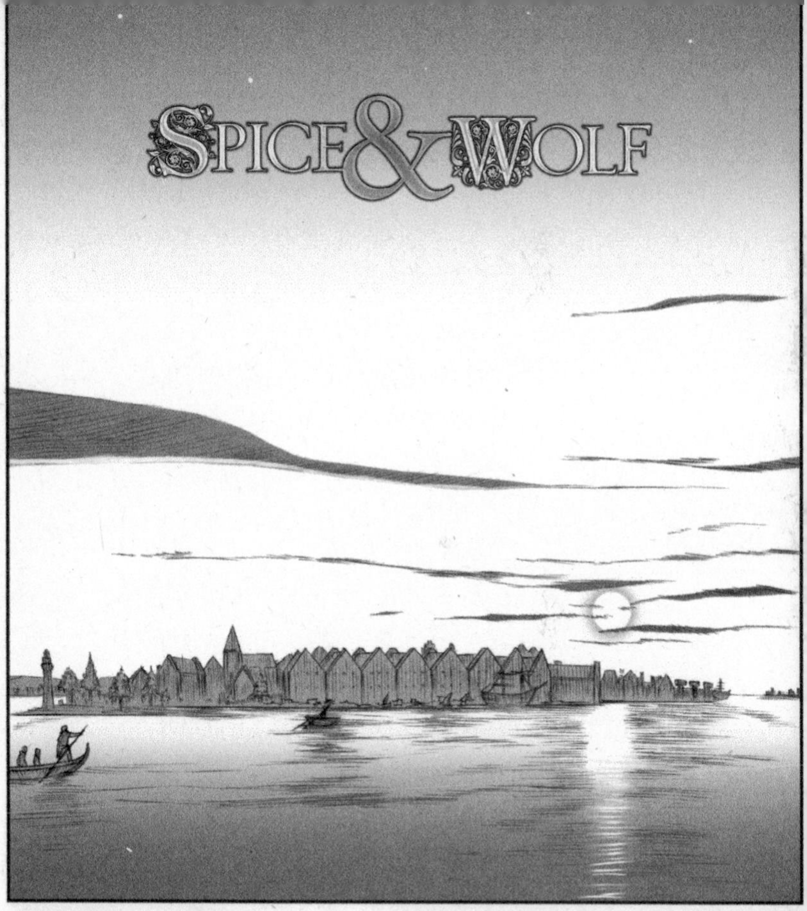
SPICE & WOLF
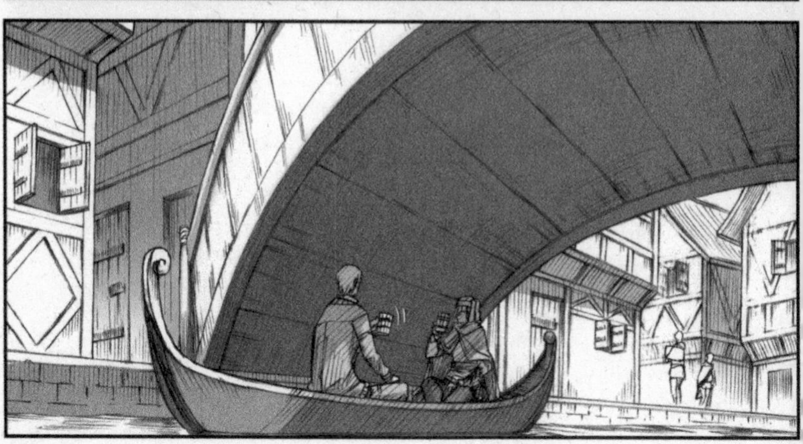

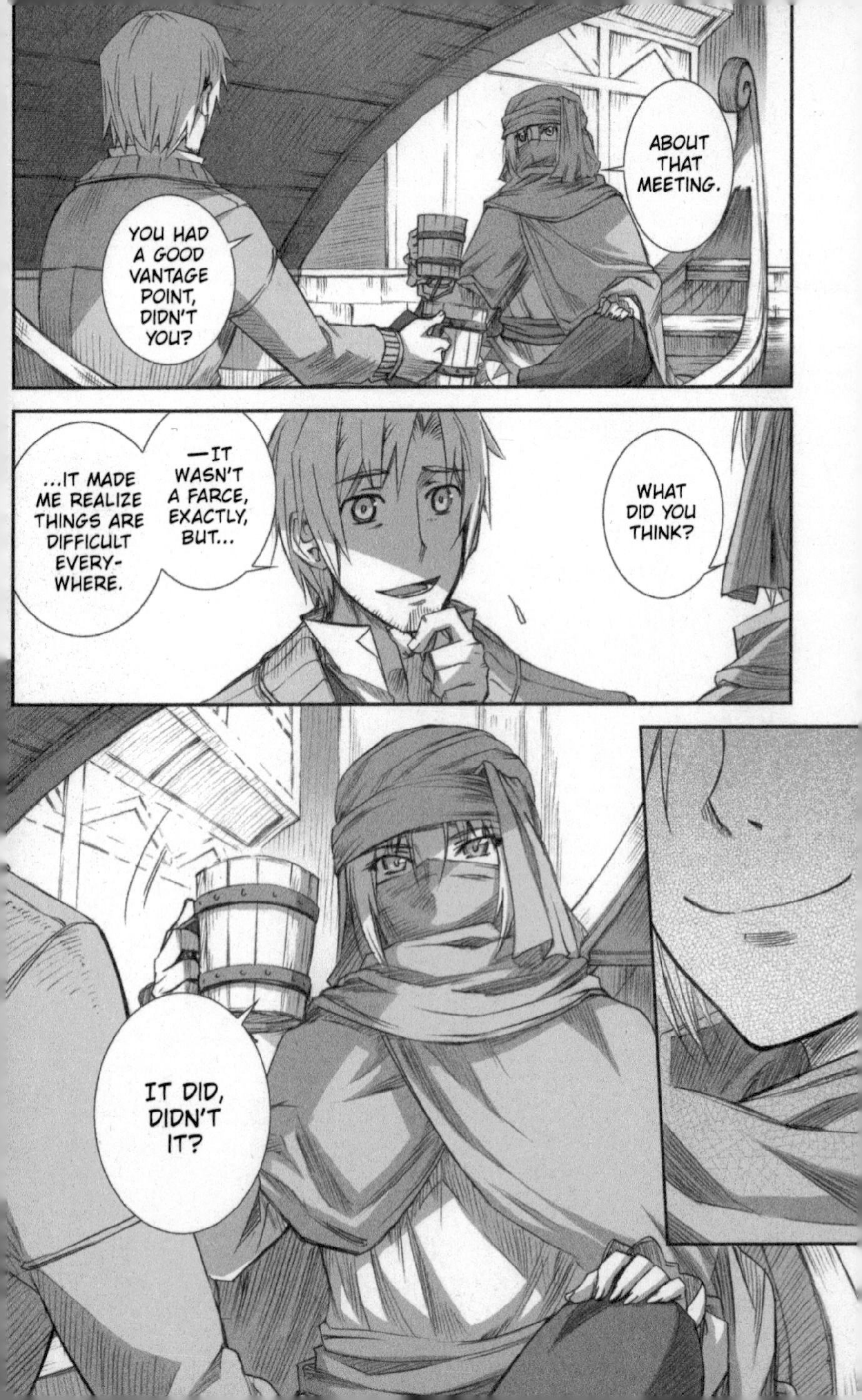
ABOUT THAT MEETING.
YOU HAD A GOOD VANTAGE POINT, DIDN'T YOU?
WHAT DID YOU THINK?
—IT WASN'T A FARCE, EXACTLY, BUT...
...IT MADE ME REALIZE THINGS ARE DIFFICULT EVERY-WHERE.
IT DID, DIDN'T IT?

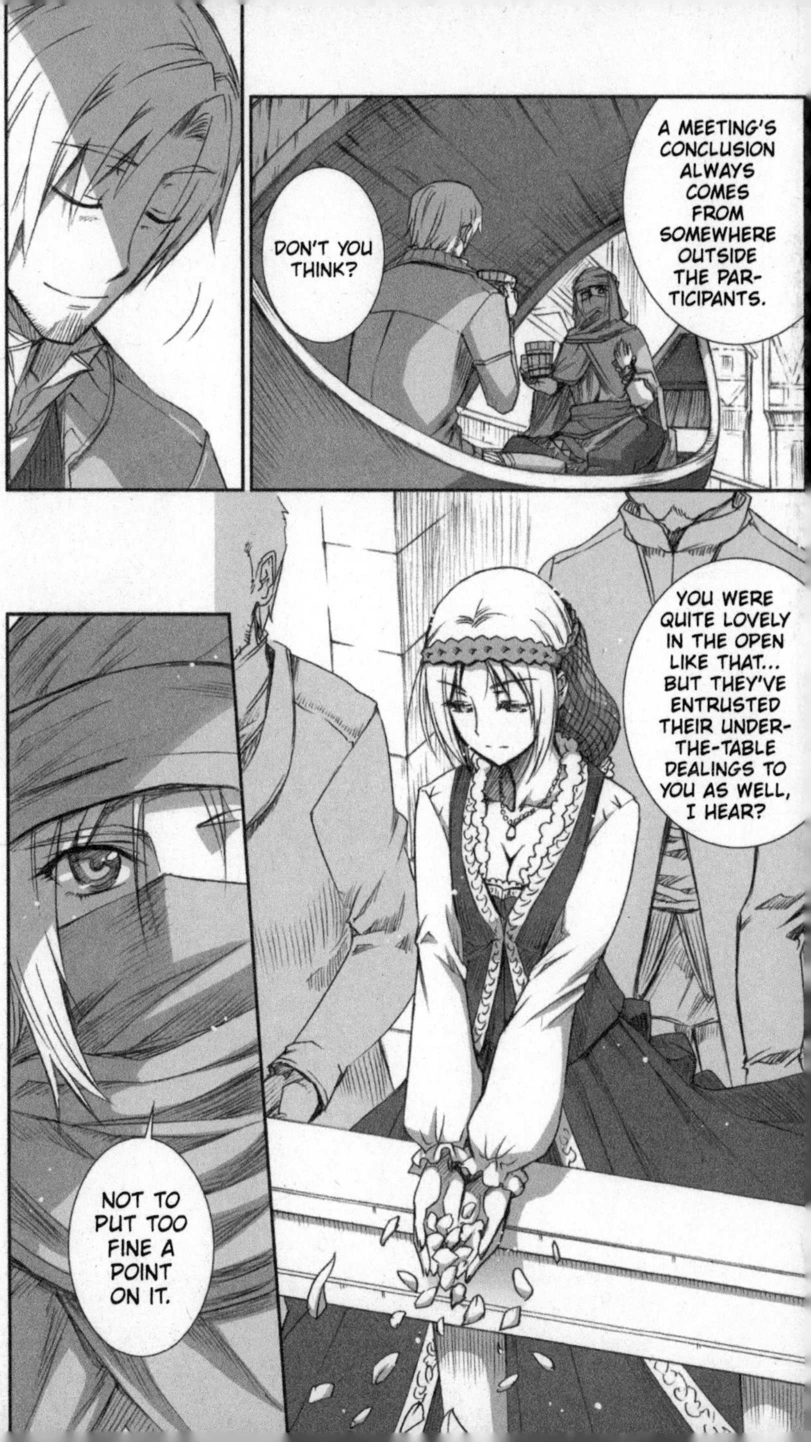
A MEETING'S CONCLUSION ALWAYS COMES FROM SOMEWHERE OUTSIDE THE PARTICIPANTS.
DON'T YOU THINK?
YOU WERE QUITE LOVELY IN THE OPEN LIKE THAT... BUT THEY'VE ENTRUSTED THEIR UNDER-THE-TABLE DEALINGS TO YOU AS WELL, I HEAR?
NOT TO PUT TOO FINE A POINT ON IT.

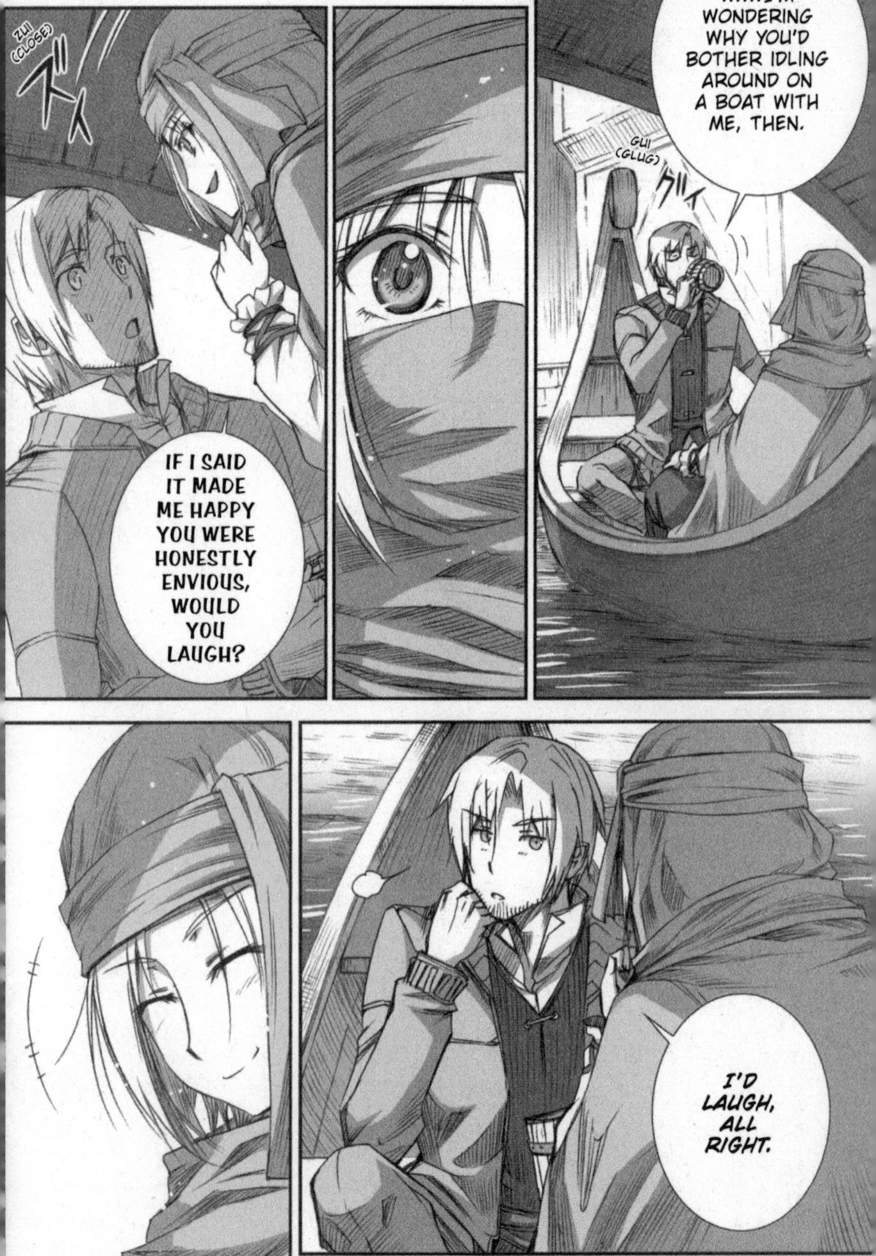
......I'M WONDERING WHY YOU'D BOTHER IDLING AROUND ON A BOAT WITH ME, THEN.
GUI (GLUG)
ZUI (CLOSE)
IF I SAID IT MADE ME HAPPY YOU WERE HONESTLY ENVIOUS, WOULD YOU LAUGH?
I'D LAUGH, ALL RIGHT.

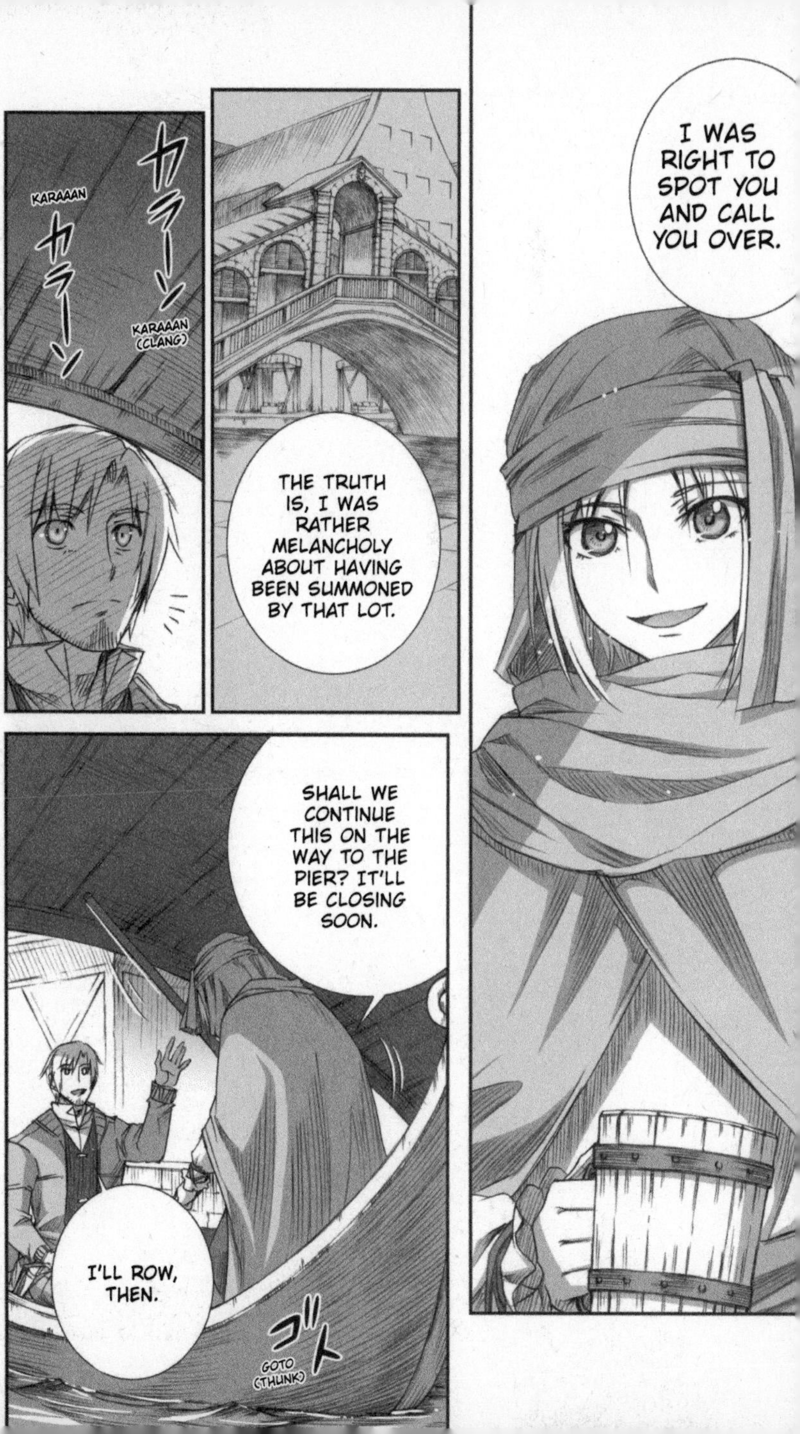
I WAS RIGHT TO SPOT YOU AND CALL YOU OVER.
THE TRUTH IS, I WAS RATHER MELANCHOLY ABOUT HAVING BEEN SUMMONED BY THAT LOT.
カラーン
KARAAAN (CLANG)
カラーン
KARAAAN
SHALL WE CONTINUE THIS ON THE WAY TO THE PIER? IT'LL BE CLOSING SOON.
I'LL ROW, THEN.
ゴト
GOTO (THUNK)

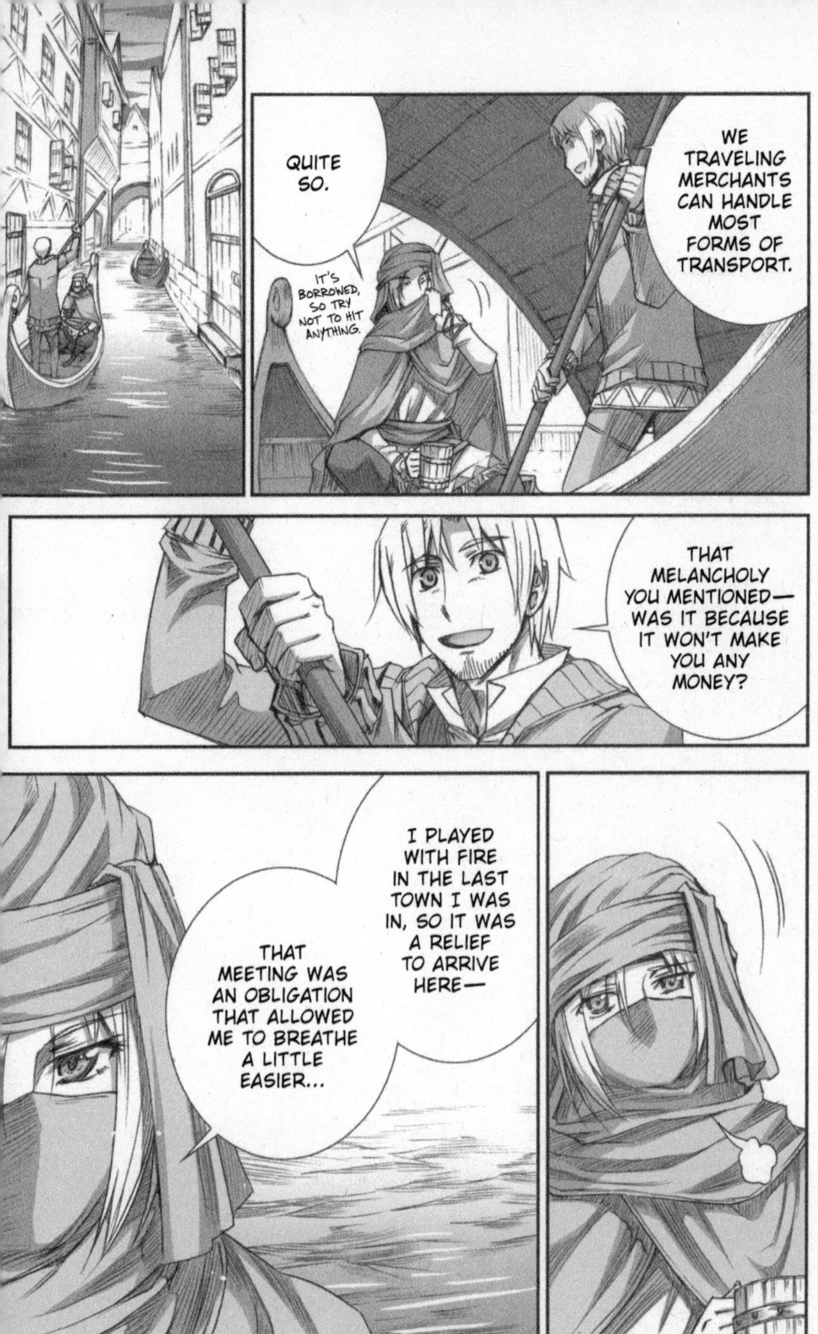
WE TRAVELING MERCHANTS CAN HANDLE MOST FORMS OF TRANSPORT.
QUITE SO.
IT'S BORROWED, SO TRY NOT TO HIT ANYTHING.
THAT MELANCHOLY YOU MENTIONED—WAS IT BECAUSE IT WON'T MAKE YOU ANY MONEY?
I PLAYED WITH FIRE IN THE LAST TOWN I WAS IN, SO IT WAS A RELIEF TO ARRIVE HERE—
THAT MEETING WAS AN OBLIGATION THAT ALLOWED ME TO BREATHE A LITTLE EASIER...

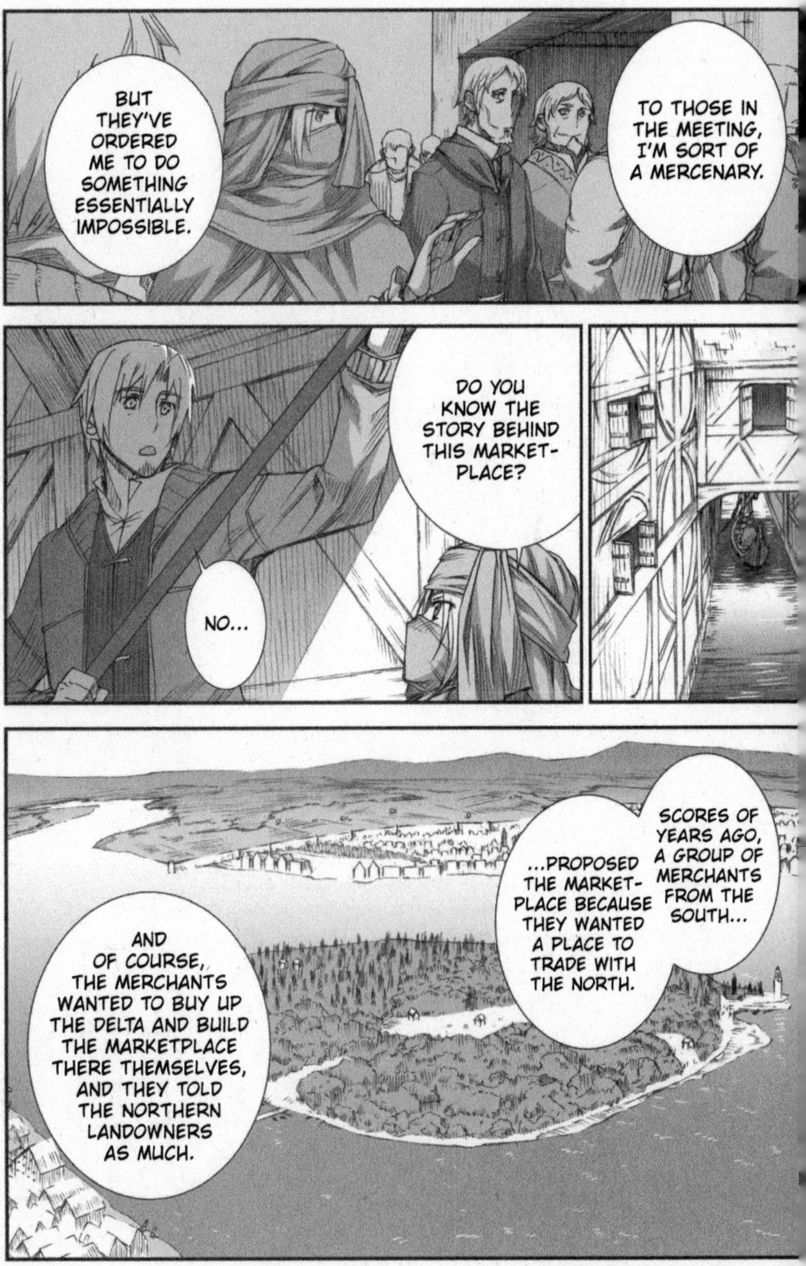
TO THOSE IN THE MEETING, I'M SORT OF A MERCENARY.
BUT THEY'VE ORDERED ME TO DO SOMETHING ESSENTIALLY IMPOSSIBLE.
DO YOU KNOW THE STORY BEHIND THIS MARKET-PLACE?
NO...
SCORES OF YEARS AGO, A GROUP OF MERCHANTS FROM THE SOUTH...
...PROPOSED THE MARKET-PLACE BECAUSE THEY WANTED A PLACE TO TRADE WITH THE NORTH.
AND OF COURSE, THE MERCHANTS WANTED TO BUY UP THE DELTA AND BUILD THE MARKETPLACE THERE THEMSELVES, AND THEY TOLD THE NORTHERN LANDOWNERS AS MUCH.

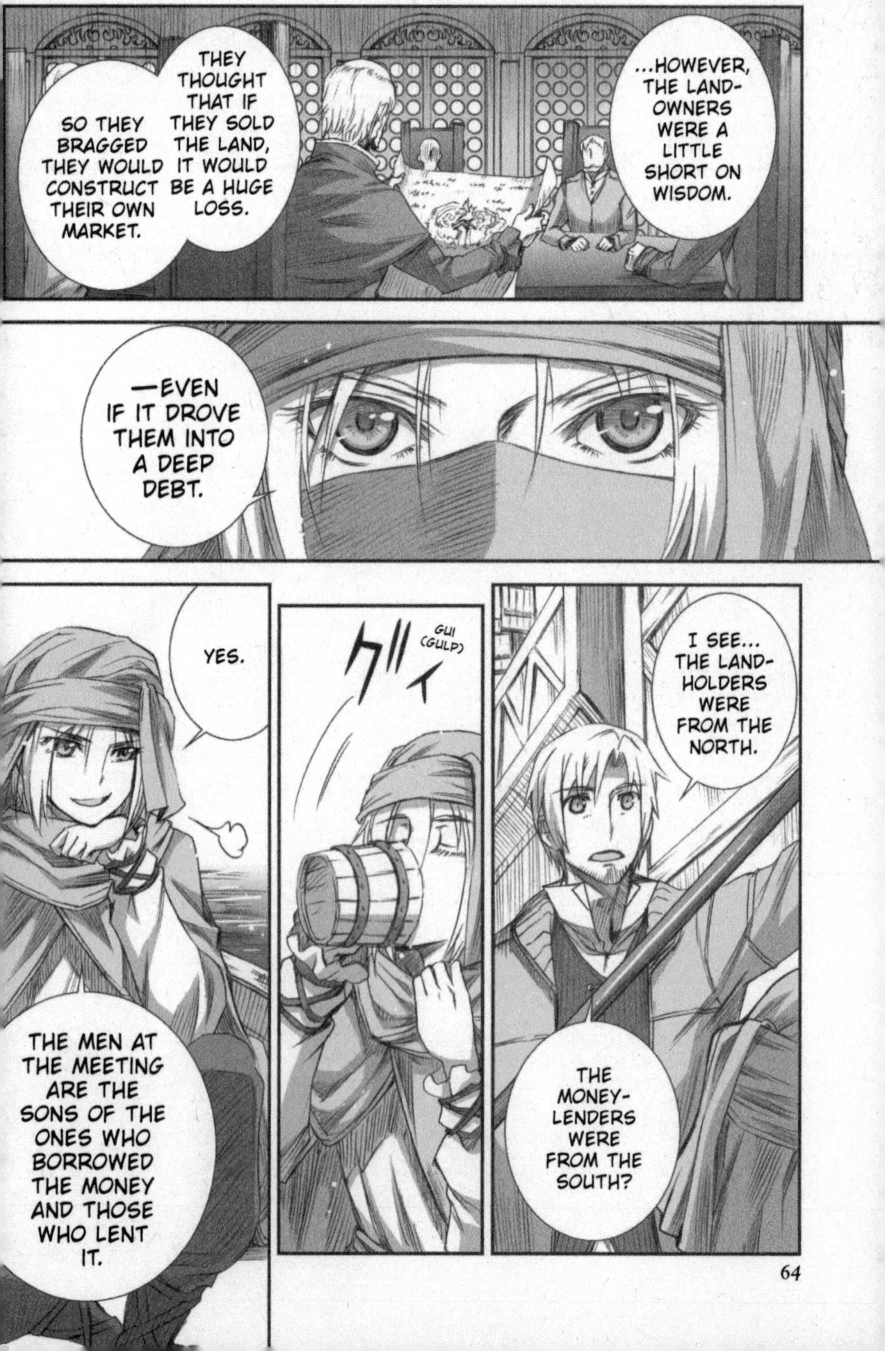
...HOWEVER, THE LAND-OWNERS WERE A LITTLE SHORT ON WISDOM.
THEY THOUGHT THAT IF THEY SOLD THE LAND, IT WOULD BE A HUGE LOSS.
SO THEY BRAGGED THEY WOULD CONSTRUCT THEIR OWN MARKET.
—EVEN IF IT DROVE THEM INTO A DEEP DEBT.
I SEE... THE LAND-HOLDERS WERE FROM THE NORTH.
THE MONEY-LENDERS WERE FROM THE SOUTH?
グイ
GUI (GULP)
YES.
THE MEN AT THE MEETING ARE THE SONS OF THE ONES WHO BORROWED THE MONEY AND THOSE WHO LENT IT.

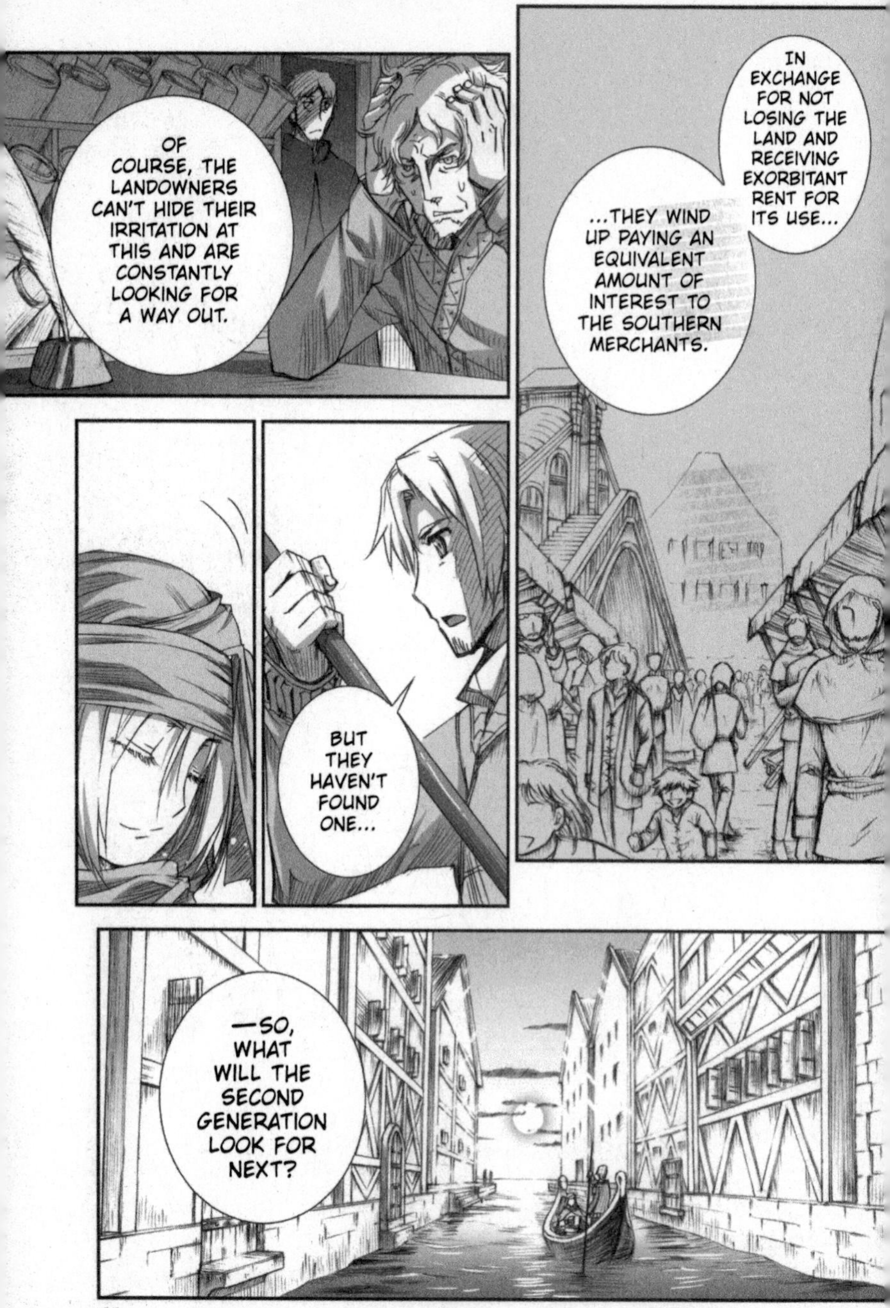
IN EXCHANGE FOR NOT LOSING THE LAND AND RECEIVING EXORBITANT RENT FOR ITS USE...
...THEY WIND UP PAYING AN EQUIVALENT AMOUNT OF INTEREST TO THE SOUTHERN MERCHANTS.
OF COURSE, THE LANDOWNERS CAN'T HIDE THEIR IRRITATION AT THIS AND ARE CONSTANTLY LOOKING FOR A WAY OUT.
BUT THEY HAVEN'T FOUND ONE...
—SO, WHAT WILL THE SECOND GENERATION LOOK FOR NEXT?

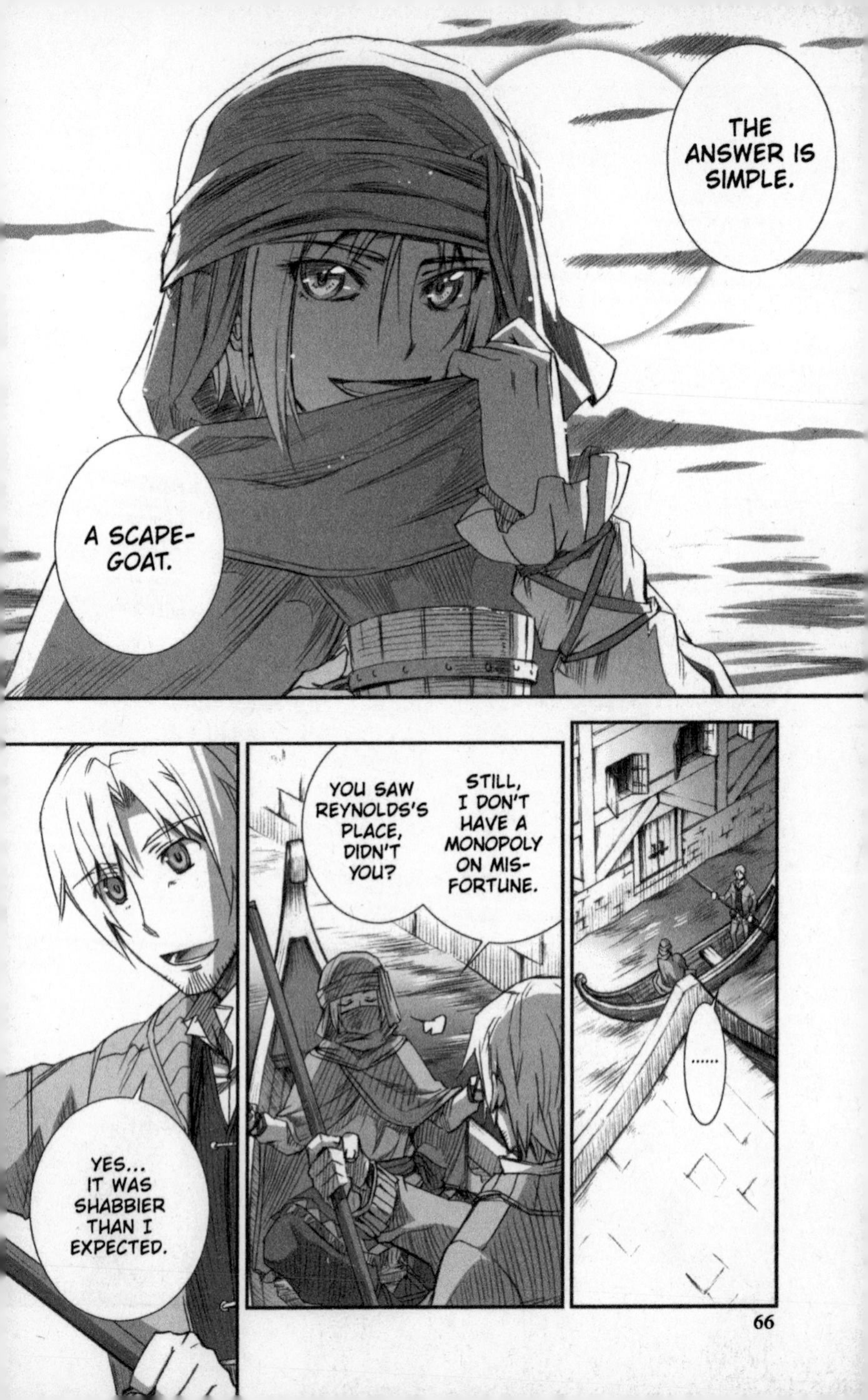
THE ANSWER IS SIMPLE.
A SCAPE-GOAT.
......
STILL, I DON'T HAVE A MONOPOLY ON MIS-FORTUNE.
YOU SAW REYNOLDS'S PLACE, DIDN'T YOU?
YES... IT WAS SHABBIER THAN I EXPECTED.

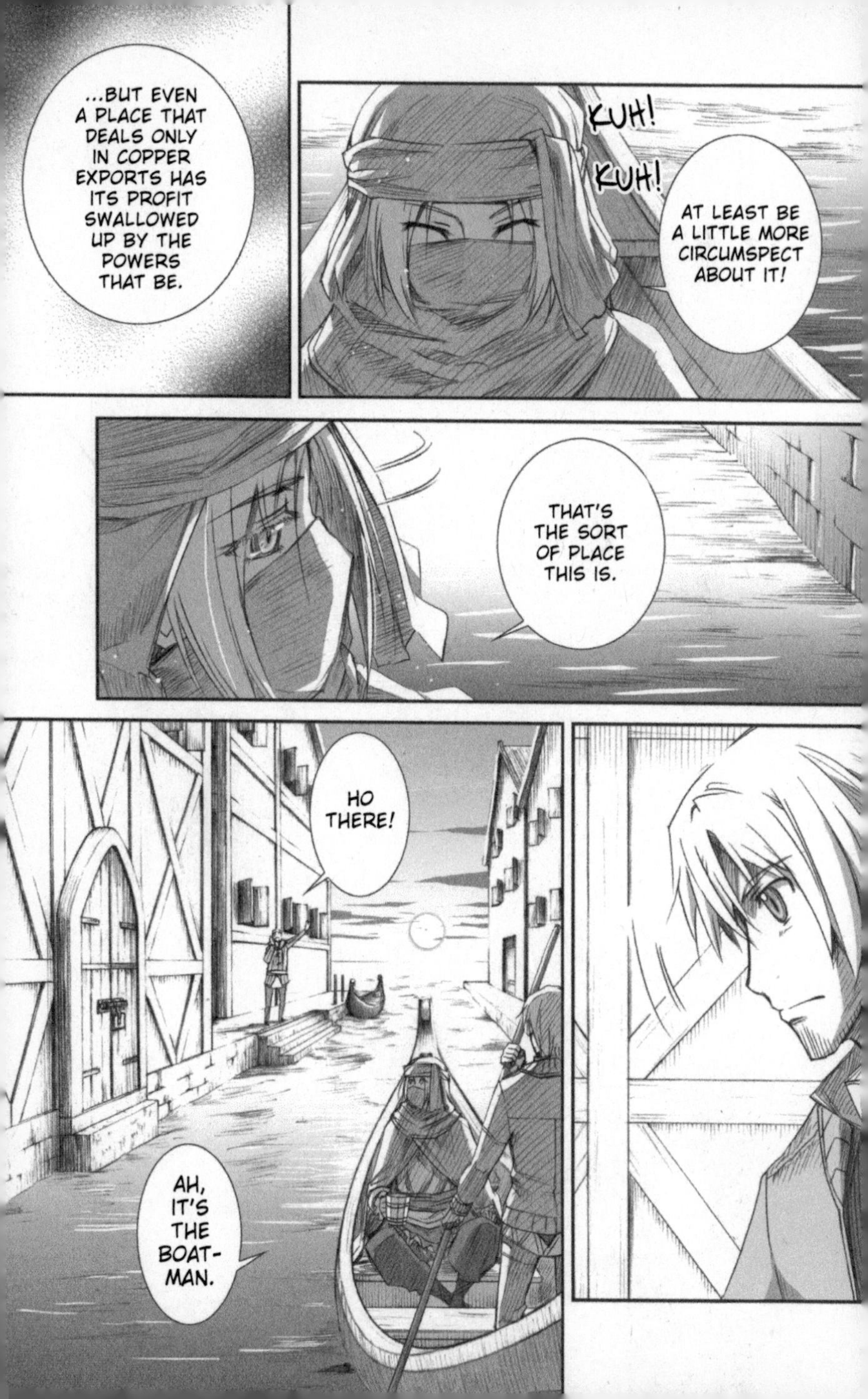
KUH!
KUH!
AT LEAST BE A LITTLE MORE CIRCUMSPECT ABOUT IT!
...BUT EVEN A PLACE THAT DEALS ONLY IN COPPER EXPORTS HAS ITS PROFIT SWALLOWED UP BY THE POWERS THAT BE.
THAT'S THE SORT OF PLACE THIS IS.
HO THERE!
AH, IT'S THE BOAT-MAN.

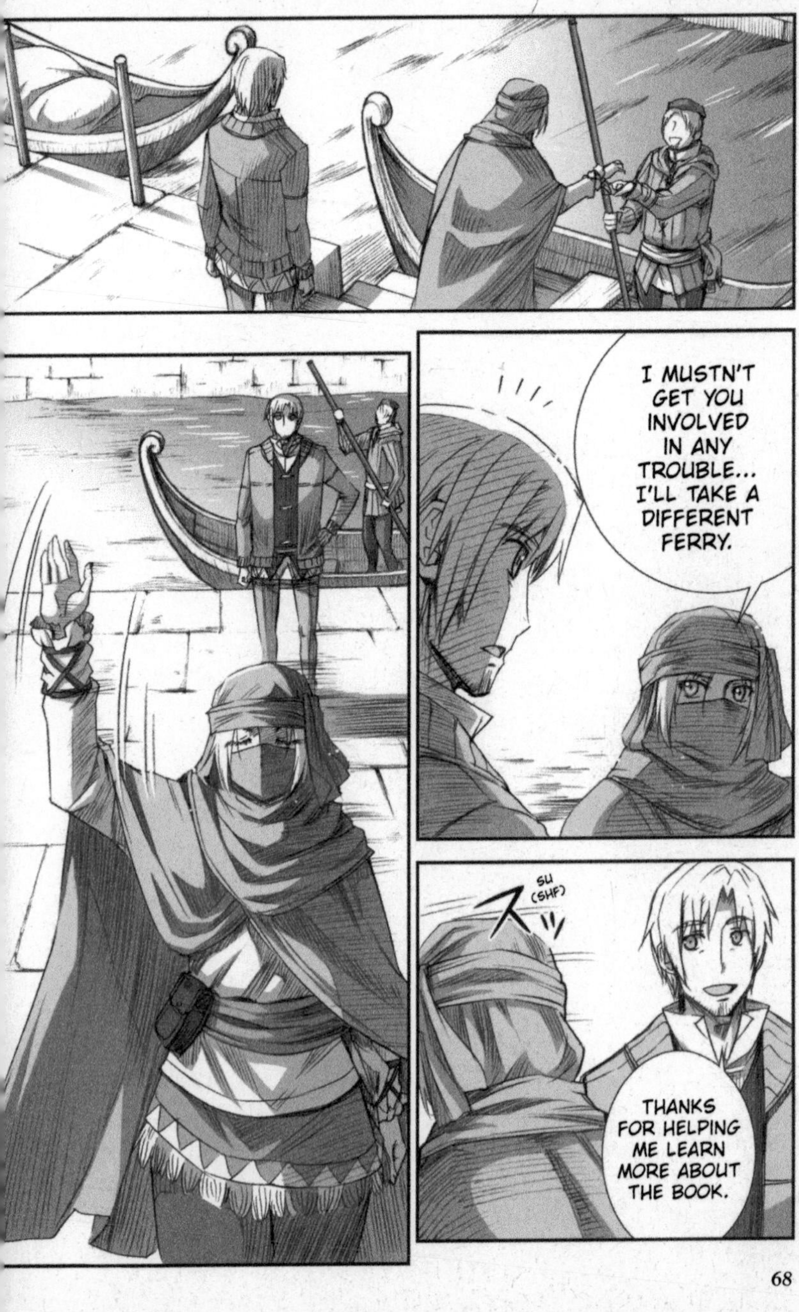
I MUSTN'T GET YOU INVOLVED IN ANY TROUBLE... I'LL TAKE A DIFFERENT FERRY.
SU (SHF)
THANKS FOR HELPING ME LEARN MORE ABOUT THE BOOK.

SPICE & WOLF

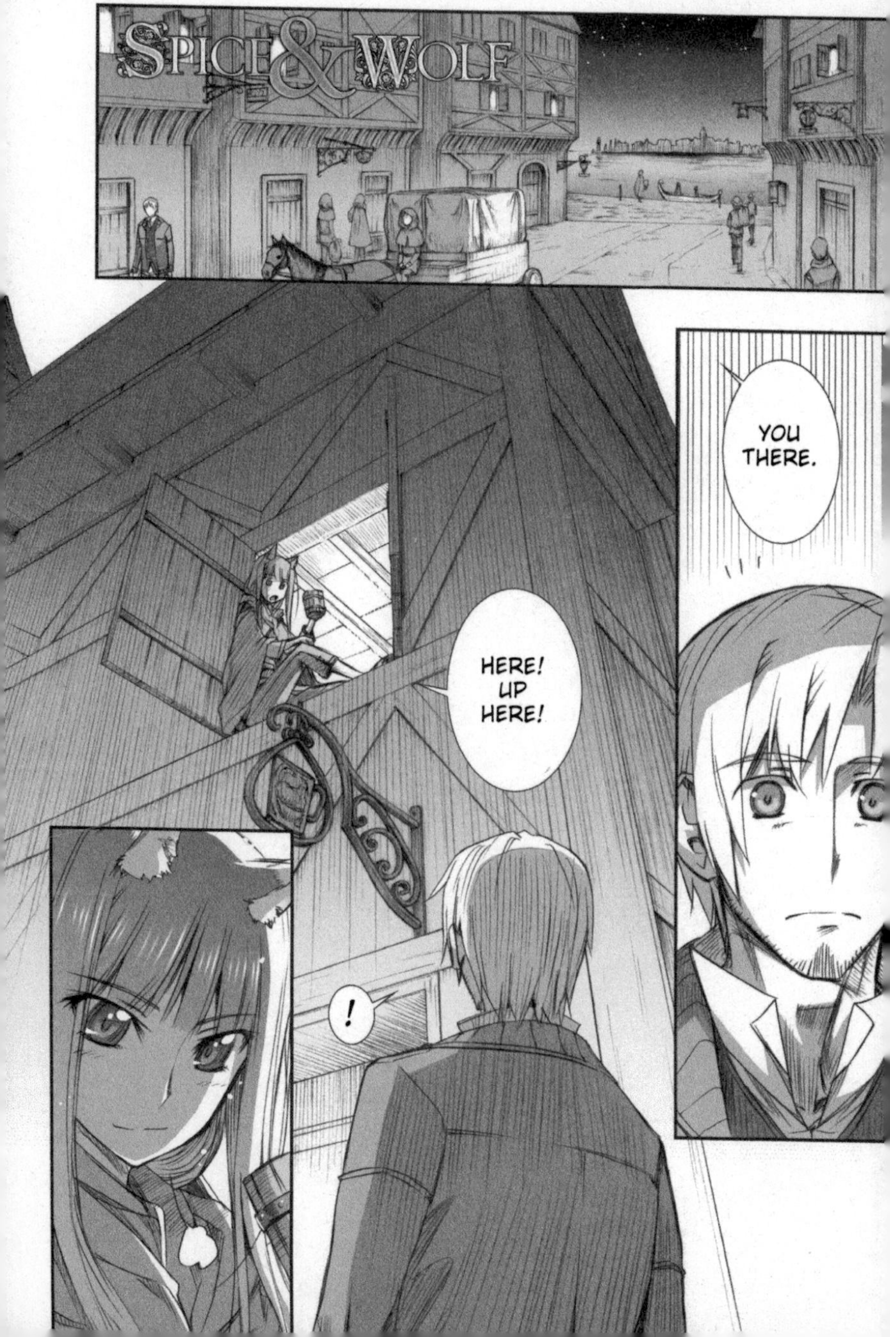
SPICE & WOLF
YOU THERE.
HERE! UP HERE!
!

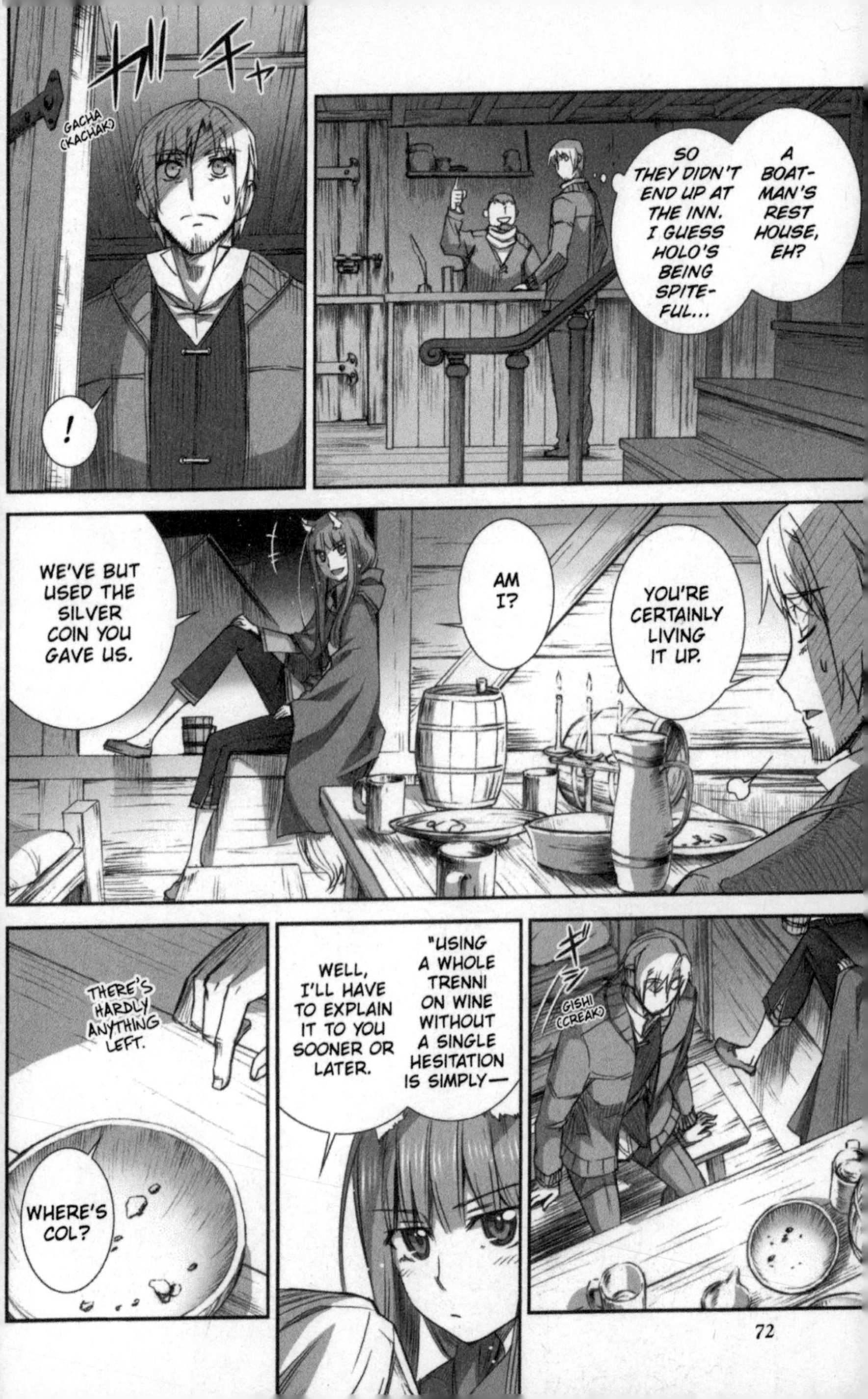
A BOAT-MAN'S REST HOUSE, EH?
SO THEY DIDN'T END UP AT THE INN. I GUESS HOLO'S BEING SPITE-FUL...
GACHA (KACHAK)
!
YOU'RE CERTAINLY LIVING IT UP.
AM I?
WE'VE BUT USED THE SILVER COIN YOU GAVE US.
GISHI (CREAK)
"USING A WHOLE TRENNI ON WINE WITHOUT A SINGLE HESITATION IS SIMPLY—
WELL, I'LL HAVE TO EXPLAIN IT TO YOU SOONER OR LATER.
THERE'S HARDLY ANYTHING LEFT.
WHERE'S COL?

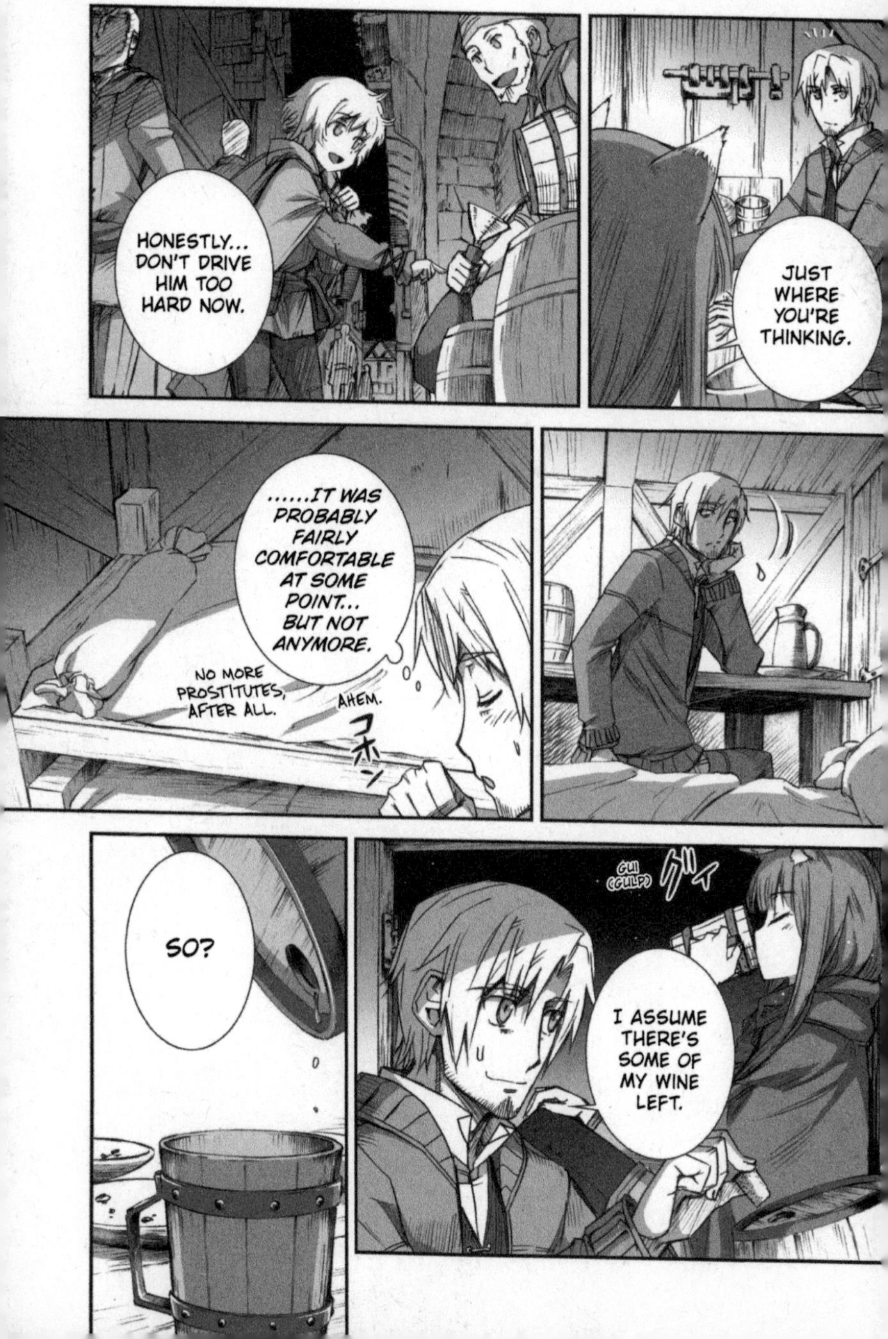
JUST WHERE YOU'RE THINKING.
HONESTLY... DON'T DRIVE HIM TOO HARD NOW.
......IT WAS PROBABLY FAIRLY COMFORTABLE AT SOME POINT... BUT NOT ANYMORE.
NO MORE PROSTITUTES, AFTER ALL.
AHEM.
コホン
GUI (GULP)
グイ
I ASSUME THERE'S SOME OF MY WINE LEFT.
SO?

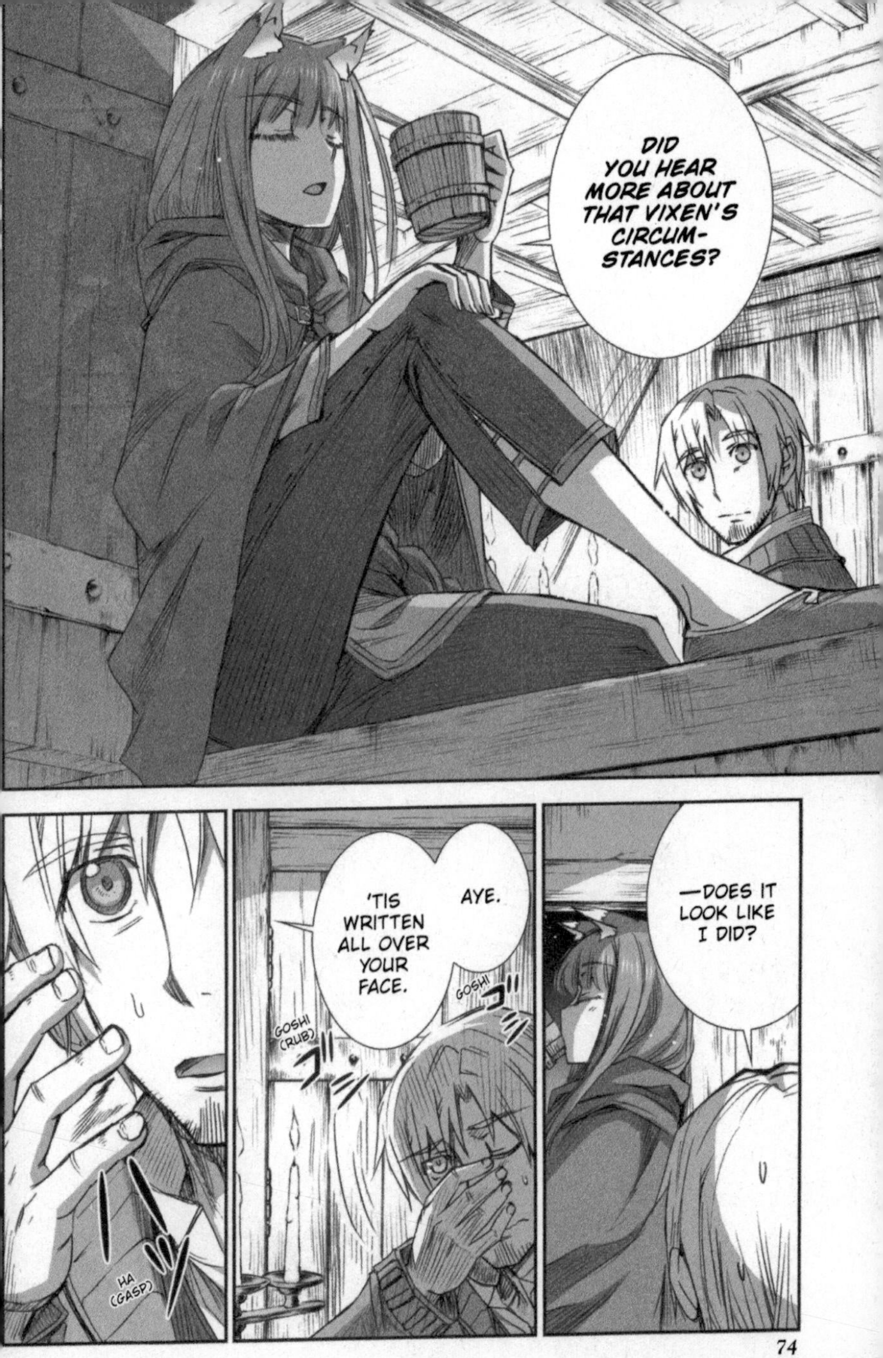
DID YOU HEAR MORE ABOUT THAT VIXEN'S CIRCUM-STANCES?
—DOES IT LOOK LIKE I DID?
AYE.
'TIS WRITTEN ALL OVER YOUR FACE.
GOSHI
GOSHI (RUB)
HA (GASP)

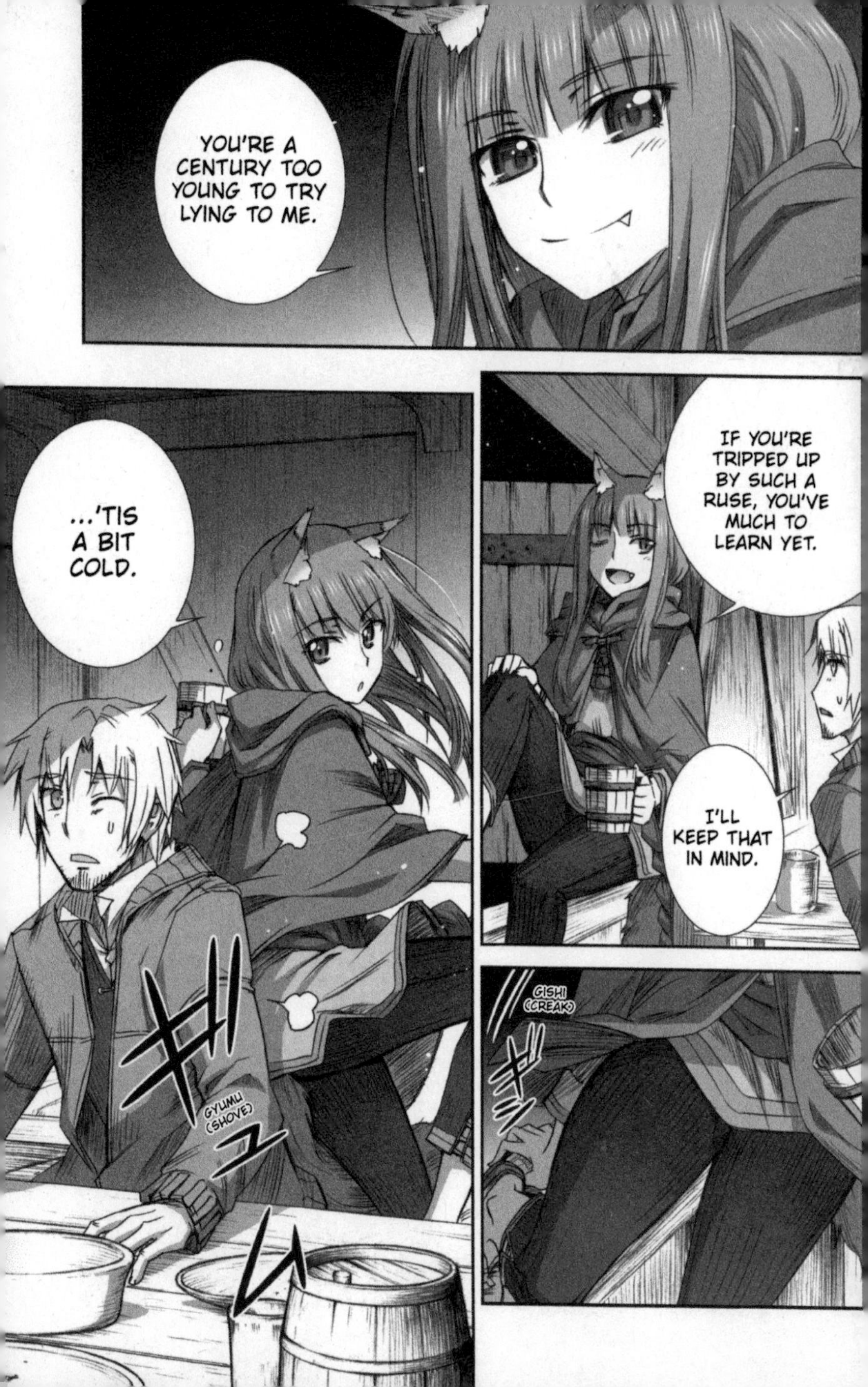
YOU'RE A CENTURY TOO YOUNG TO TRY LYING TO ME.
IF YOU'RE TRIPPED UP BY SUCH A RUSE, YOU'VE MUCH TO LEARN YET.
I'LL KEEP THAT IN MIND.
GISHI (CREAK)
...'TIS A BIT COLD.
GYUMU (SHOVE)

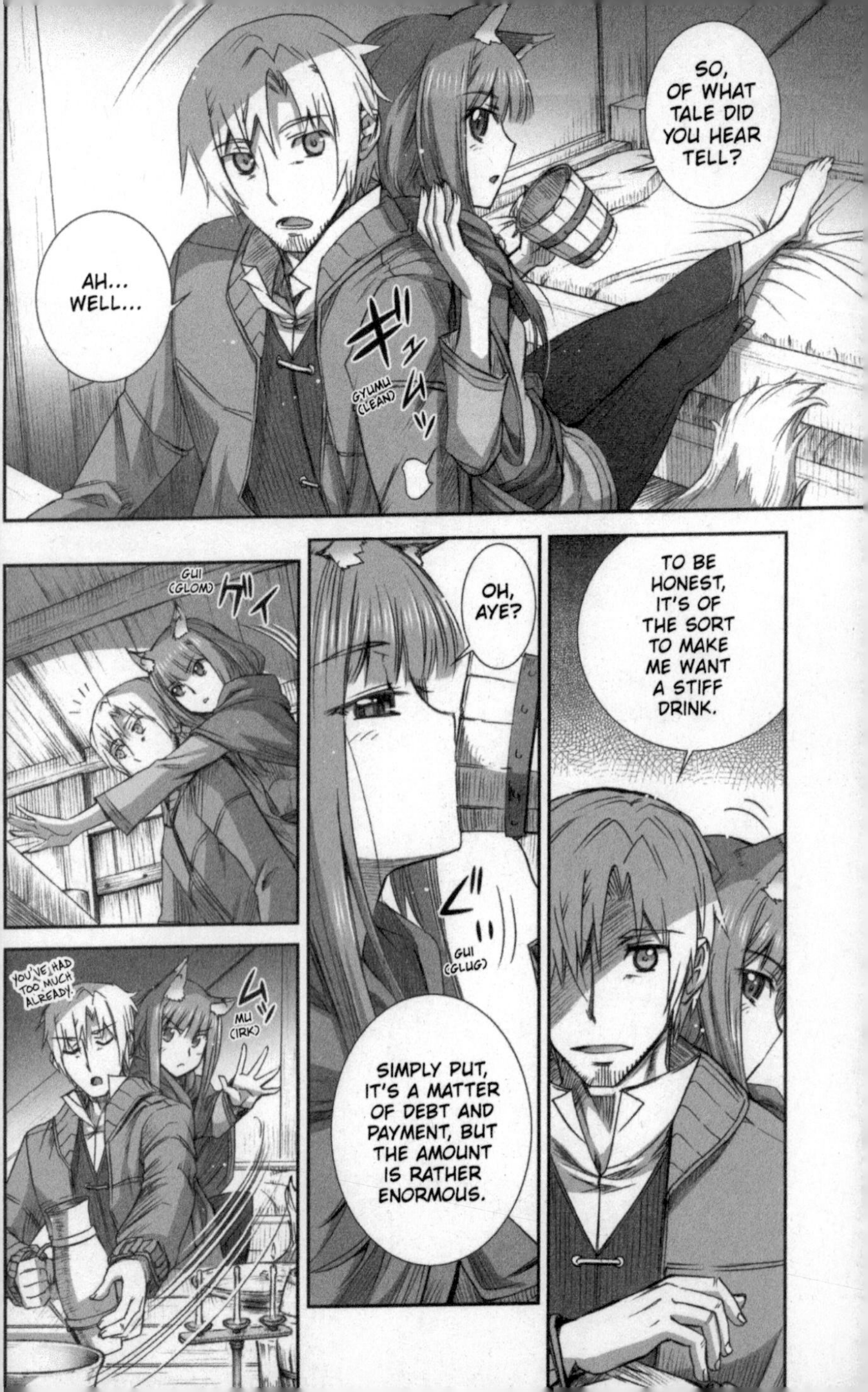
SO, OF WHAT TALE DID YOU HEAR TELL?
GYUMU (LEAN)
AH... WELL...
TO BE HONEST, IT'S OF THE SORT TO MAKE ME WANT A STIFF DRINK.
OH, AYE?
GUI (GLUG)
SIMPLY PUT, IT'S A MATTER OF DEBT AND PAYMENT, BUT THE AMOUNT IS RATHER ENORMOUS.
GUI (GLOM)
MU (IRK)
YOU'VE HAD TOO MUCH ALREADY.

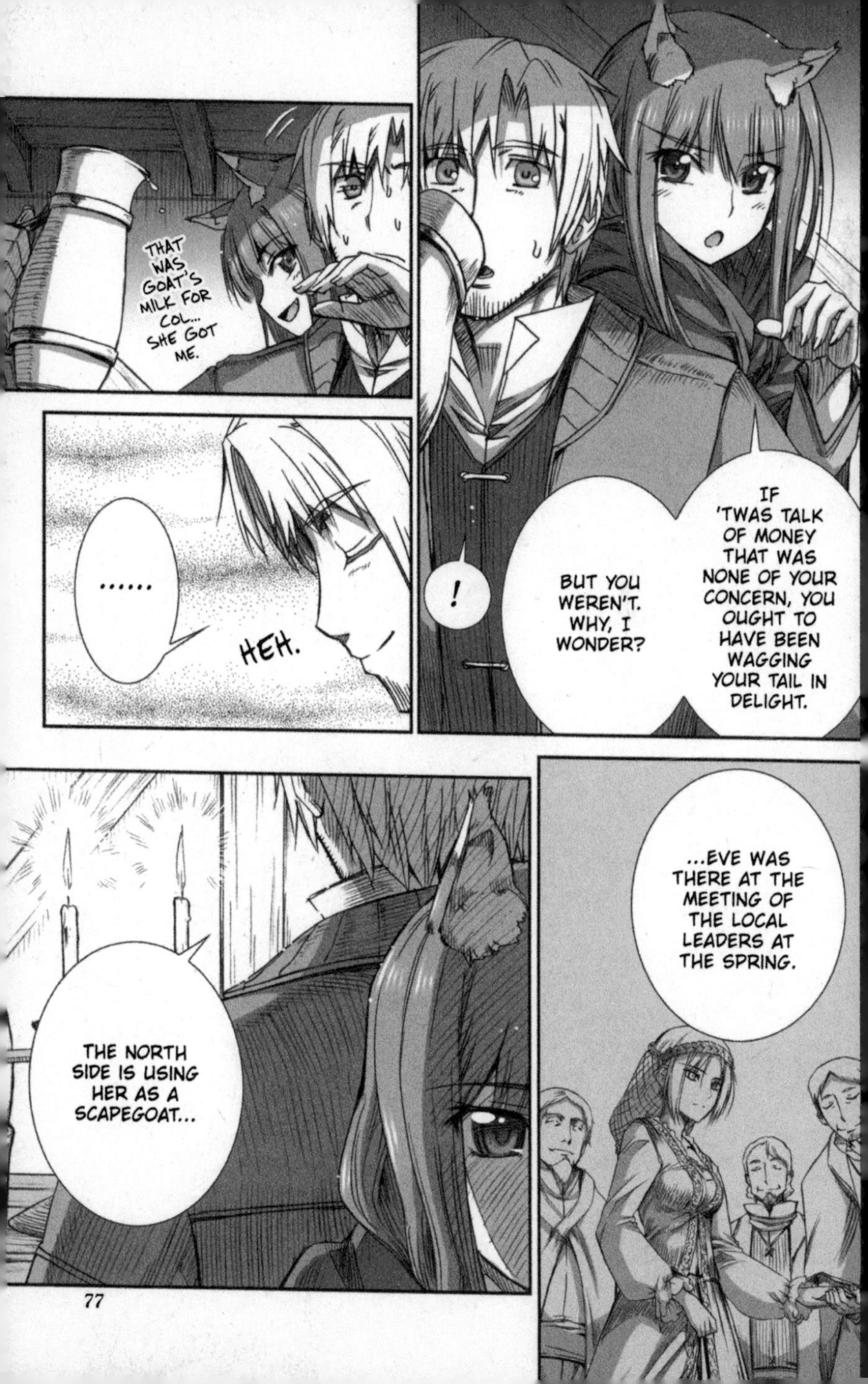
IF 'TWAS TALK OF MONEY THAT WAS NONE OF YOUR CONCERN, YOU OUGHT TO HAVE BEEN WAGGING YOUR TAIL IN DELIGHT.
BUT YOU WEREN'T. WHY, I WONDER?
!
THAT WAS GOAT'S MILK FOR COL... SHE GOT ME.
......
HEH.
...EVE WAS THERE AT THE MEETING OF THE LOCAL LEADERS AT THE SPRING.
THE NORTH SIDE IS USING HER AS A SCAPEGOAT...

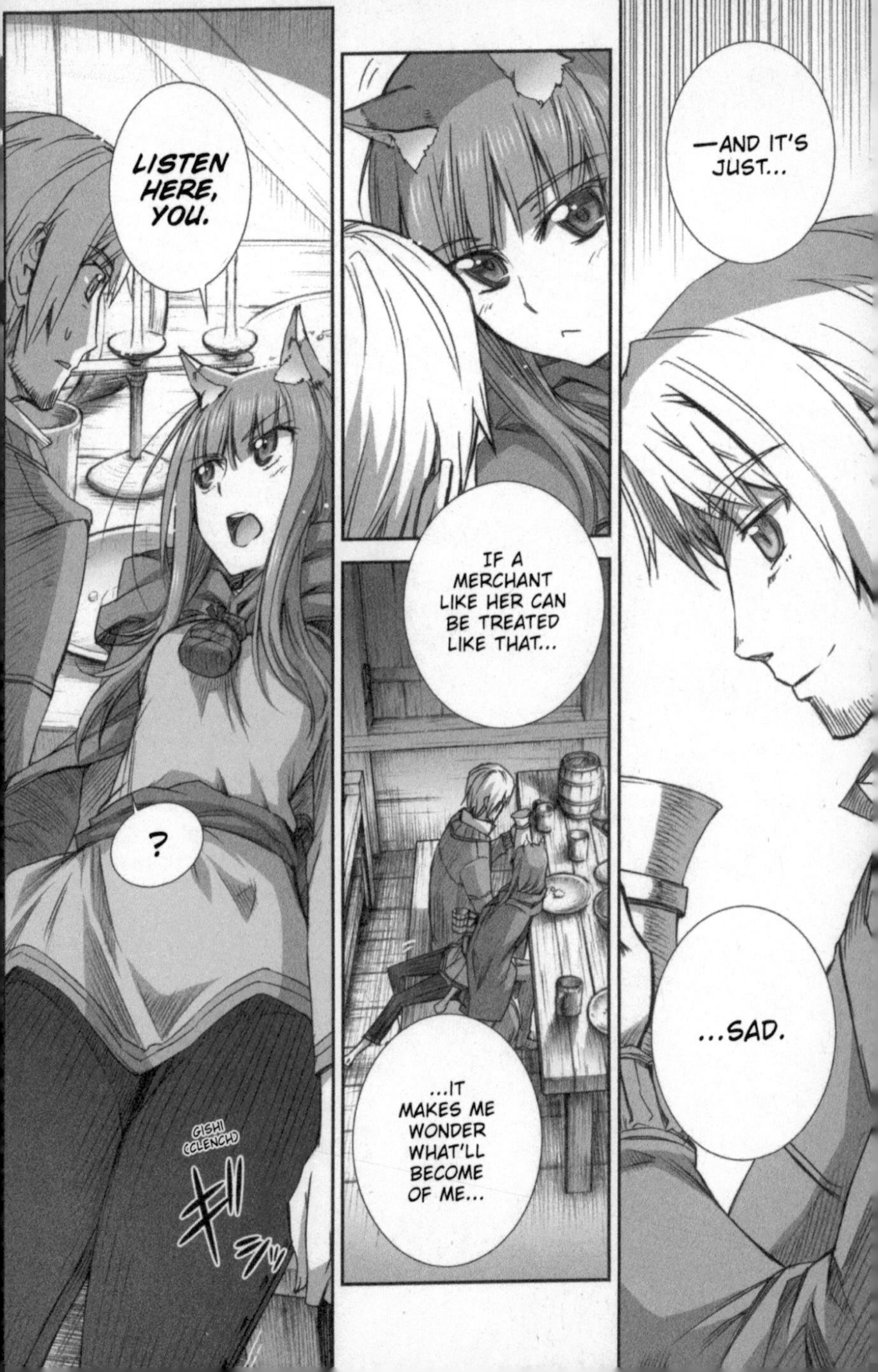
—AND IT'S JUST...
...SAD.
IF A MERCHANT LIKE HER CAN BE TREATED LIKE THAT...
...IT MAKES ME WONDER WHAT'LL BECOME OF ME...
LISTEN HERE, YOU.
?
GISHI (CLENCH)

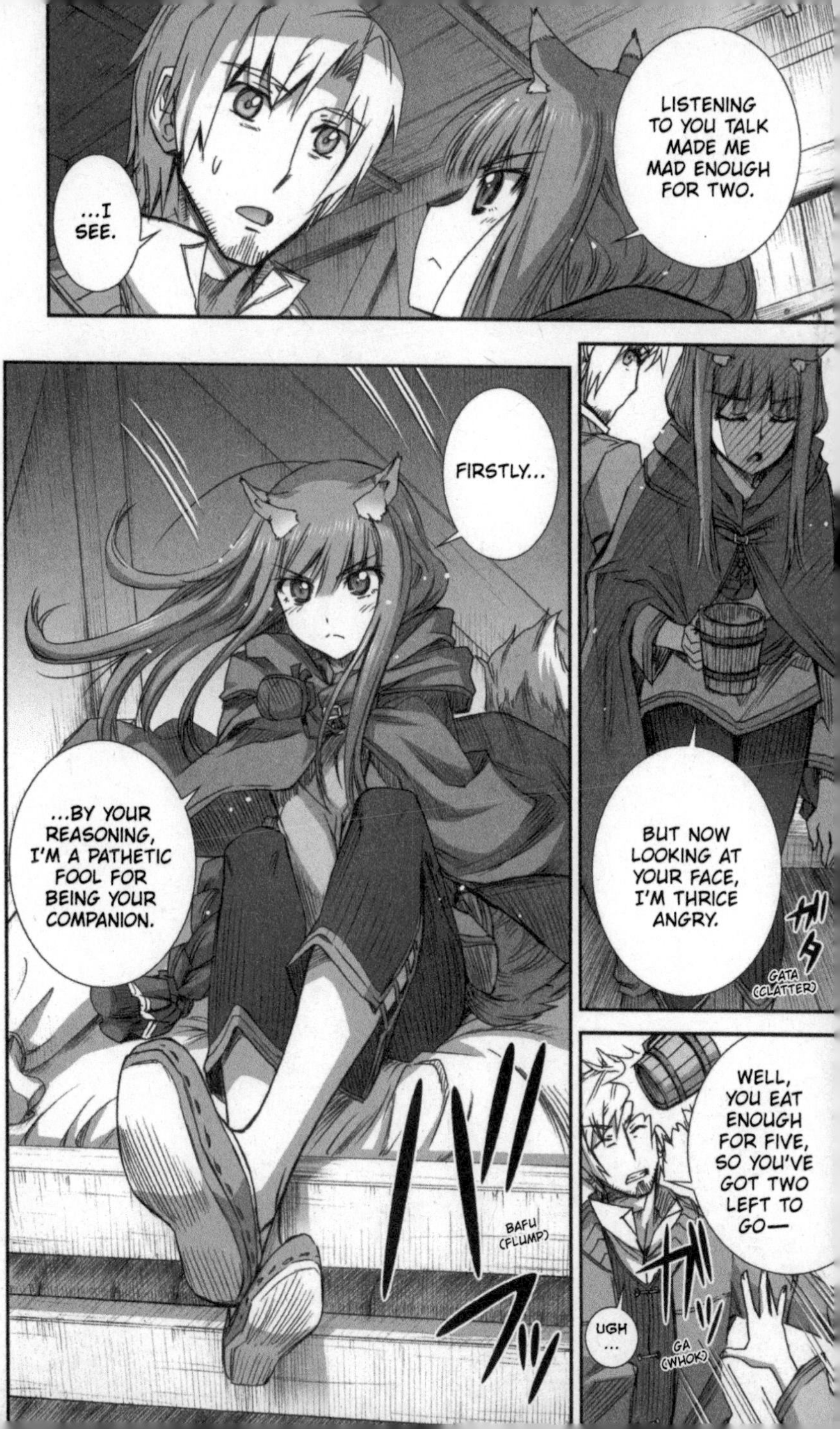
LISTENING TO YOU TALK MADE ME MAD ENOUGH FOR TWO.
...I SEE.
BUT NOW LOOKING AT YOUR FACE, I'M THRICE ANGRY.
GATA (CLATTER)
WELL, YOU EAT ENOUGH FOR FIVE, SO YOU'VE GOT TWO LEFT TO GO—
UGH ...
GA (WHOK)
FIRSTLY...
...BY YOUR REASONING, I'M A PATHETIC FOOL FOR BEING YOUR COMPANION.
BAFU (FLUMP)

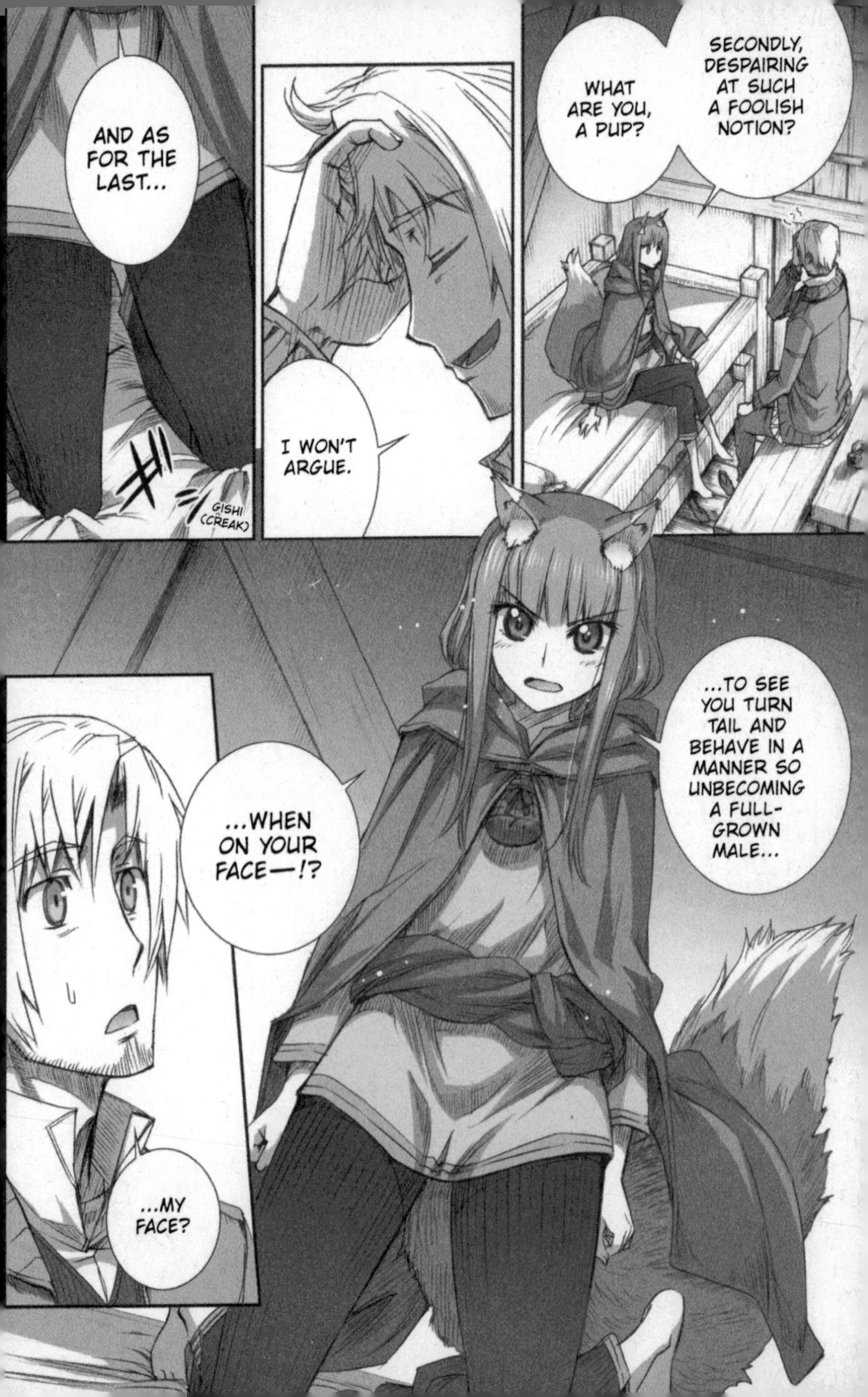
SECONDLY, DESPAIRING AT SUCH A FOOLISH NOTION?
WHAT ARE YOU, A PUP?
I WON'T ARGUE.
AND AS FOR THE LAST...
GISHI (CREAK)
...TO SEE YOU TURN TAIL AND BEHAVE IN A MANNER SO UNBECOMING A FULL-GROWN MALE...
...WHEN ON YOUR FACE—!?
...MY FACE?

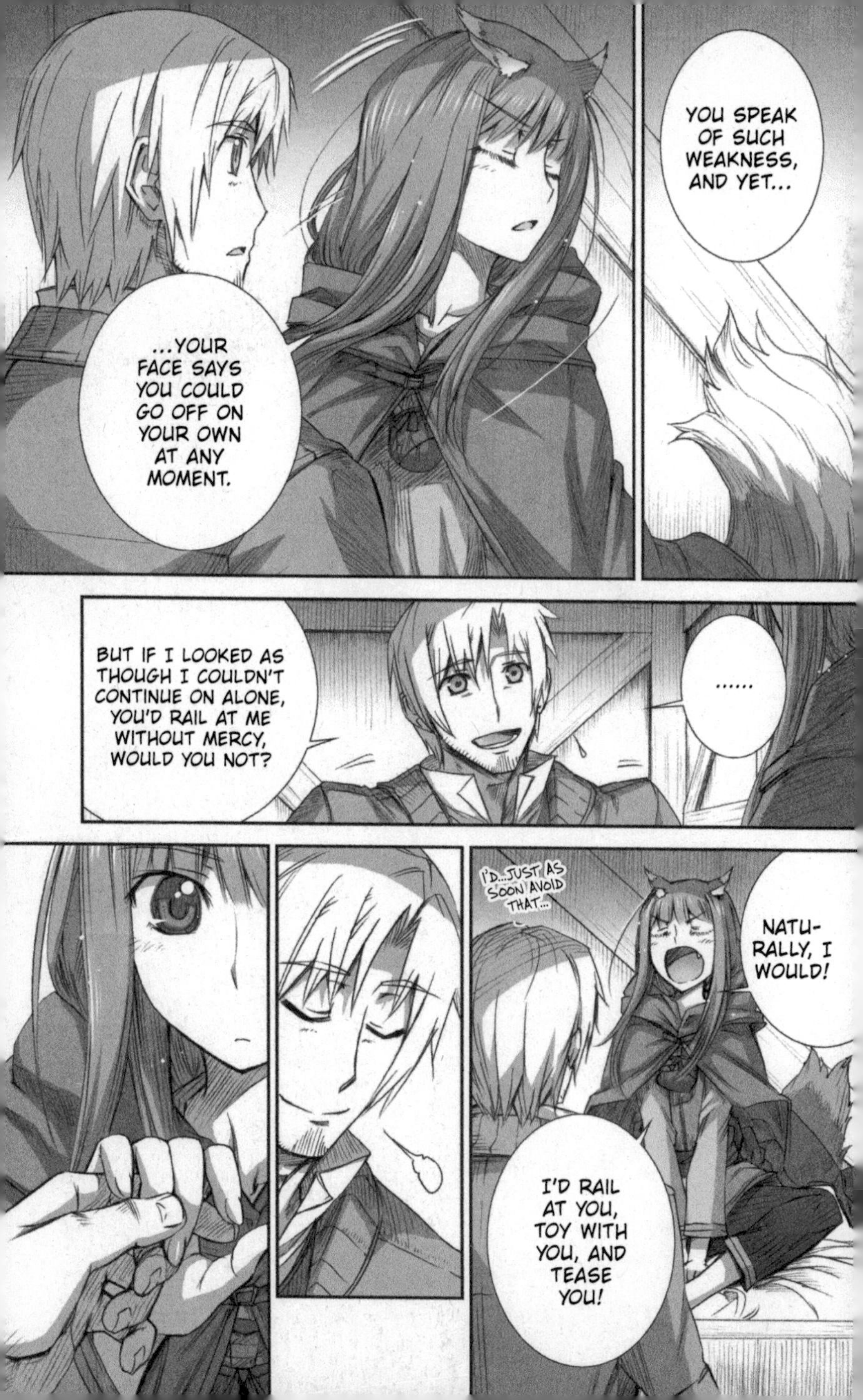
YOU SPEAK OF SUCH WEAKNESS, AND YET...
...YOUR FACE SAYS YOU COULD GO OFF ON YOUR OWN AT ANY MOMENT.
BUT IF I LOOKED AS THOUGH I COULDN'T CONTINUE ON ALONE, YOU'D RAIL AT ME WITHOUT MERCY, WOULD YOU NOT?
......
NATU-RALLY, I WOULD!
I'D RAIL AT YOU, TOY WITH YOU, AND TEASE YOU!
I'D...JUST AS SOON AVOID THAT...

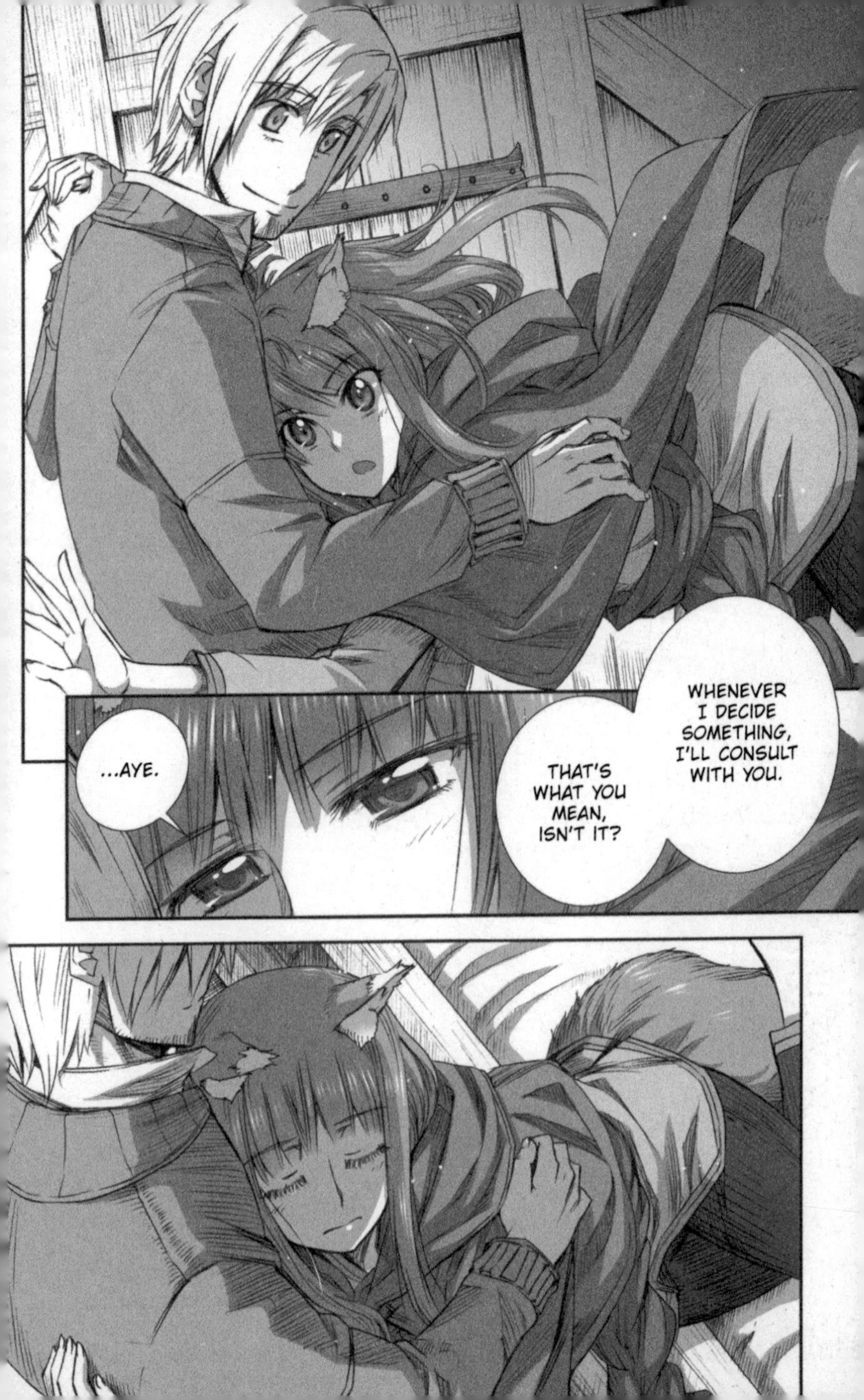
WHENEVER I DECIDE SOMETHING, I'LL CONSULT WITH YOU.
THAT'S WHAT YOU MEAN, ISN'T IT?
...AYE.

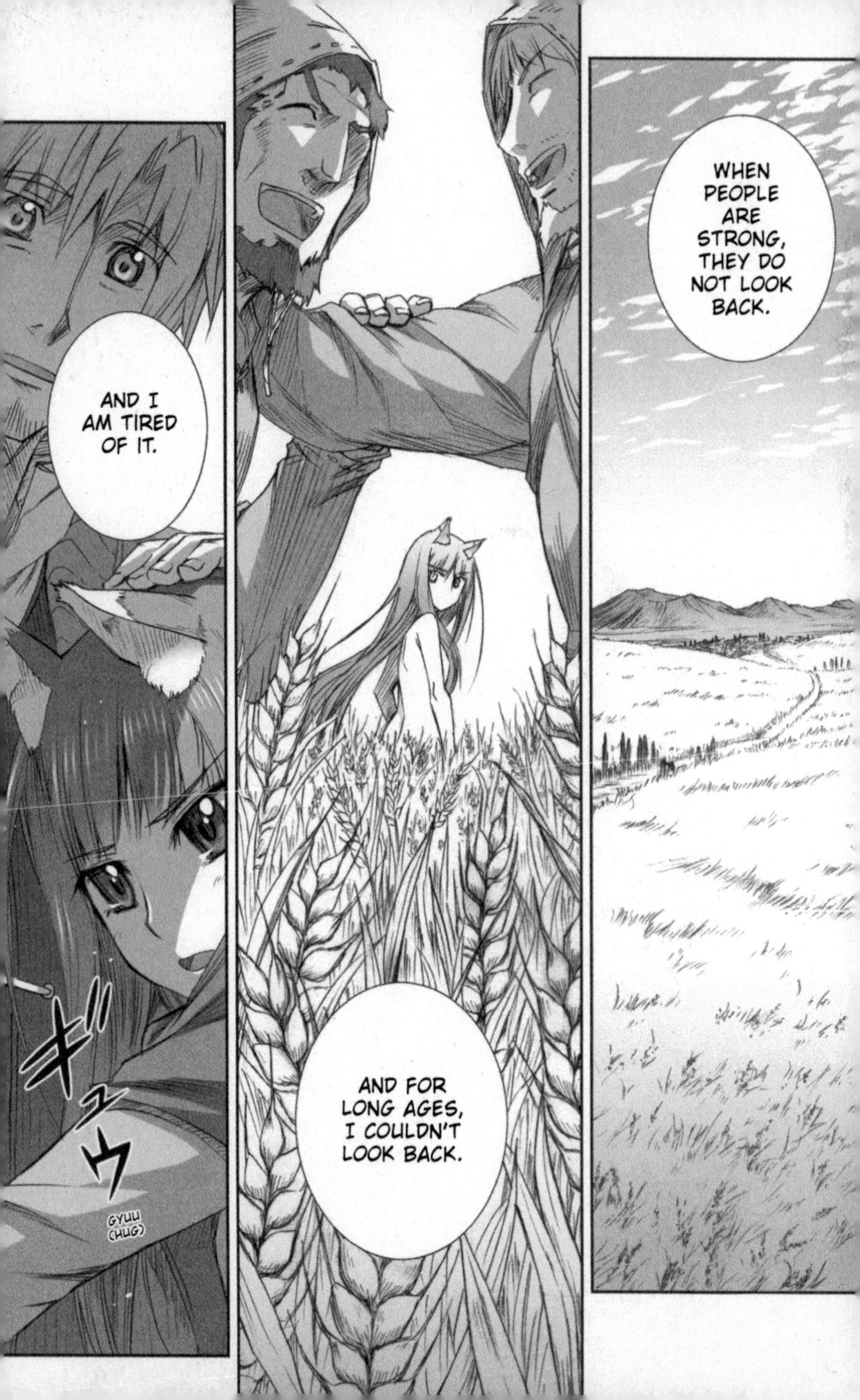
WHEN PEOPLE ARE STRONG, THEY DO NOT LOOK BACK.
AND FOR LONG AGES, I COULDN'T LOOK BACK.
AND I AM TIRED OF IT.
GYUU (HUG)

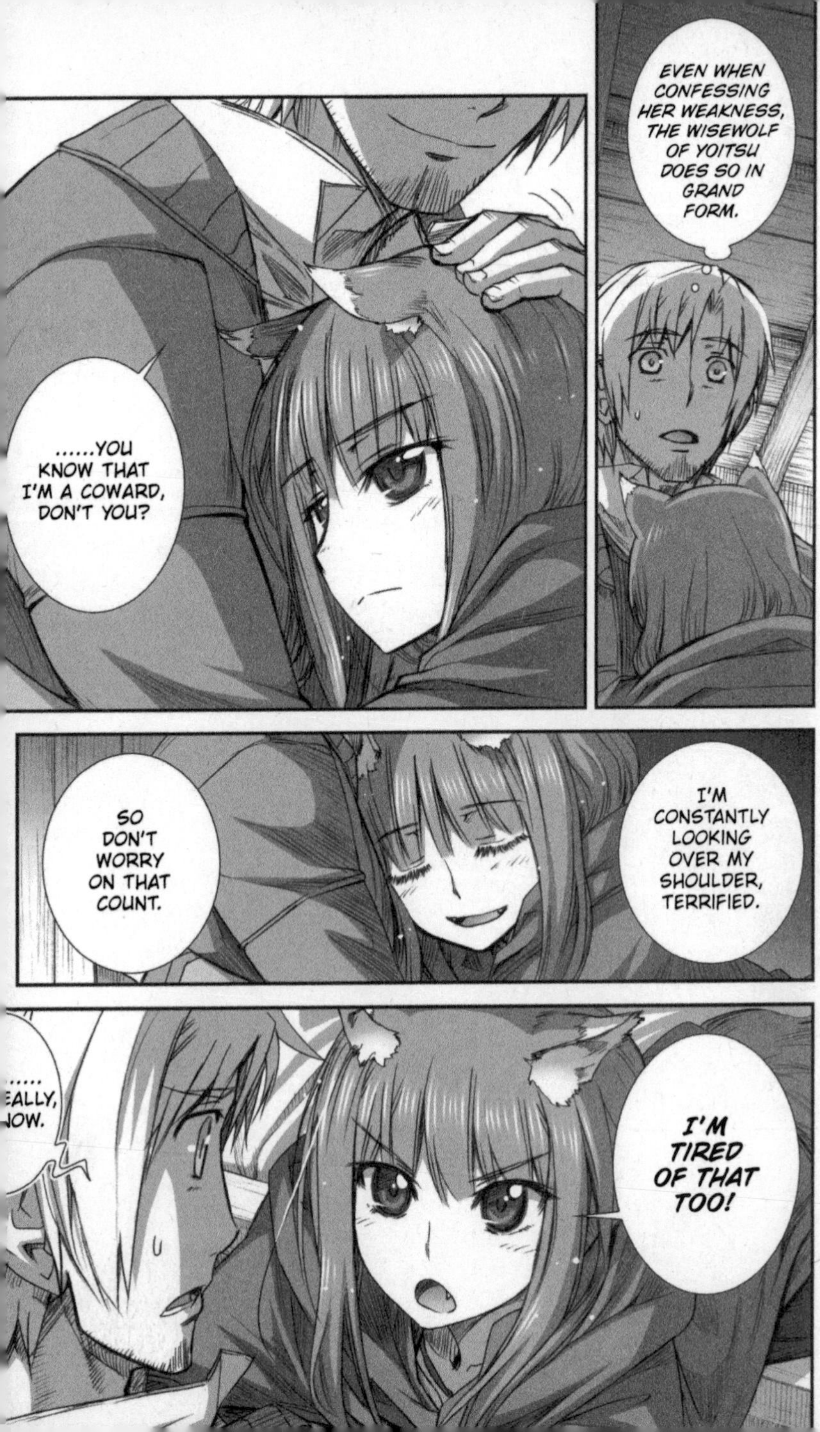
EVEN WHEN CONFESSING HER WEAKNESS, THE WISEWOLF OF YOITSU DOES SO IN GRAND FORM.
......YOU KNOW THAT I'M A COWARD, DON'T YOU?
I'M CONSTANTLY LOOKING OVER MY SHOULDER, TERRIFIED.
SO DON'T WORRY ON THAT COUNT.
I'M TIRED OF THAT TOO!
......EALLY, NOW.

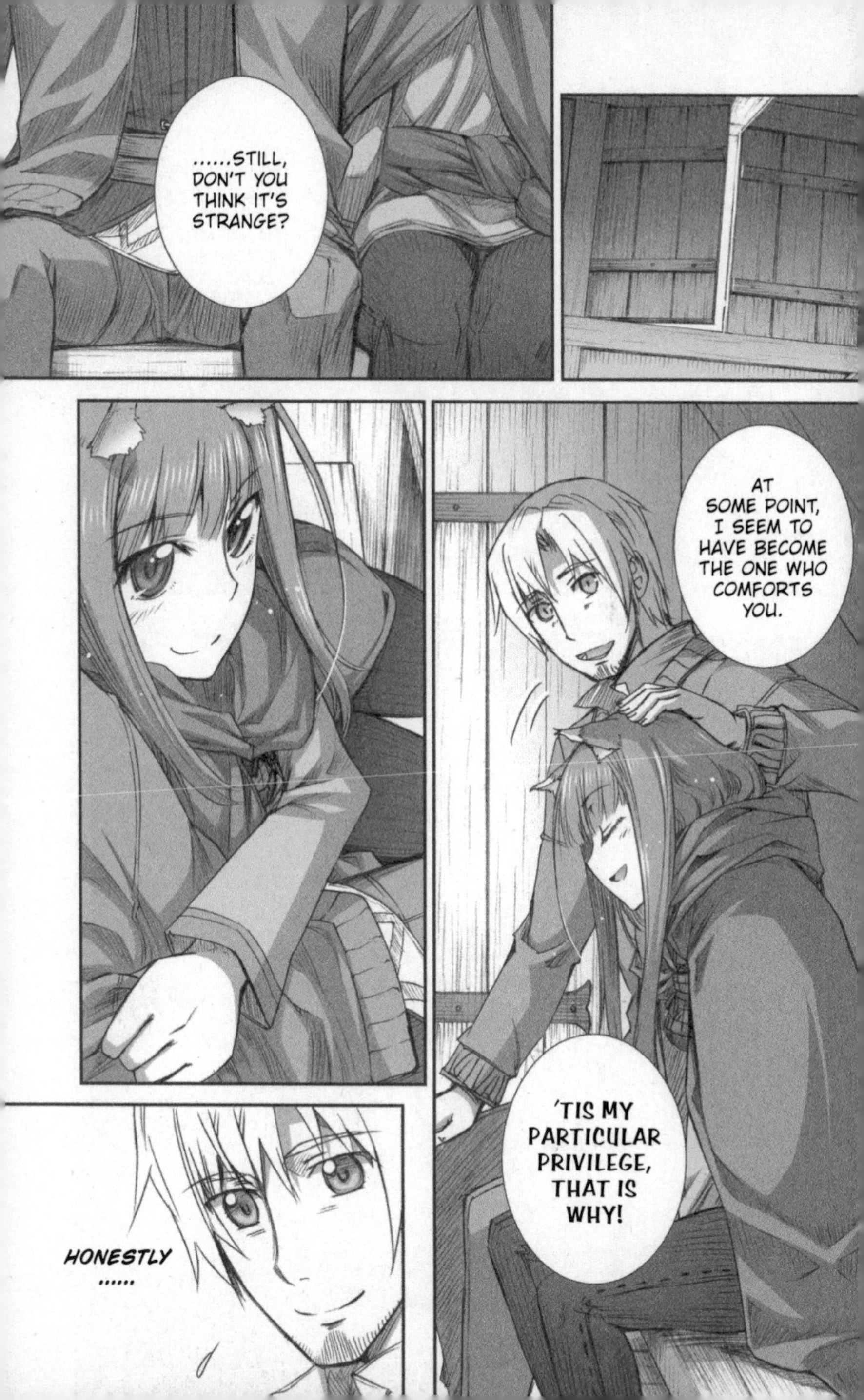
......STILL, DON'T YOU THINK IT'S STRANGE?
AT SOME POINT, I SEEM TO HAVE BECOME THE ONE WHO COMFORTS YOU.
'TIS MY PARTICULAR PRIVILEGE, THAT IS WHY!
HONESTLY ......

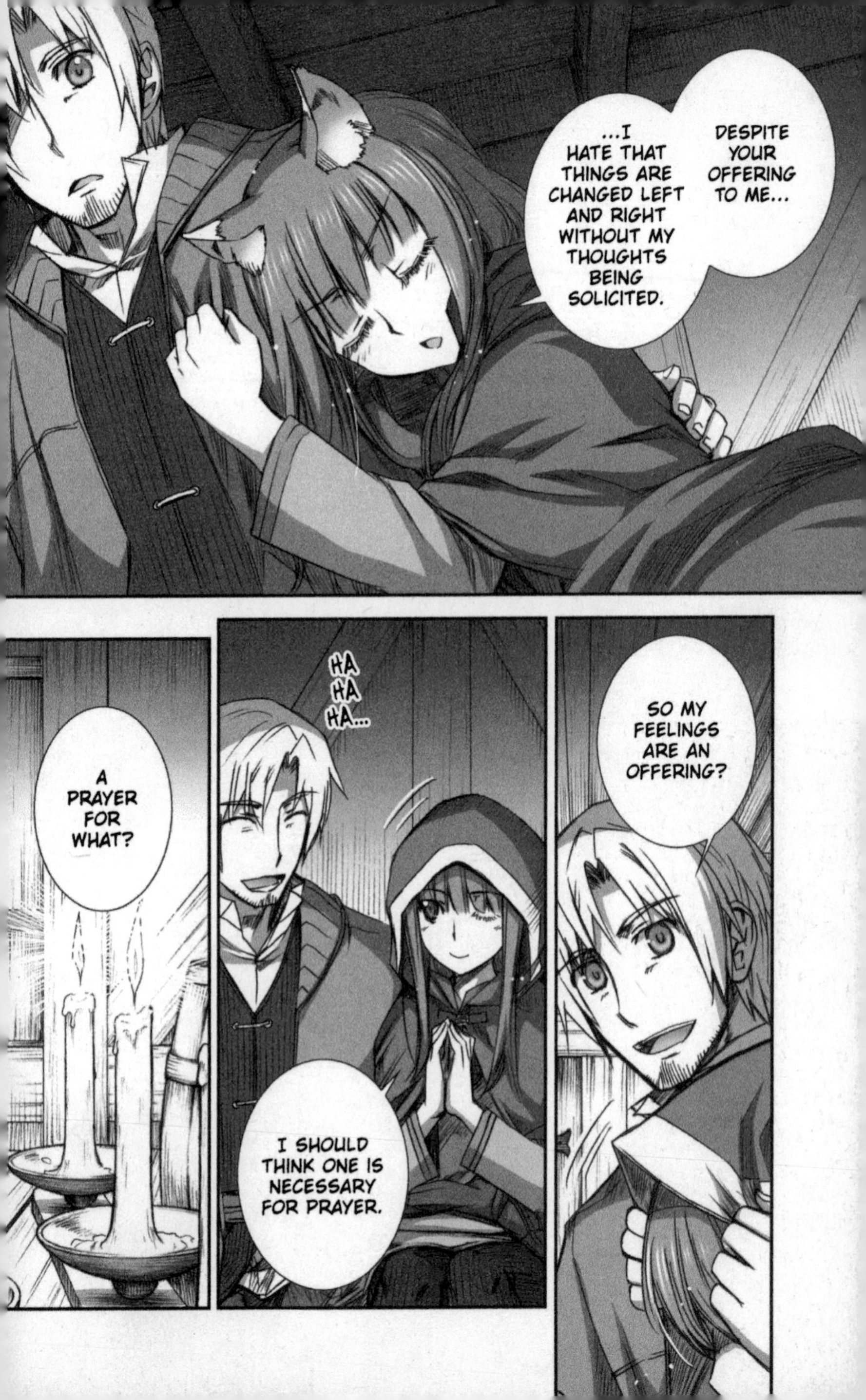
DESPITE YOUR OFFERING TO ME...
...I HATE THAT THINGS ARE CHANGED LEFT AND RIGHT WITHOUT MY THOUGHTS BEING SOLICITED.
SO MY FEELINGS ARE AN OFFERING?
HA HA HA...
I SHOULD THINK ONE IS NECESSARY FOR PRAYER.
A PRAYER FOR WHAT?

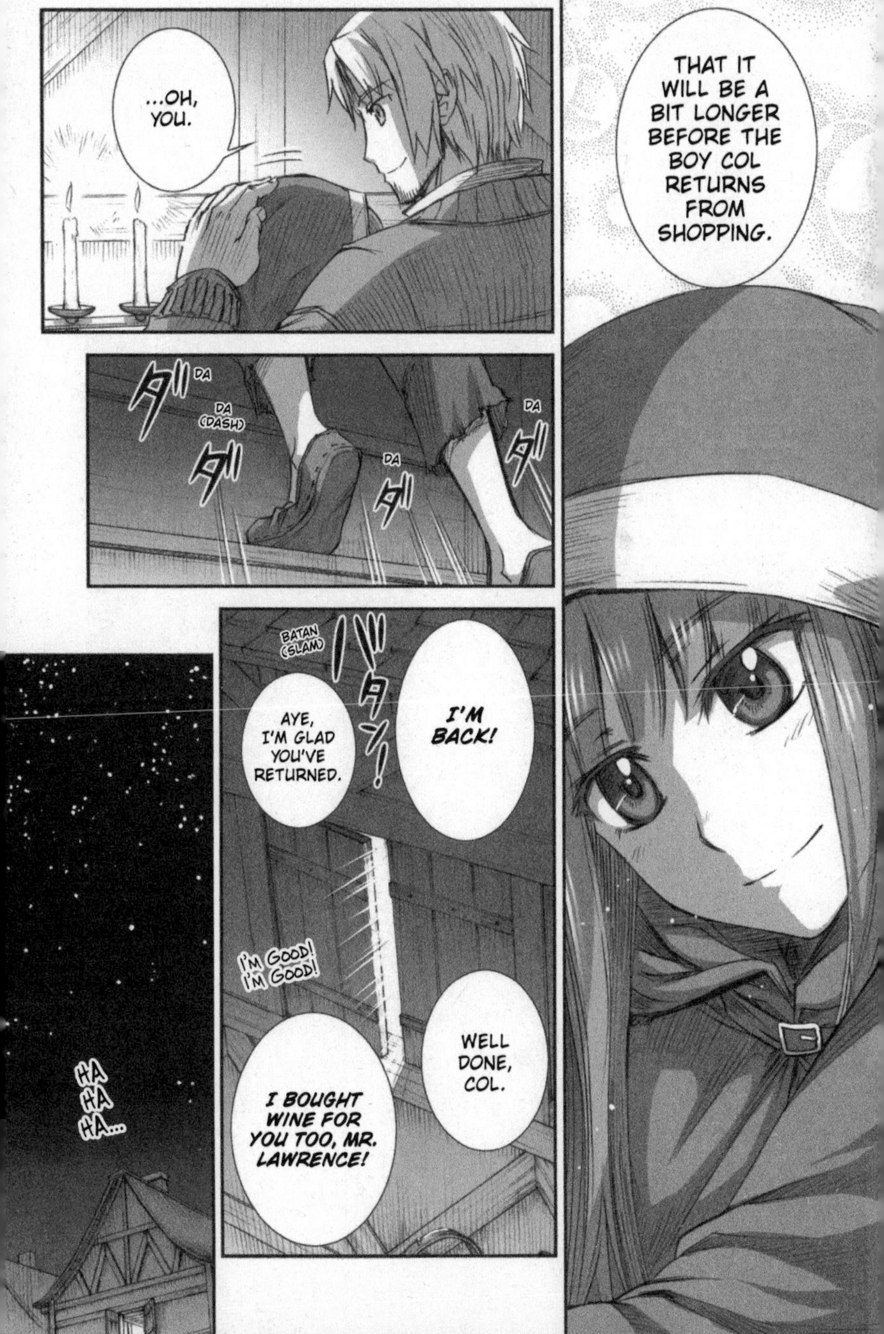
THAT IT WILL BE A BIT LONGER BEFORE THE BOY COL RETURNS FROM SHOPPING.
...OH, YOU.
DA
DA (DASH)
DA
DA
BATAN (SLAM)
I'M BACK!
AYE, I'M GLAD YOU'VE RETURNED.
I'M GOOD! I'M GOOD!
WELL DONE, COL.
I BOUGHT WINE FOR YOU TOO, MR. LAWRENCE!
HA HA HA...

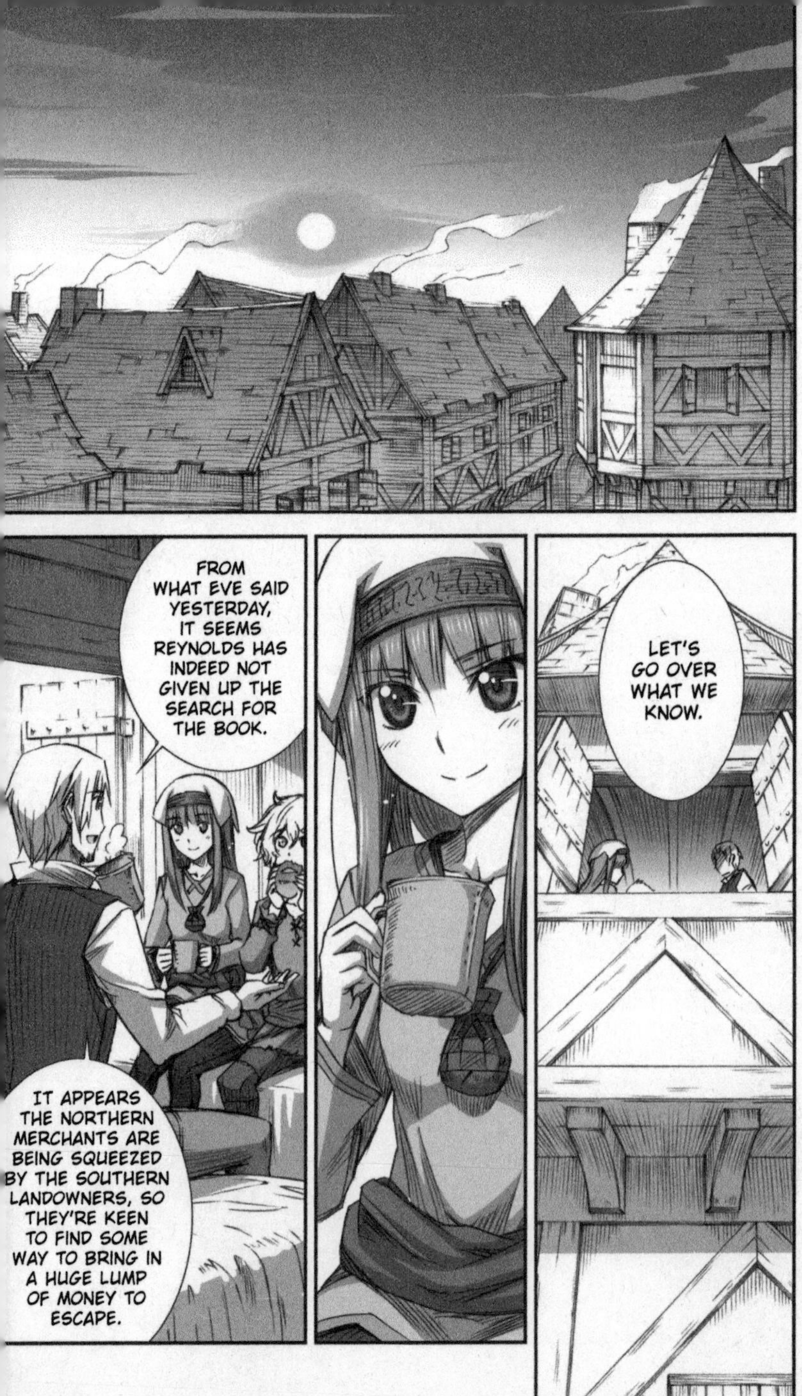
LET'S GO OVER WHAT WE KNOW.
FROM WHAT EVE SAID YESTERDAY, IT SEEMS REYNOLDS HAS INDEED NOT GIVEN UP THE SEARCH FOR THE BOOK.
IT APPEARS THE NORTHERN MERCHANTS ARE BEING SQUEEZED BY THE SOUTHERN LANDOWNERS, SO THEY'RE KEEN TO FIND SOME WAY TO BRING IN A HUGE LUMP OF MONEY TO ESCAPE.

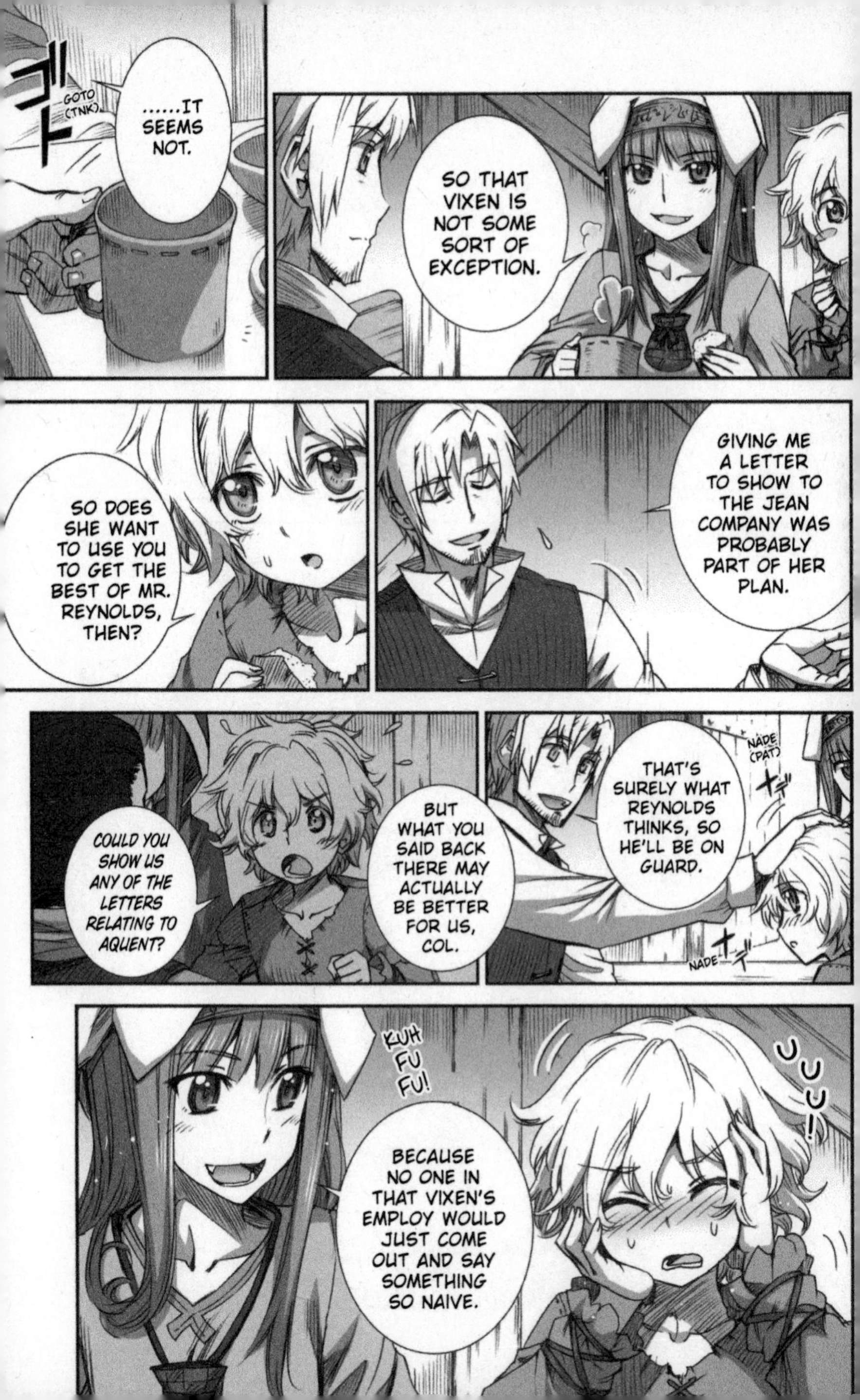
SO THAT VIXEN IS NOT SOME SORT OF EXCEPTION.
GOTO (TNK)
......IT SEEMS NOT.
GIVING ME A LETTER TO SHOW TO THE JEAN COMPANY WAS PROBABLY PART OF HER PLAN.
SO DOES SHE WANT TO USE YOU TO GET THE BEST OF MR. REYNOLDS, THEN?
NADE (PAT)
THAT'S SURELY WHAT REYNOLDS THINKS, SO HE'LL BE ON GUARD.
NADE
BUT WHAT YOU SAID BACK THERE MAY ACTUALLY BE BETTER FOR US, COL.
COULD YOU SHOW US ANY OF THE LETTERS RELATING TO AQUENT?
UUU!
KUH FU FU!
BECAUSE NO ONE IN THAT VIXEN'S EMPLOY WOULD JUST COME OUT AND SAY SOMETHING SO NAIVE.

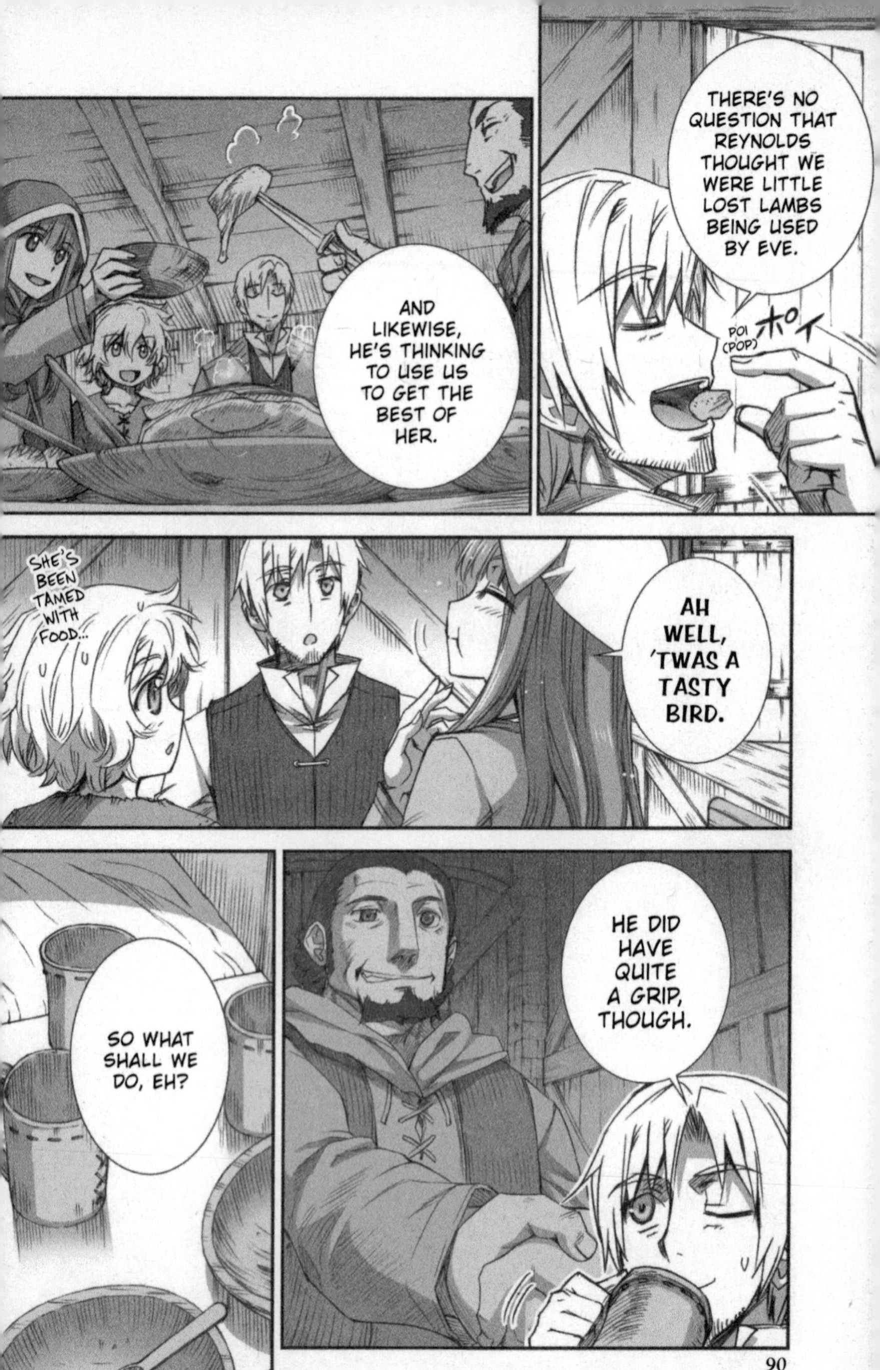
THERE'S NO QUESTION THAT REYNOLDS THOUGHT WE WERE LITTLE LOST LAMBS BEING USED BY EVE.
POI (POP)
AND LIKEWISE, HE'S THINKING TO USE US TO GET THE BEST OF HER.
AH WELL, 'TWAS A TASTY BIRD.
SHE'S BEEN TAMED WITH FOOD...
HE DID HAVE QUITE A GRIP, THOUGH.
SO WHAT SHALL WE DO, EH?

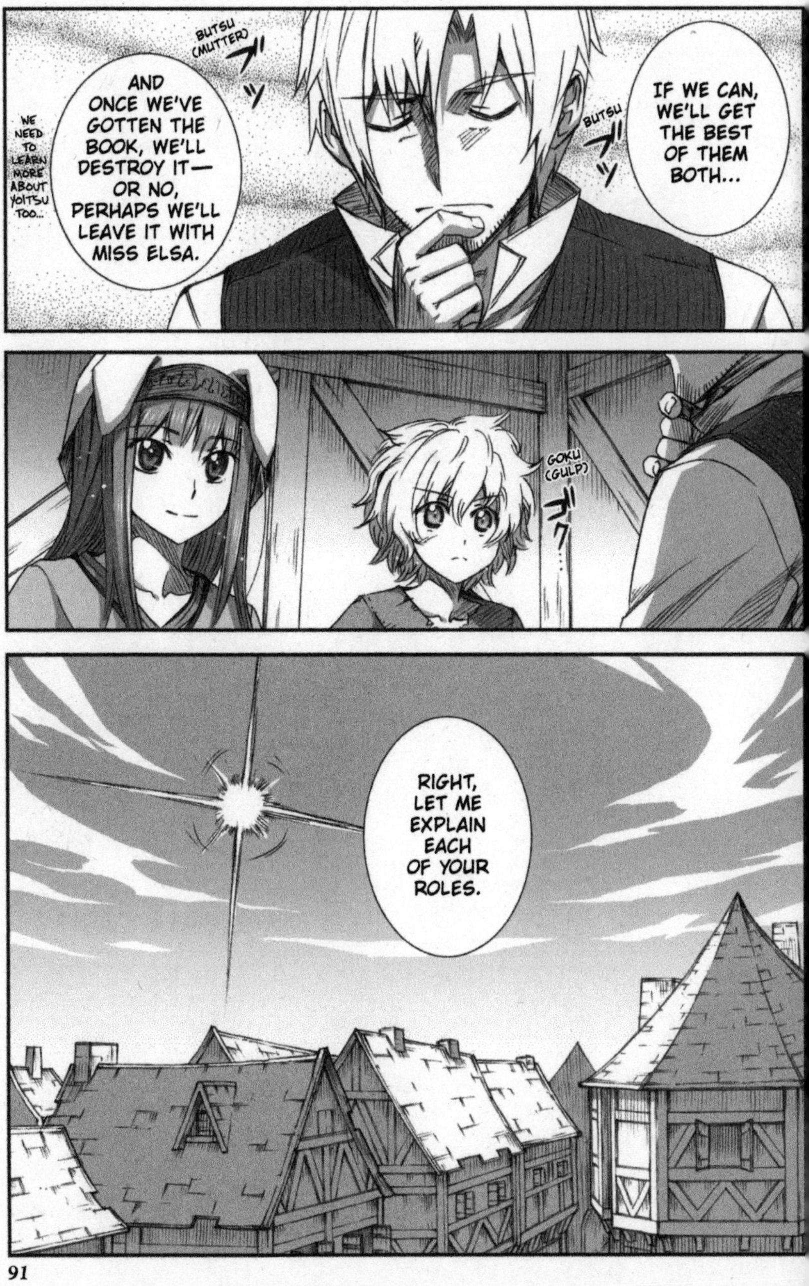
IF WE CAN, WE'LL GET THE BEST OF THEM BOTH...
BUTSU
BUTSU (MUTTER)
AND ONCE WE'VE GOTTEN THE BOOK, WE'LL DESTROY IT— OR NO, PERHAPS WE'LL LEAVE IT WITH MISS ELSA.
WE NEED TO LEARN MORE ABOUT YOITSU TOO...
GOKU (GULP)
RIGHT, LET ME EXPLAIN EACH OF YOUR ROLES.

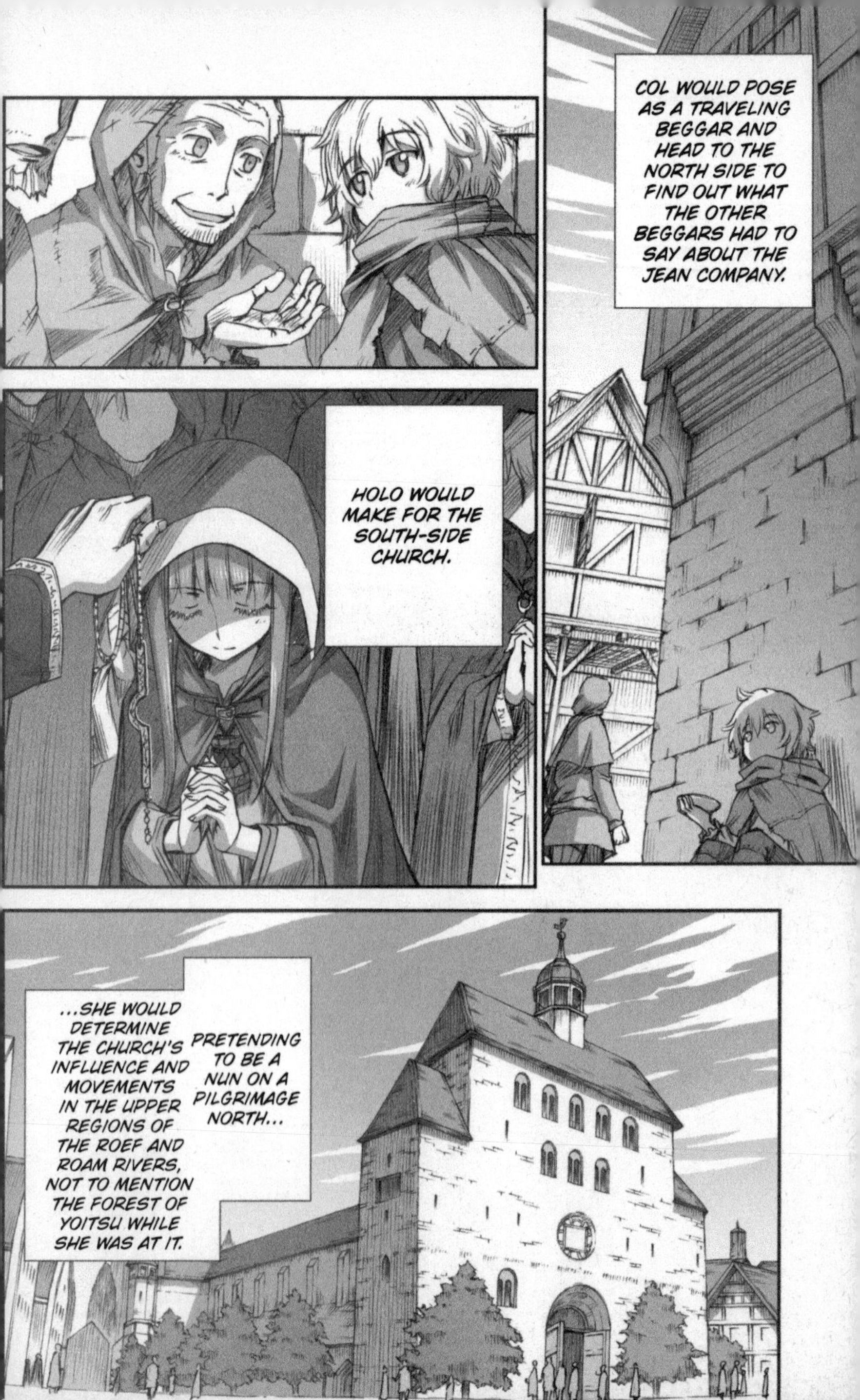
COL WOULD POSE AS A TRAVELING BEGGAR AND HEAD TO THE NORTH SIDE TO FIND OUT WHAT THE OTHER BEGGARS HAD TO SAY ABOUT THE JEAN COMPANY.
HOLO WOULD MAKE FOR THE SOUTH-SIDE CHURCH.
PRETENDING TO BE A NUN ON A PILGRIMAGE NORTH...
...SHE WOULD DETERMINE THE CHURCH'S INFLUENCE AND MOVEMENTS IN THE UPPER REGIONS OF THE ROEF AND ROAM RIVERS, NOT TO MENTION THE FOREST OF YOITSU WHILE SHE WAS AT IT.

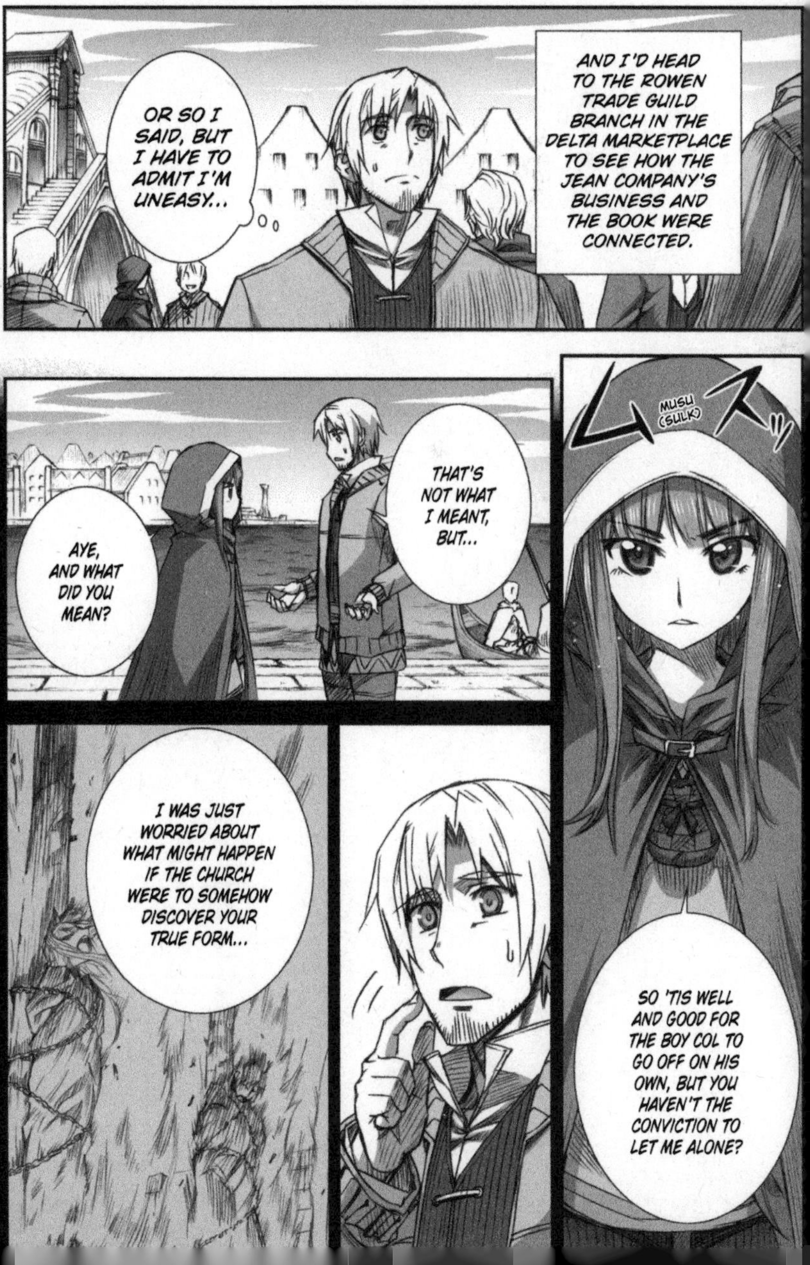
AND I'D HEAD TO THE ROWEN TRADE GUILD BRANCH IN THE DELTA MARKETPLACE TO SEE HOW THE JEAN COMPANY'S BUSINESS AND THE BOOK WERE CONNECTED.
OR SO I SAID, BUT I HAVE TO ADMIT I'M UNEASY...
ムスッ
MUSU (SULK)
SO 'TIS WELL AND GOOD FOR THE BOY COL TO GO OFF ON HIS OWN, BUT YOU HAVEN'T THE CONVICTION TO LET ME ALONE?
THAT'S NOT WHAT I MEANT, BUT...
AYE, AND WHAT DID YOU MEAN?
I WAS JUST WORRIED ABOUT WHAT MIGHT HAPPEN IF THE CHURCH WERE TO SOMEHOW DISCOVER YOUR TRUE FORM...

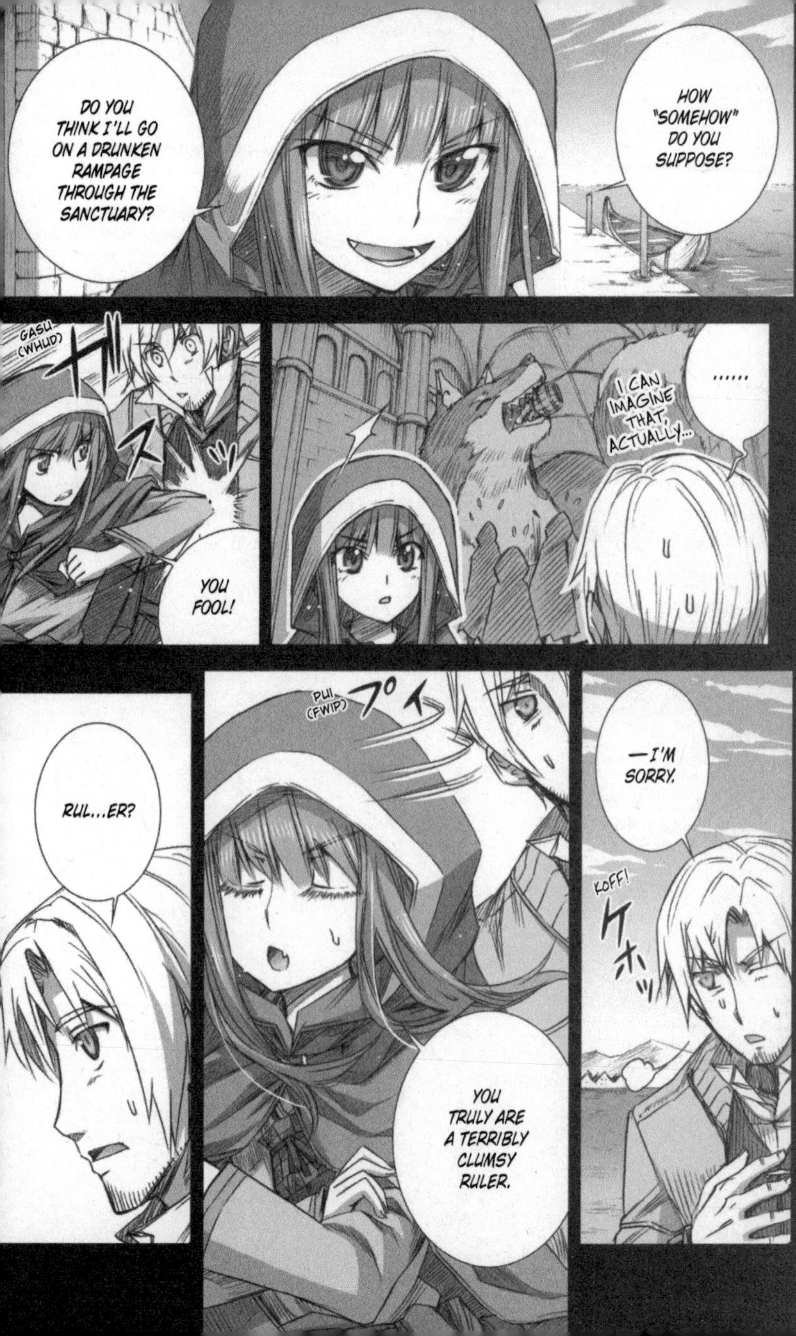
HOW "SOMEHOW" DO YOU SUPPOSE?
DO YOU THINK I'LL GO ON A DRUNKEN RAMPAGE THROUGH THE SANCTUARY?
......
I CAN IMAGINE THAT, ACTUALLY...
GASU (WHUD)
YOU FOOL!
—I'M SORRY.
KOFF!
PUI (FWIP)
YOU TRULY ARE A TERRIBLY CLUMSY RULER.
RUL...ER?

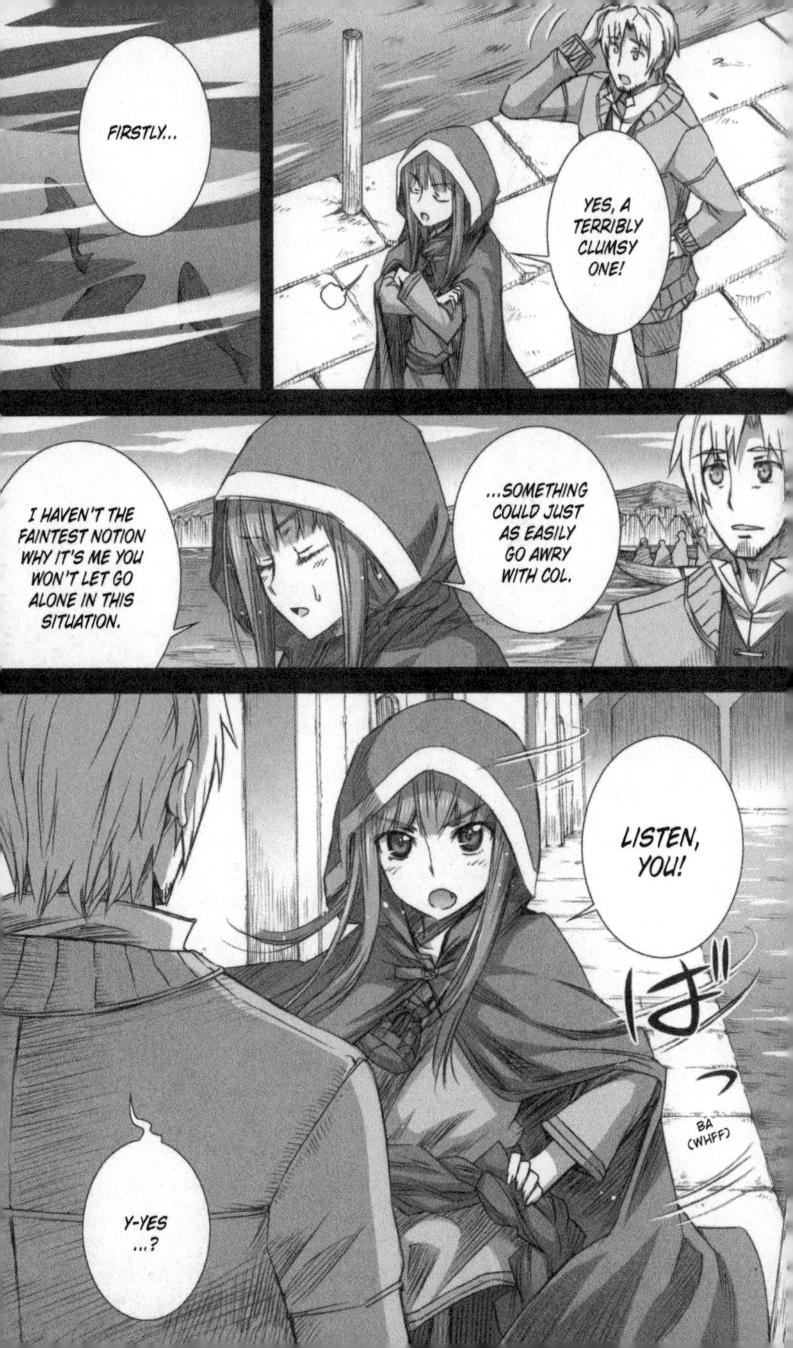
YES, A TERRIBLY CLUMSY ONE!
FIRSTLY...
...SOMETHING COULD JUST AS EASILY GO AWRY WITH COL.
I HAVEN'T THE FAINTEST NOTION WHY IT'S ME YOU WON'T LET GO ALONE IN THIS SITUATION.
LISTEN, YOU!
ばっ
BA (WHFF)
Y-YES ...?

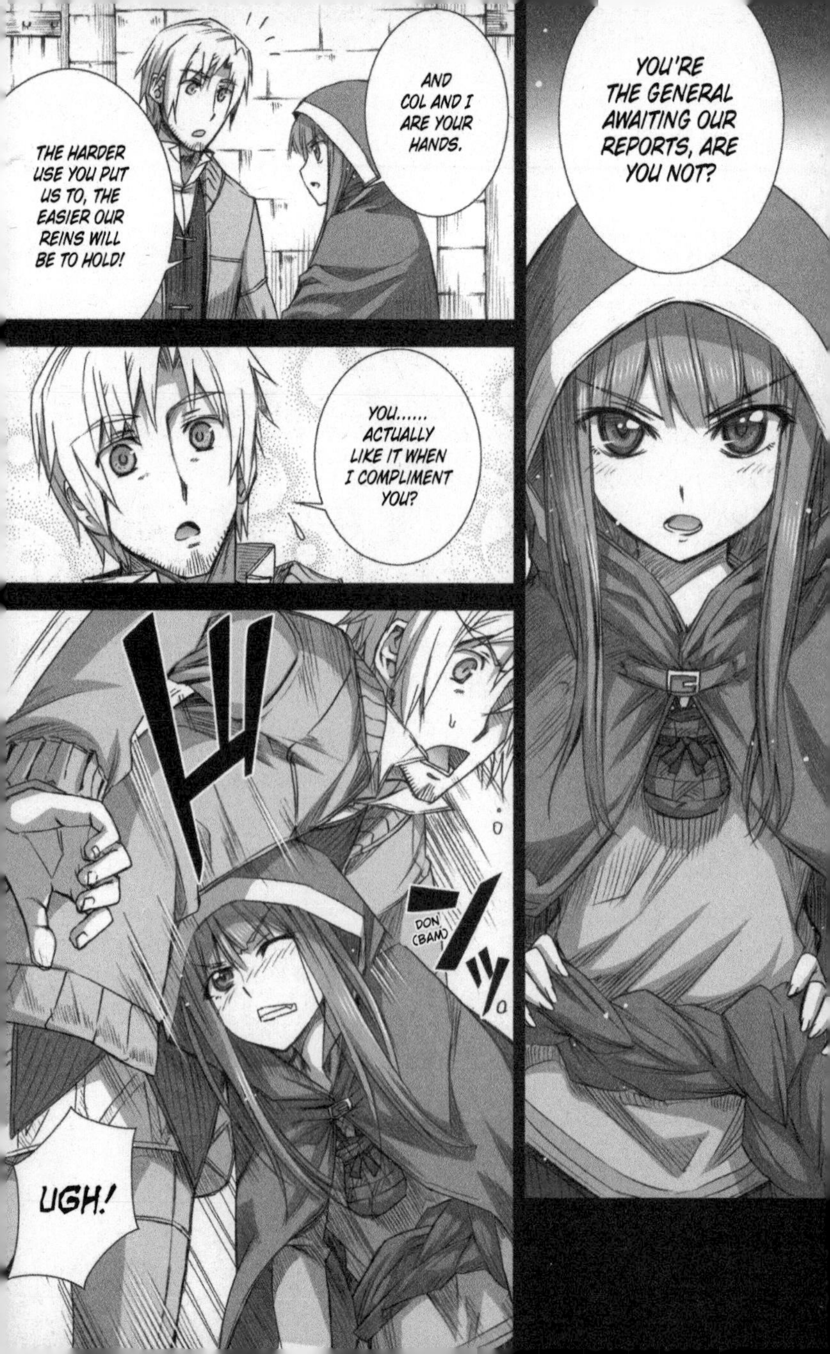
YOU'RE THE GENERAL AWAITING OUR REPORTS, ARE YOU NOT?
AND COL AND I ARE YOUR HANDS.
THE HARDER USE YOU PUT US TO, THE EASIER OUR REINS WILL BE TO HOLD!
YOU...... ACTUALLY LIKE IT WHEN I COMPLIMENT YOU?
DON (BAM)
UGH!

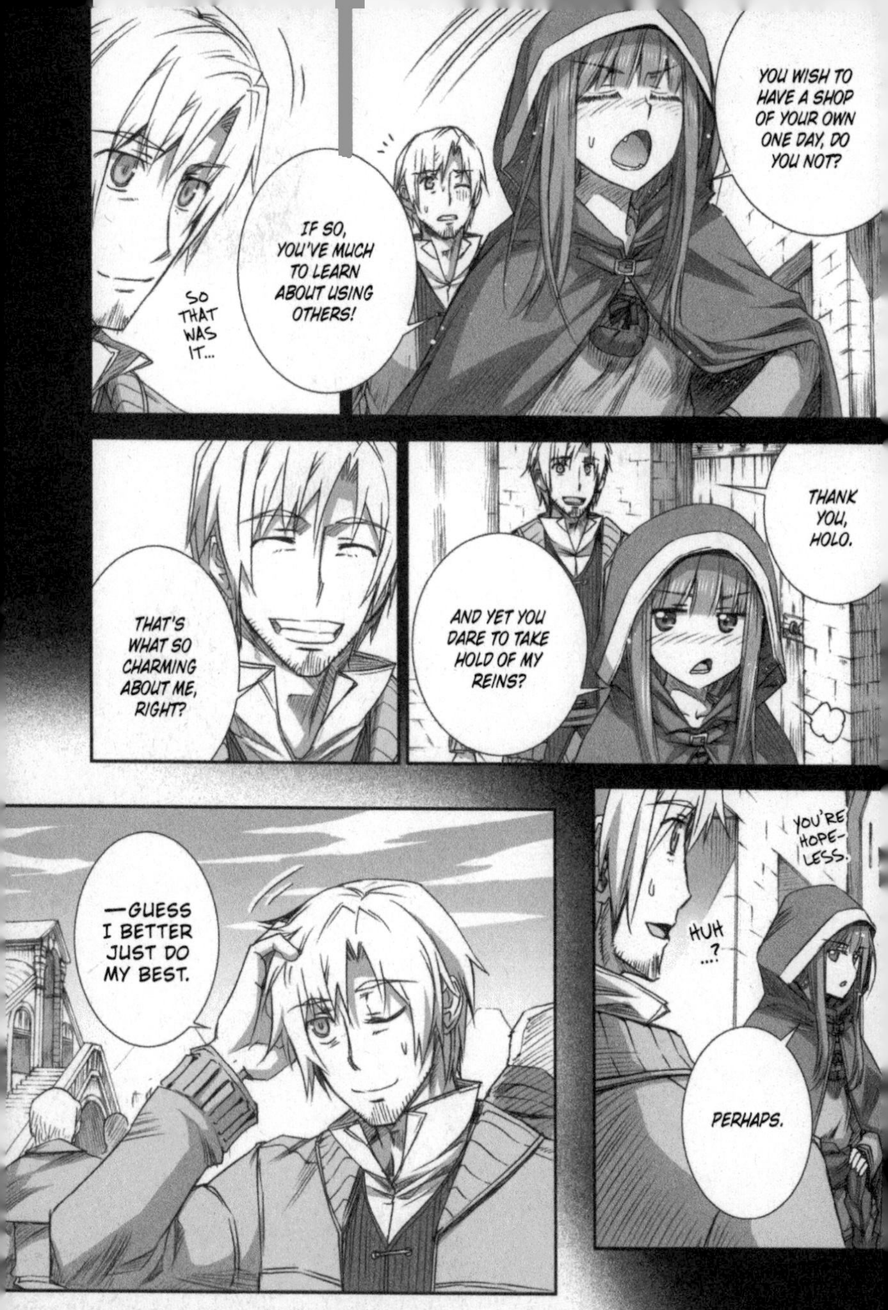
YOU WISH TO HAVE A SHOP OF YOUR OWN ONE DAY, DO YOU NOT?
IF SO, YOU'VE MUCH TO LEARN ABOUT USING OTHERS!
SO THAT WAS IT...
THANK YOU, HOLO.
AND YET YOU DARE TO TAKE HOLD OF MY REINS?
THAT'S WHAT SO CHARMING ABOUT ME, RIGHT?
YOU'RE HOPELESS.
HUH ...?
PERHAPS.
—GUESS I BETTER JUST DO MY BEST.

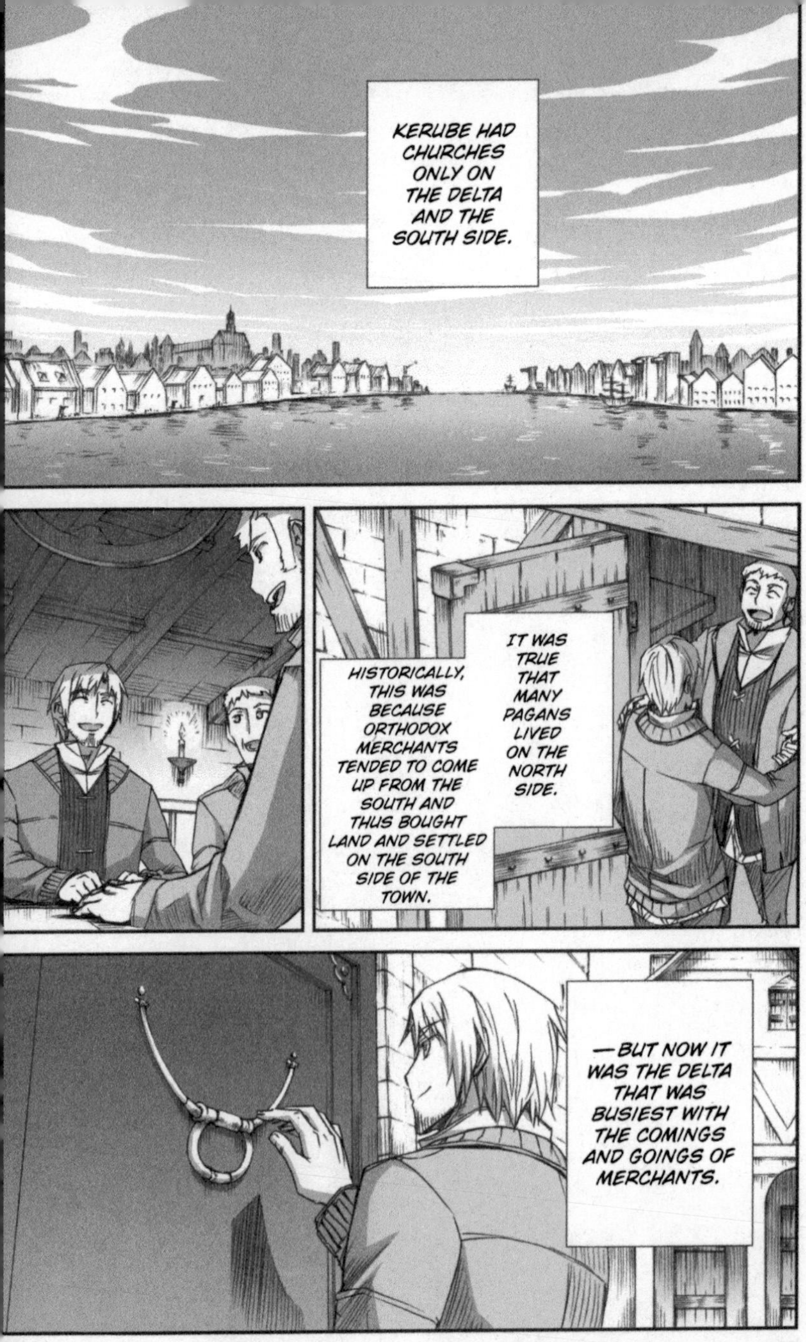
KERUBE HAD CHURCHES ONLY ON THE DELTA AND THE SOUTH SIDE.
IT WAS TRUE THAT MANY PAGANS LIVED ON THE NORTH SIDE.
HISTORICALLY, THIS WAS BECAUSE ORTHODOX MERCHANTS TENDED TO COME UP FROM THE SOUTH AND THUS BOUGHT LAND AND SETTLED ON THE SOUTH SIDE OF THE TOWN.
—BUT NOW IT WAS THE DELTA THAT WAS BUSIEST WITH THE COMINGS AND GOINGS OF MERCHANTS.

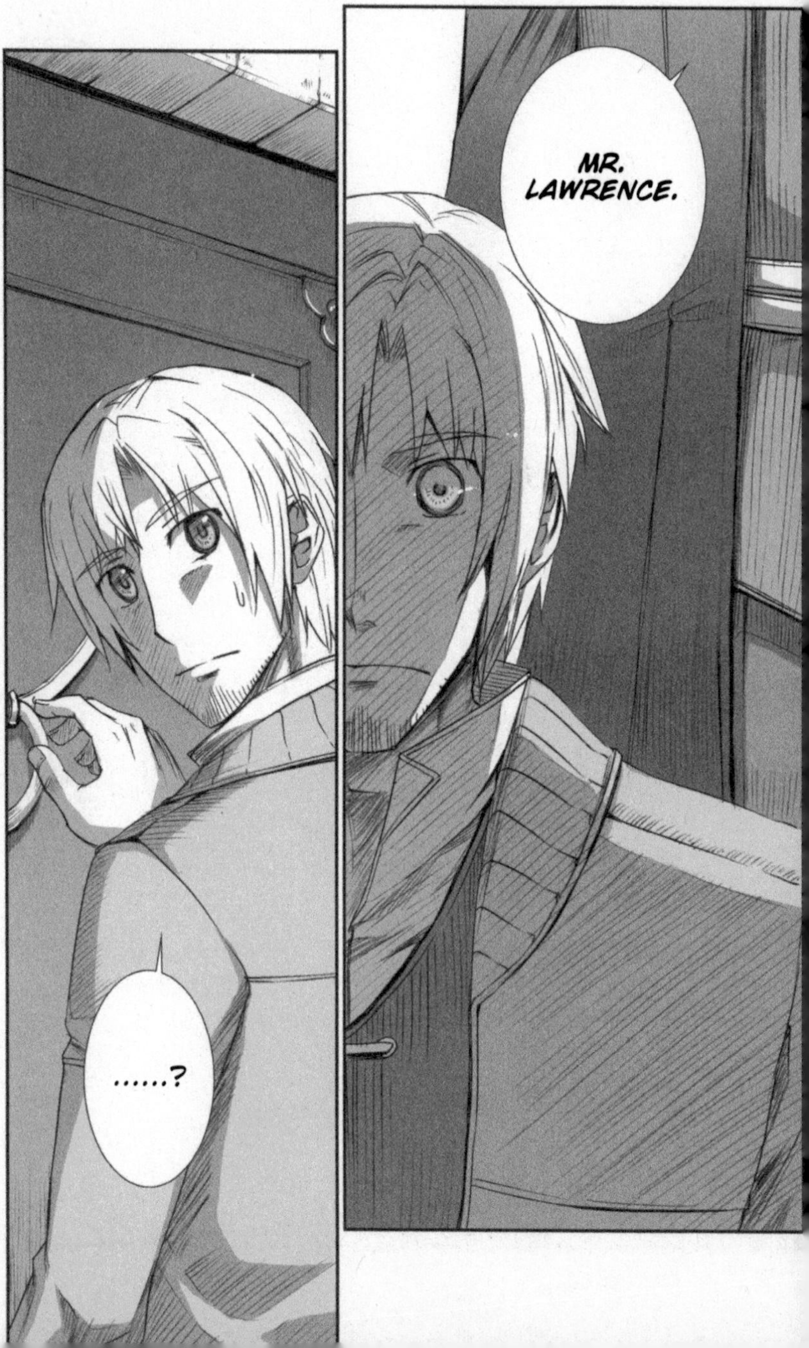
MR. LAWRENCE.
......?

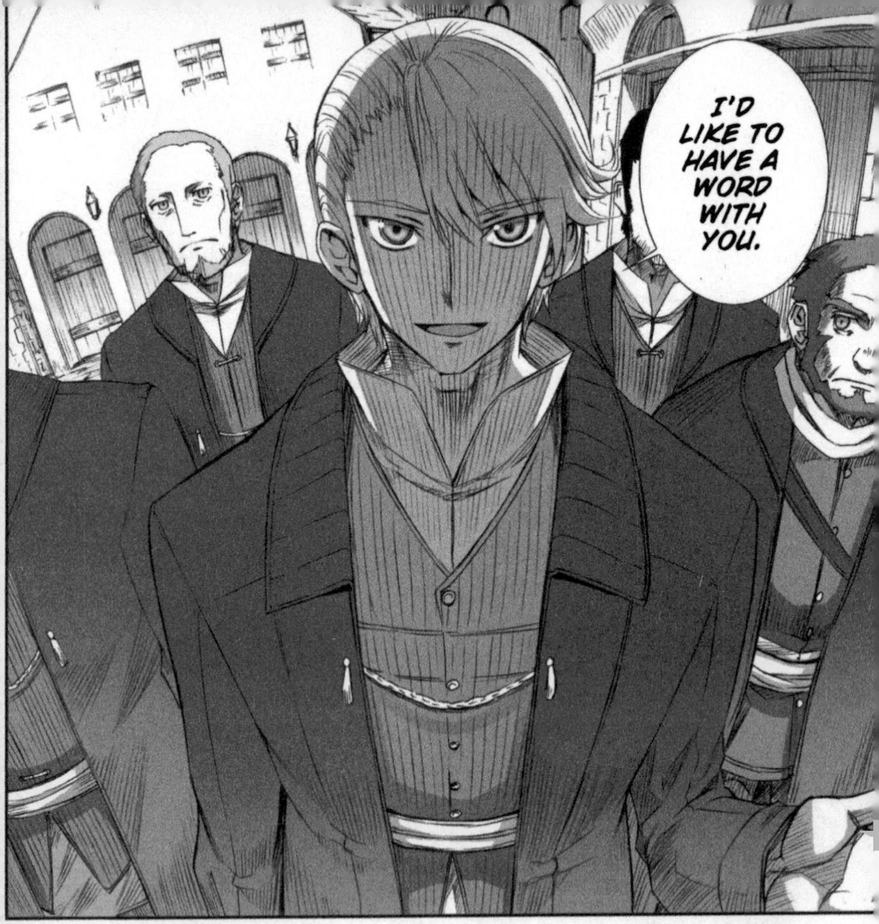
I'D LIKE TO HAVE A WORD WITH YOU.
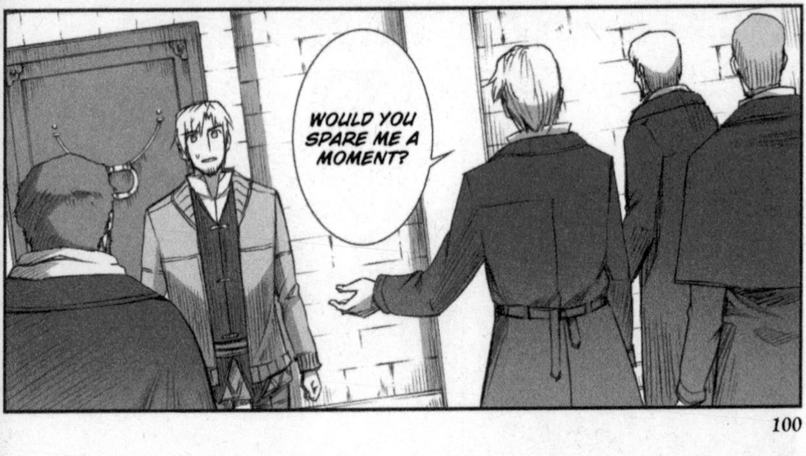
WOULD YOU SPARE ME A MOMENT?

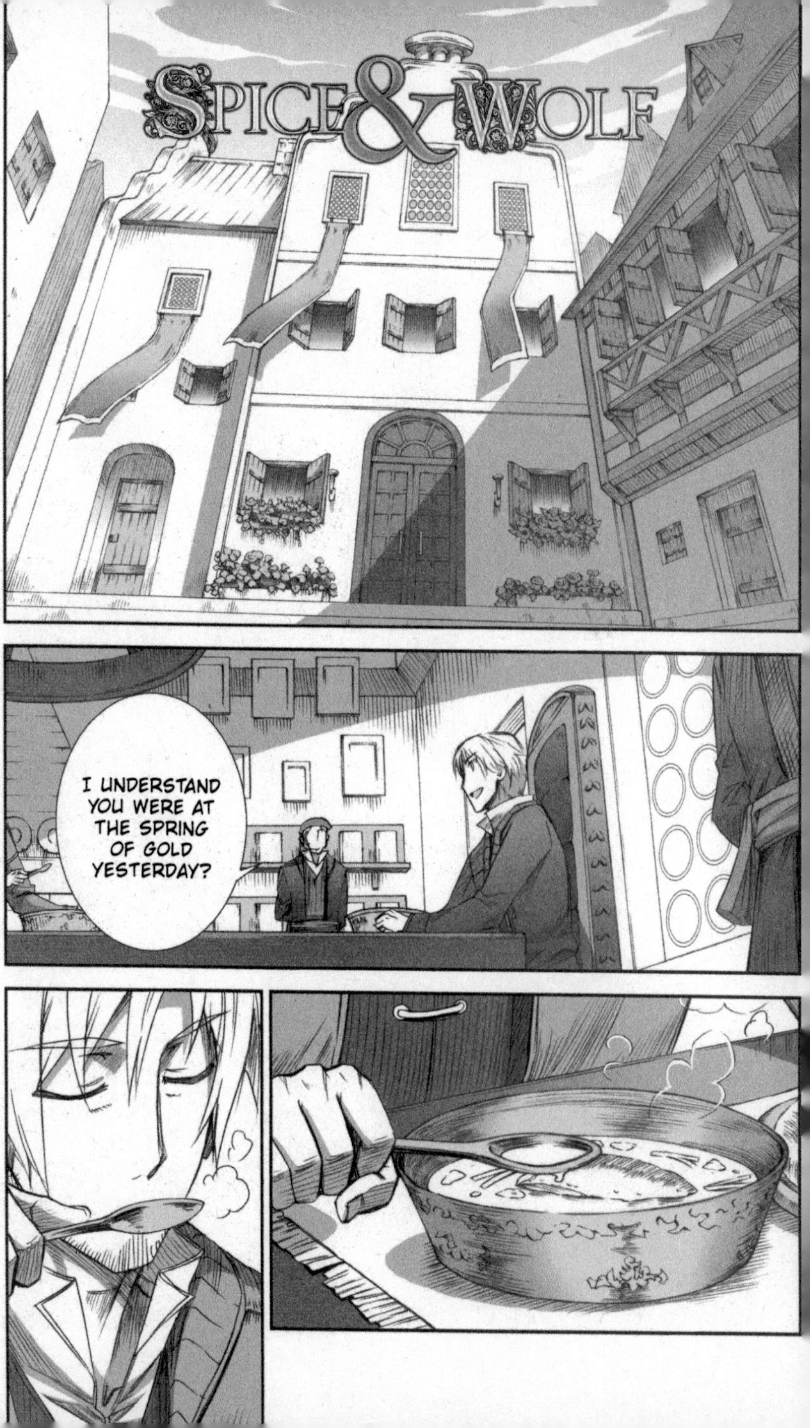
SPICE & WOLF
I UNDERSTAND YOU WERE AT THE SPRING OF GOLD YESTERDAY?

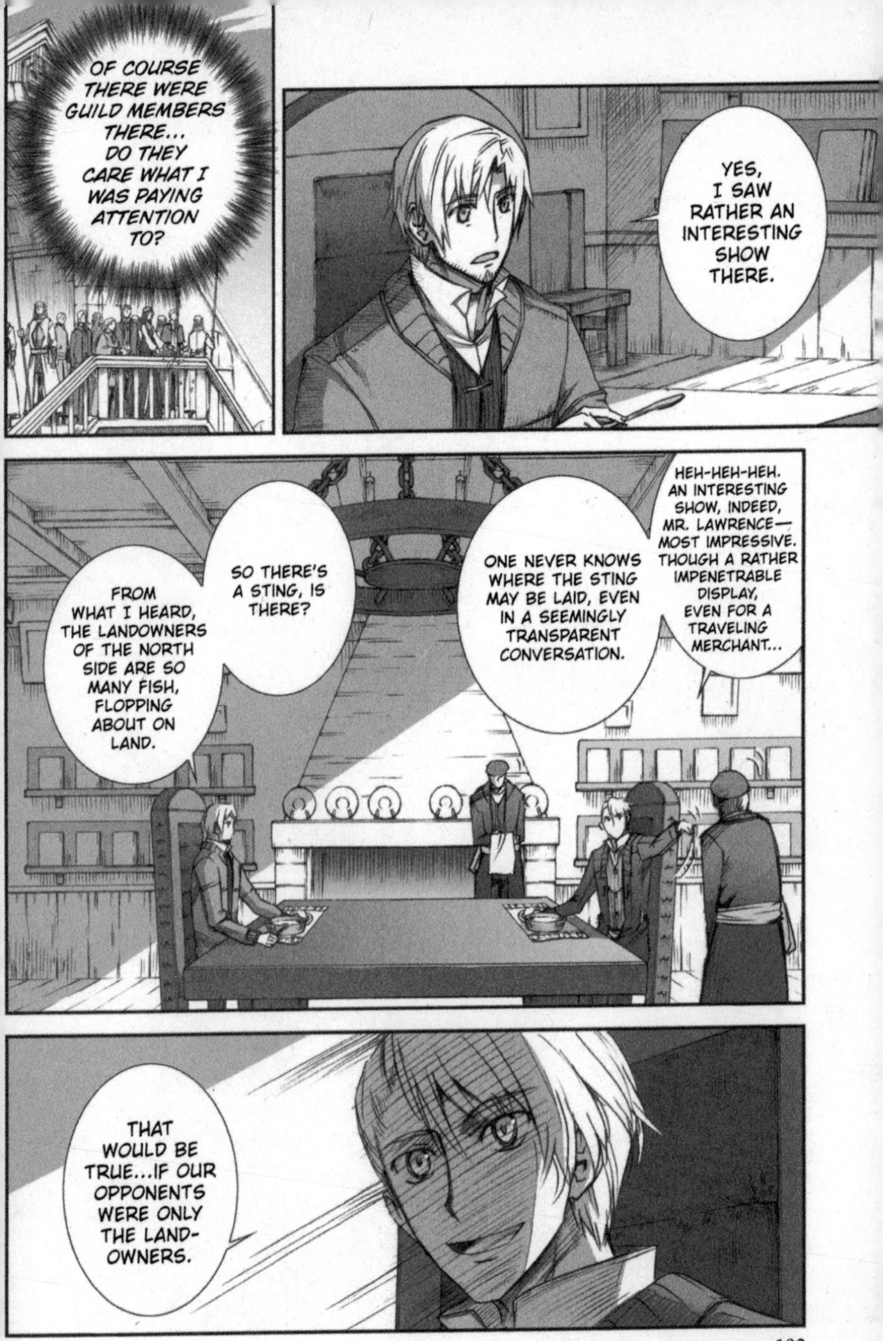
YES, I SAW RATHER AN INTERESTING SHOW THERE.
OF COURSE THERE WERE GUILD MEMBERS THERE... DO THEY CARE WHAT I WAS PAYING ATTENTION TO?
HEH-HEH-HEH. AN INTERESTING SHOW, INDEED, MR. LAWRENCE—MOST IMPRESSIVE. THOUGH A RATHER IMPENETRABLE DISPLAY, EVEN FOR A TRAVELING MERCHANT...
ONE NEVER KNOWS WHERE THE STING MAY BE LAID, EVEN IN A SEEMINGLY TRANSPARENT CONVERSATION.
SO THERE'S A STING, IS THERE?
FROM WHAT I HEARD, THE LANDOWNERS OF THE NORTH SIDE ARE SO MANY FISH, FLOPPING ABOUT ON LAND.
THAT WOULD BE TRUE...IF OUR OPPONENTS WERE ONLY THE LAND-OWNERS.

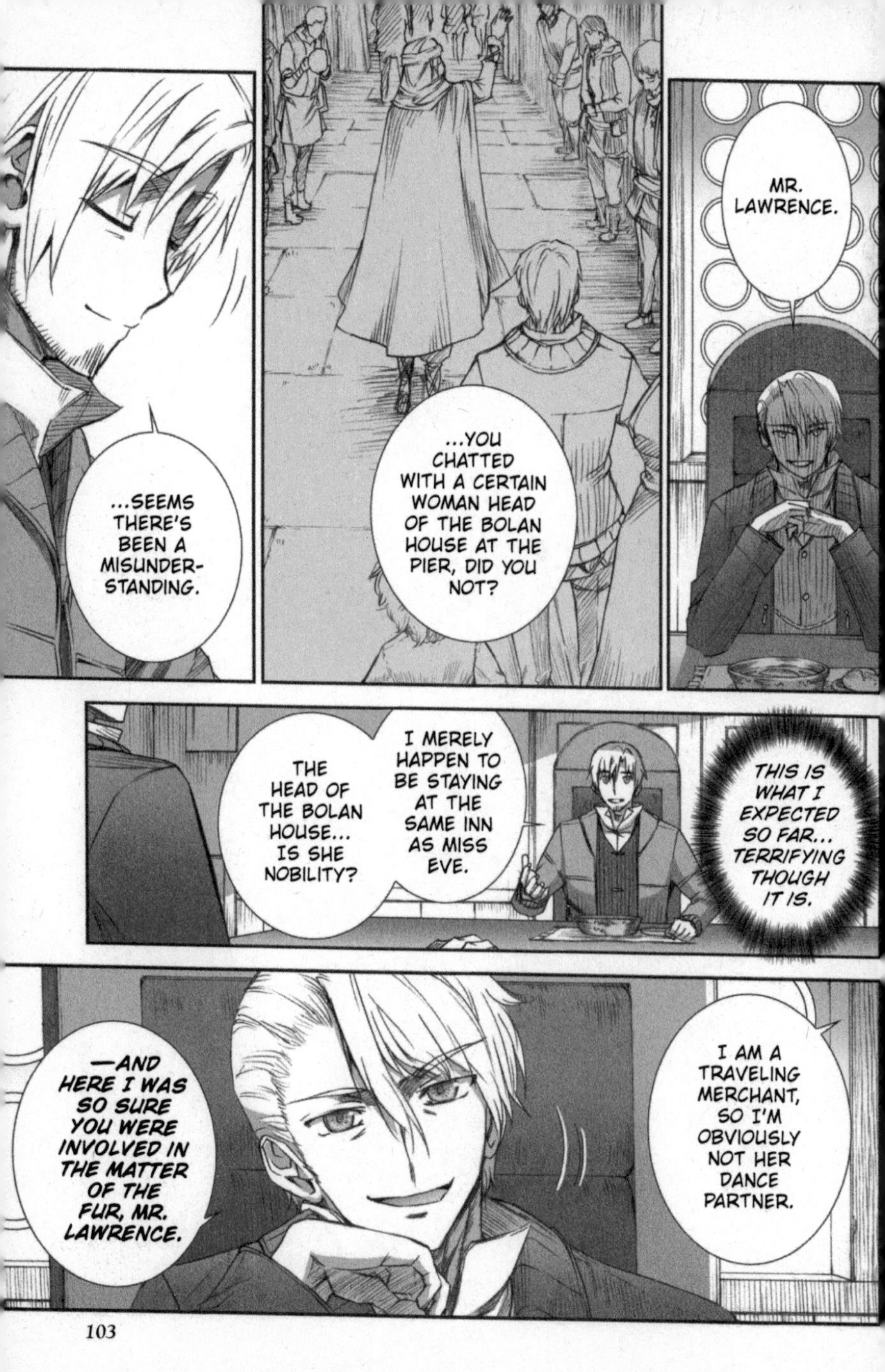
MR. LAWRENCE.
...YOU CHATTED WITH A CERTAIN WOMAN HEAD OF THE BOLAN HOUSE AT THE PIER, DID YOU NOT?
...SEEMS THERE'S BEEN A MISUNDERSTANDING.
THIS IS WHAT I EXPECTED SO FAR... TERRIFYING THOUGH IT IS.
I MERELY HAPPEN TO BE STAYING AT THE SAME INN AS MISS EVE.
THE HEAD OF THE BOLAN HOUSE... IS SHE NOBILITY?
I AM A TRAVELING MERCHANT, SO I'M OBVIOUSLY NOT HER DANCE PARTNER.
—AND HERE I WAS SO SURE YOU WERE INVOLVED IN THE MATTER OF THE FUR, MR. LAWRENCE.

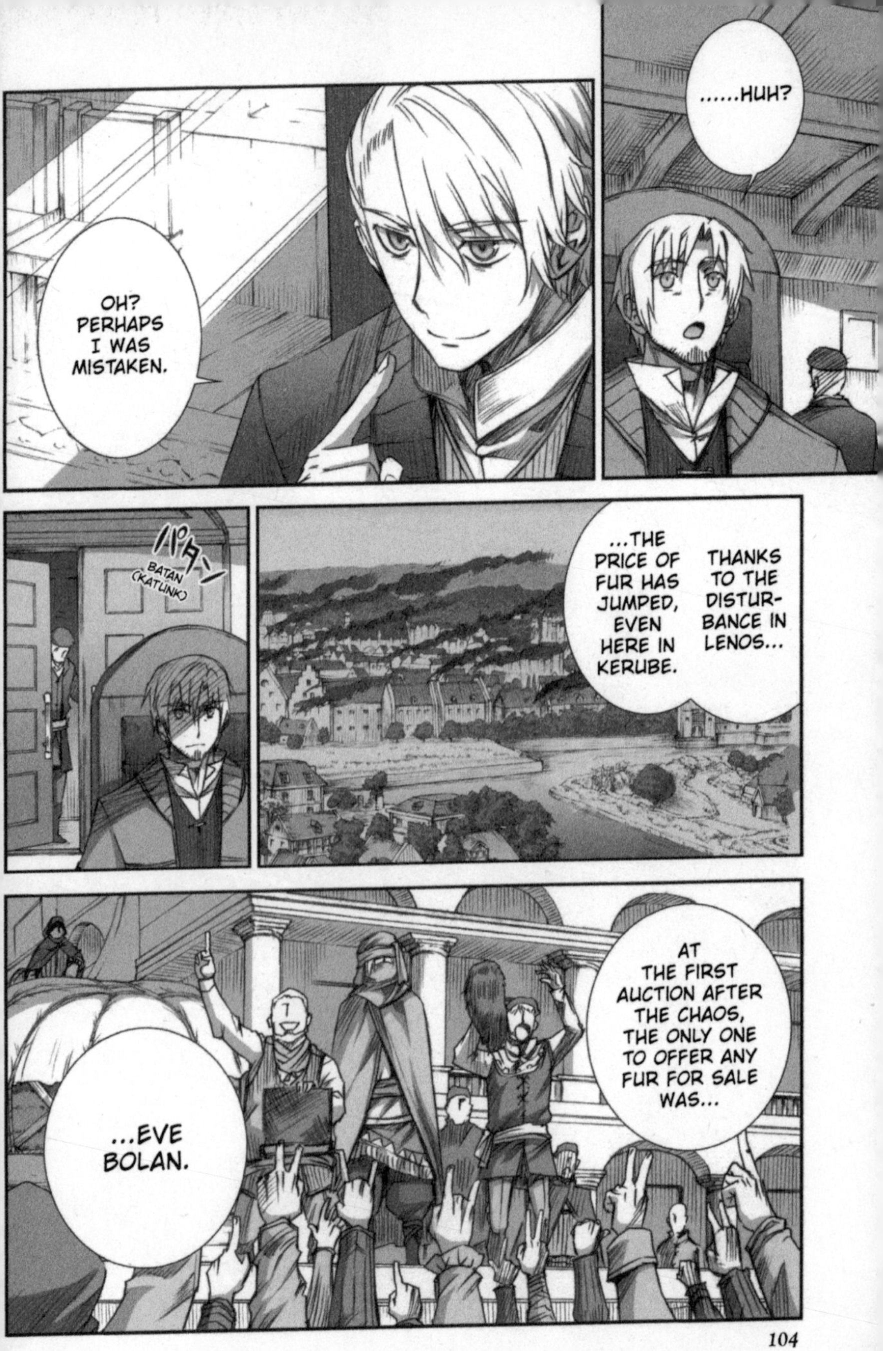

......HUH?
OH? PERHAPS I WAS MISTAKEN.
THANKS TO THE DISTUR-BANCE IN LENOS...
...THE PRICE OF FUR HAS JUMPED, EVEN HERE IN KERUBE.
パタン
BATAN (KATLINK)
AT THE FIRST AUCTION AFTER THE CHAOS, THE ONLY ONE TO OFFER ANY FUR FOR SALE WAS...
...EVE BOLAN.

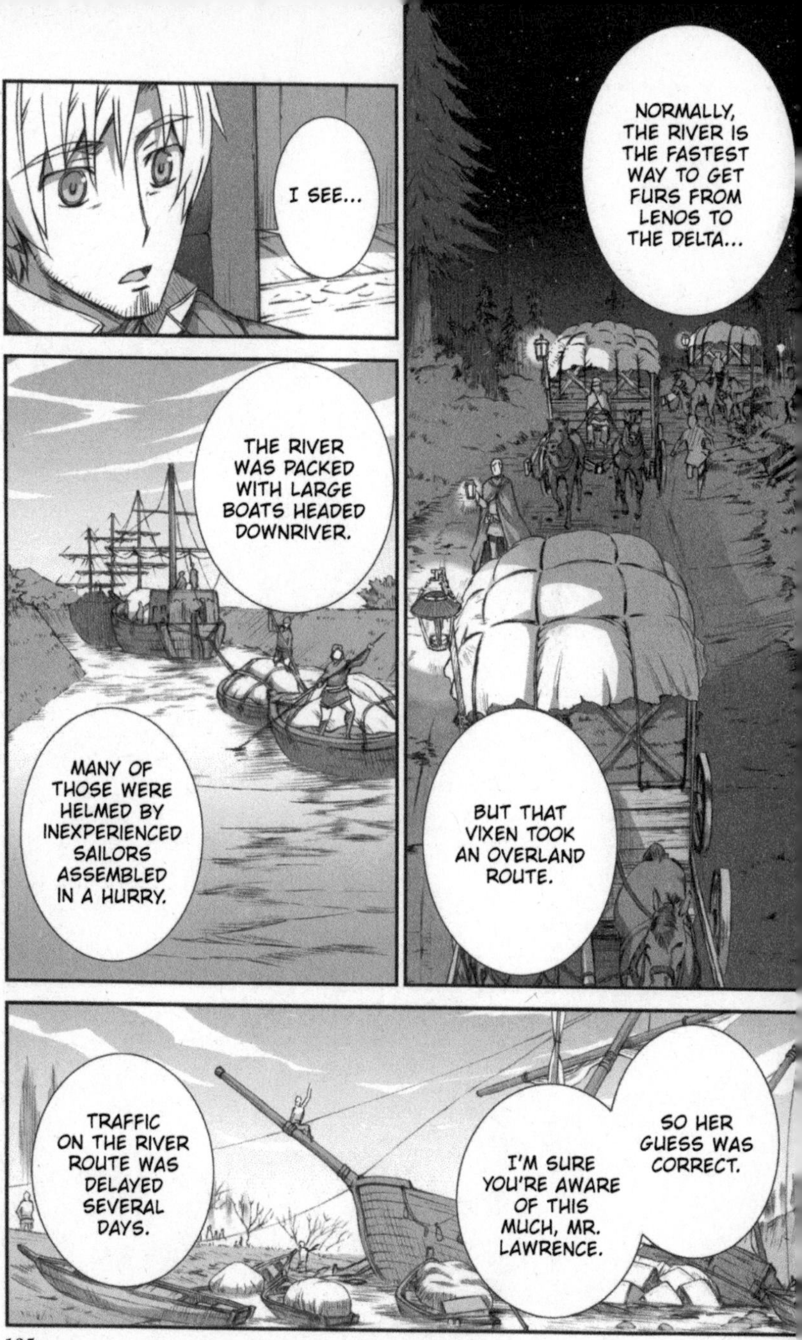
NORMALLY, THE RIVER IS THE FASTEST WAY TO GET FURS FROM LENOS TO THE DELTA...
BUT THAT VIXEN TOOK AN OVERLAND ROUTE.
I SEE...
THE RIVER WAS PACKED WITH LARGE BOATS HEADED DOWNRIVER.
MANY OF THOSE WERE HELMED BY INEXPERIENCED SAILORS ASSEMBLED IN A HURRY.
SO HER GUESS WAS CORRECT.
I'M SURE YOU'RE AWARE OF THIS MUCH, MR. LAWRENCE.
TRAFFIC ON THE RIVER ROUTE WAS DELAYED SEVERAL DAYS.

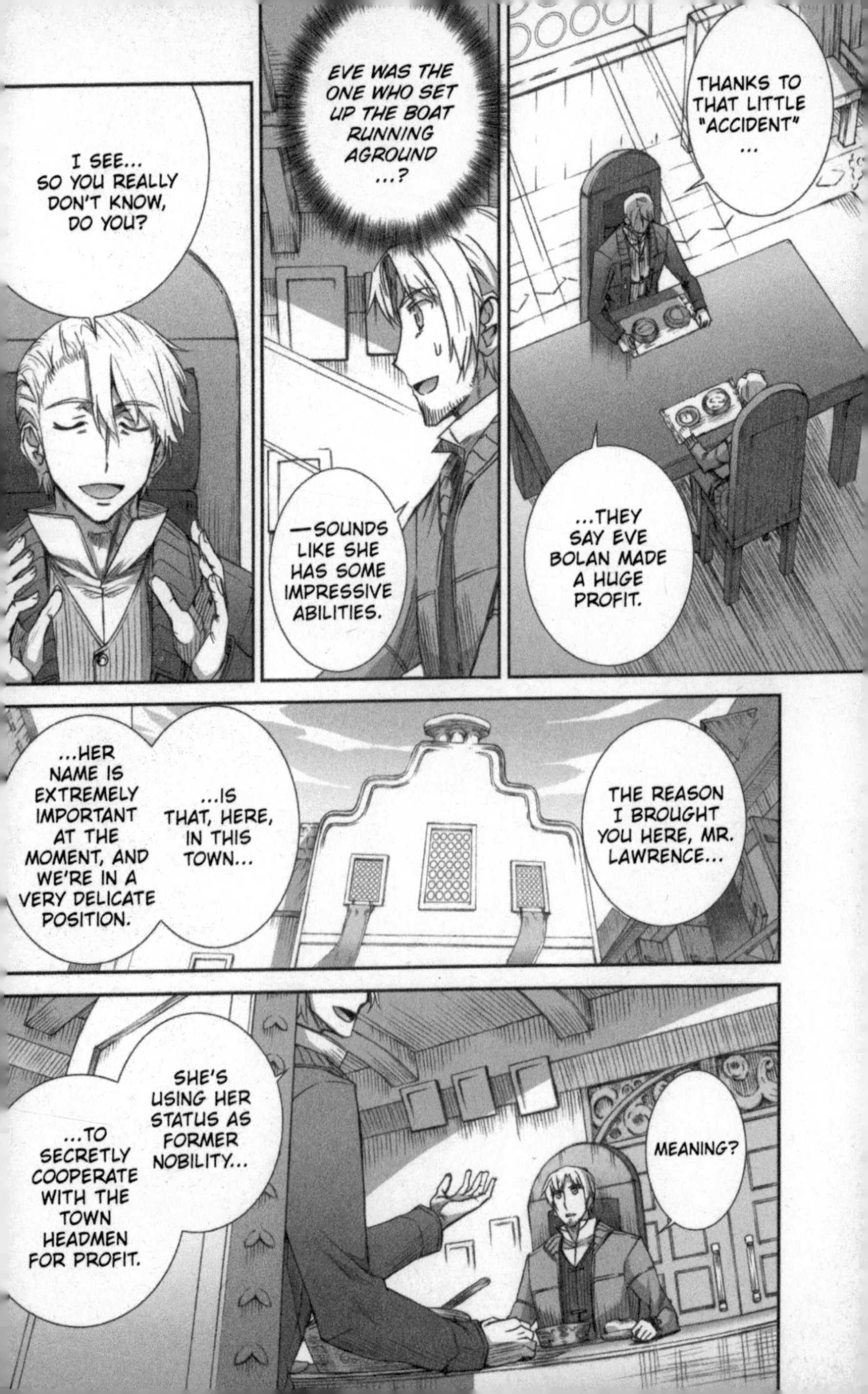
THANKS TO THAT LITTLE "ACCIDENT" ...
...THEY SAY EVE BOLAN MADE A HUGE PROFIT.
EVE WAS THE ONE WHO SET UP THE BOAT RUNNING AGROUND ...?
—SOUNDS LIKE SHE HAS SOME IMPRESSIVE ABILITIES.
I SEE... SO YOU REALLY DON'T KNOW, DO YOU?
THE REASON I BROUGHT YOU HERE, MR. LAWRENCE...
...IS THAT, HERE, IN THIS TOWN...
...HER NAME IS EXTREMELY IMPORTANT AT THE MOMENT, AND WE'RE IN A VERY DELICATE POSITION.
MEANING?
SHE'S USING HER STATUS AS FORMER NOBILITY...
...TO SECRETLY COOPERATE WITH THE TOWN HEADMEN FOR PROFIT.

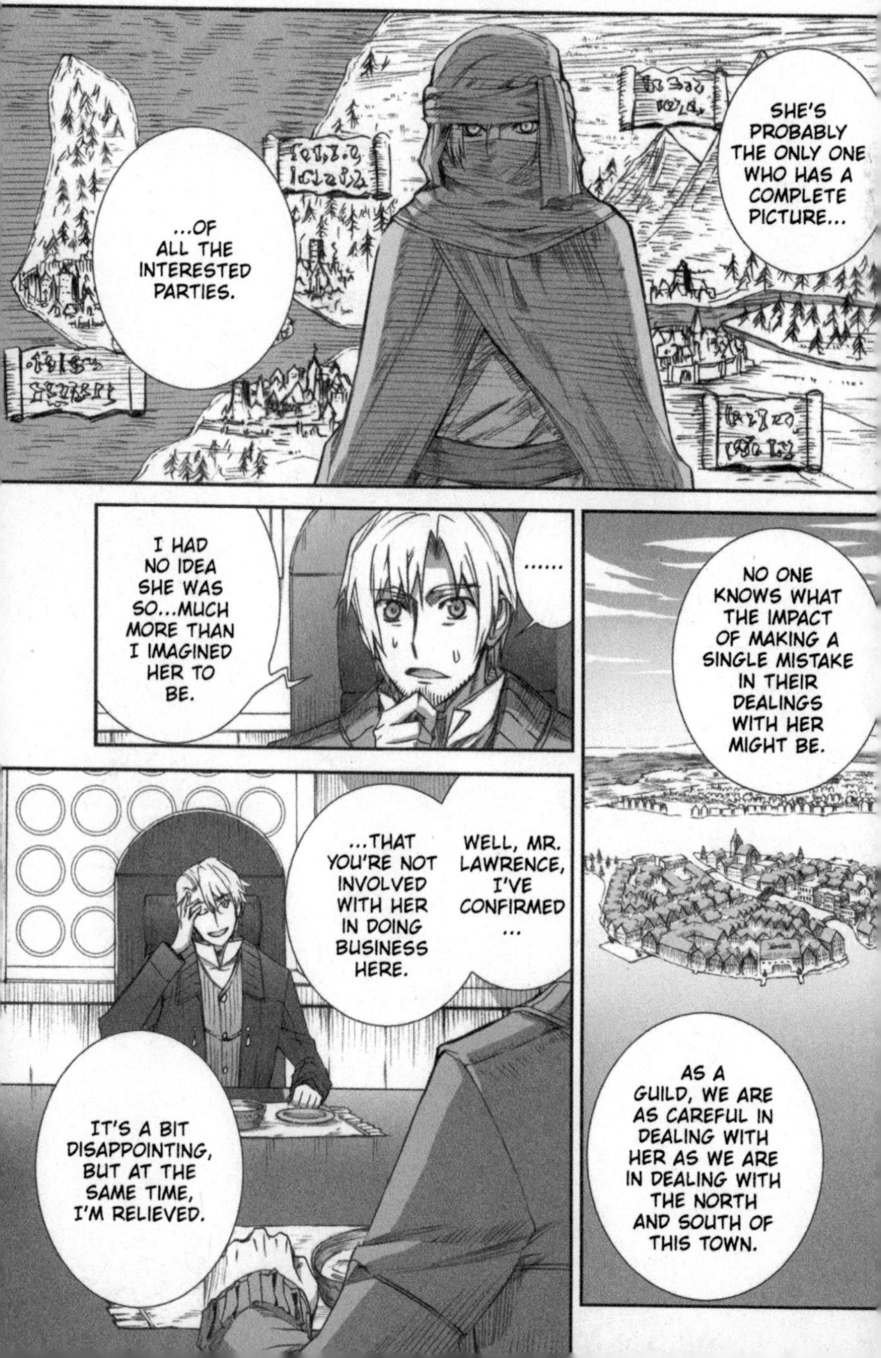
SHE'S PROBABLY THE ONLY ONE WHO HAS A COMPLETE PICTURE...
...OF ALL THE INTERESTED PARTIES.
NO ONE KNOWS WHAT THE IMPACT OF MAKING A SINGLE MISTAKE IN THEIR DEALINGS WITH HER MIGHT BE.
AS A GUILD, WE ARE AS CAREFUL IN DEALING WITH HER AS WE ARE IN DEALING WITH THE NORTH AND SOUTH OF THIS TOWN.
......
I HAD NO IDEA SHE WAS SO...MUCH MORE THAN I IMAGINED HER TO BE.
WELL, MR. LAWRENCE, I'VE CONFIRMED...
...THAT YOU'RE NOT INVOLVED WITH HER IN DOING BUSINESS HERE.
IT'S A BIT DISAPPOINTING, BUT AT THE SAME TIME, I'M RELIEVED.

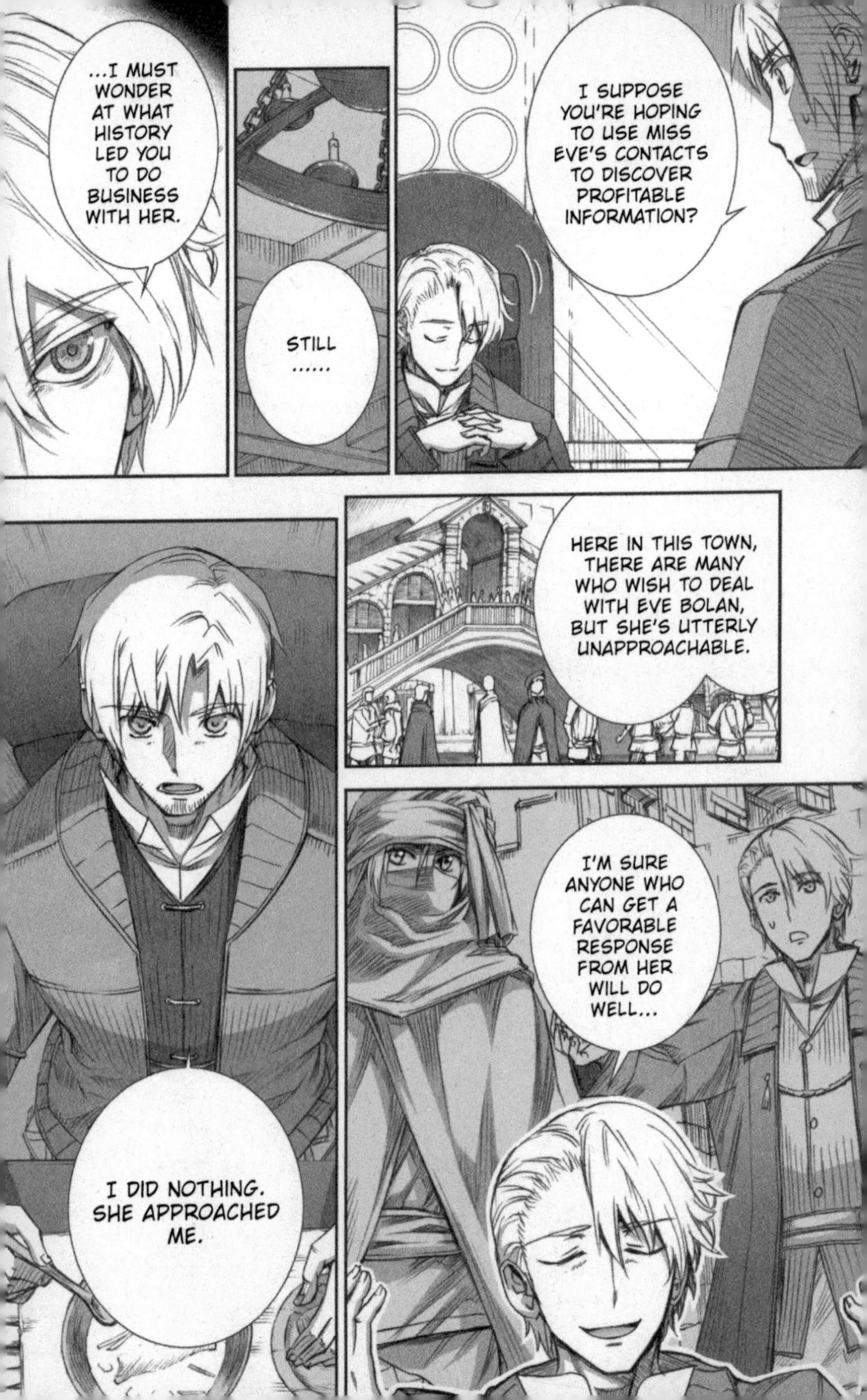
I SUPPOSE YOU'RE HOPING TO USE MISS EVE'S CONTACTS TO DISCOVER PROFITABLE INFORMATION?
STILL ......
...I MUST WONDER AT WHAT HISTORY LED YOU TO DO BUSINESS WITH HER.
HERE IN THIS TOWN, THERE ARE MANY WHO WISH TO DEAL WITH EVE BOLAN, BUT SHE'S UTTERLY UNAPPROACHABLE.
I'M SURE ANYONE WHO CAN GET A FAVORABLE RESPONSE FROM HER WILL DO WELL...
I DID NOTHING. SHE APPROACHED ME.

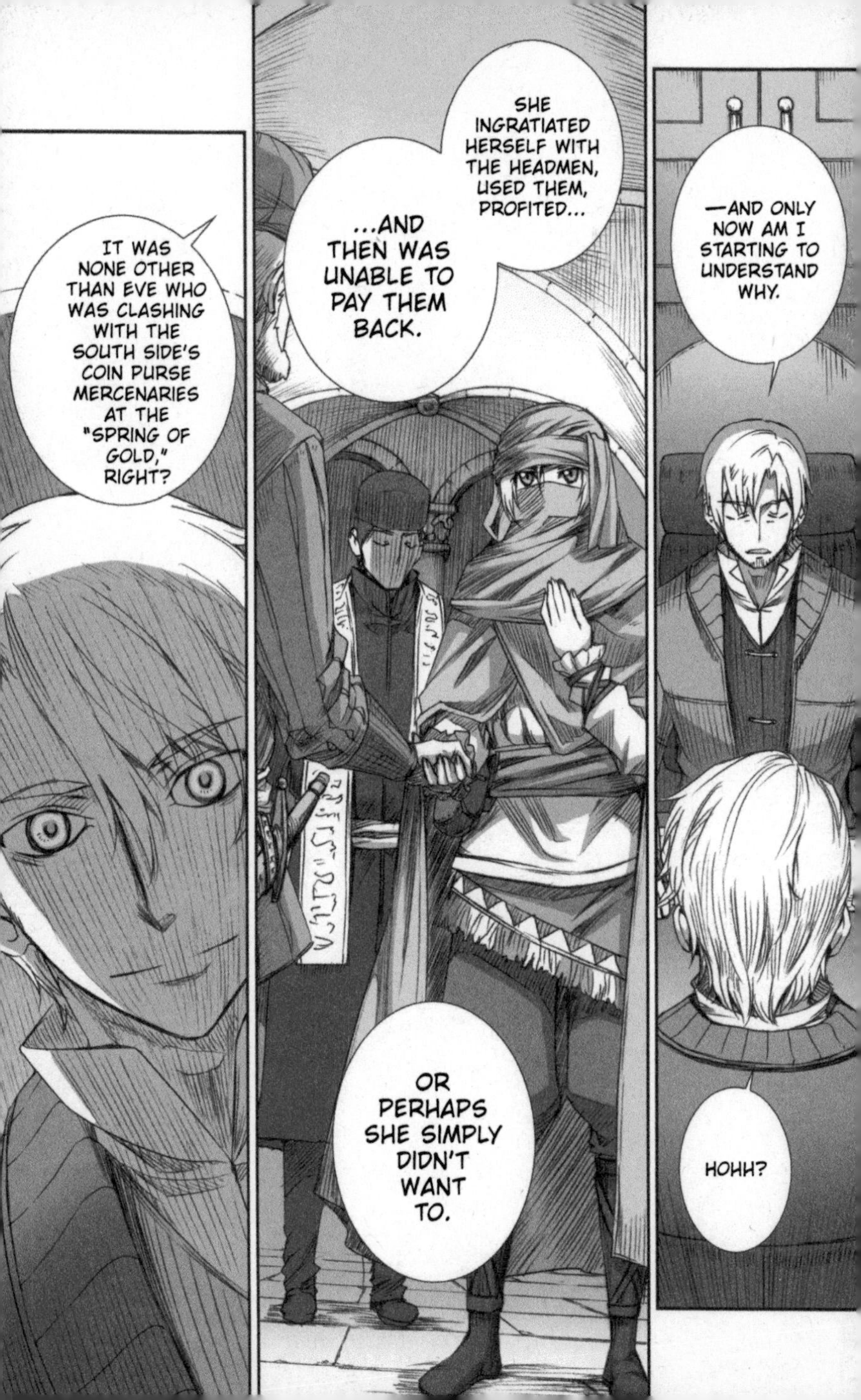
—AND ONLY NOW AM I STARTING TO UNDERSTAND WHY.
HOHH?
SHE INGRATIATED HERSELF WITH THE HEADMEN, USED THEM, PROFITED...
...AND THEN WAS UNABLE TO PAY THEM BACK.
OR PERHAPS SHE SIMPLY DIDN'T WANT TO.
IT WAS NONE OTHER THAN EVE WHO WAS CLASHING WITH THE SOUTH SIDE'S COIN PURSE MERCENARIES AT THE "SPRING OF GOLD," RIGHT?

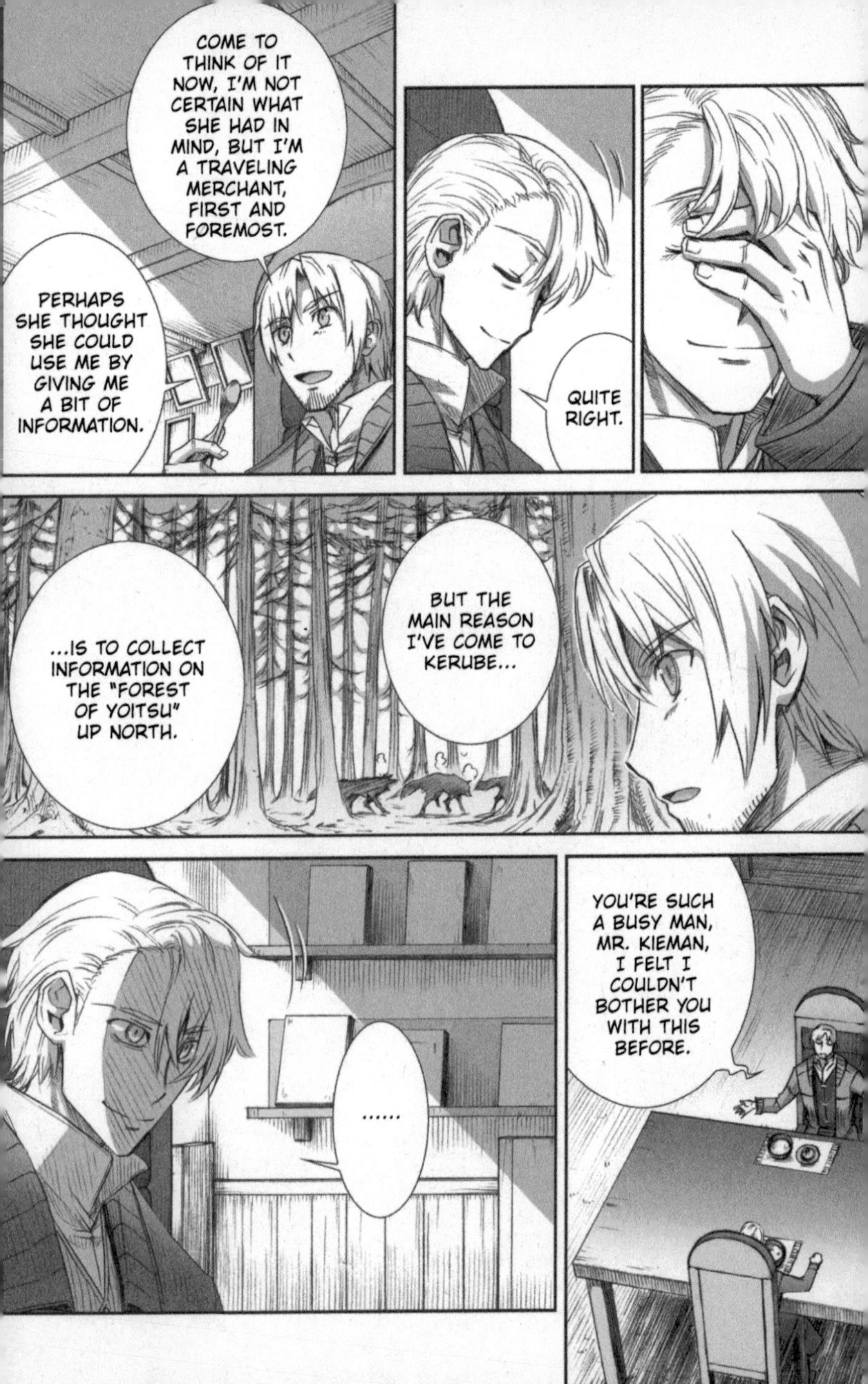
QUITE RIGHT.
COME TO THINK OF IT NOW, I'M NOT CERTAIN WHAT SHE HAD IN MIND, BUT I'M A TRAVELING MERCHANT, FIRST AND FOREMOST.
PERHAPS SHE THOUGHT SHE COULD USE ME BY GIVING ME A BIT OF INFORMATION.
BUT THE MAIN REASON I'VE COME TO KERUBE...
...IS TO COLLECT INFORMATION ON THE "FOREST OF YOITSU" UP NORTH.
YOU'RE SUCH A BUSY MAN, MR. KIEMAN, I FELT I COULDN'T BOTHER YOU WITH THIS BEFORE.
......

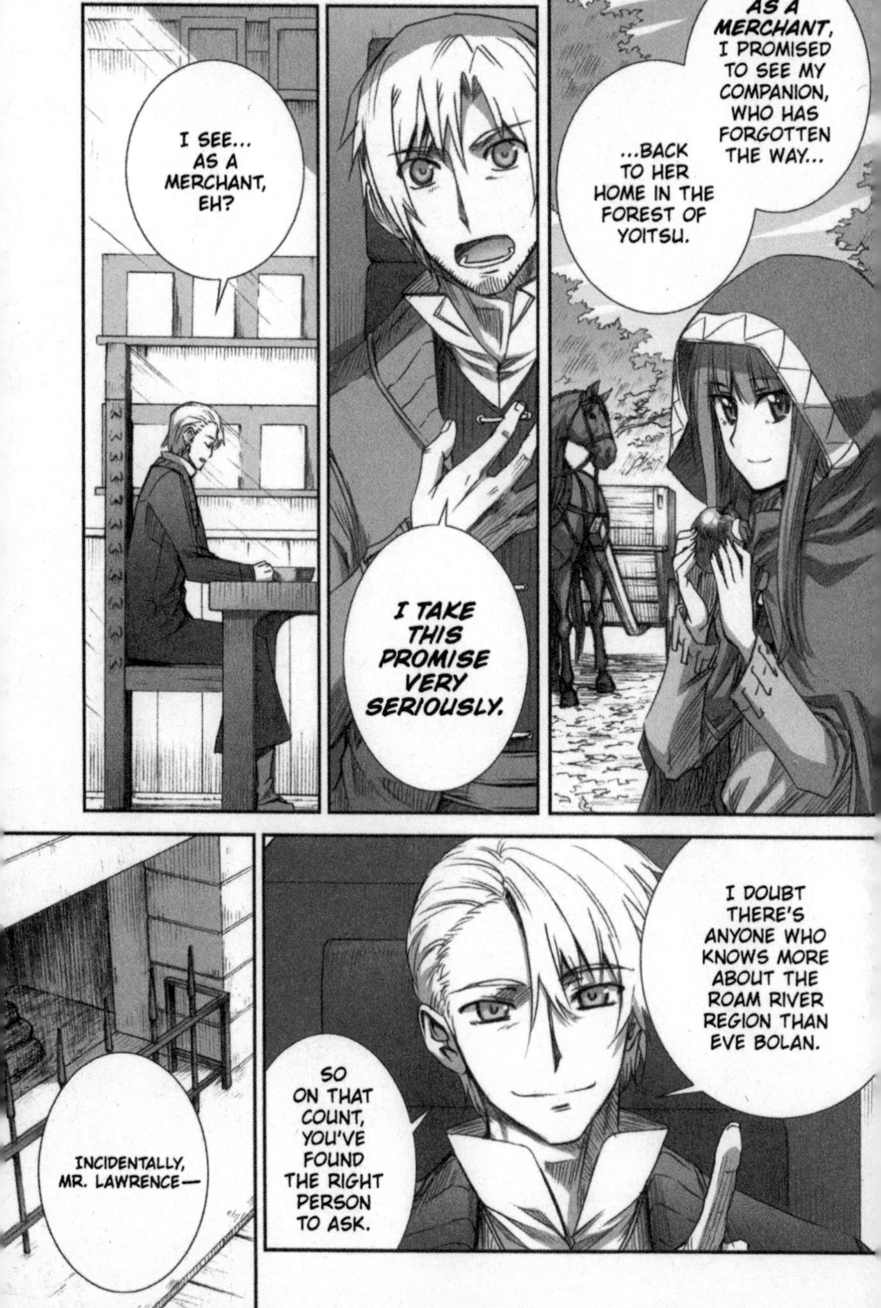

AS A MERCHANT, I PROMISED TO SEE MY COMPANION, WHO HAS FORGOTTEN THE WAY...
...BACK TO HER HOME IN THE FOREST OF YOITSU.
I TAKE THIS PROMISE VERY SERIOUSLY.
I SEE... AS A MERCHANT, EH?
I DOUBT THERE'S ANYONE WHO KNOWS MORE ABOUT THE ROAM RIVER REGION THAN EVE BOLAN.
SO ON THAT COUNT, YOU'VE FOUND THE RIGHT PERSON TO ASK.
INCIDENTALLY, MR. LAWRENCE—

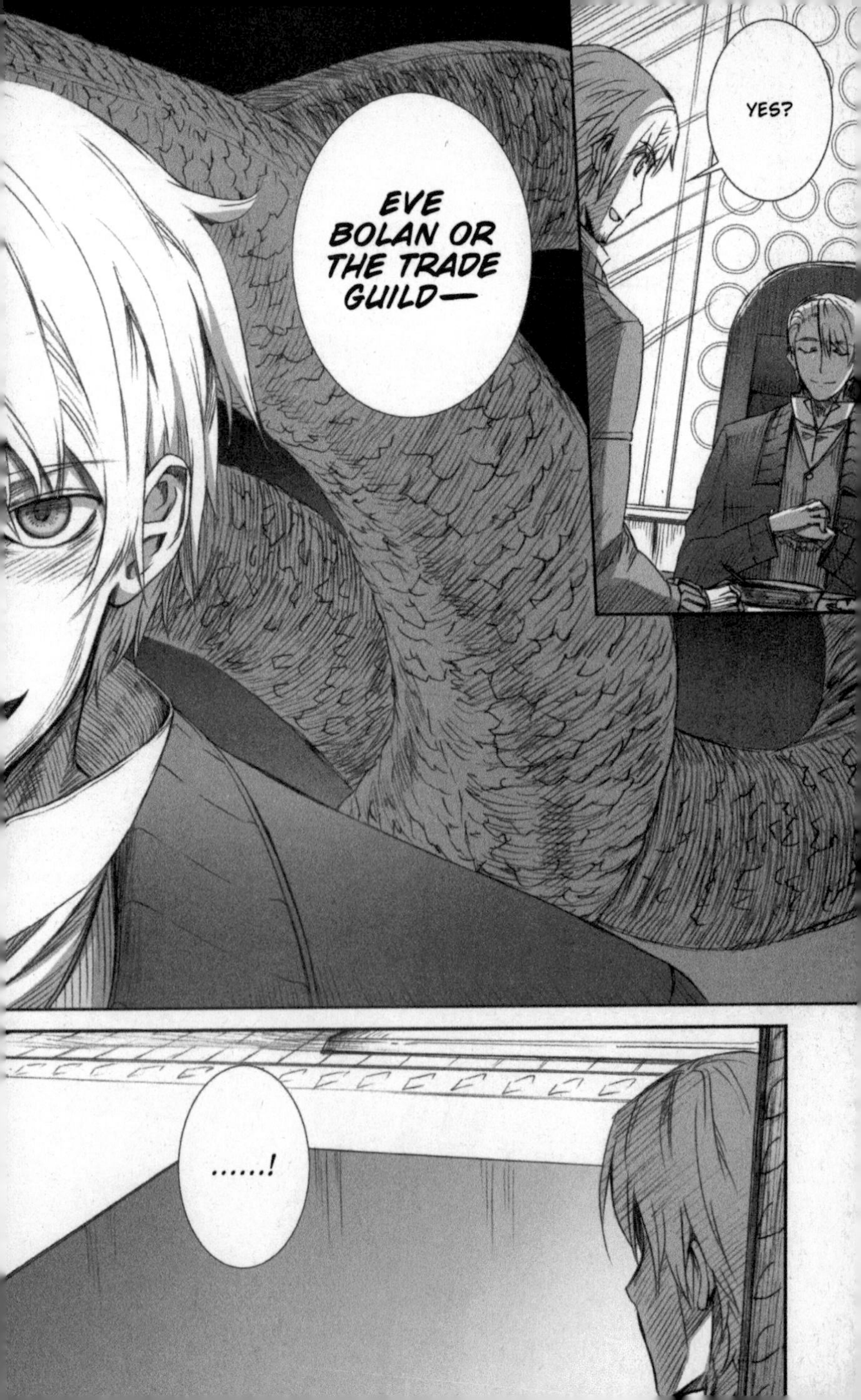
YES?
EVE BOLAN OR THE TRADE GUILD—
......!

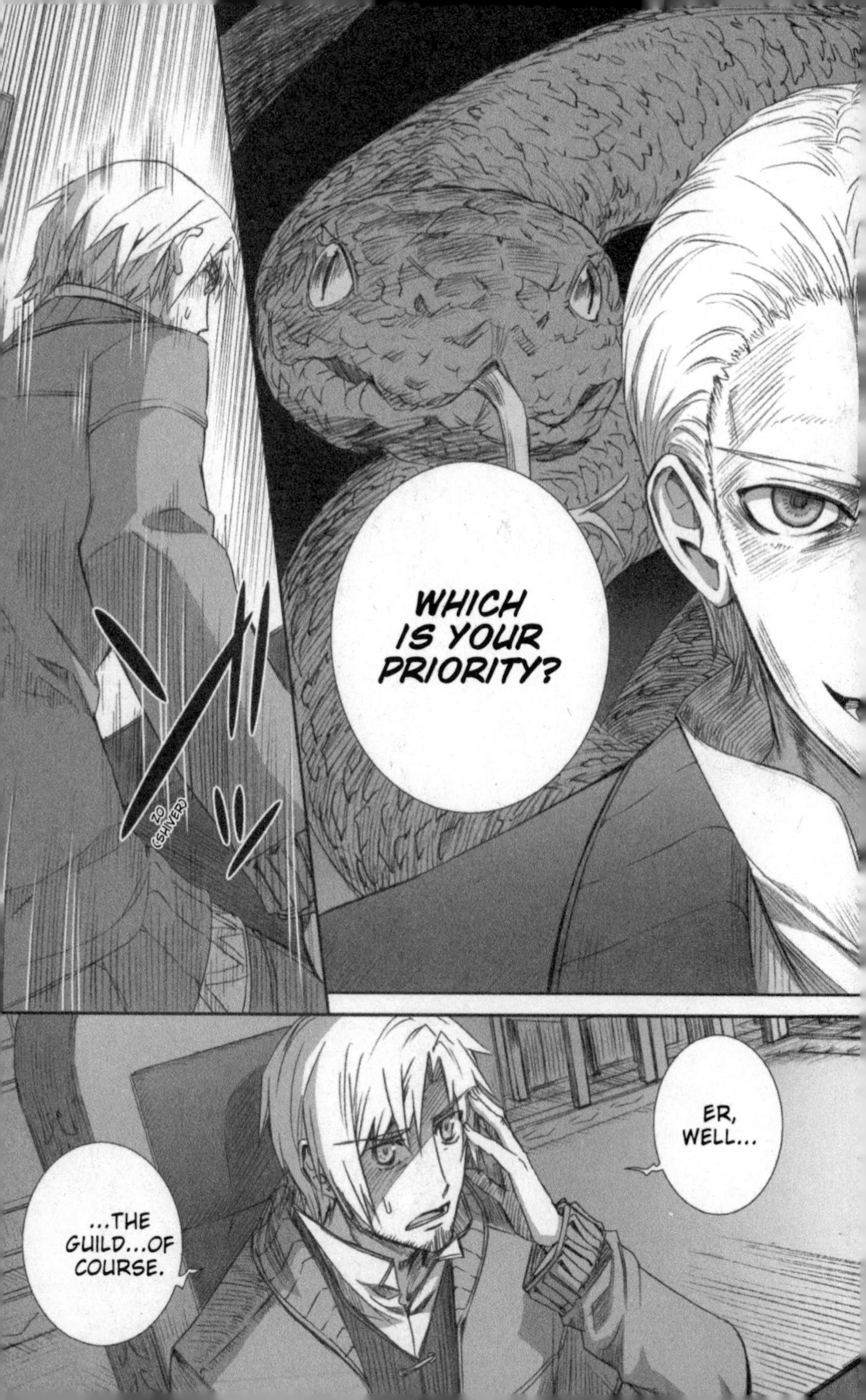
WHICH IS YOUR PRIORITY?
ZO (SHIVER)
ER, WELL...
...THE GUILD...OF COURSE.

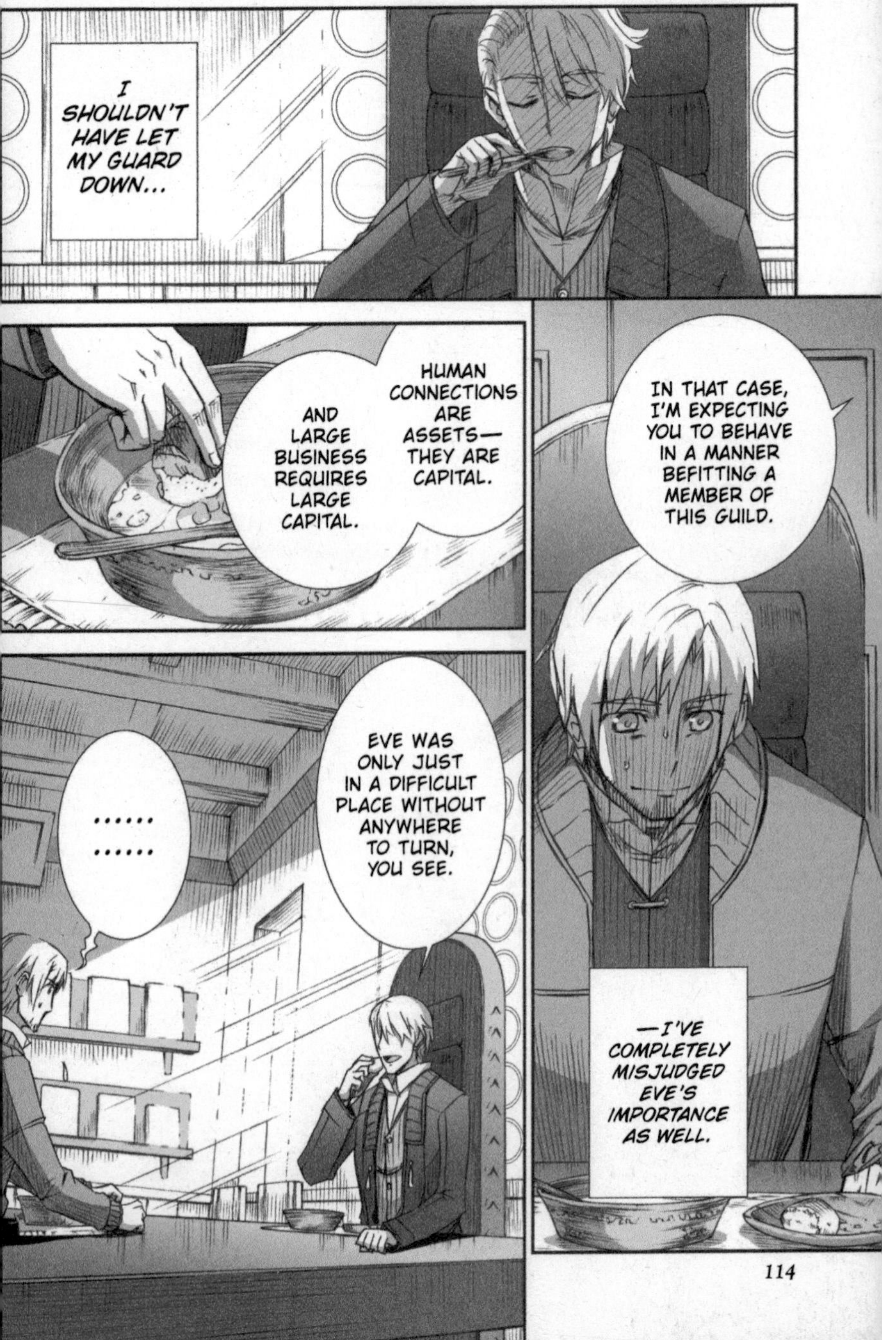
I SHOULDN'T HAVE LET MY GUARD DOWN...
IN THAT CASE, I'M EXPECTING YOU TO BEHAVE IN A MANNER BEFITTING A MEMBER OF THIS GUILD.
—I'VE COMPLETELY MISJUDGED EVE'S IMPORTANCE AS WELL.
HUMAN CONNECTIONS ARE ASSETS— THEY ARE CAPITAL.
AND LARGE BUSINESS REQUIRES LARGE CAPITAL.
EVE WAS ONLY JUST IN A DIFFICULT PLACE WITHOUT ANYWHERE TO TURN, YOU SEE.
....

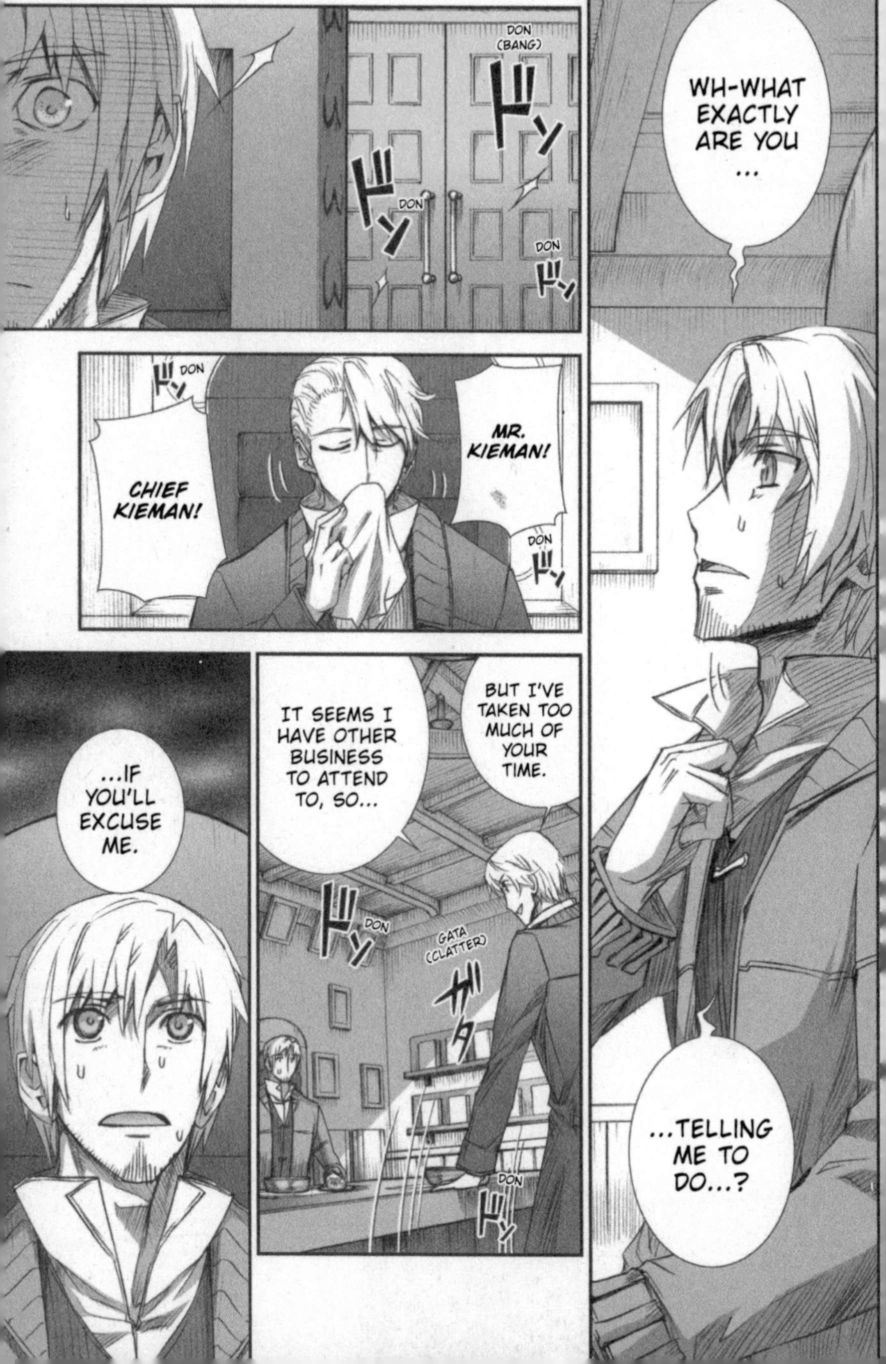
WH-WHAT EXACTLY ARE YOU ...
...TELLING ME TO DO...?
ドッ DON (BANG)
ドッ DON
ドッ DON
ドッ DON
MR. KIEMAN!
CHIEF KIEMAN!
ドッ DON
BUT I'VE TAKEN TOO MUCH OF YOUR TIME.
IT SEEMS I HAVE OTHER BUSINESS TO ATTEND TO, SO...
ドッ DON
ガタ GATA (CLATTER)
ドッ DON
...IF YOU'LL EXCUSE ME.

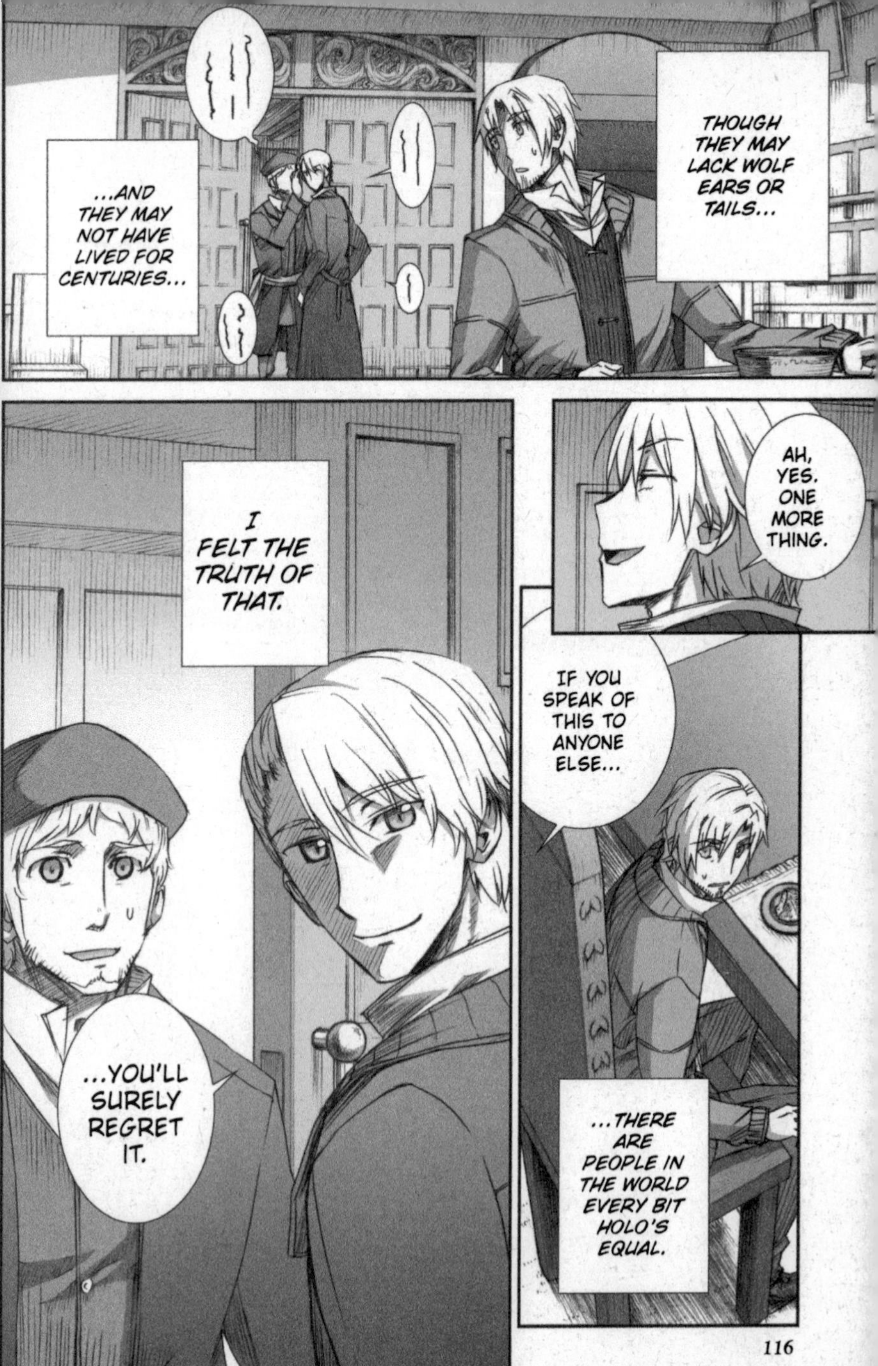
THOUGH THEY MAY LACK WOLF EARS OR TAILS...
...AND THEY MAY NOT HAVE LIVED FOR CENTURIES...
AH, YES. ONE MORE THING.
IF YOU SPEAK OF THIS TO ANYONE ELSE...
...THERE ARE PEOPLE IN THE WORLD EVERY BIT HOLO'S EQUAL.
I FELT THE TRUTH OF THAT.
...YOU'LL SURELY REGRET IT.

SPICE & WOLF

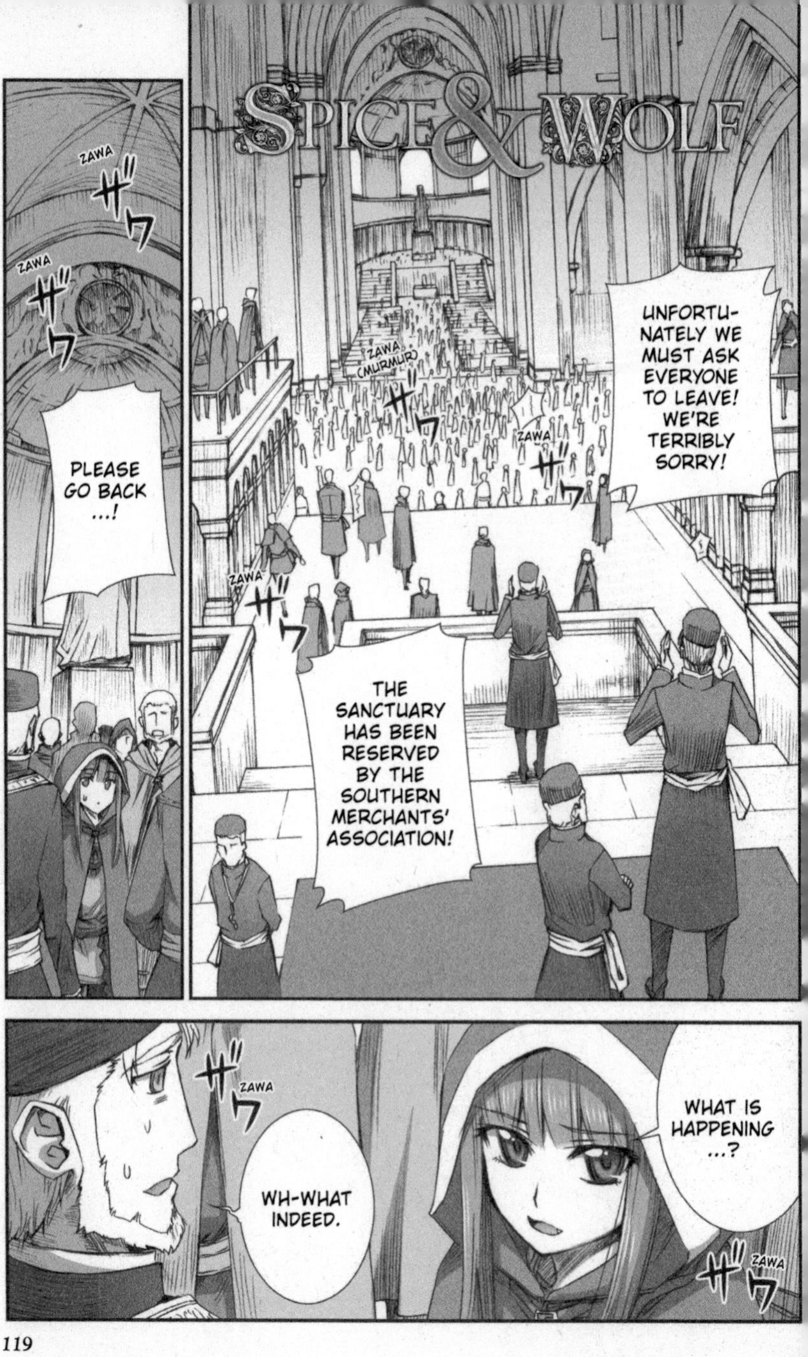
SPICE & WOLF
UNFORTUNATELY WE MUST ASK EVERYONE TO LEAVE! WE'RE TERRIBLY SORRY!
ZAWA (MURMUR)
ZAWA
ZAWA
THE SANCTUARY HAS BEEN RESERVED BY THE SOUTHERN MERCHANTS' ASSOCIATION!
ZAWA
ZAWA
PLEASE GO BACK ...!
WHAT IS HAPPENING ...?
ZAWA
ZAWA
WH-WHAT INDEED.

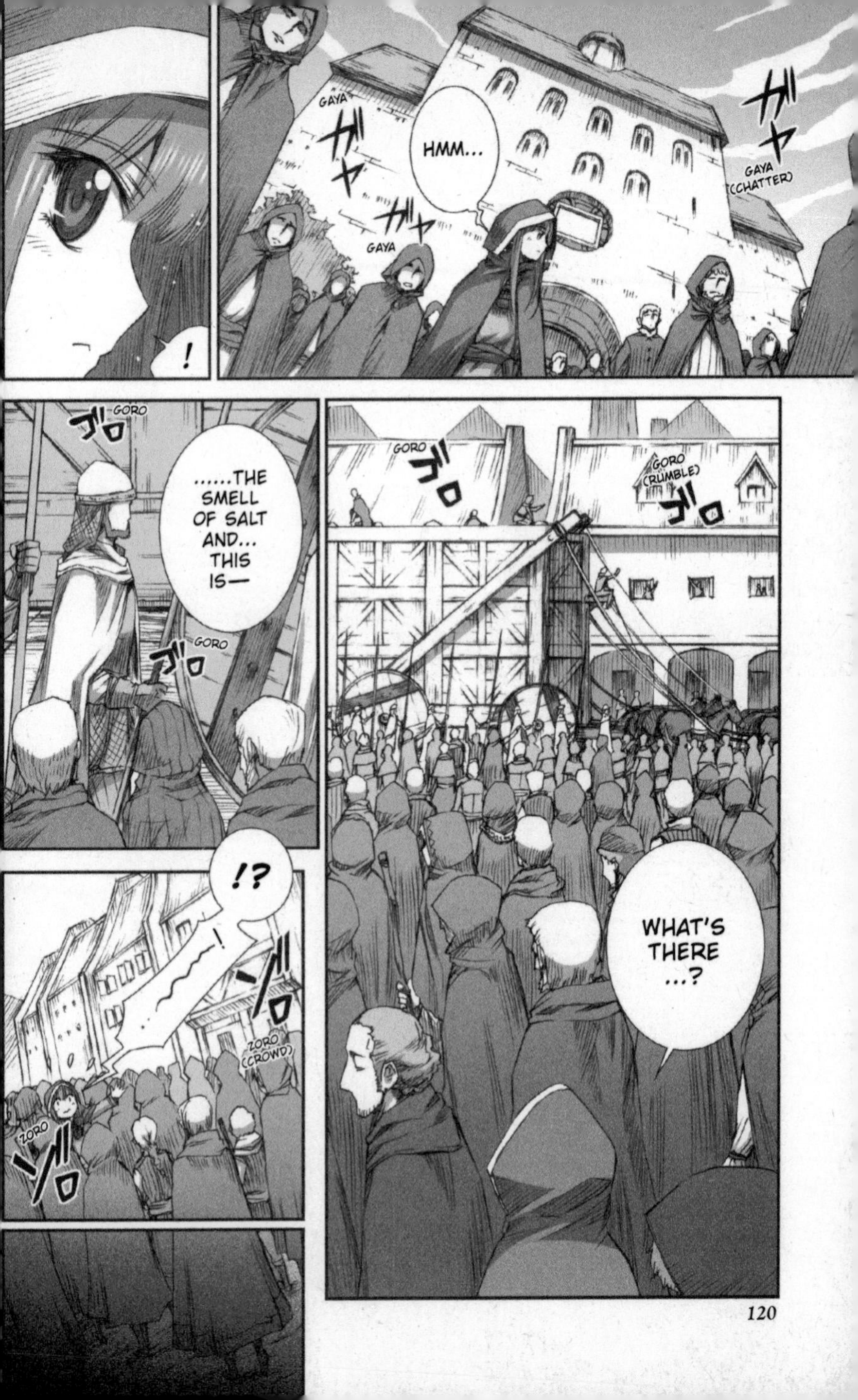
GAYA (CHATTER)
GAYA
HMM...
GAYA
!
GORO
GORO (RUMBLE)
WHAT'S THERE ...?
GORO
......THE SMELL OF SALT AND... THIS IS—
GORO
!?
!
ZORO (CROWD)
ZORO

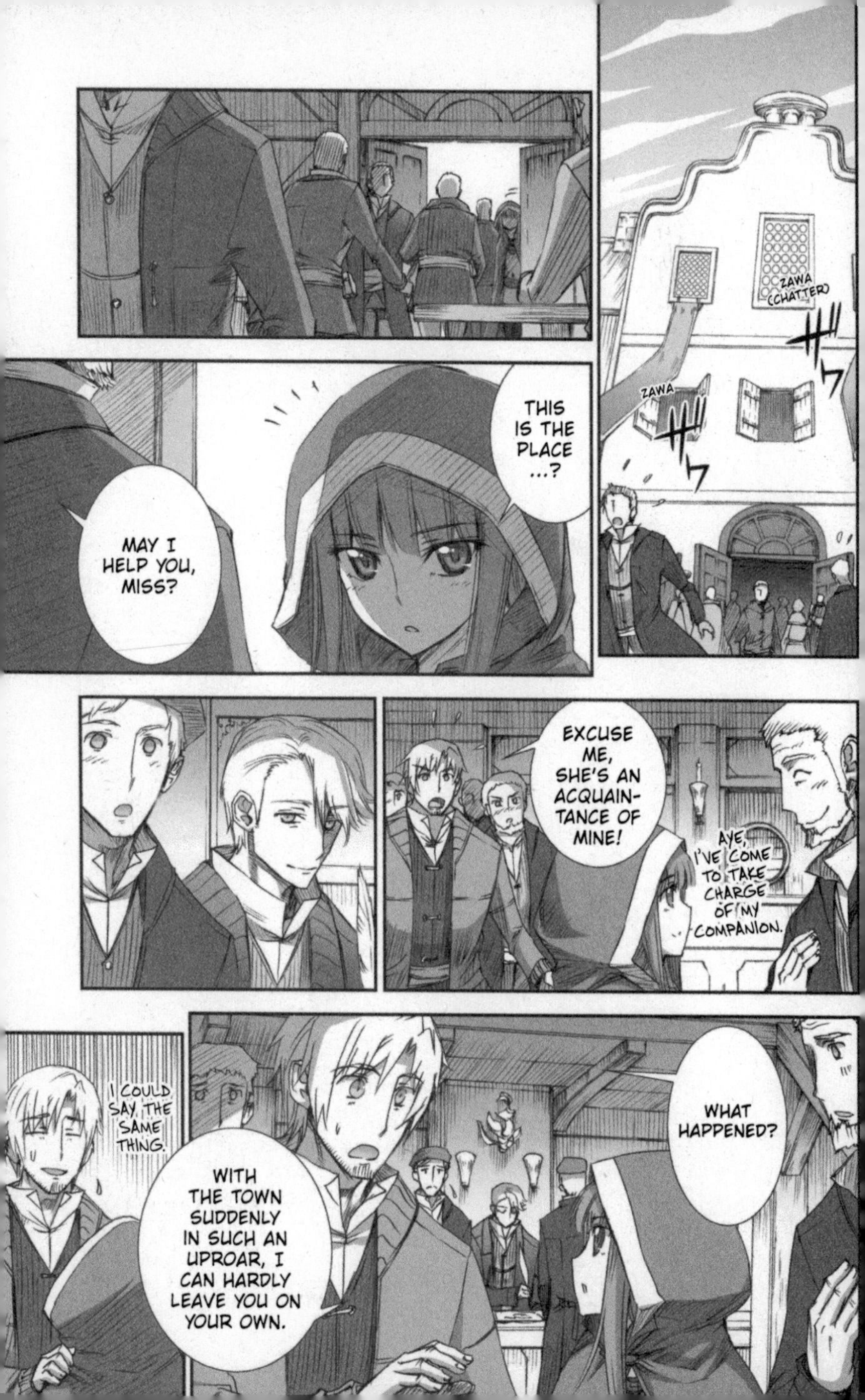
ZAWA (CHATTER)
ZAWA
THIS IS THE PLACE ...?
MAY I HELP YOU, MISS?
EXCUSE ME, SHE'S AN ACQUAINTANCE OF MINE!
AYE, I'VE COME TO TAKE CHARGE OF MY COMPANION.
WHAT HAPPENED?
WITH THE TOWN SUDDENLY IN SUCH AN UPROAR, I CAN HARDLY LEAVE YOU ON YOUR OWN.
I COULD SAY THE SAME THING.

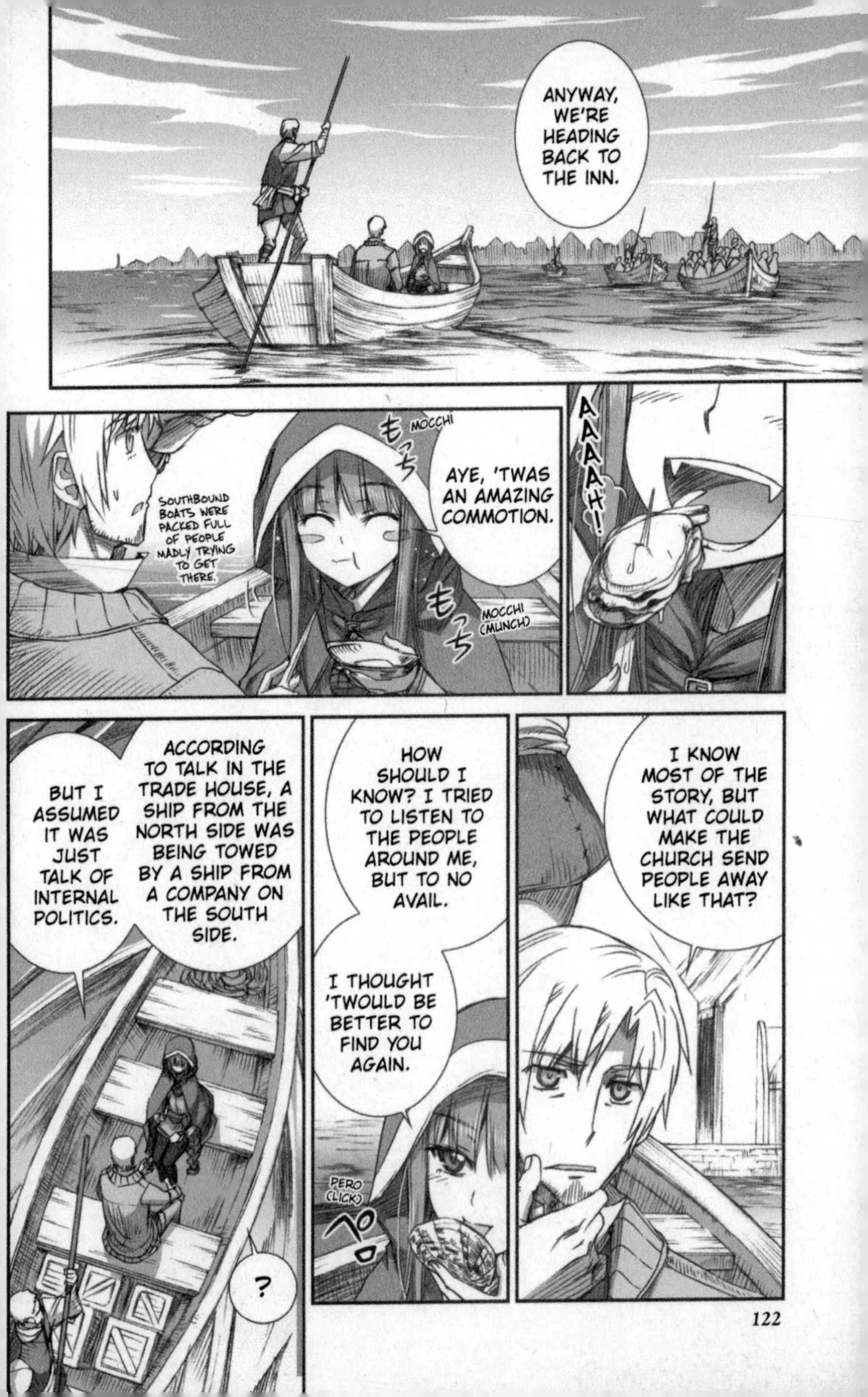
ANYWAY, WE'RE HEADING BACK TO THE INN.
AAAAH!
MOCCHI
AYE, 'TWAS AN AMAZING COMMOTION.
MOCCHI (MUNCH)
SOUTHBOUND BOATS WERE PACKED FULL OF PEOPLE MADLY TRYING TO GET THERE.
I KNOW MOST OF THE STORY, BUT WHAT COULD MAKE THE CHURCH SEND PEOPLE AWAY LIKE THAT?
HOW SHOULD I KNOW? I TRIED TO LISTEN TO THE PEOPLE AROUND ME, BUT TO NO AVAIL.
I THOUGHT 'TWOULD BE BETTER TO FIND YOU AGAIN.
PERO (CLICK)
ACCORDING TO TALK IN THE TRADE HOUSE, A SHIP FROM THE NORTH SIDE WAS BEING TOWED BY A SHIP FROM A COMPANY ON THE SOUTH SIDE.
BUT I ASSUMED IT WAS JUST TALK OF INTERNAL POLITICS.
?

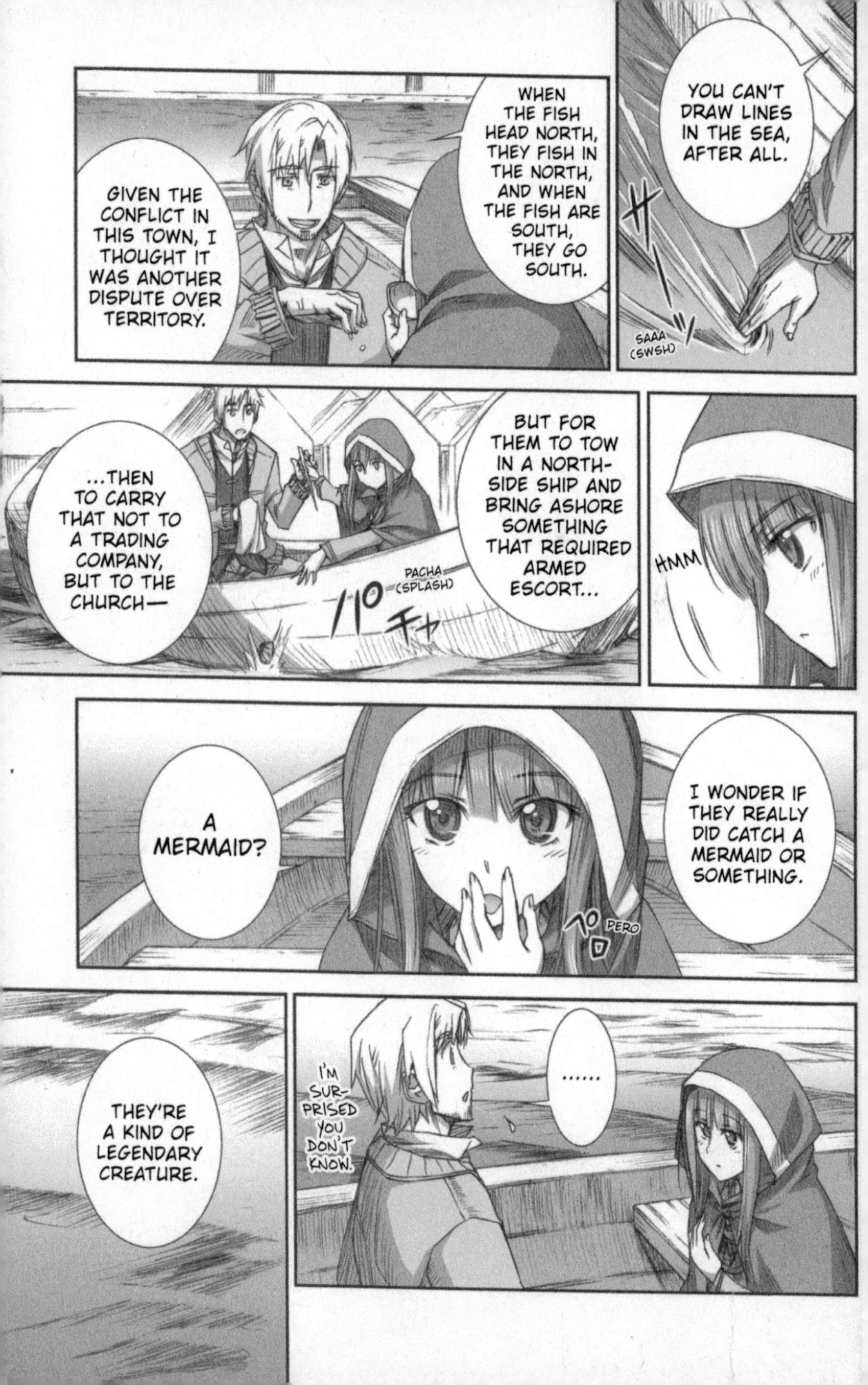
YOU CAN'T DRAW LINES IN THE SEA, AFTER ALL.
SAAA (SWSH)
WHEN THE FISH HEAD NORTH, THEY FISH IN THE NORTH, AND WHEN THE FISH ARE SOUTH, THEY GO SOUTH.
GIVEN THE CONFLICT IN THIS TOWN, I THOUGHT IT WAS ANOTHER DISPUTE OVER TERRITORY.
HMM
BUT FOR THEM TO TOW IN A NORTH-SIDE SHIP AND BRING ASHORE SOMETHING THAT REQUIRED ARMED ESCORT...
PACHA (SPLASH)
...THEN TO CARRY THAT NOT TO A TRADING COMPANY, BUT TO THE CHURCH—
I WONDER IF THEY REALLY DID CATCH A MERMAID OR SOMETHING.
PERO
A MERMAID?
......
I'M SURPRISED YOU DON'T KNOW.
THEY'RE A KIND OF LEGENDARY CREATURE.

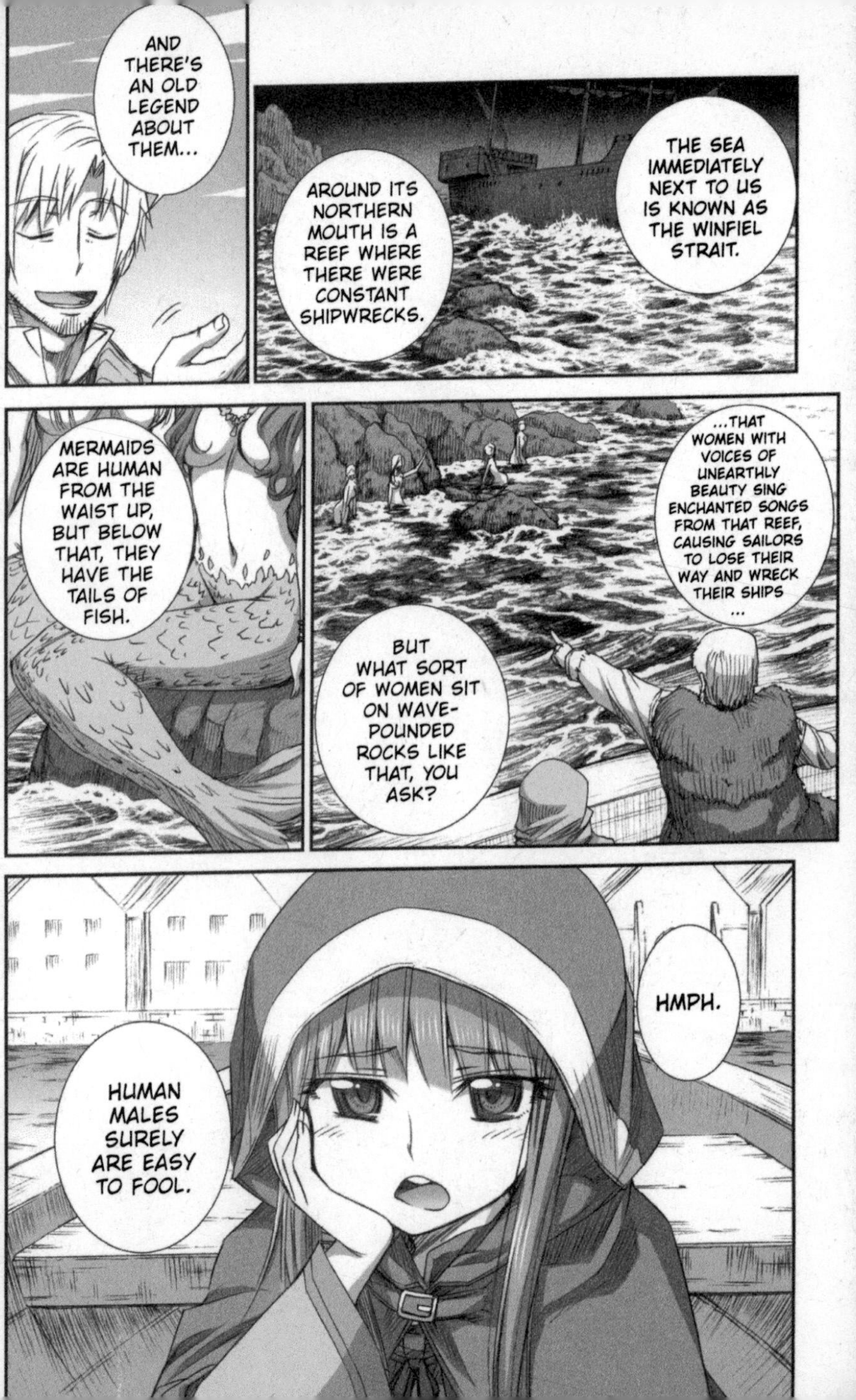
THE SEA IMMEDIATELY NEXT TO US IS KNOWN AS THE WINFIEL STRAIT.
AROUND ITS NORTHERN MOUTH IS A REEF WHERE THERE WERE CONSTANT SHIPWRECKS.
AND THERE'S AN OLD LEGEND ABOUT THEM...
...THAT WOMEN WITH VOICES OF UNEARTHLY BEAUTY SING ENCHANTED SONGS FROM THAT REEF, CAUSING SAILORS TO LOSE THEIR WAY AND WRECK THEIR SHIPS...
BUT WHAT SORT OF WOMEN SIT ON WAVE-POUNDED ROCKS LIKE THAT, YOU ASK?
MERMAIDS ARE HUMAN FROM THE WAIST UP, BUT BELOW THAT, THEY HAVE THE TAILS OF FISH.
HMPH.
HUMAN MALES SURELY ARE EASY TO FOOL.

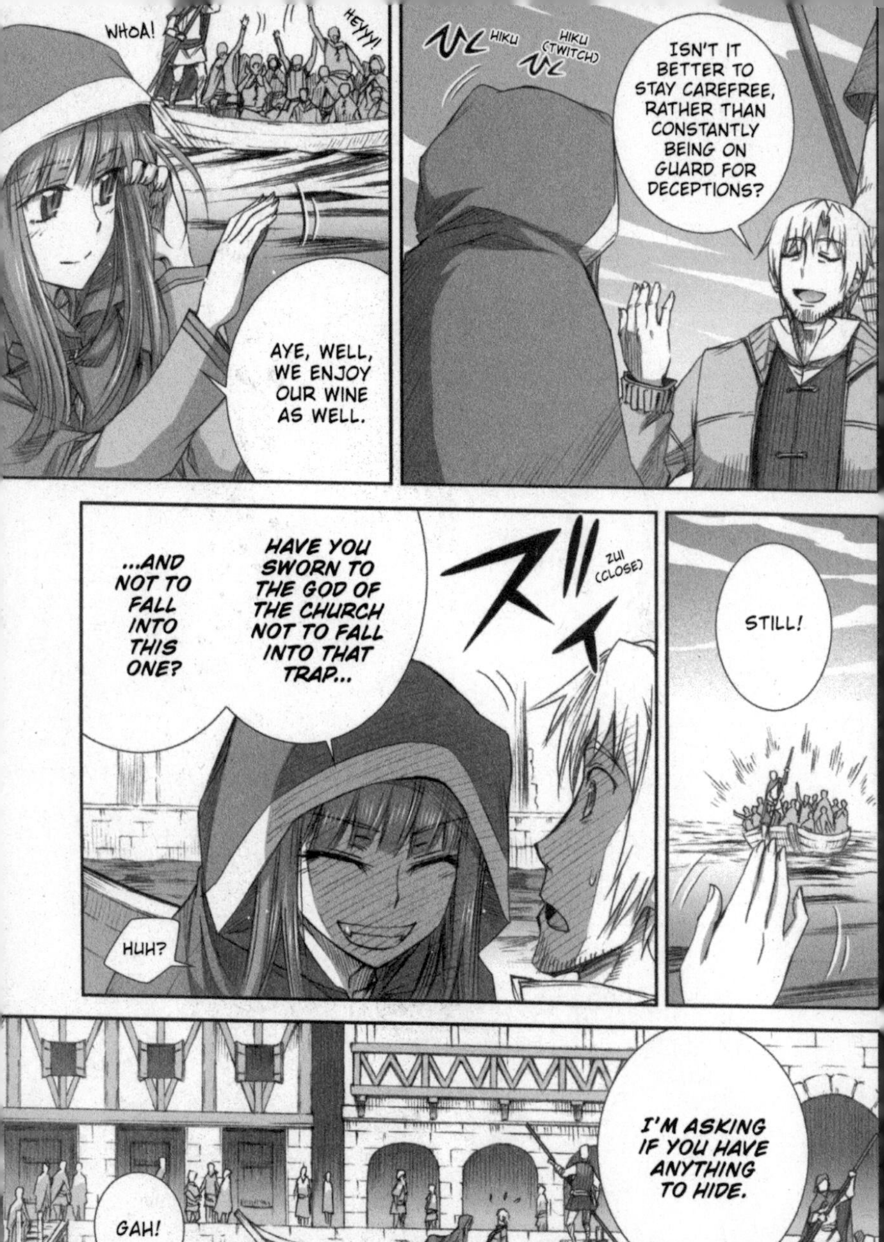
ISN'T IT BETTER TO STAY CAREFREE, RATHER THAN CONSTANTLY BEING ON GUARD FOR DECEPTIONS?
HIKU
HIKU (TWITCH)
HEYYY!
WHOA!
AYE, WELL, WE ENJOY OUR WINE AS WELL.
STILL!
ZUI (CLOSE)
HAVE YOU SWORN TO THE GOD OF THE CHURCH NOT TO FALL INTO THAT TRAP...
...AND NOT TO FALL INTO THIS ONE?
HUH?
I'M ASKING IF YOU HAVE ANYTHING TO HIDE.
GAH!

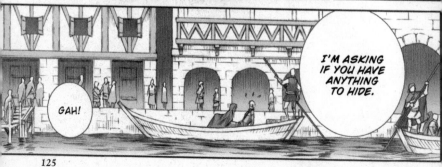

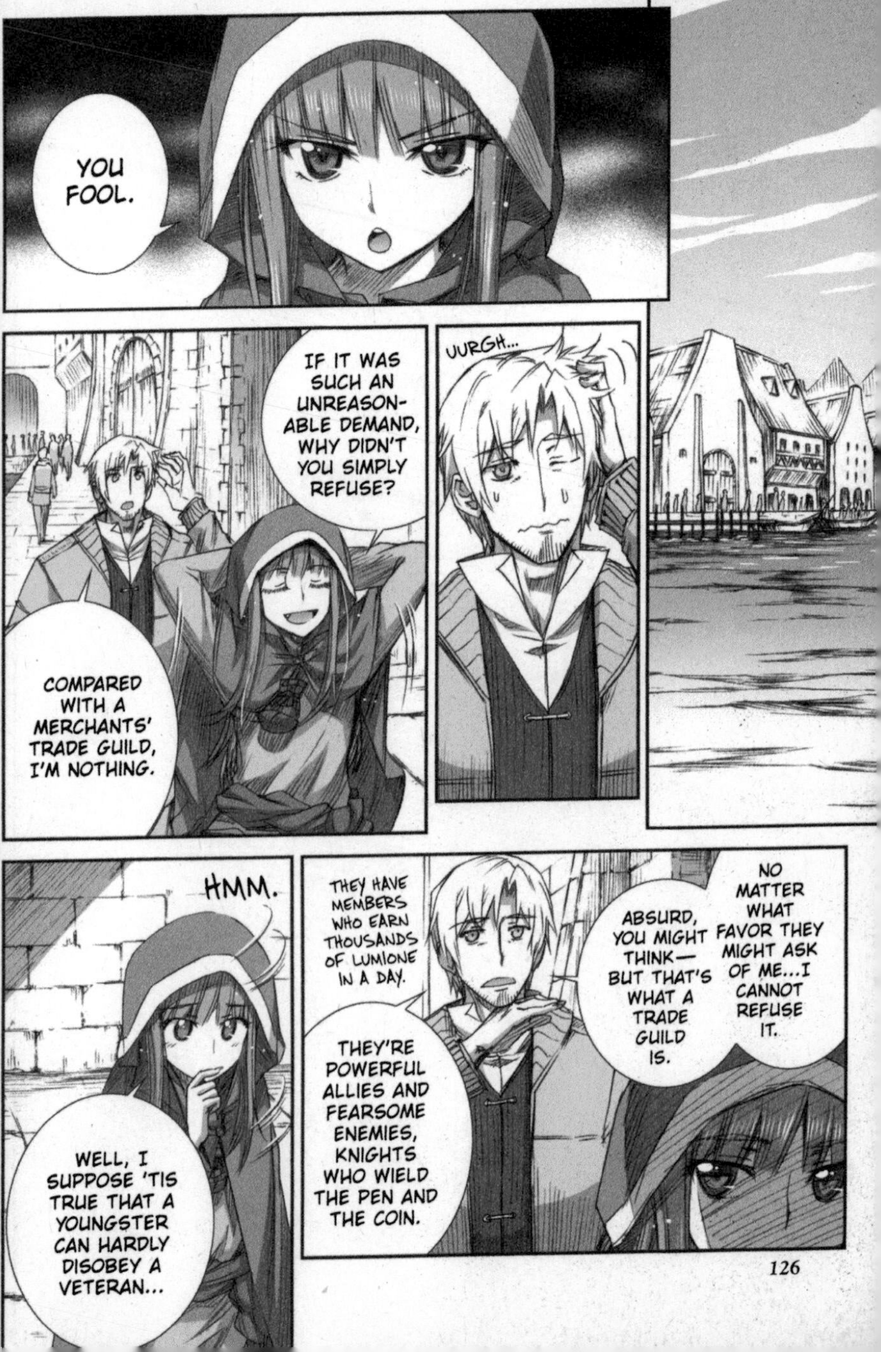
YOU FOOL.
UURGH...
IF IT WAS SUCH AN UNREASON-ABLE DEMAND, WHY DIDN'T YOU SIMPLY REFUSE?
COMPARED WITH A MERCHANTS' TRADE GUILD, I'M NOTHING.
NO MATTER WHAT FAVOR THEY MIGHT ASK OF ME...I CANNOT REFUSE IT.
ABSURD, YOU MIGHT THINK— BUT THAT'S WHAT A TRADE GUILD IS.
THEY HAVE MEMBERS WHO EARN THOUSANDS OF LUMIONE IN A DAY.
THEY'RE POWERFUL ALLIES AND FEARSOME ENEMIES, KNIGHTS WHO WIELD THE PEN AND THE COIN.
HMM.
WELL, I SUPPOSE 'TIS TRUE THAT A YOUNGSTER CAN HARDLY DISOBEY A VETERAN...

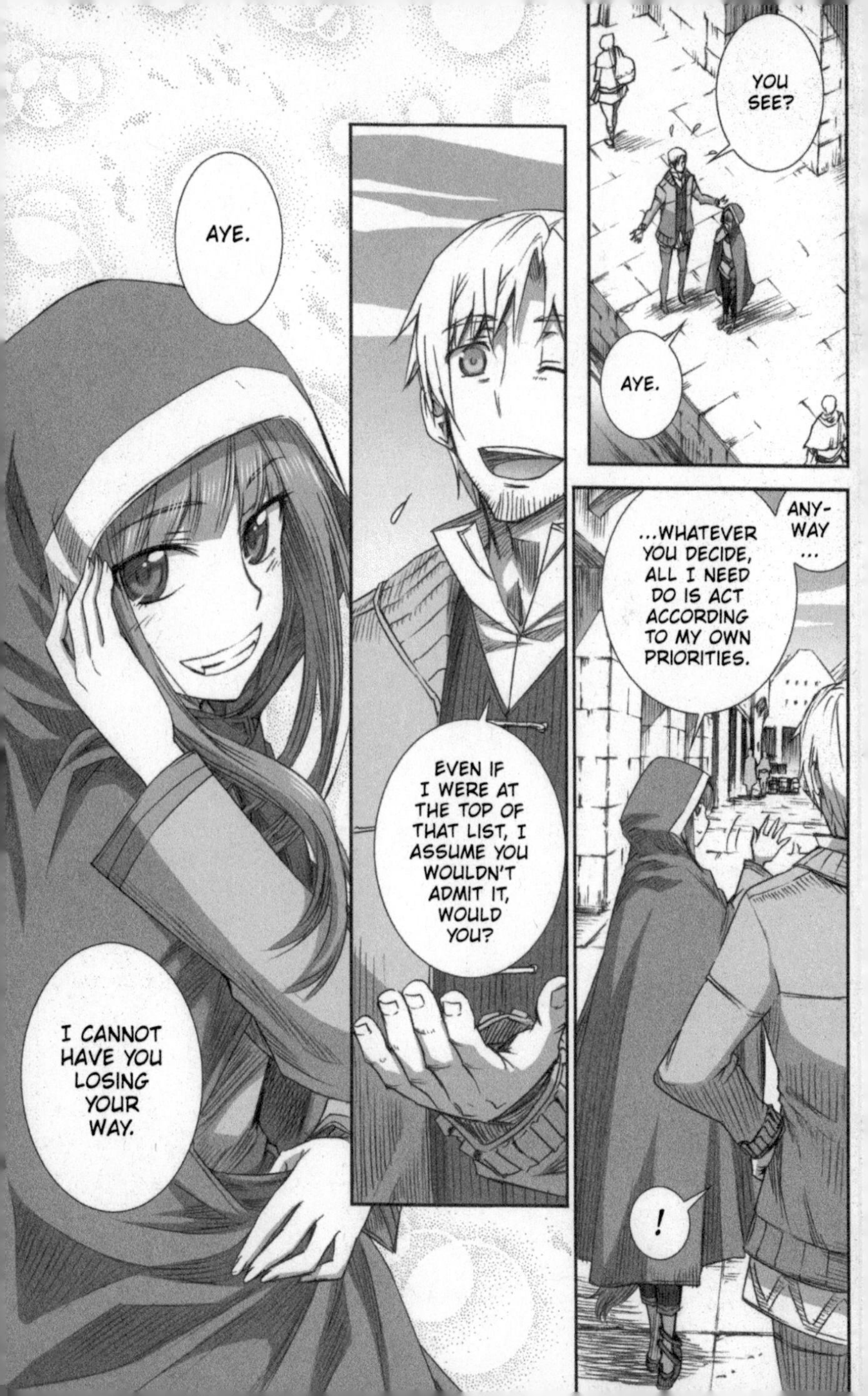
YOU SEE?
AYE.
ANY-WAY ...
...WHATEVER YOU DECIDE, ALL I NEED DO IS ACT ACCORDING TO MY OWN PRIORITIES.
!
EVEN IF I WERE AT THE TOP OF THAT LIST, I ASSUME YOU WOULDN'T ADMIT IT, WOULD YOU?
AYE.
I CANNOT HAVE YOU LOSING YOUR WAY.

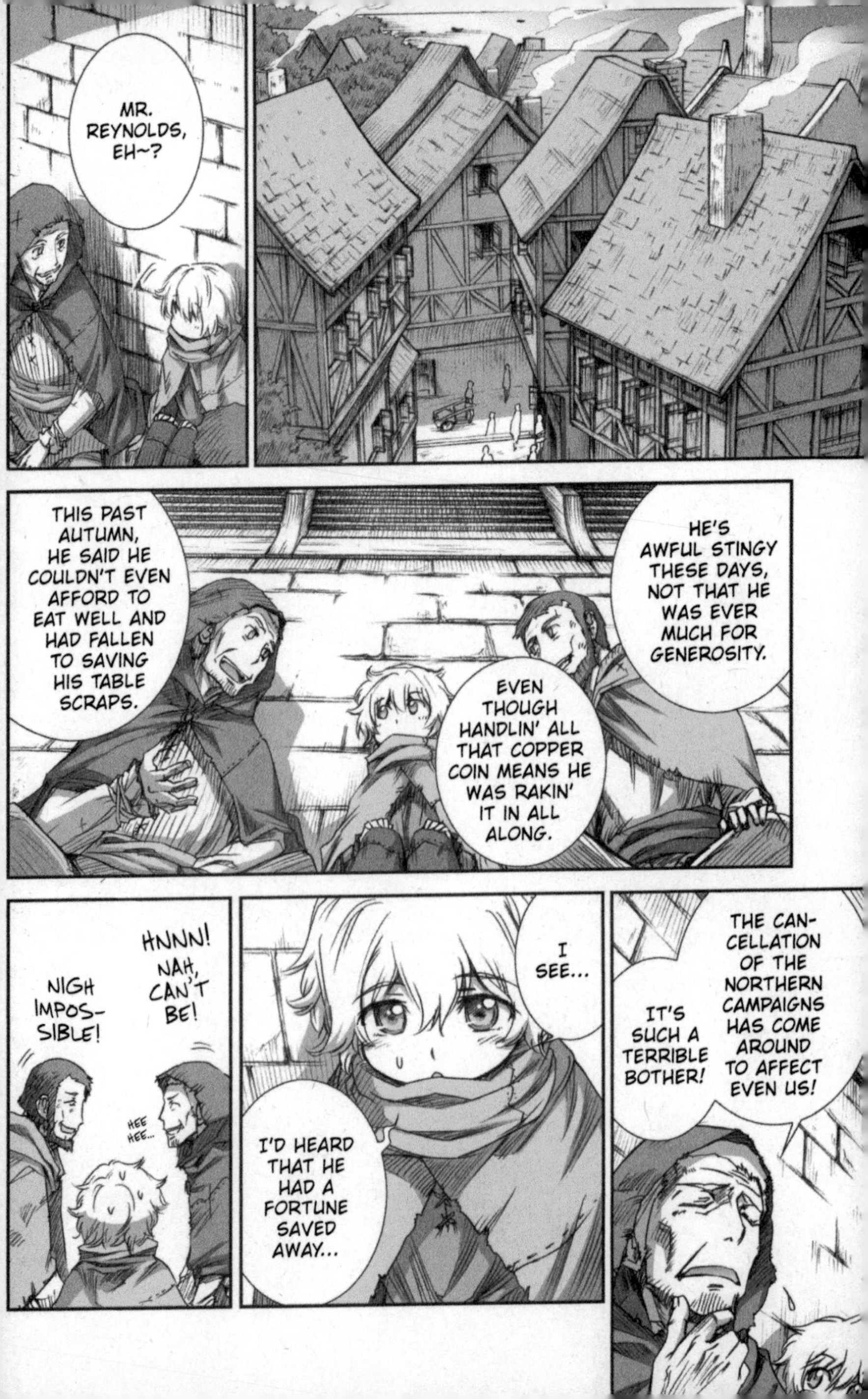
MR. REYNOLDS, EH~?
HE'S AWFUL STINGY THESE DAYS, NOT THAT HE WAS EVER MUCH FOR GENEROSITY.
EVEN THOUGH HANDLIN' ALL THAT COPPER COIN MEANS HE WAS RAKIN' IT IN ALL ALONG.
THIS PAST AUTUMN, HE SAID HE COULDN'T EVEN AFFORD TO EAT WELL AND HAD FALLEN TO SAVING HIS TABLE SCRAPS.
THE CAN-CELLATION OF THE NORTHERN CAMPAIGNS HAS COME AROUND TO AFFECT EVEN US!
IT'S SUCH A TERRIBLE BOTHER!
I SEE...
I'D HEARD THAT HE HAD A FORTUNE SAVED AWAY...
HNNN! NAH, CAN'T BE!
NIGH IMPOS-SIBLE!
HEE HEE...

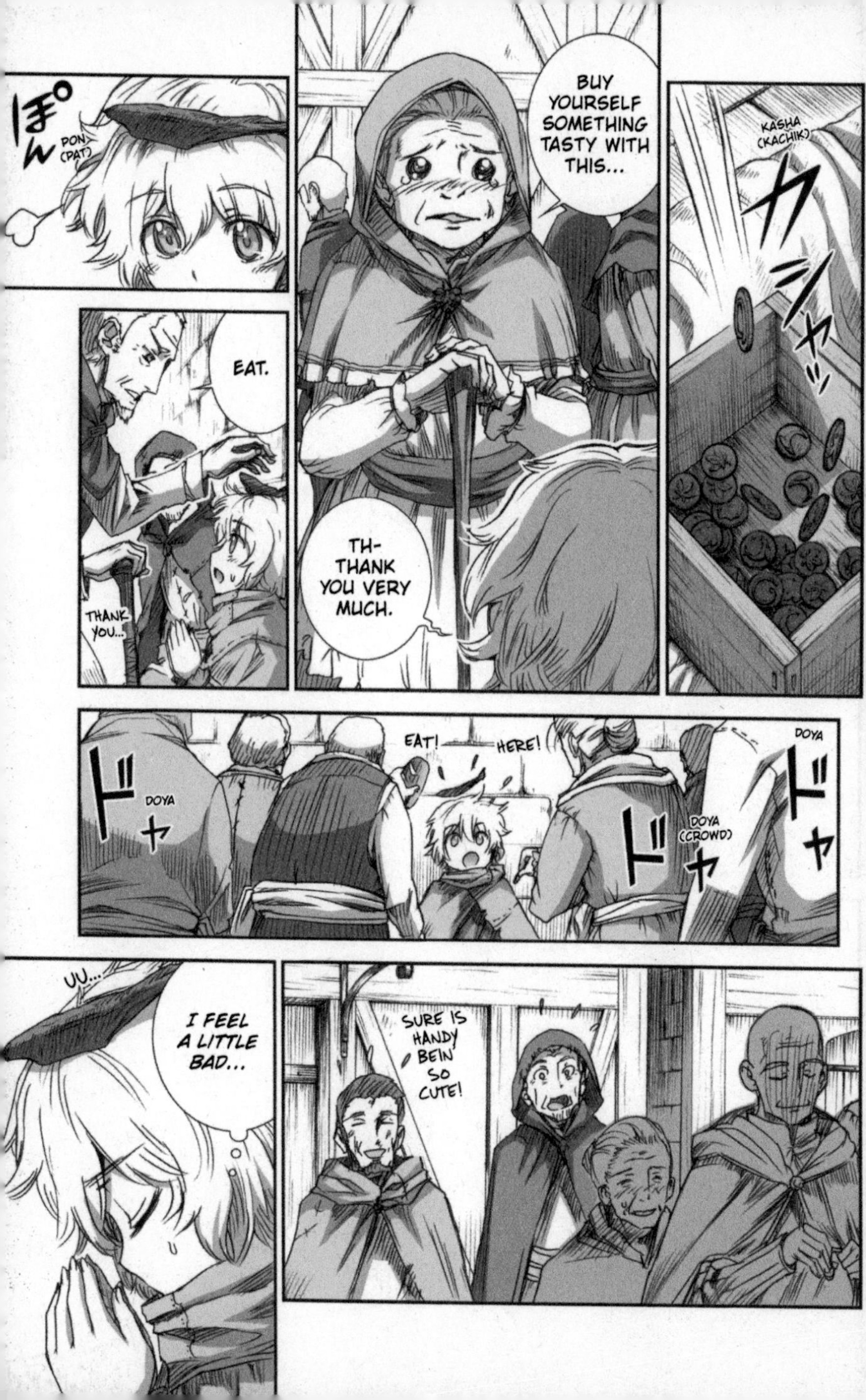
KASHA (KACHIK)
カシャッ
BUY YOURSELF SOMETHING TASTY WITH THIS...
TH-THANK YOU VERY MUCH.
ぽん
PON (PAT)
EAT.
THANK YOU...
ドヤ
DOYA
ドヤ
DOYA (CROWD)
HERE!
EAT!
ドヤ
DOYA
SURE IS HANDY BEIN SO CUTE!
UU...
I FEEL A LITTLE BAD...

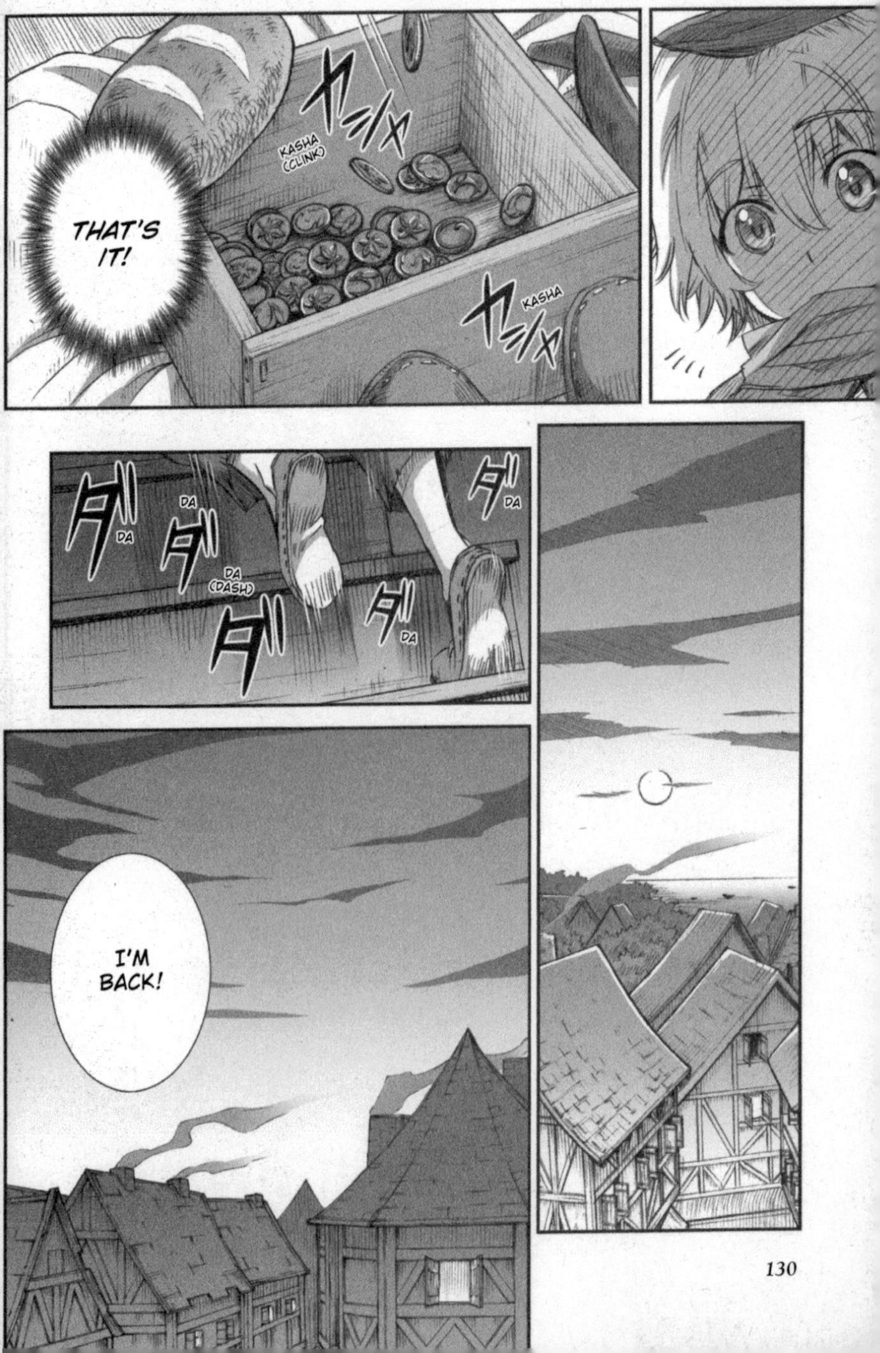
KASHA (CLINK)
THAT'S IT!
KASHA
DA
DA
DA
DA (DASH)
DA
I'M BACK!

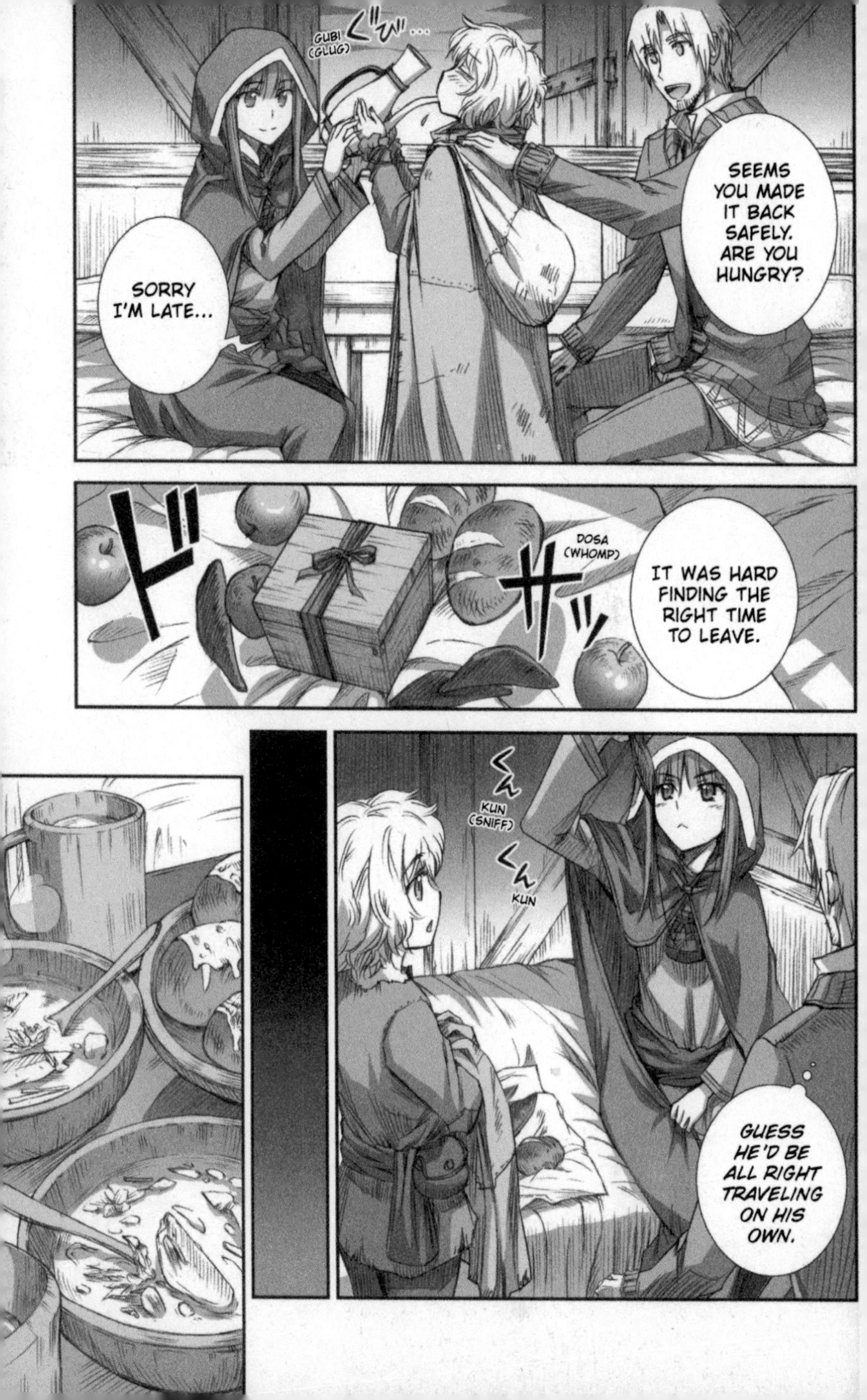
GUBI (GLUG)
SEEMS YOU MADE IT BACK SAFELY. ARE YOU HUNGRY?
SORRY I'M LATE...
DOSA (WHOMP)
IT WAS HARD FINDING THE RIGHT TIME TO LEAVE.
KUN (SNIFF)
KUN
GUESS HE'D BE ALL RIGHT TRAVELING ON HIS OWN.

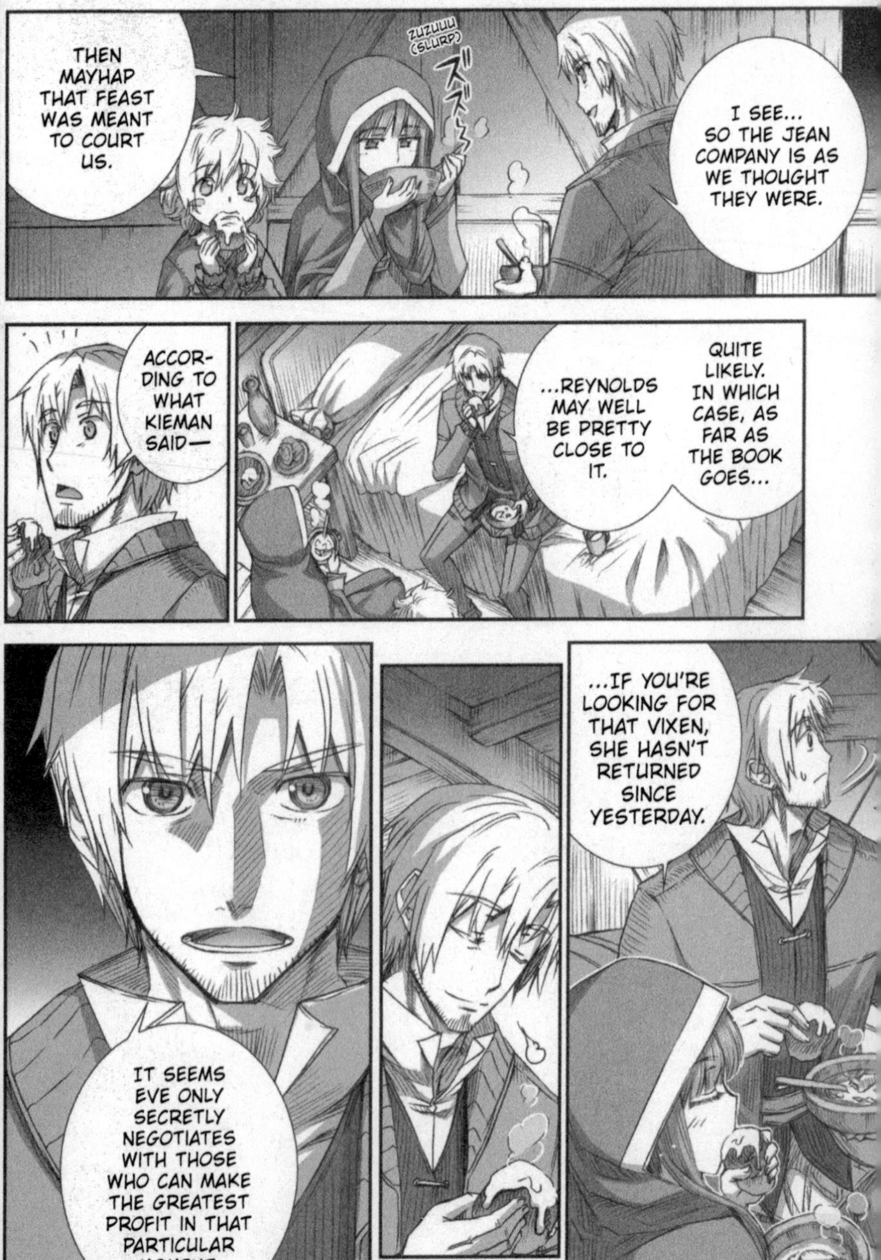
I SEE... SO THE JEAN COMPANY IS AS WE THOUGHT THEY WERE.
ZUZUUU (SLURP)
THEN MAYHAP THAT FEAST WAS MEANT TO COURT US.
QUITE LIKELY. IN WHICH CASE, AS FAR AS THE BOOK GOES...
...REYNOLDS MAY WELL BE PRETTY CLOSE TO IT.
ACCOR-DING TO WHAT KIEMAN SAID—
...IF YOU'RE LOOKING FOR THAT VIXEN, SHE HASN'T RETURNED SINCE YESTERDAY.
IT SEEMS EVE ONLY SECRETLY NEGOTIATES WITH THOSE WHO CAN MAKE THE GREATEST PROFIT IN THAT PARTICULAR MOMENT.

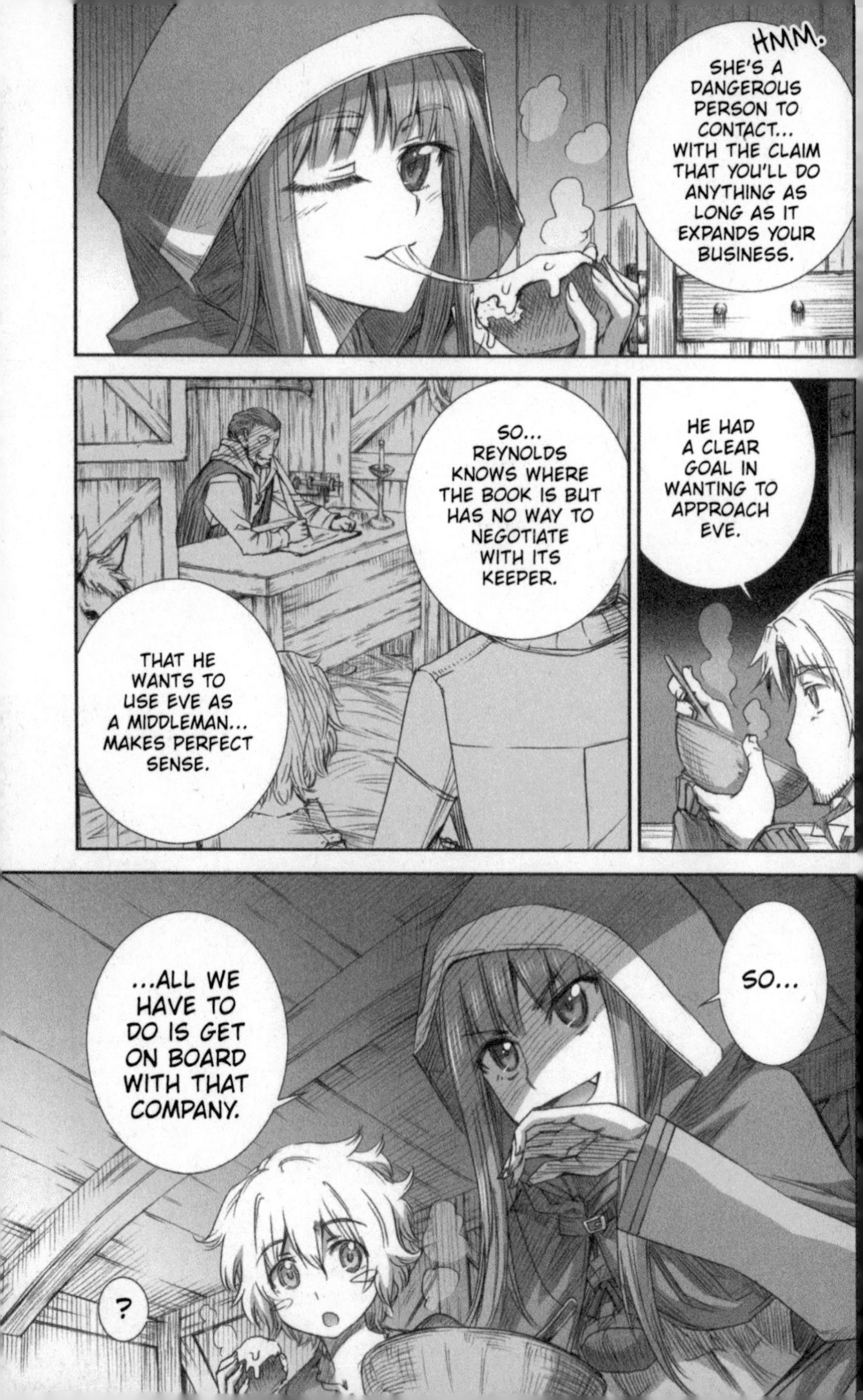
HMM.
SHE'S A DANGEROUS PERSON TO CONTACT... WITH THE CLAIM THAT YOU'LL DO ANYTHING AS LONG AS IT EXPANDS YOUR BUSINESS.
HE HAD A CLEAR GOAL IN WANTING TO APPROACH EVE.
SO... REYNOLDS KNOWS WHERE THE BOOK IS BUT HAS NO WAY TO NEGOTIATE WITH ITS KEEPER.
THAT HE WANTS TO USE EVE AS A MIDDLEMAN... MAKES PERFECT SENSE.
SO...
...ALL WE HAVE TO DO IS GET ON BOARD WITH THAT COMPANY.
?

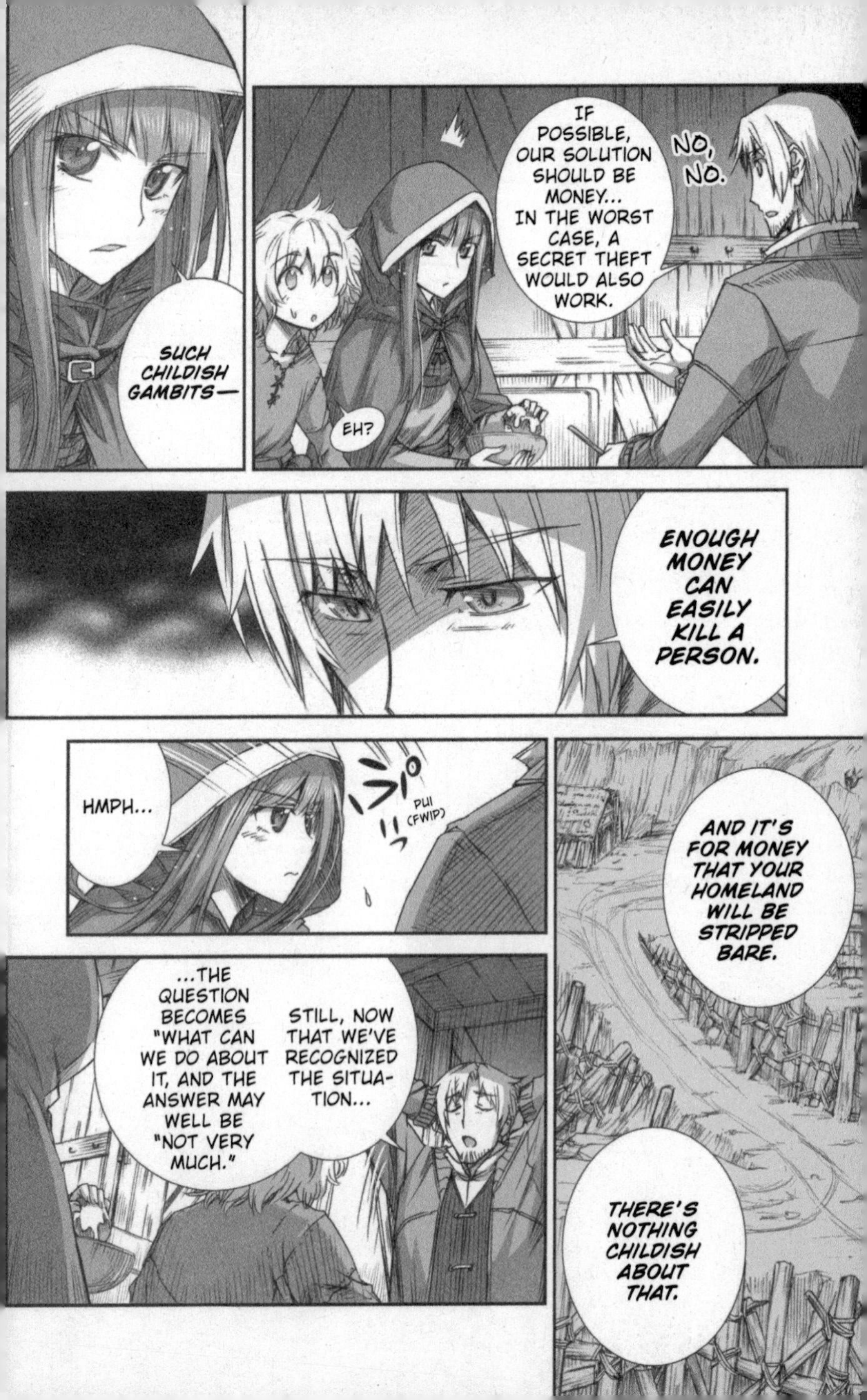
IF POSSIBLE, OUR SOLUTION SHOULD BE MONEY... IN THE WORST CASE, A SECRET THEFT WOULD ALSO WORK.
NO, NO.
EH?
SUCH CHILDISH GAMBITS—
ENOUGH MONEY CAN EASILY KILL A PERSON.
AND IT'S FOR MONEY THAT YOUR HOMELAND WILL BE STRIPPED BARE.
THERE'S NOTHING CHILDISH ABOUT THAT.
PUI (FWIP)
HMPH...
STILL, NOW THAT WE'VE RECOGNIZED THE SITUA-TION...
...THE QUESTION BECOMES "WHAT CAN WE DO ABOUT IT, AND THE ANSWER MAY WELL BE "NOT VERY MUCH."

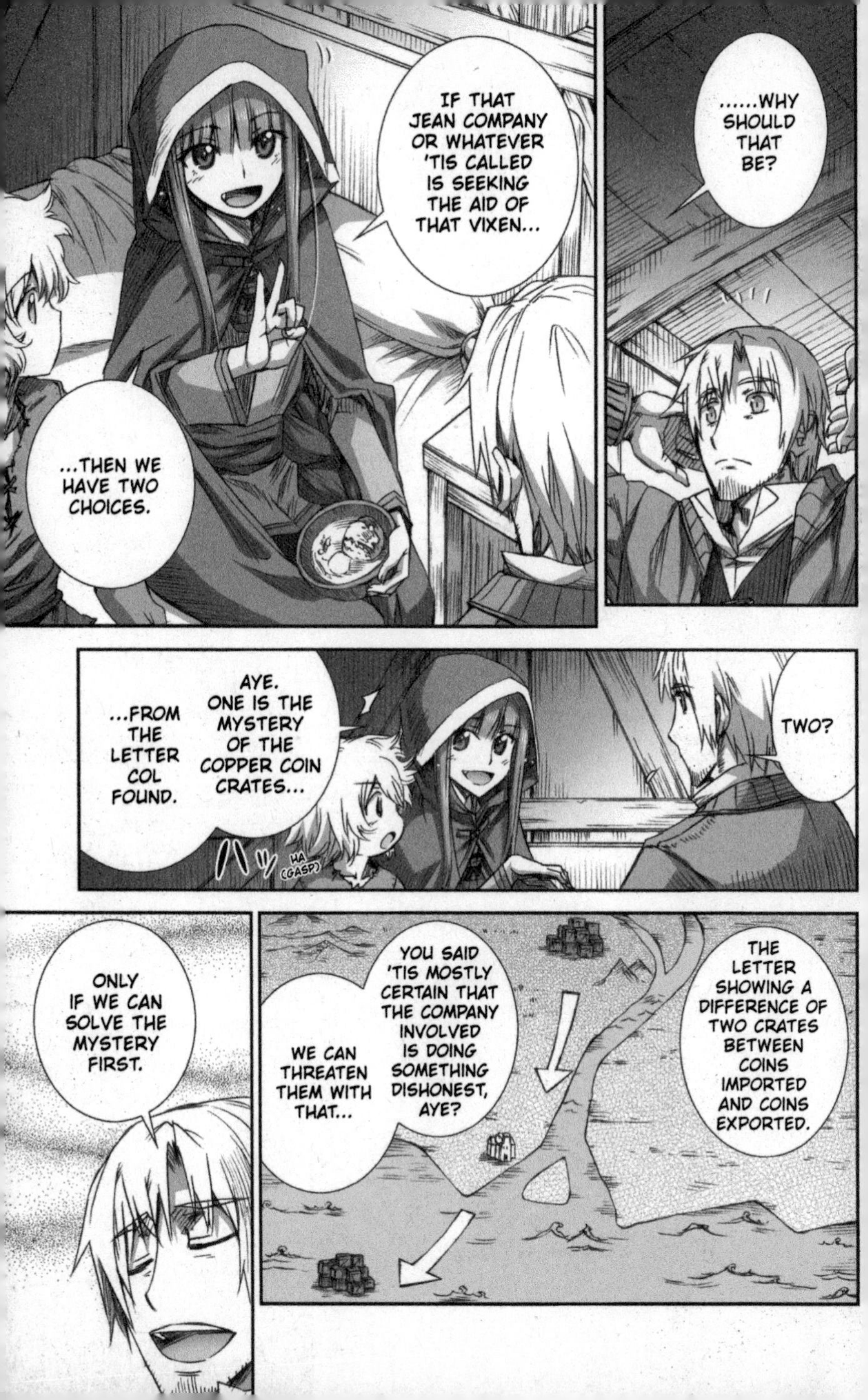
......WHY SHOULD THAT BE?
IF THAT JEAN COMPANY OR WHATEVER 'TIS CALLED IS SEEKING THE AID OF THAT VIXEN...
...THEN WE HAVE TWO CHOICES.
TWO?
AYE. ONE IS THE MYSTERY OF THE COPPER COIN CRATES...
...FROM THE LETTER COL FOUND.
HA (GASP)
THE LETTER SHOWING A DIFFERENCE OF TWO CRATES BETWEEN COINS IMPORTED AND COINS EXPORTED.
YOU SAID 'TIS MOSTLY CERTAIN THAT THE COMPANY INVOLVED IS DOING SOMETHING DISHONEST, AYE?
WE CAN THREATEN THEM WITH THAT...
ONLY IF WE CAN SOLVE THE MYSTERY FIRST.

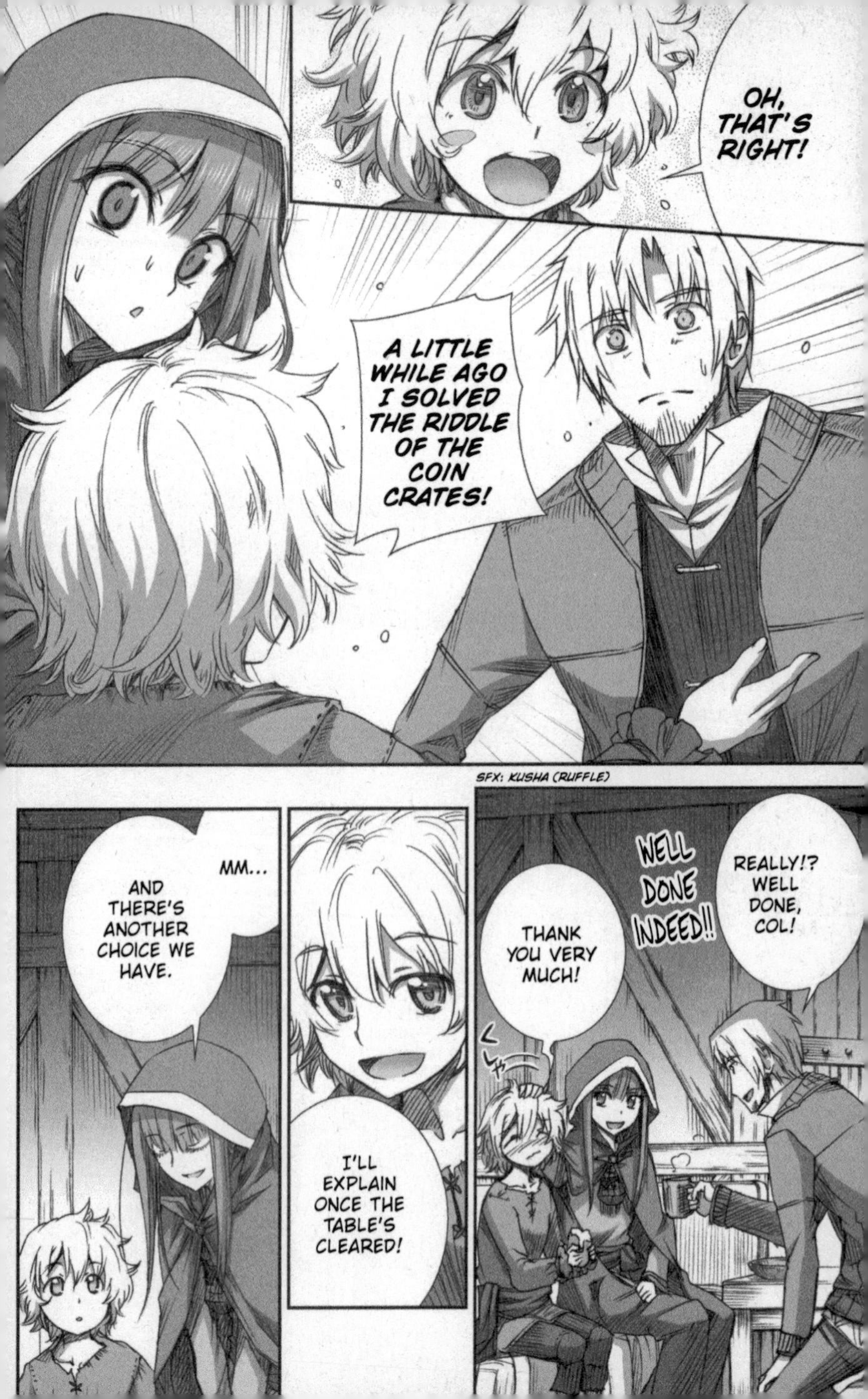
OH, THAT'S RIGHT!
A LITTLE WHILE AGO I SOLVED THE RIDDLE OF THE COIN CRATES!
SFX: KUSHA (RUFFLE)
REALLY!? WELL DONE, COL!
WELL DONE INDEED!!
THANK YOU VERY MUCH!
I'LL EXPLAIN ONCE THE TABLE'S CLEARED!
MM...
AND THERE'S ANOTHER CHOICE WE HAVE.

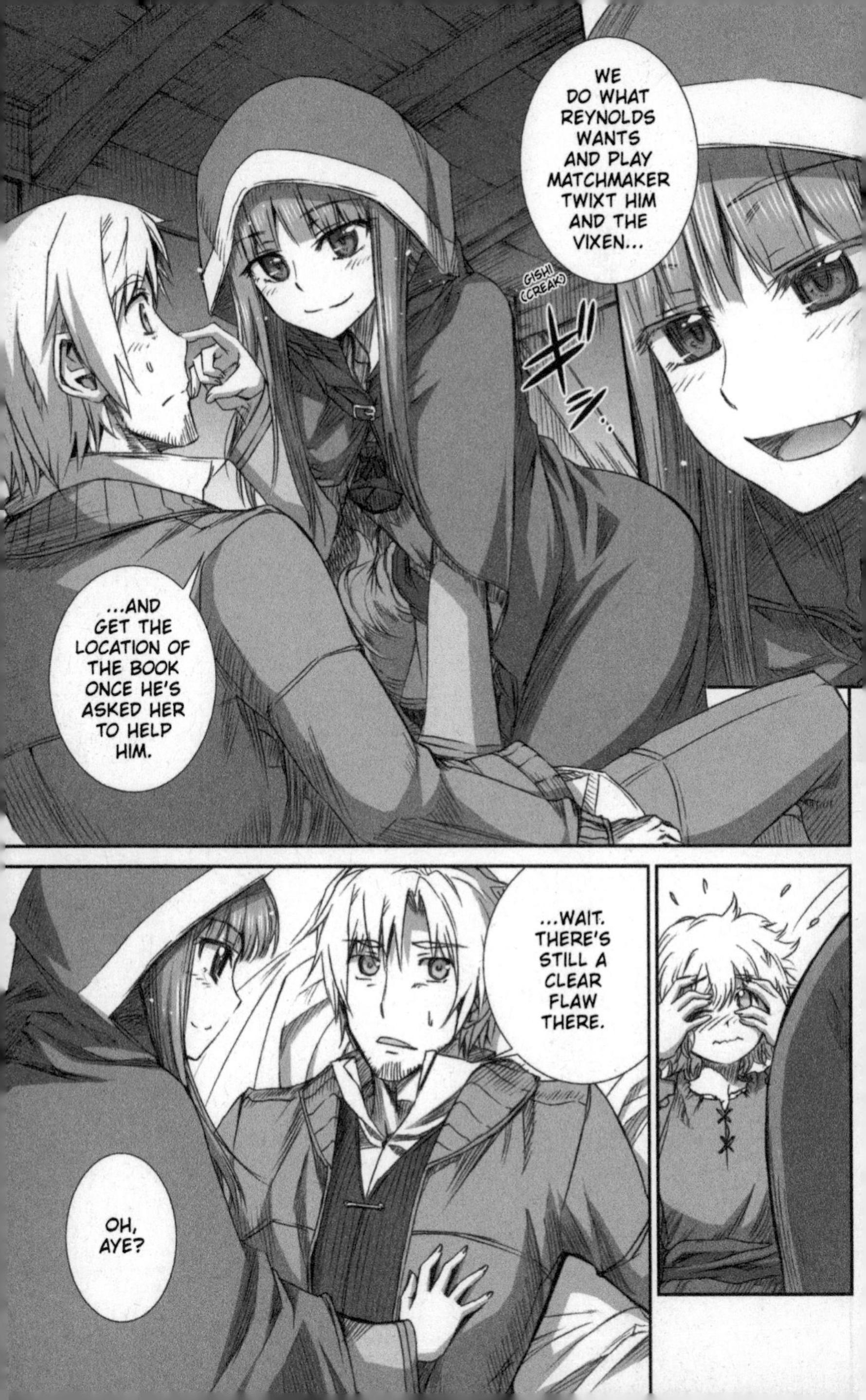
WE DO WHAT REYNOLDS WANTS AND PLAY MATCHMAKER TWIXT HIM AND THE VIXEN...
GISHI (CREAK)
ギシ…
...AND GET THE LOCATION OF THE BOOK ONCE HE'S ASKED HER TO HELP HIM.
...WAIT. THERE'S STILL A CLEAR FLAW THERE.
OH, AYE?

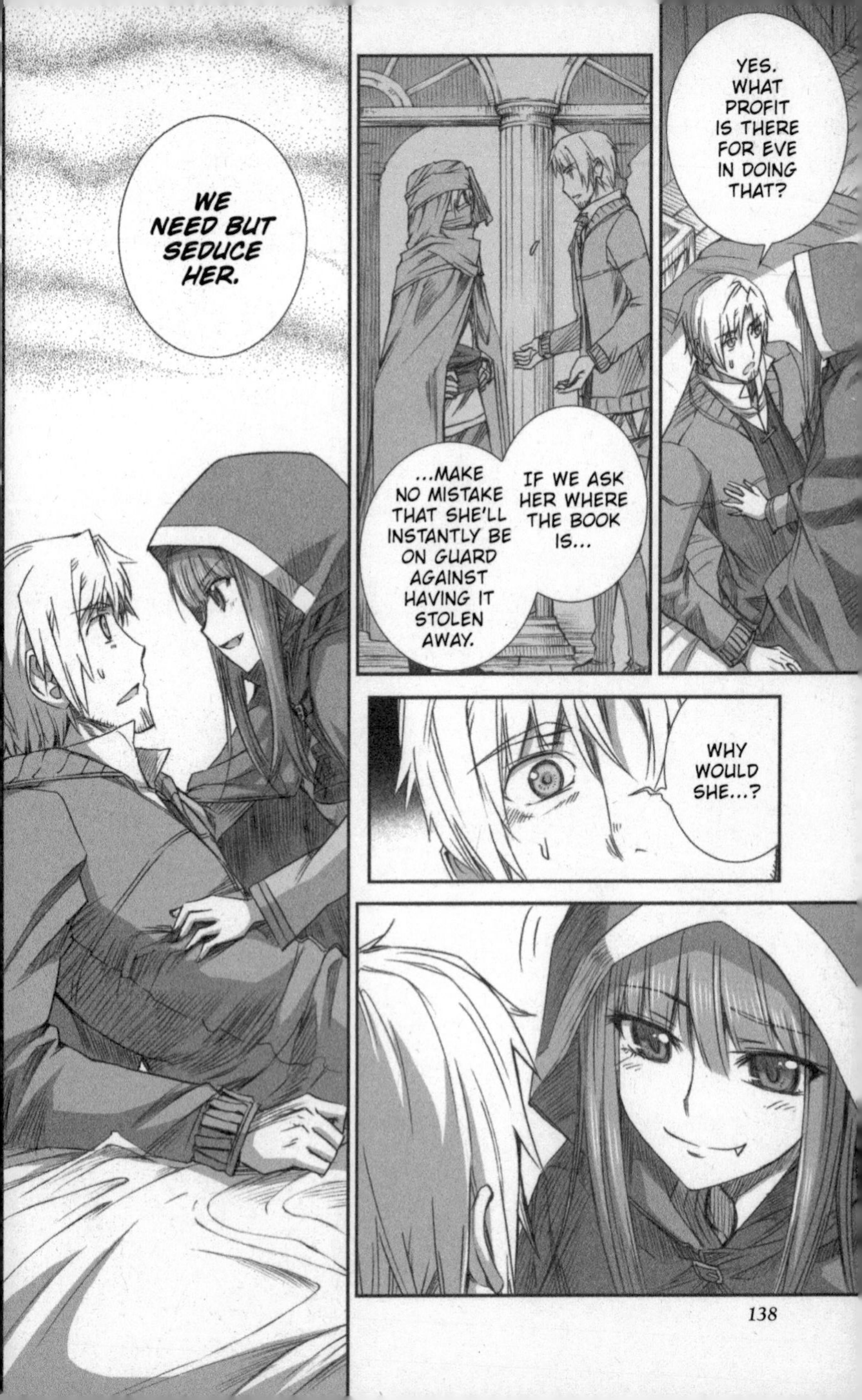
YES. WHAT PROFIT IS THERE FOR EVE IN DOING THAT?
IF WE ASK HER WHERE THE BOOK IS...
...MAKE NO MISTAKE THAT SHE'LL INSTANTLY BE ON GUARD AGAINST HAVING IT STOLEN AWAY.
WHY WOULD SHE...?
WE NEED BUT SEDUCE HER.

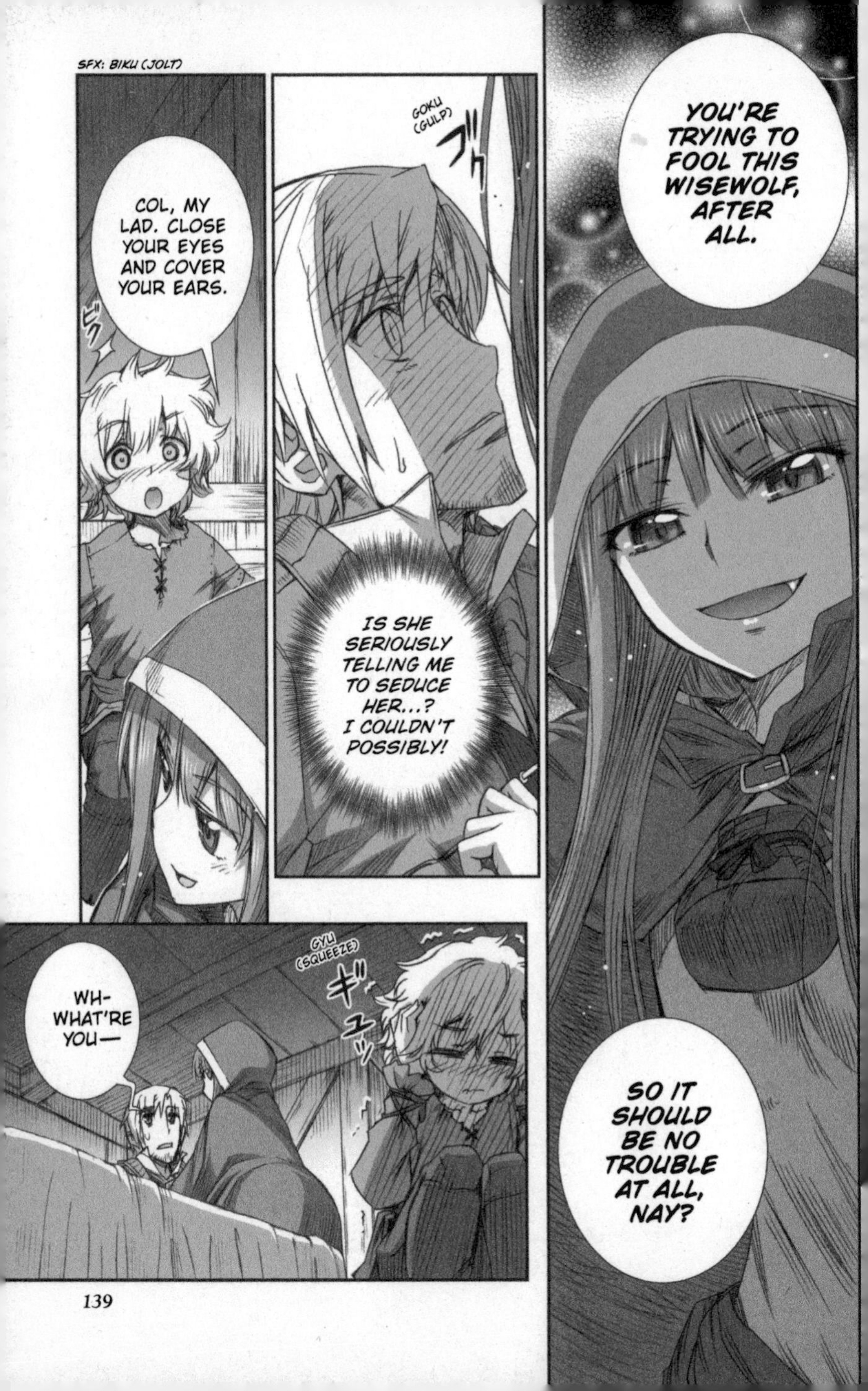
SFX: BIKU (JOLT)
YOU'RE TRYING TO FOOL THIS WISEWOLF, AFTER ALL.
SO IT SHOULD BE NO TROUBLE AT ALL, NAY?
GOKU (GULP)
IS SHE SERIOUSLY TELLING ME TO SEDUCE HER...? I COULDN'T POSSIBLY!
COL, MY LAD. CLOSE YOUR EYES AND COVER YOUR EARS.
GYU (SQUEEZE)
WH- WHAT'RE YOU—

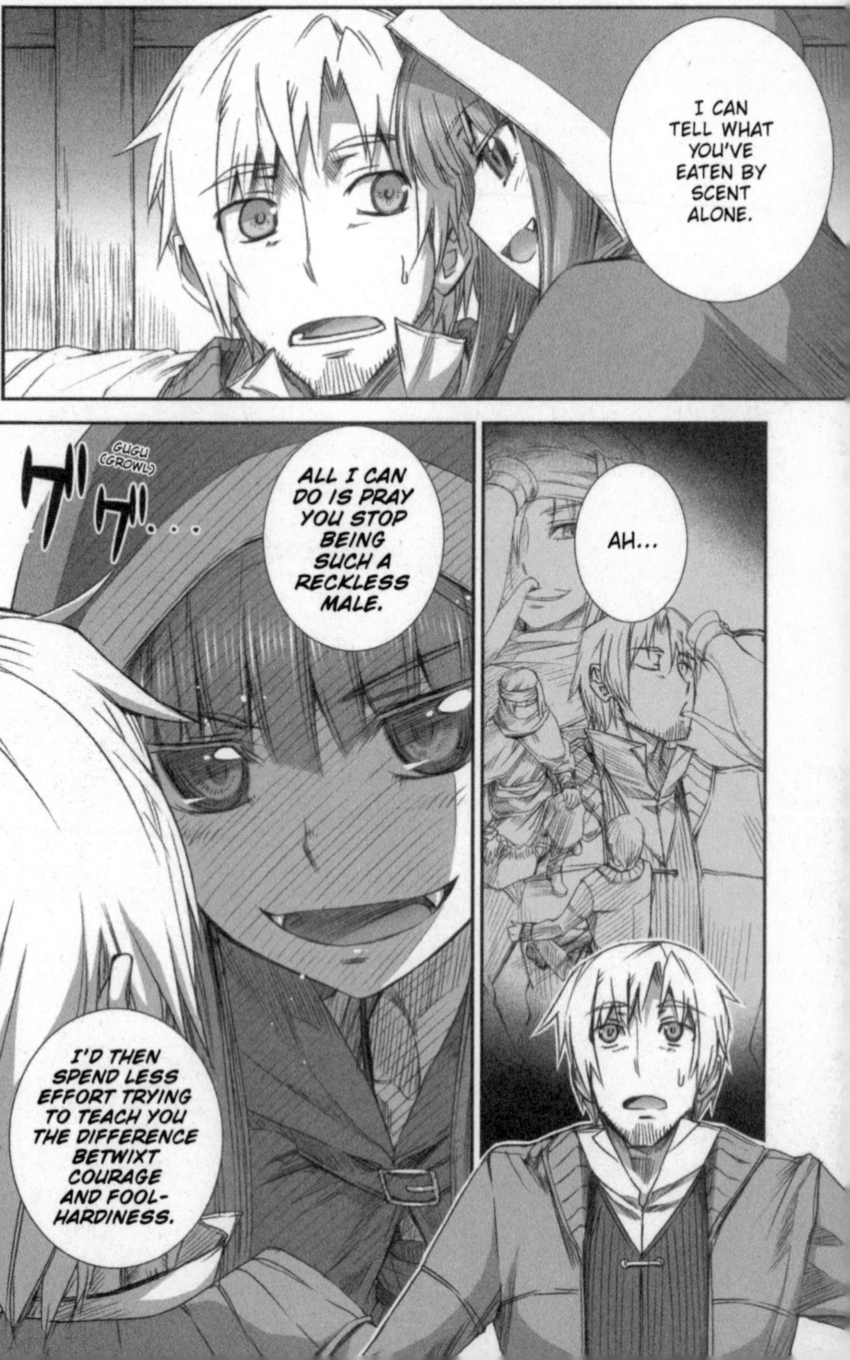
I CAN TELL WHAT YOU'VE EATEN BY SCENT ALONE.
AH...
GUGU (GROWL)
ALL I CAN DO IS PRAY YOU STOP BEING SUCH A RECKLESS MALE.
I'D THEN SPEND LESS EFFORT TRYING TO TEACH YOU THE DIFFERENCE BETWIXT COURAGE AND FOOL-HARDINESS.

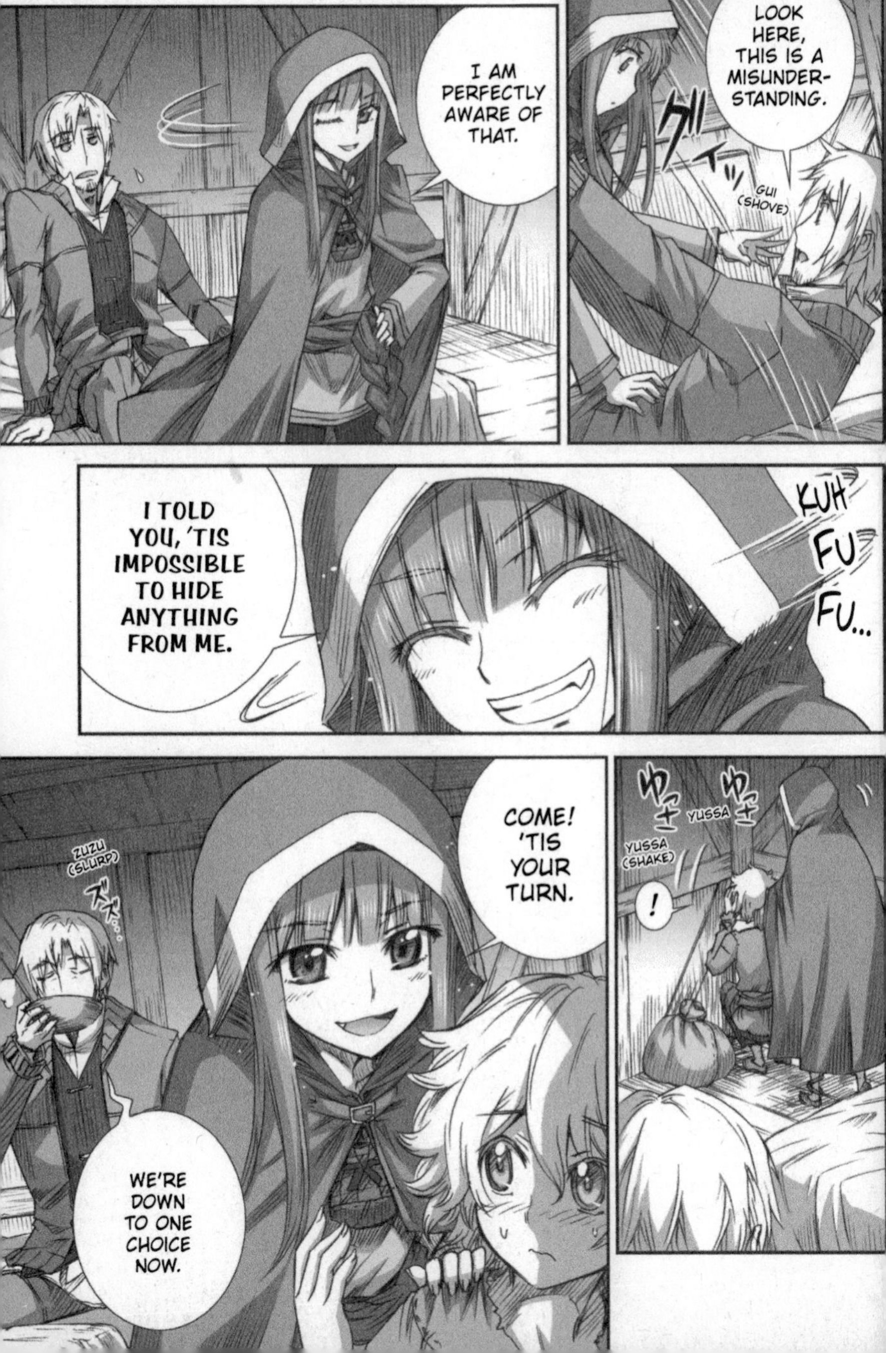
LOOK HERE, THIS IS A MISUNDER-STANDING.
GUI (SHOVE)
I AM PERFECTLY AWARE OF THAT.
KUH FU FU...
I TOLD YOU, 'TIS IMPOSSIBLE TO HIDE ANYTHING FROM ME.
YUSSA
YUSSA (SHAKE)
!
COME! 'TIS YOUR TURN.
ZUZU (SLURP)
WE'RE DOWN TO ONE CHOICE NOW.

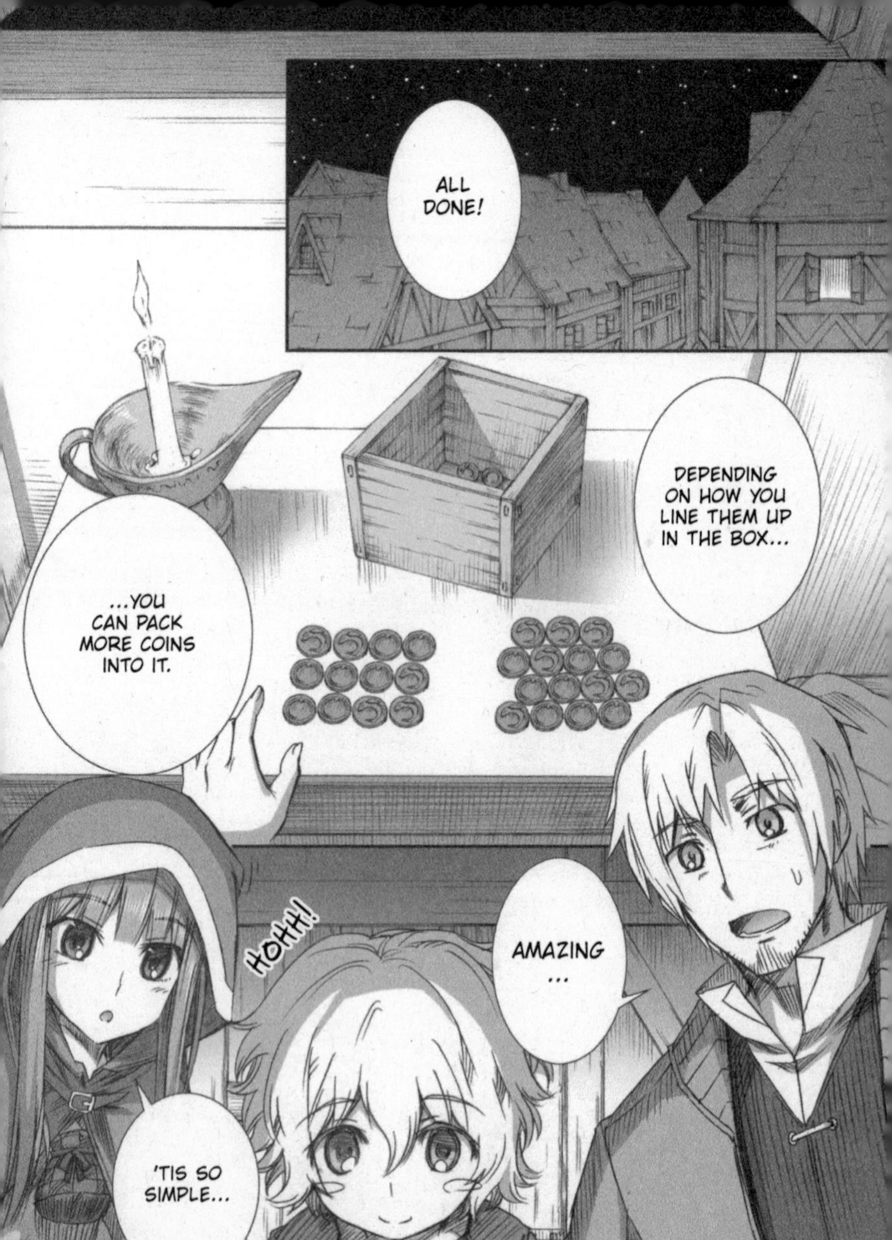
ALL DONE!
DEPENDING ON HOW YOU LINE THEM UP IN THE BOX...
...YOU CAN PACK MORE COINS INTO IT.
AMAZING...
HOHH!
'TIS SO SIMPLE...

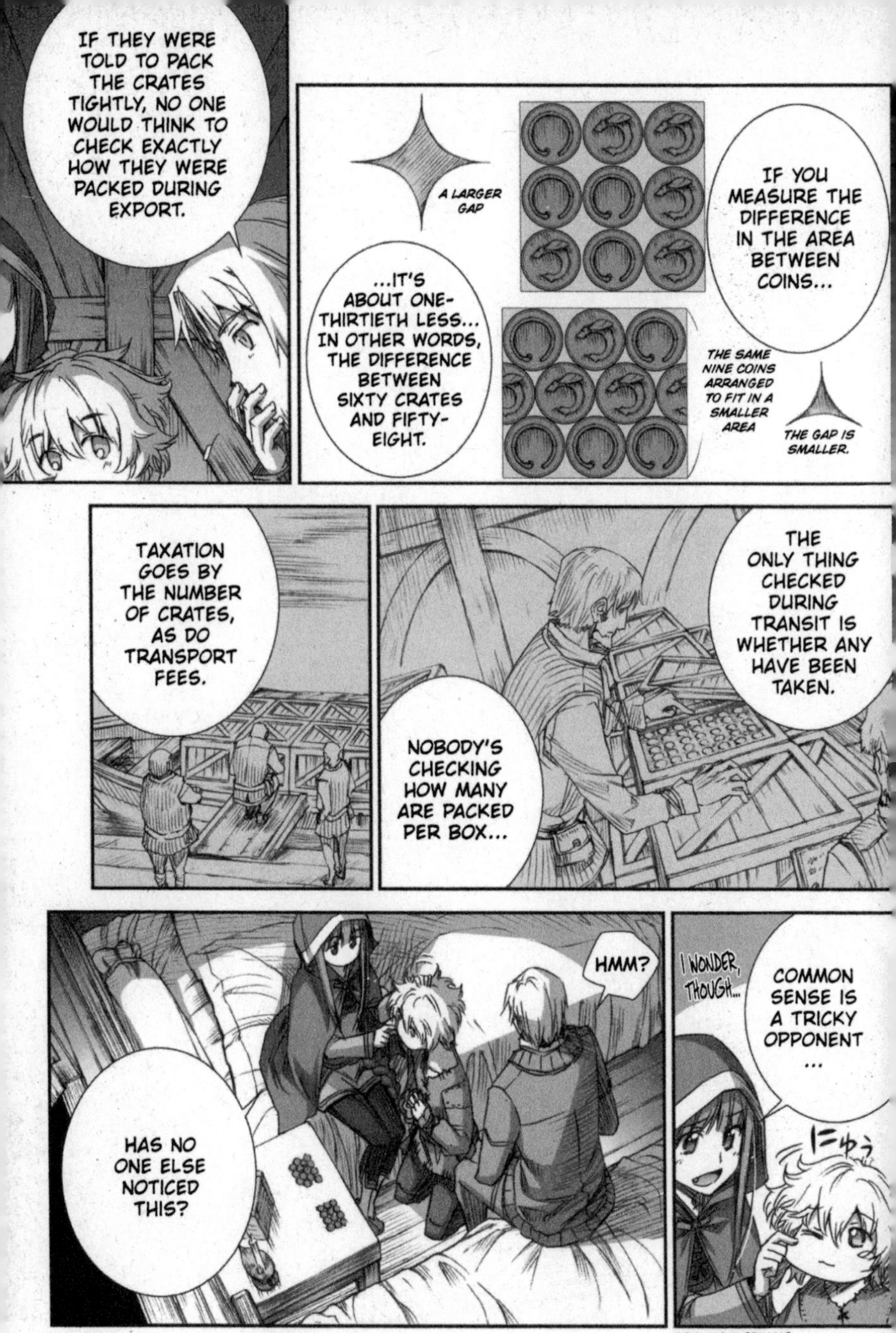
IF YOU MEASURE THE DIFFERENCE IN THE AREA BETWEEN COINS...
A LARGER GAP
...IT'S ABOUT ONE-THIRTIETH LESS... IN OTHER WORDS, THE DIFFERENCE BETWEEN SIXTY CRATES AND FIFTY-EIGHT.
THE SAME NINE COINS ARRANGED TO FIT IN A SMALLER AREA
THE GAP IS SMALLER.
IF THEY WERE TOLD TO PACK THE CRATES TIGHTLY, NO ONE WOULD THINK TO CHECK EXACTLY HOW THEY WERE PACKED DURING EXPORT.
THE ONLY THING CHECKED DURING TRANSIT IS WHETHER ANY HAVE BEEN TAKEN.
NOBODY'S CHECKING HOW MANY ARE PACKED PER BOX...
TAXATION GOES BY THE NUMBER OF CRATES, AS DO TRANSPORT FEES.
COMMON SENSE IS A TRICKY OPPONENT...
I WONDER, THOUGH...
にゅう
HMM?
HAS NO ONE ELSE NOTICED THIS?
SFX: NYUU (PINCH)

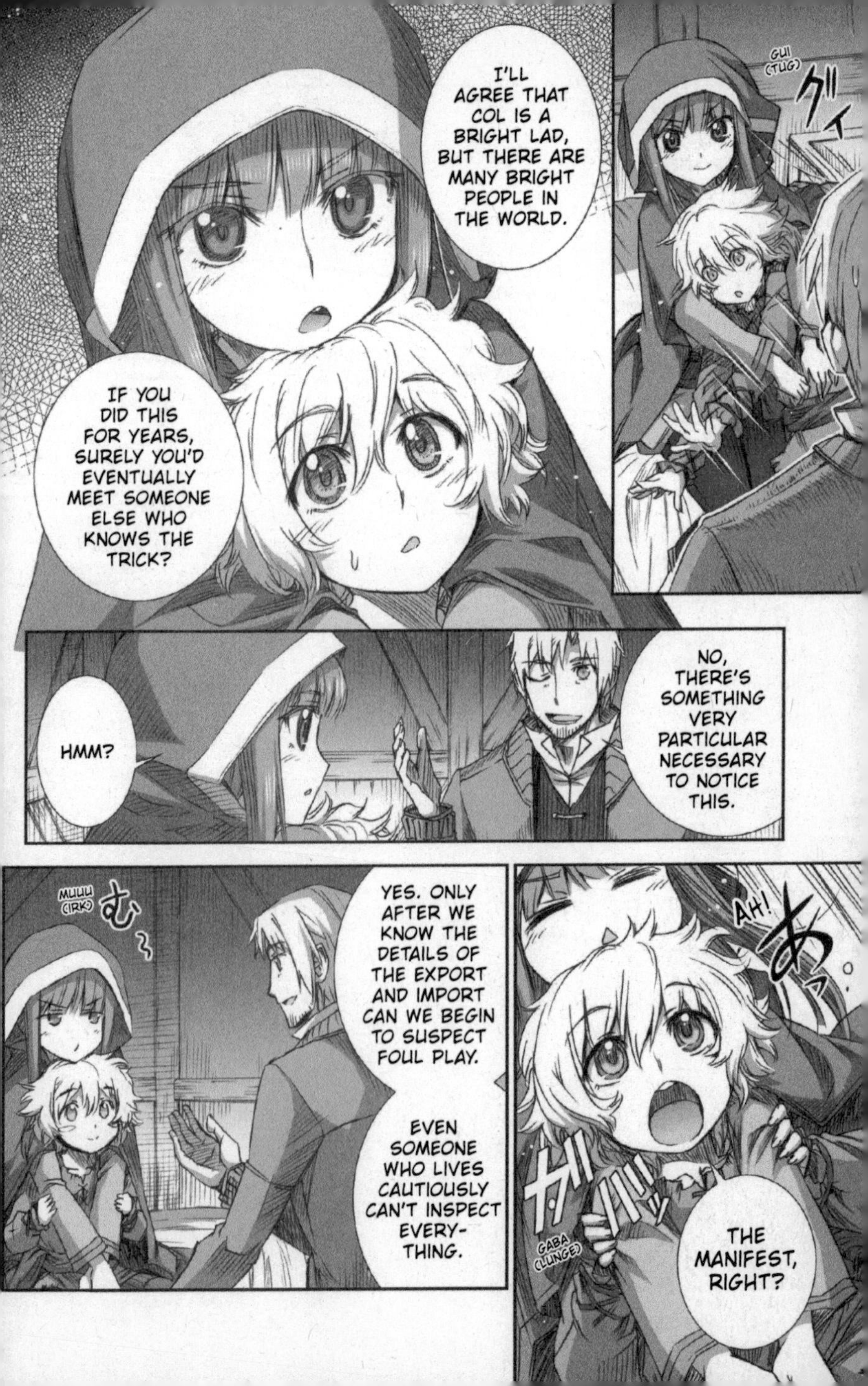
GUI (TUG)
I'LL AGREE THAT COL IS A BRIGHT LAD, BUT THERE ARE MANY BRIGHT PEOPLE IN THE WORLD.
IF YOU DID THIS FOR YEARS, SURELY YOU'D EVENTUALLY MEET SOMEONE ELSE WHO KNOWS THE TRICK?
NO, THERE'S SOMETHING VERY PARTICULAR NECESSARY TO NOTICE THIS.
HMM?
AH!
GABA (LUNGE)
THE MANIFEST, RIGHT?
MUUU (IRK)
YES. ONLY AFTER WE KNOW THE DETAILS OF THE EXPORT AND IMPORT CAN WE BEGIN TO SUSPECT FOUL PLAY.
EVEN SOMEONE WHO LIVES CAUTIOUSLY CAN'T INSPECT EVERY-THING.

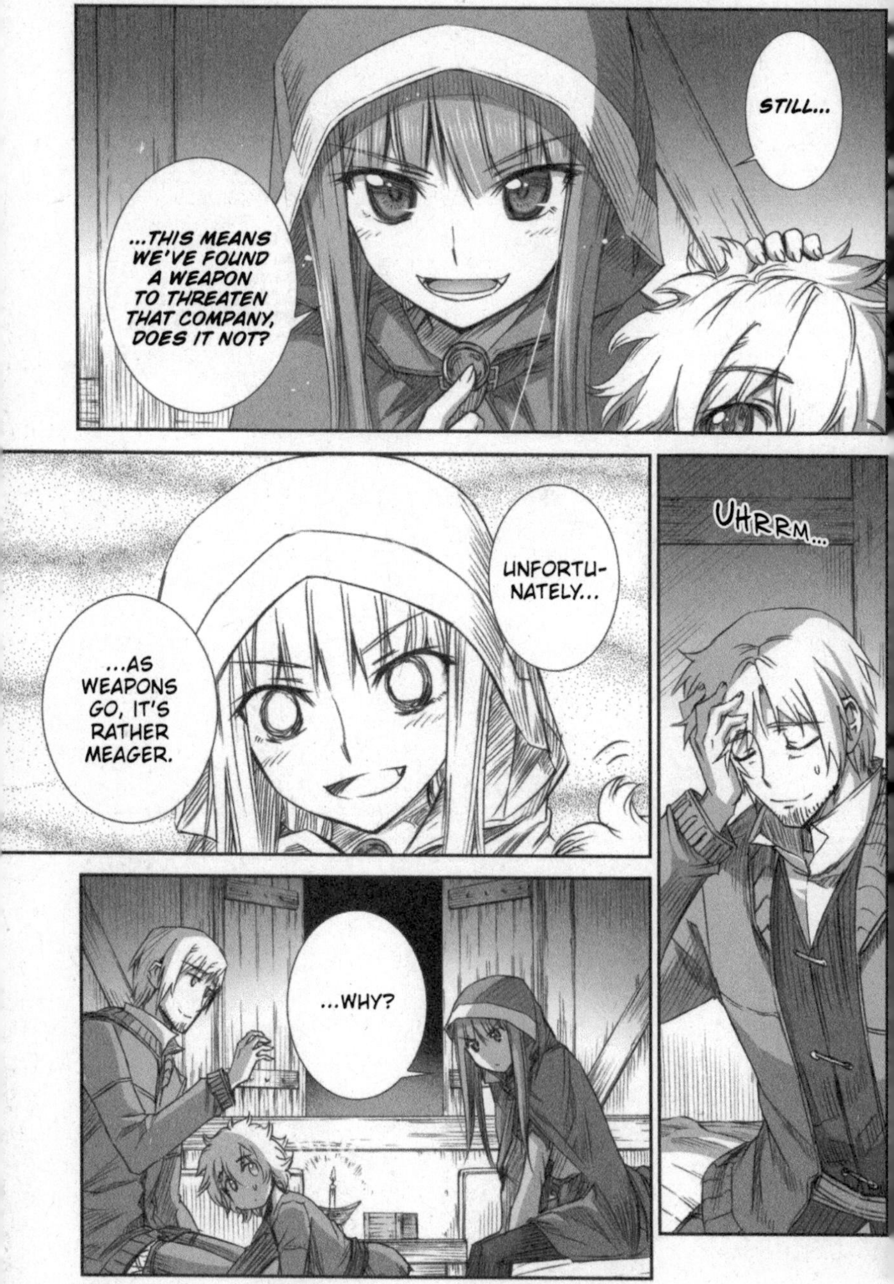
STILL...
...THIS MEANS WE'VE FOUND A WEAPON TO THREATEN THAT COMPANY, DOES IT NOT?
UHRRM...
UNFORTU-NATELY...
...AS WEAPONS GO, IT'S RATHER MEAGER.
...WHY?

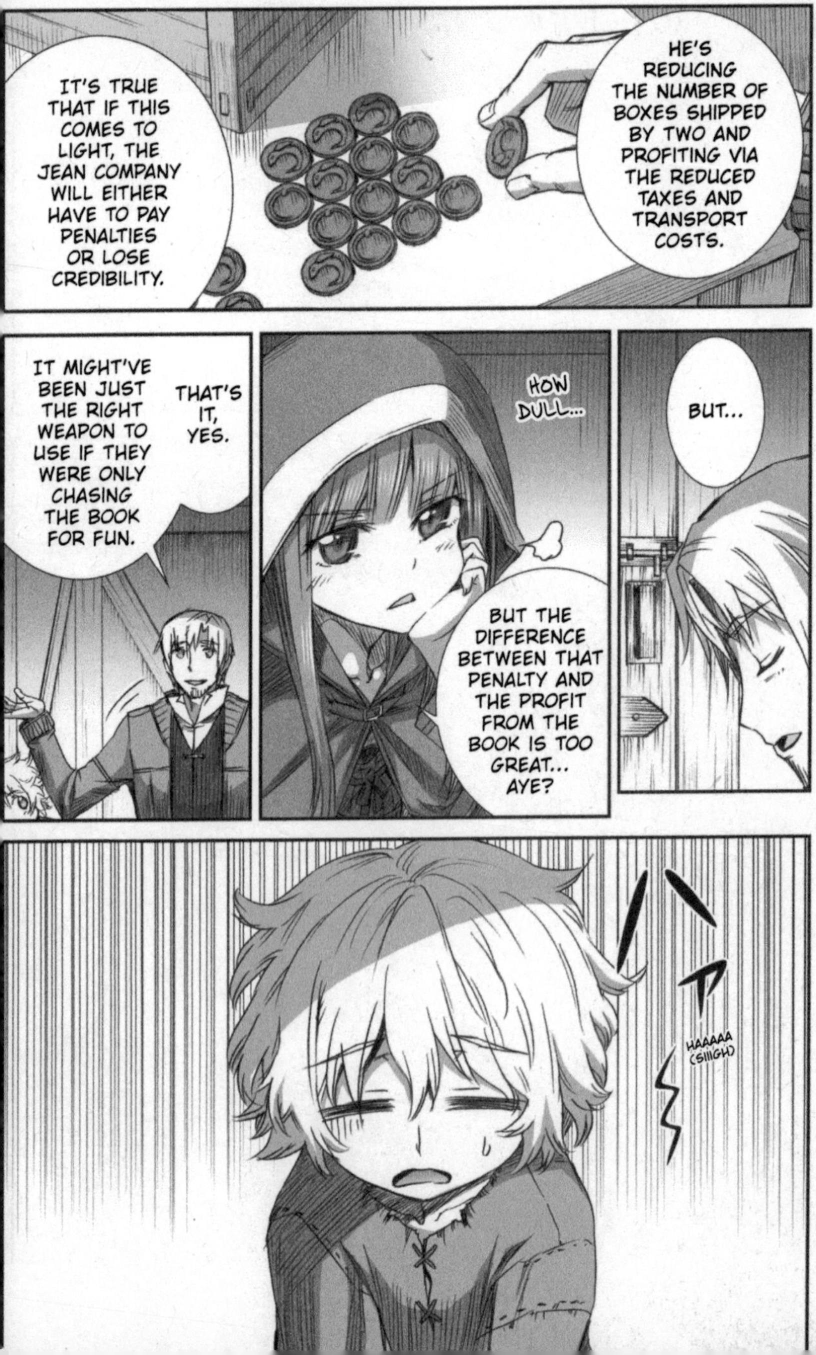
HE'S REDUCING THE NUMBER OF BOXES SHIPPED BY TWO AND PROFITING VIA THE REDUCED TAXES AND TRANSPORT COSTS.
IT'S TRUE THAT IF THIS COMES TO LIGHT, THE JEAN COMPANY WILL EITHER HAVE TO PAY PENALTIES OR LOSE CREDIBILITY.
BUT...
HOW DULL...
BUT THE DIFFERENCE BETWEEN THAT PENALTY AND THE PROFIT FROM THE BOOK IS TOO GREAT... AYE?
THAT'S IT, YES.
IT MIGHT'VE BEEN JUST THE RIGHT WEAPON TO USE IF THEY WERE ONLY CHASING THE BOOK FOR FUN.
HAAAAA (SIIIGH)

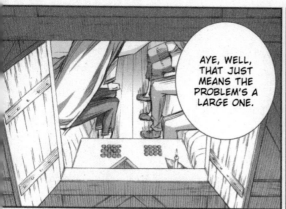

AYE, WELL, THAT JUST MEANS THE PROBLEM'S A LARGE ONE.

NADE (PAT)
ナデ

NADE
ナデ

UU...

PIKU (TWITCH)
ピク

BESIDES, 'TIS BETTER THIS THAN SOMETHING SOLVED WITH THE TRADE OF A SINGLE APPLE.

BA (WHAP)
ばっ

!

UN (NOD)
ウン ウン

QUITE RIGHT. IF ONE METHOD WON'T WORK, WE'LL JUST MOVE ON TO THE NEX—

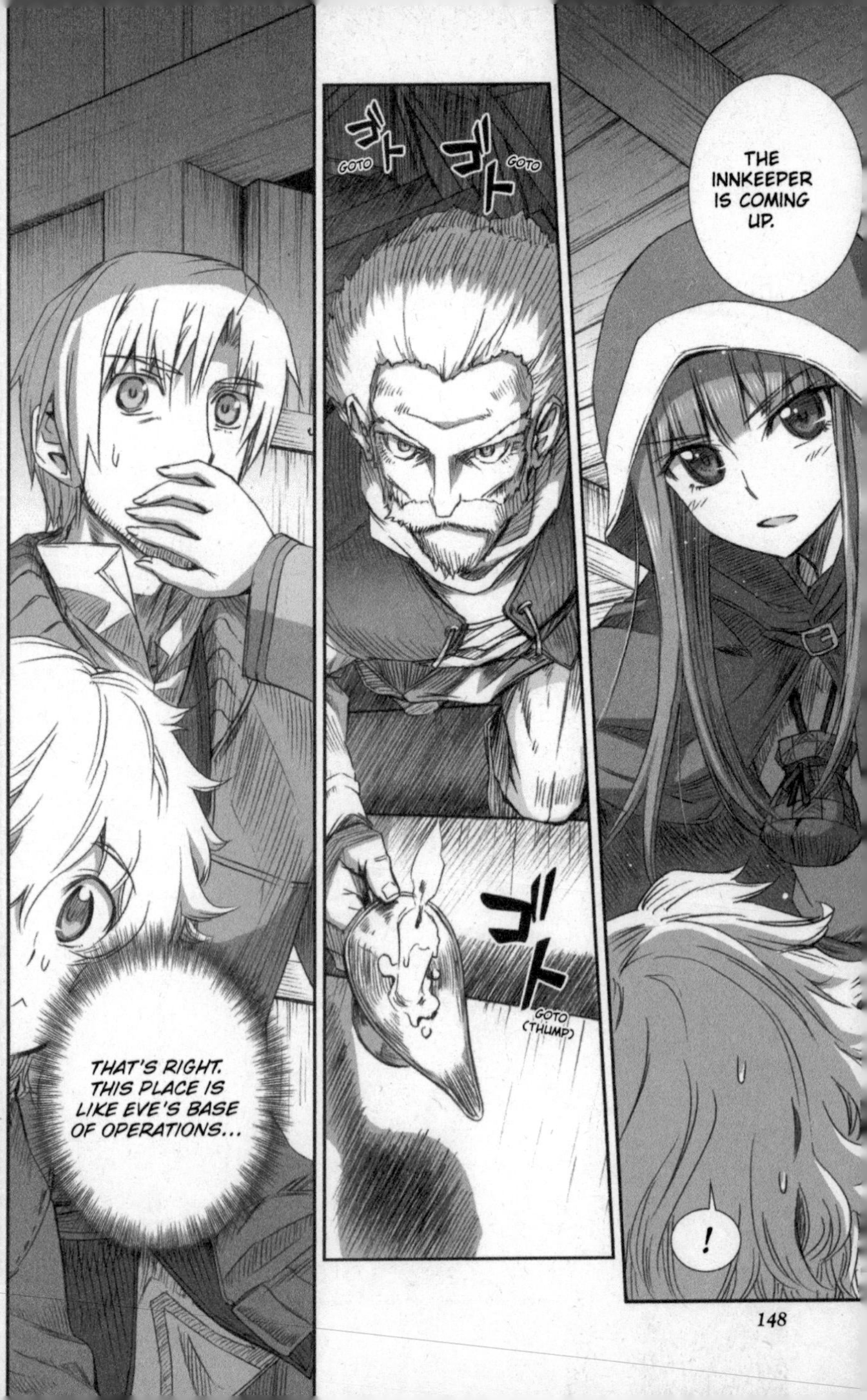
THE INNKEEPER IS COMING UP.
!
ゴト
GOTO
ゴト
GOTO
ゴト
GOTO (THUMP)
THAT'S RIGHT. THIS PLACE IS LIKE EVE'S BASE OF OPERATIONS...

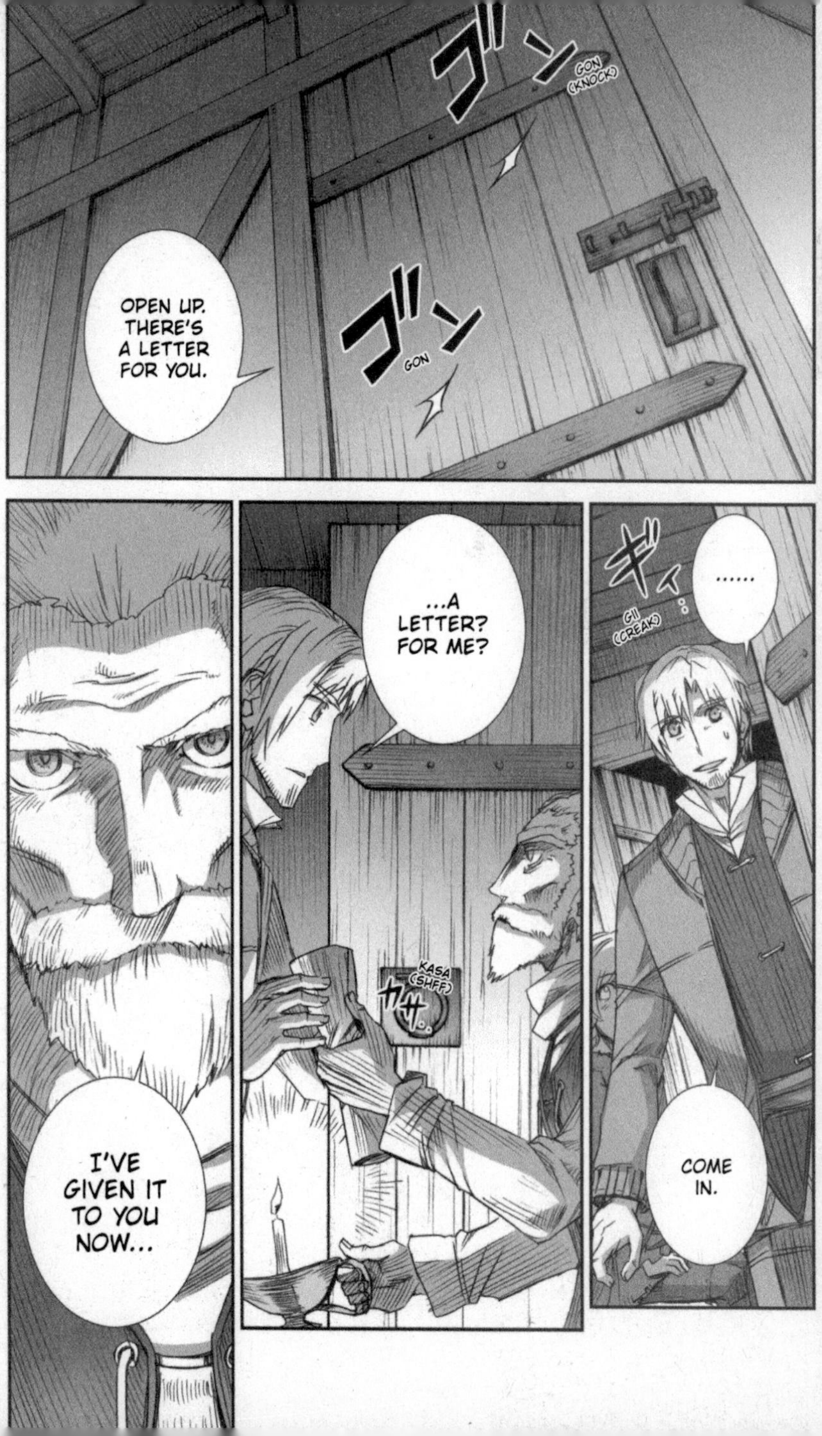
GON (KNOCK)
GON
OPEN UP. THERE'S A LETTER FOR YOU.
GII (CREAK)
......
COME IN.
KASA (SHFF)
...A LETTER? FOR ME?
I'VE GIVEN IT TO YOU NOW...

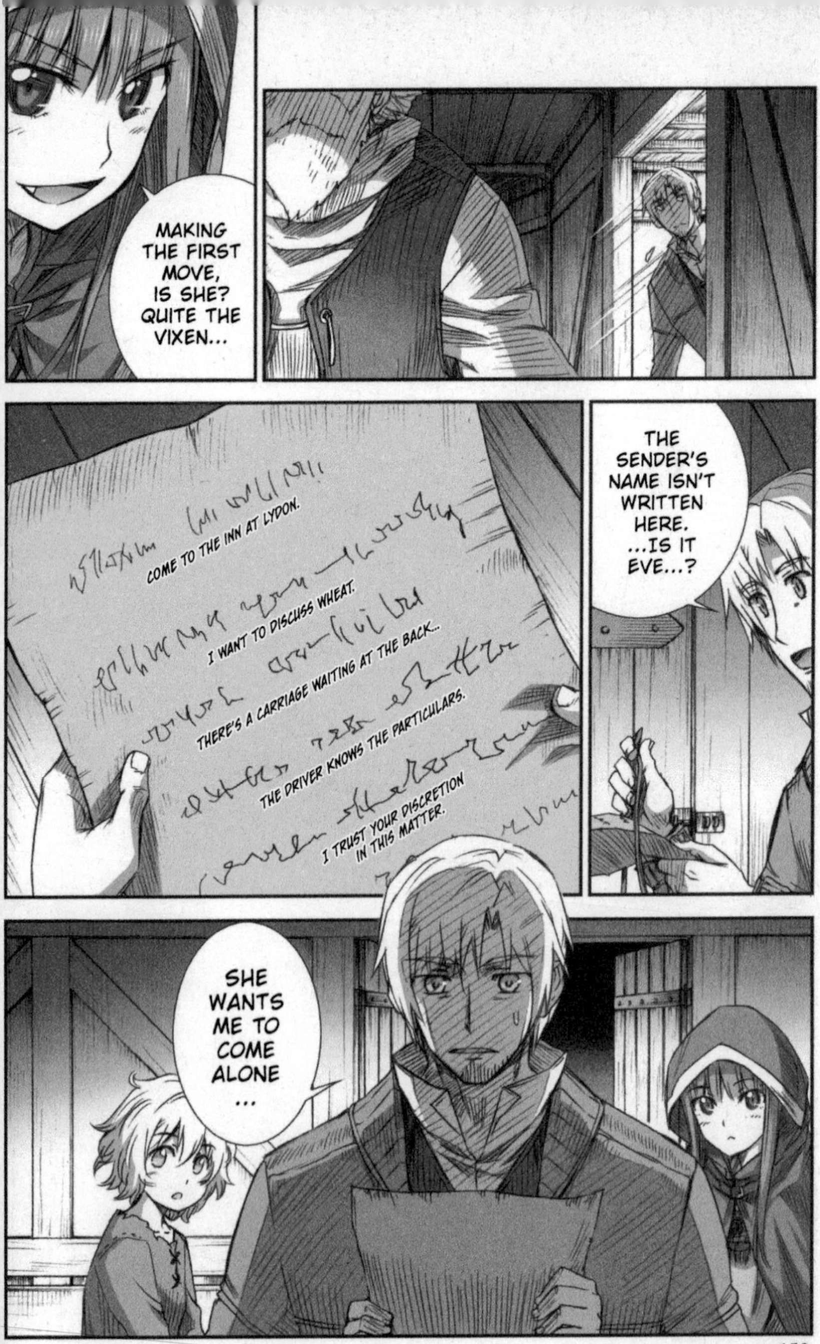
MAKING THE FIRST MOVE, IS SHE? QUITE THE VIXEN...
THE SENDER'S NAME ISN'T WRITTEN HERE. ...IS IT EVE...?
COME TO THE INN AT LYDON.
I WANT TO DISCUSS WHEAT.
THERE'S A CARRIAGE WAITING AT THE BACK...
THE DRIVER KNOWS THE PARTICULARS.
I TRUST YOUR DISCRETION IN THIS MATTER.
SHE WANTS ME TO COME ALONE ...

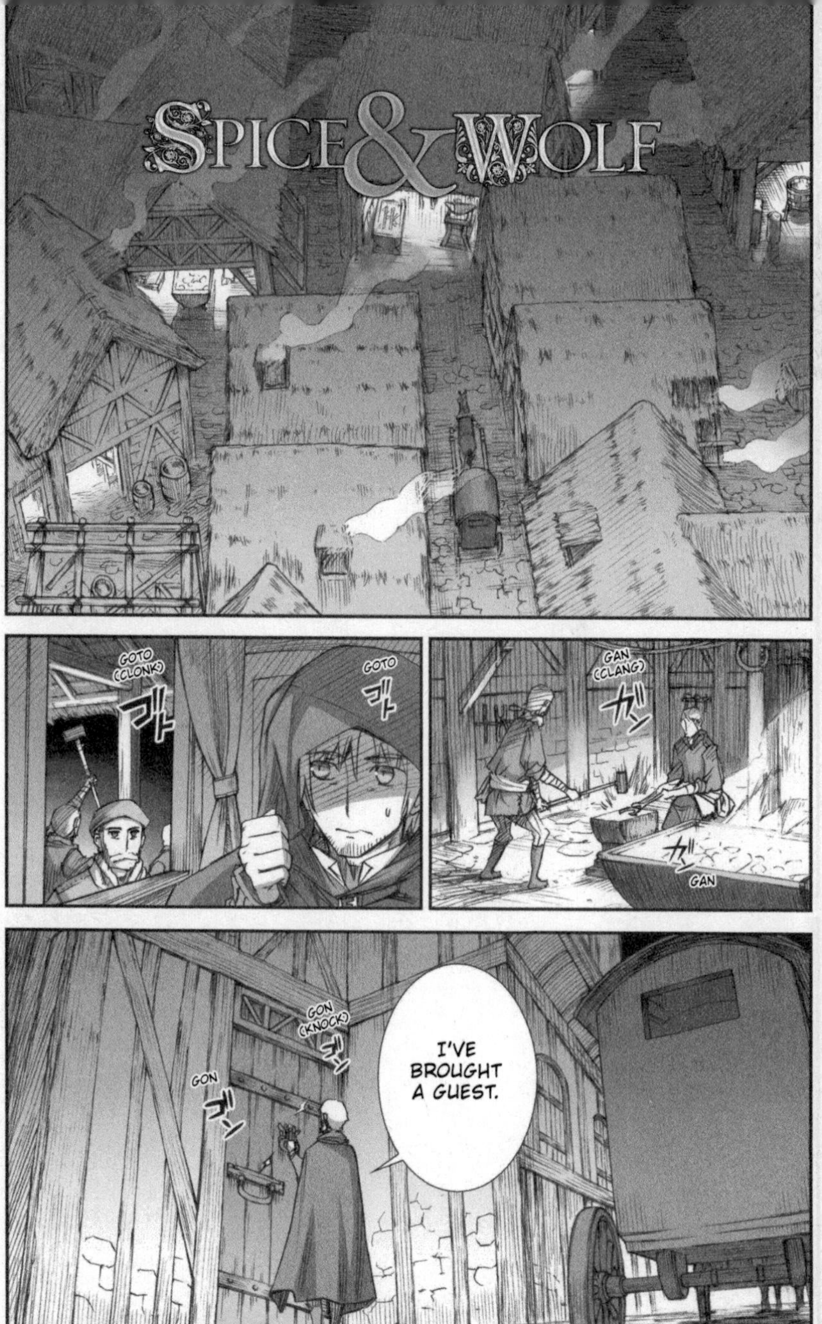
SPICE & WOLF
GAN (CLANG)
GAN
GOTO
GOTO (CLONK)
GON (KNOCK)
I'VE BROUGHT A GUEST.
GON

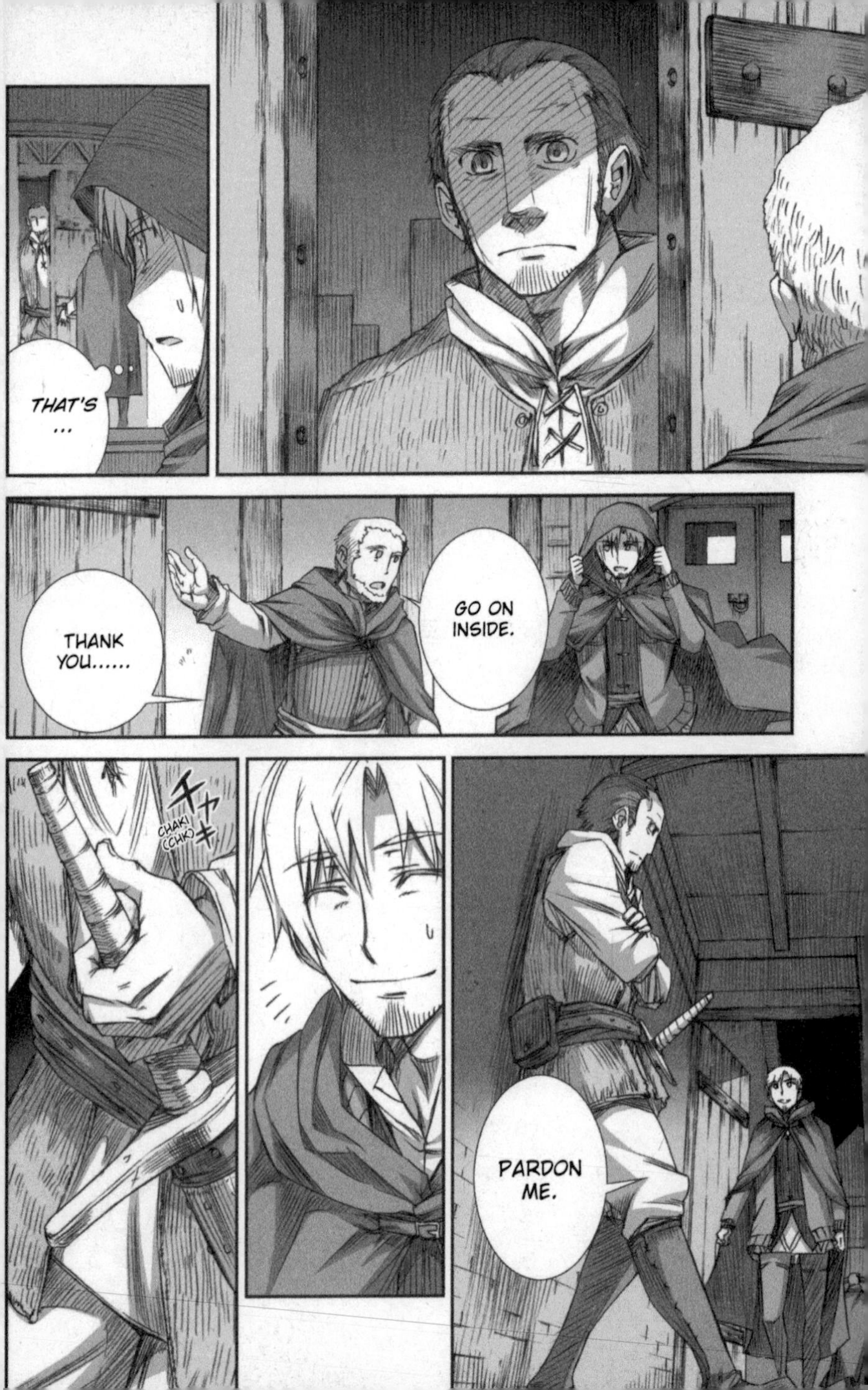
THAT'S ...
GO ON INSIDE.
THANK YOU......
PARDON ME.
チャキ
CHAKI (CHK)

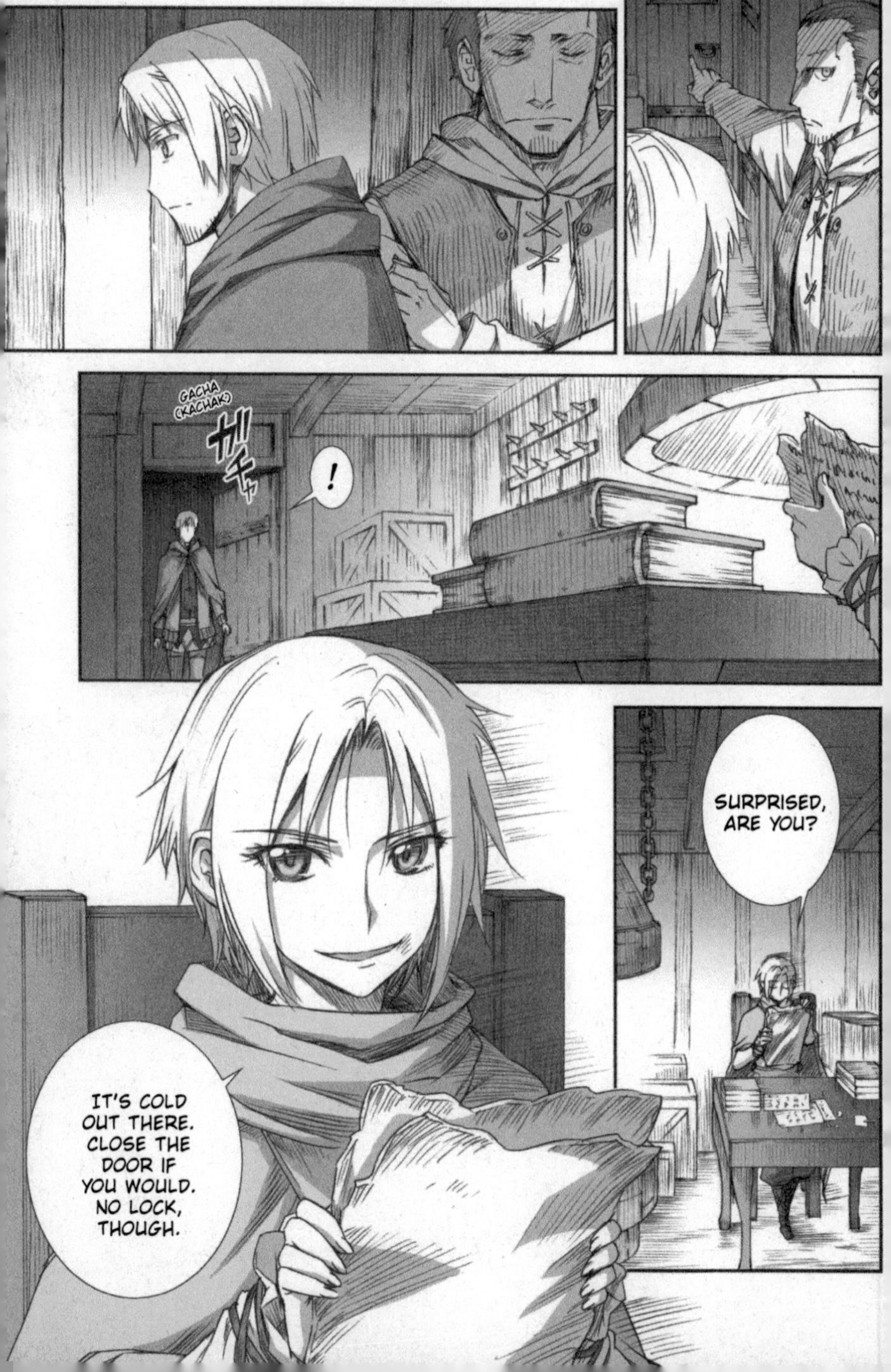
GACHA (KACHAK)
ガチャ
!
SURPRISED, ARE YOU?
IT'S COLD OUT THERE. CLOSE THE DOOR IF YOU WOULD. NO LOCK, THOUGH.

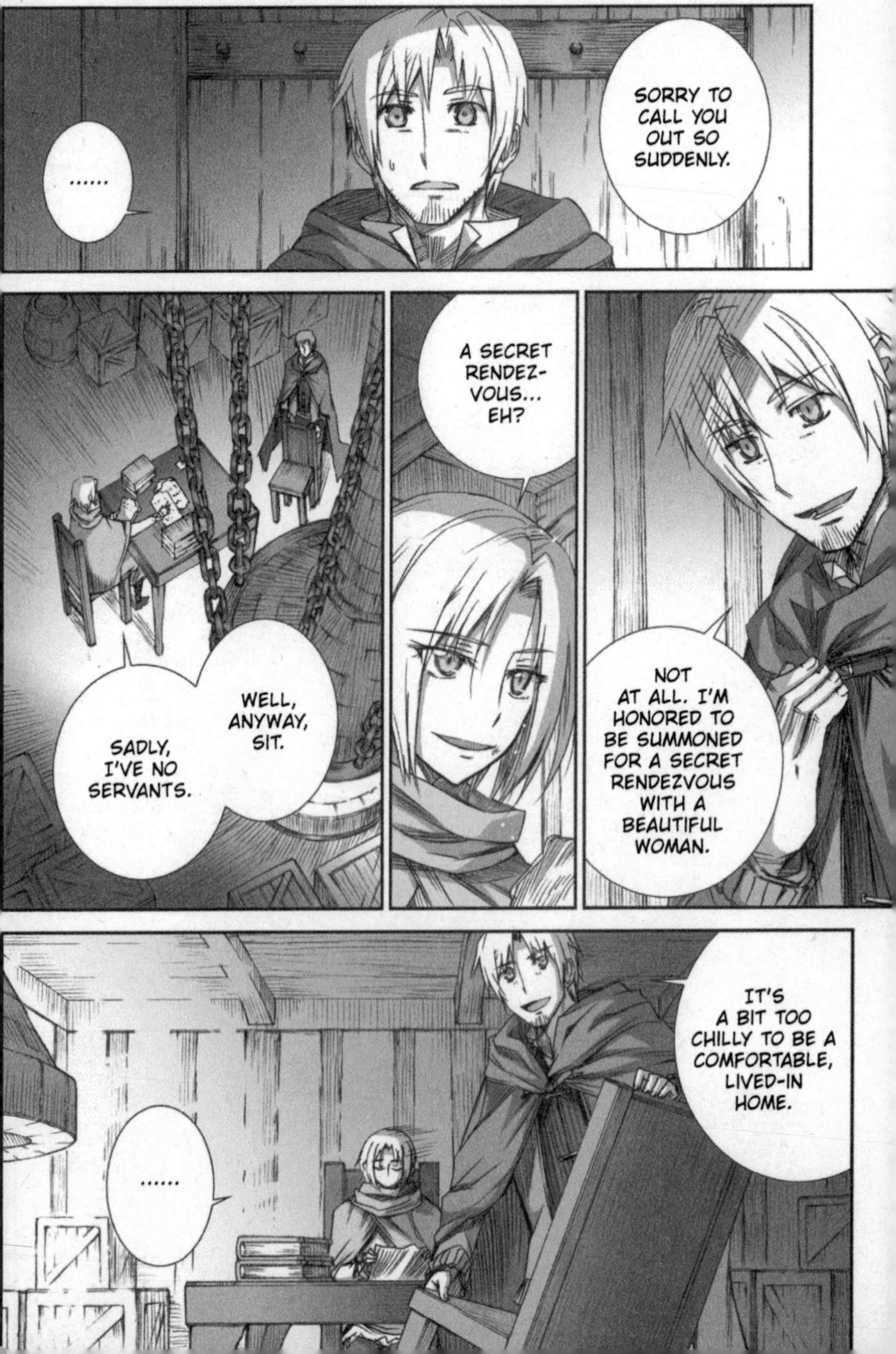
SORRY TO CALL YOU OUT SO SUDDENLY.
......
NOT AT ALL. I'M HONORED TO BE SUMMONED FOR A SECRET RENDEZVOUS WITH A BEAUTIFUL WOMAN.
A SECRET RENDEZ-VOUS... EH?
WELL, ANYWAY, SIT.
SADLY, I'VE NO SERVANTS.
IT'S A BIT TOO CHILLY TO BE A COMFORTABLE, LIVED-IN HOME.
......

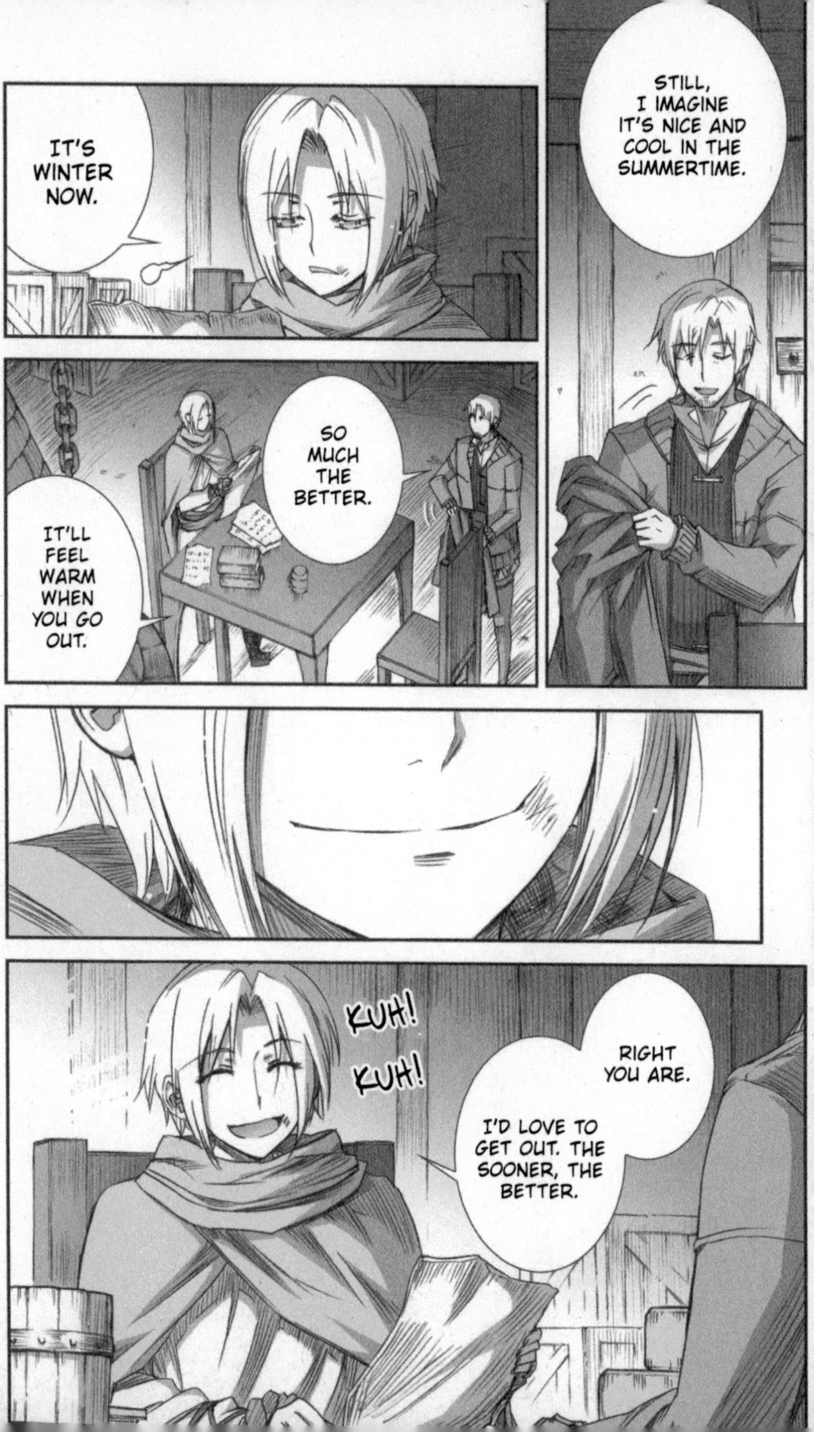
STILL, I IMAGINE IT'S NICE AND COOL IN THE SUMMERTIME.
IT'S WINTER NOW.
SO MUCH THE BETTER.
IT'LL FEEL WARM WHEN YOU GO OUT.
RIGHT YOU ARE.
I'D LOVE TO GET OUT. THE SOONER, THE BETTER.
KUH! KUH!

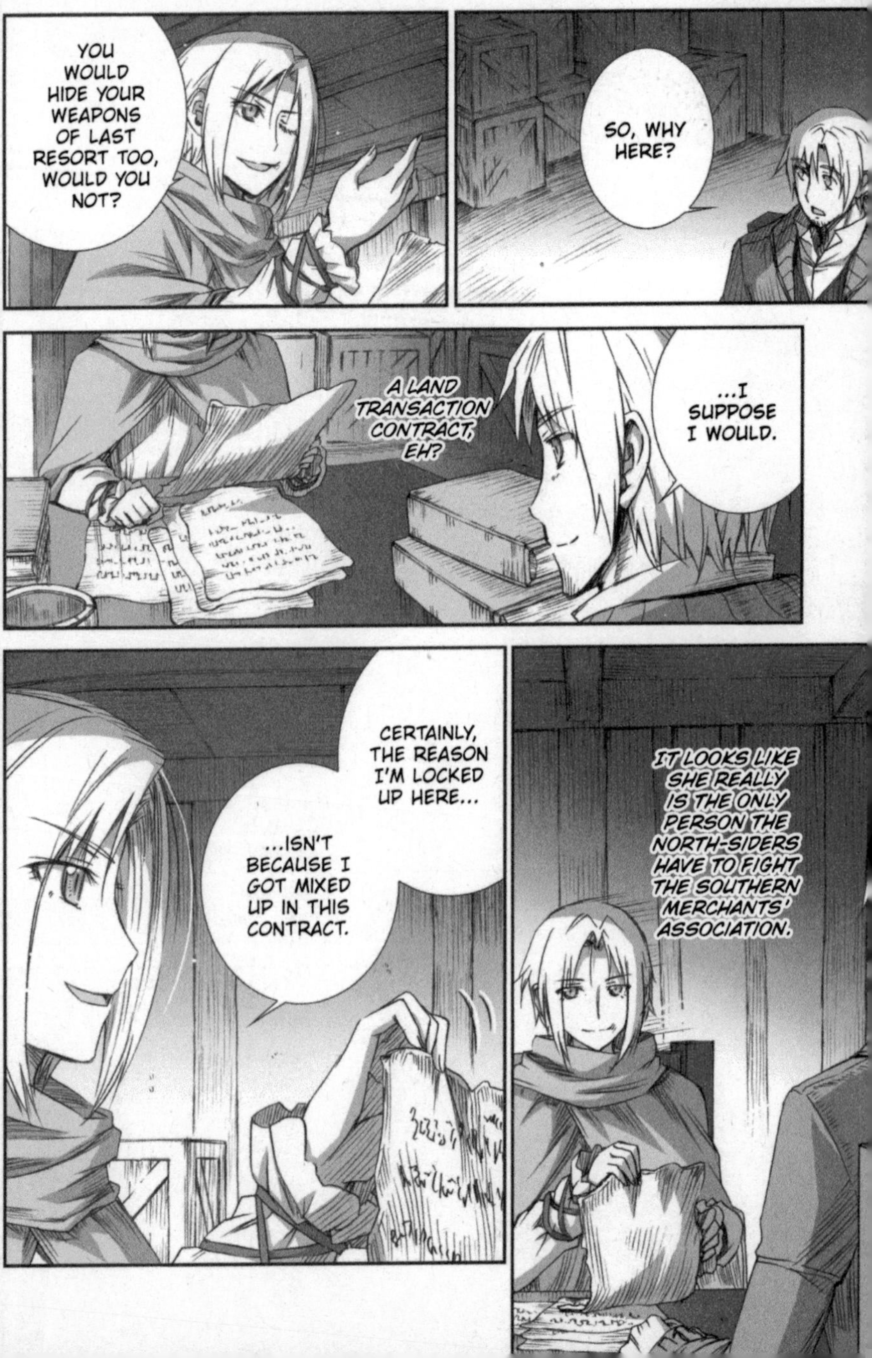
SO, WHY HERE?
YOU WOULD HIDE YOUR WEAPONS OF LAST RESORT TOO, WOULD YOU NOT?
...I SUPPOSE I WOULD.
A LAND TRANSACTION CONTRACT, EH?
IT LOOKS LIKE SHE REALLY IS THE ONLY PERSON THE NORTH-SIDERS HAVE TO FIGHT THE SOUTHERN MERCHANTS' ASSOCIATION.
CERTAINLY, THE REASON I'M LOCKED UP HERE...
...ISN'T BECAUSE I GOT MIXED UP IN THIS CONTRACT.

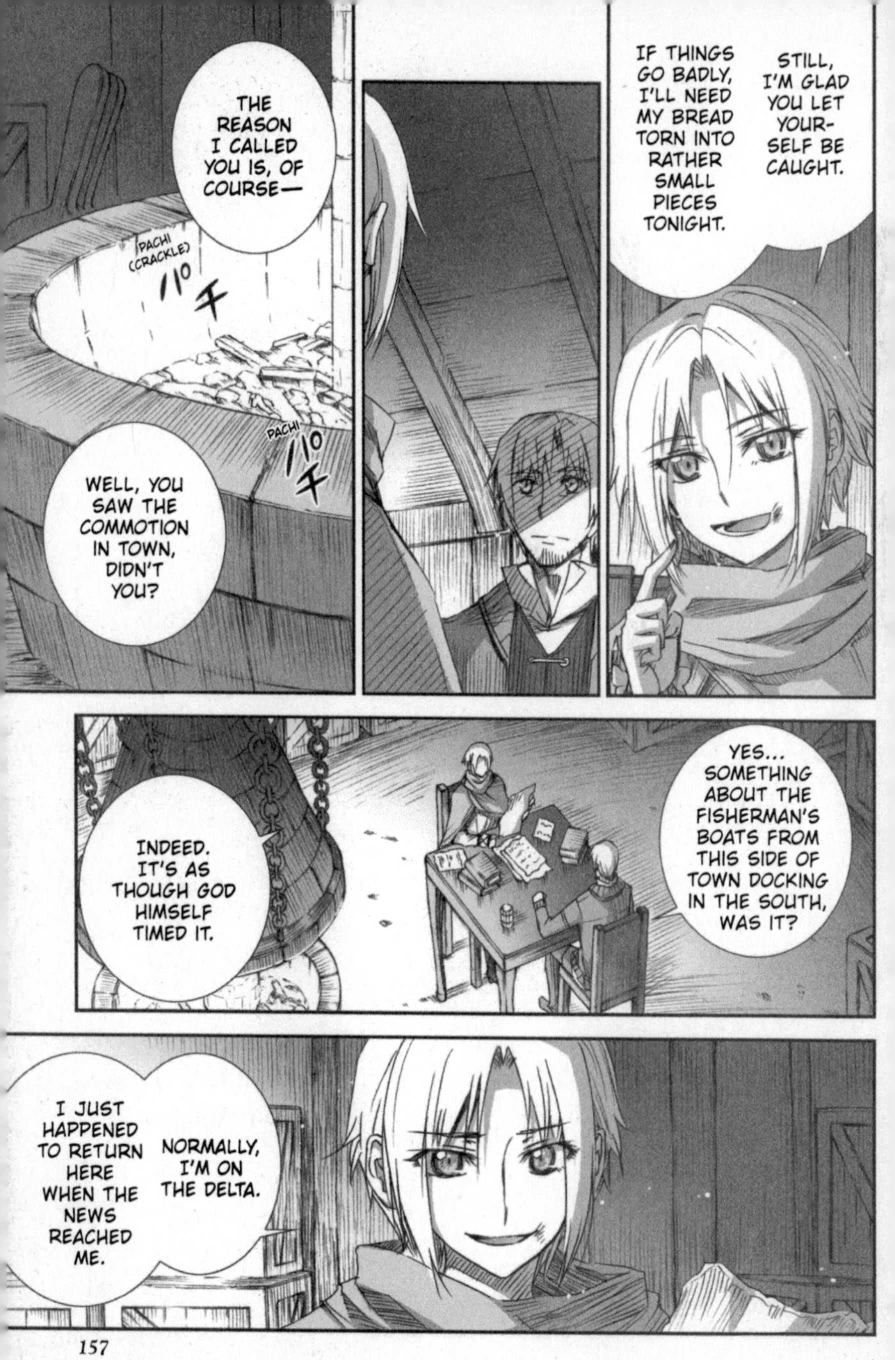
STILL, I'M GLAD YOU LET YOURSELF BE CAUGHT.
IF THINGS GO BADLY, I'LL NEED MY BREAD TORN INTO RATHER SMALL PIECES TONIGHT.
THE REASON I CALLED YOU IS, OF COURSE—
PACHI (CRACKLE)
パチ
PACHI
パチ
WELL, YOU SAW THE COMMOTION IN TOWN, DIDN'T YOU?
YES... SOMETHING ABOUT THE FISHERMAN'S BOATS FROM THIS SIDE OF TOWN DOCKING IN THE SOUTH, WAS IT?
INDEED. IT'S AS THOUGH GOD HIMSELF TIMED IT.
NORMALLY, I'M ON THE DELTA.
I JUST HAPPENED TO RETURN HERE WHEN THE NEWS REACHED ME.

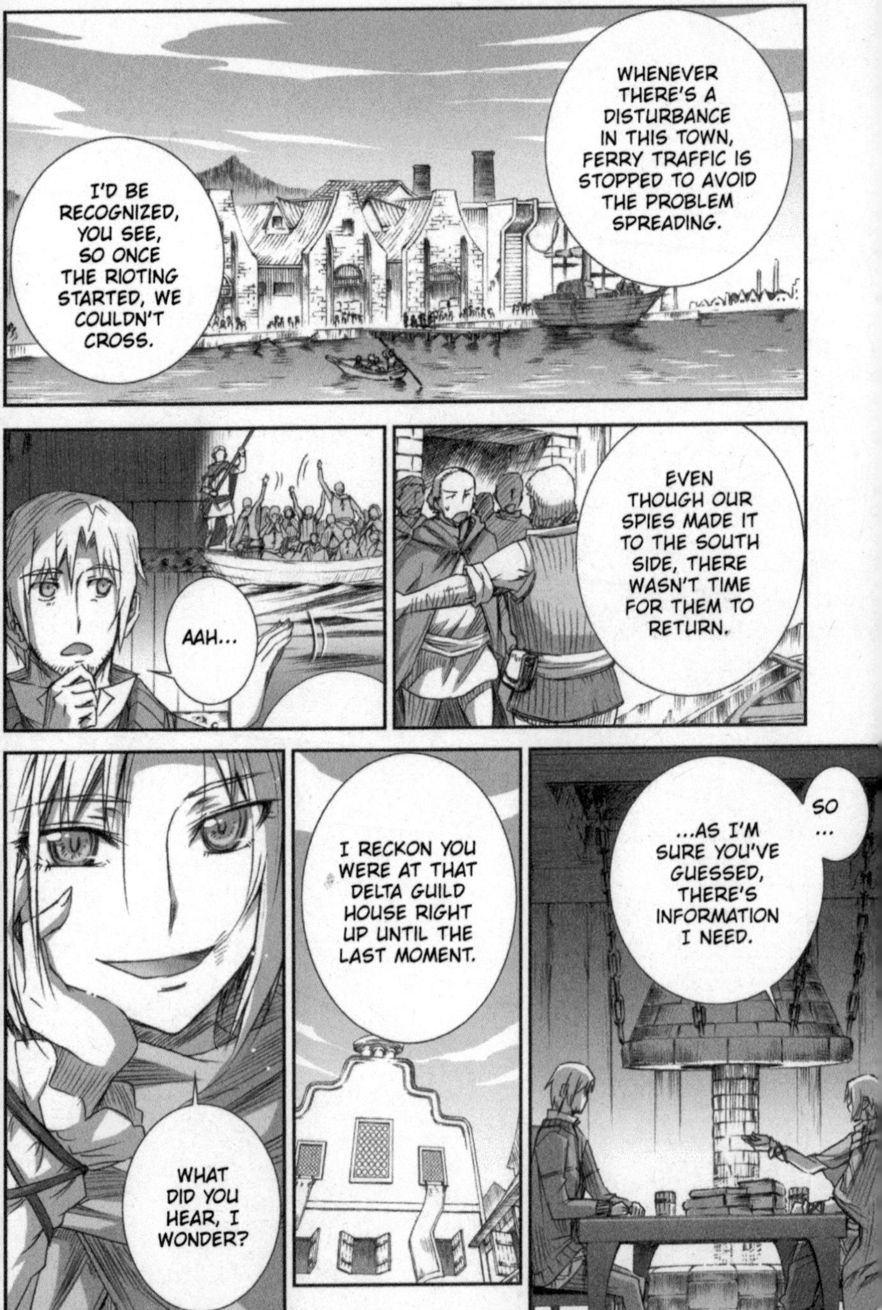
WHENEVER THERE'S A DISTURBANCE IN THIS TOWN, FERRY TRAFFIC IS STOPPED TO AVOID THE PROBLEM SPREADING.
I'D BE RECOGNIZED, YOU SEE, SO ONCE THE RIOTING STARTED, WE COULDN'T CROSS.
EVEN THOUGH OUR SPIES MADE IT TO THE SOUTH SIDE, THERE WASN'T TIME FOR THEM TO RETURN.
AAH...
SO ...
...AS I'M SURE YOU'VE GUESSED, THERE'S INFORMATION I NEED.
I RECKON YOU WERE AT THAT DELTA GUILD HOUSE RIGHT UP UNTIL THE LAST MOMENT.
WHAT DID YOU HEAR, I WONDER?

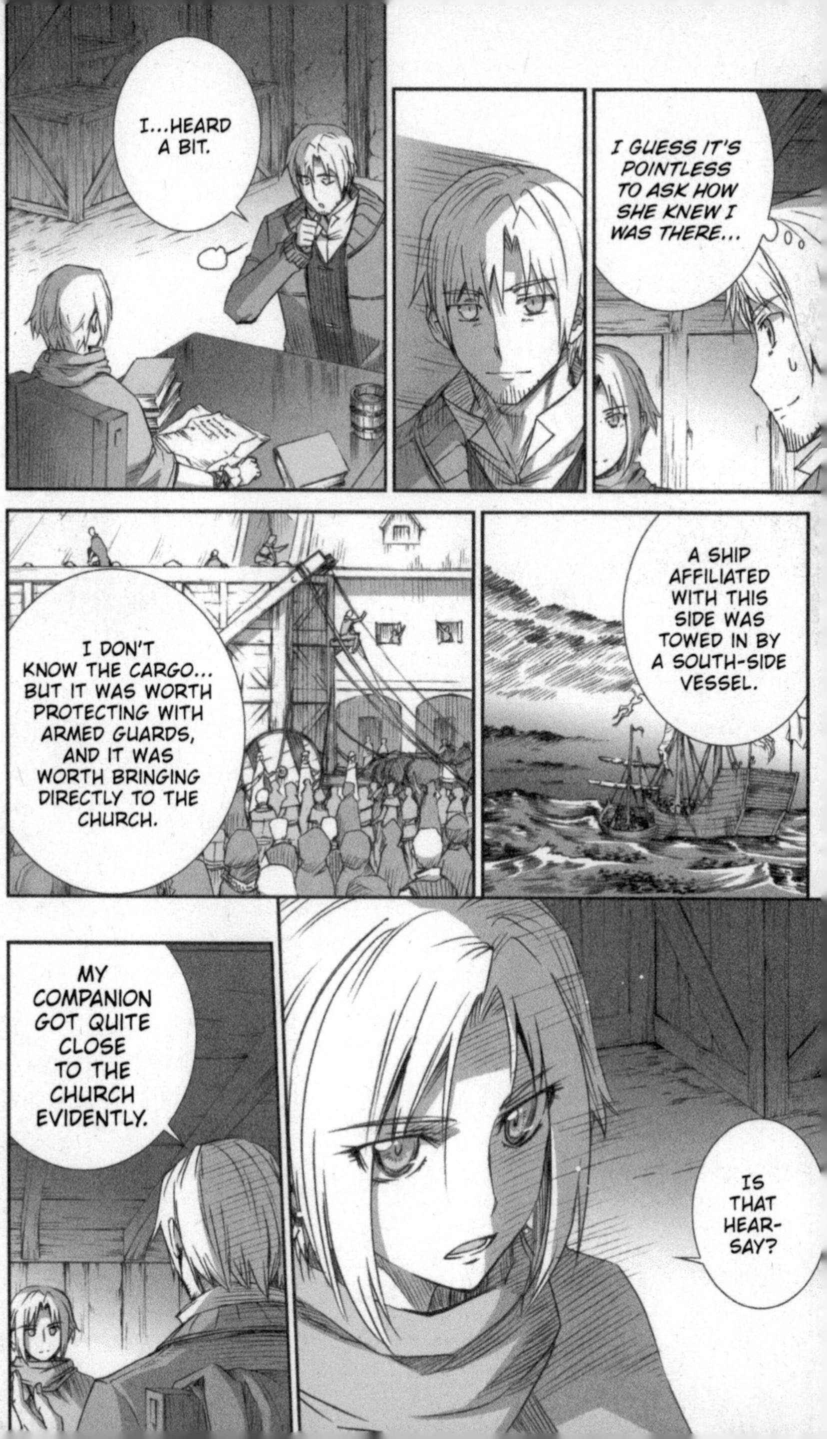
I GUESS IT'S POINTLESS TO ASK HOW SHE KNEW I WAS THERE...
I...HEARD A BIT.
A SHIP AFFILIATED WITH THIS SIDE WAS TOWED IN BY A SOUTH-SIDE VESSEL.
I DON'T KNOW THE CARGO... BUT IT WAS WORTH PROTECTING WITH ARMED GUARDS, AND IT WAS WORTH BRINGING DIRECTLY TO THE CHURCH.
IS THAT HEAR-SAY?
MY COMPANION GOT QUITE CLOSE TO THE CHURCH EVIDENTLY.

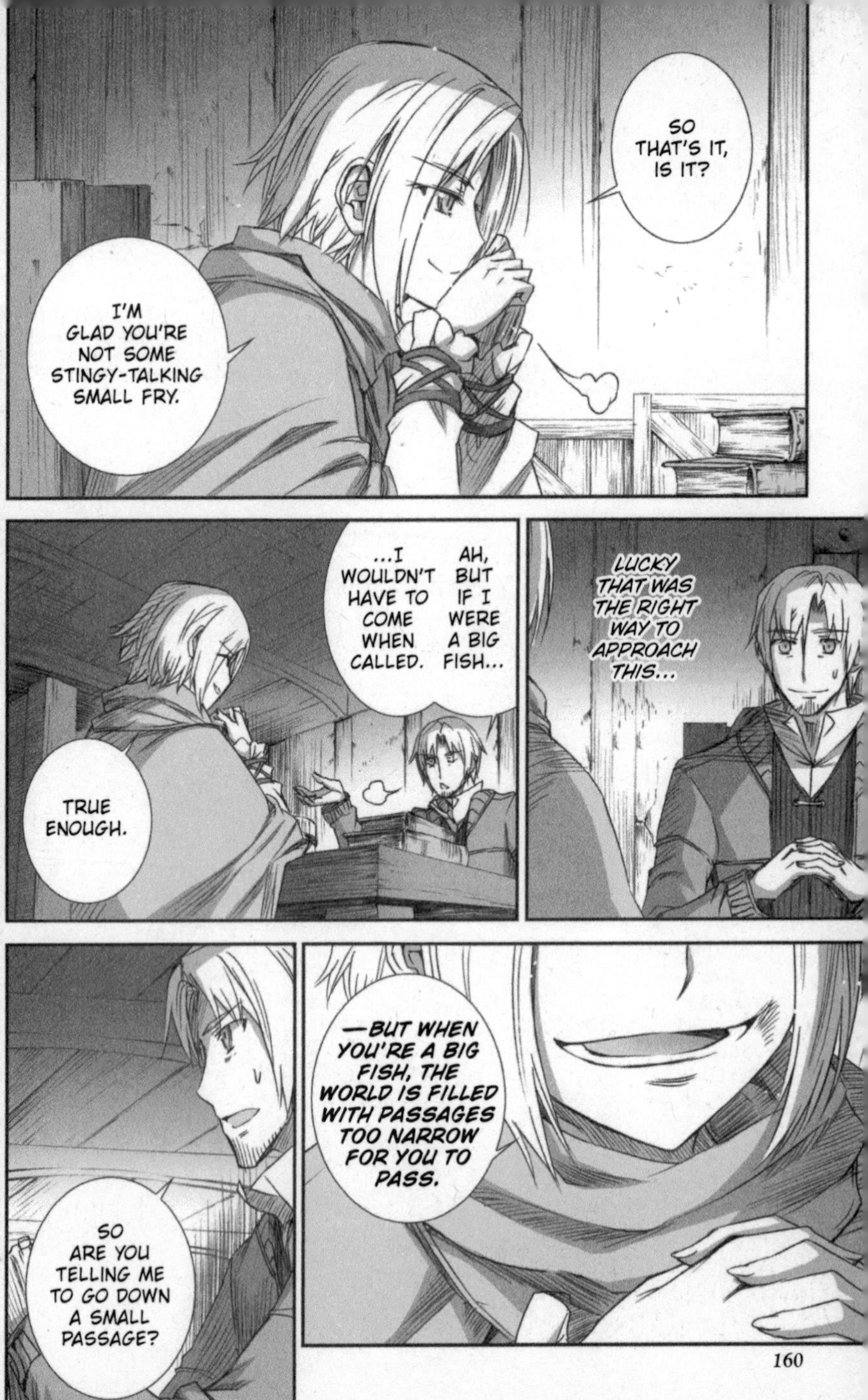
SO THAT'S IT, IS IT?
I'M GLAD YOU'RE NOT SOME STINGY-TALKING SMALL FRY.
LUCKY THAT WAS THE RIGHT WAY TO APPROACH THIS...
AH, BUT IF I WERE A BIG FISH...
...I WOULDN'T HAVE TO COME WHEN CALLED.
TRUE ENOUGH.
—BUT WHEN YOU'RE A BIG FISH, THE WORLD IS FILLED WITH PASSAGES TOO NARROW FOR YOU TO PASS.
SO ARE YOU TELLING ME TO GO DOWN A SMALL PASSAGE?

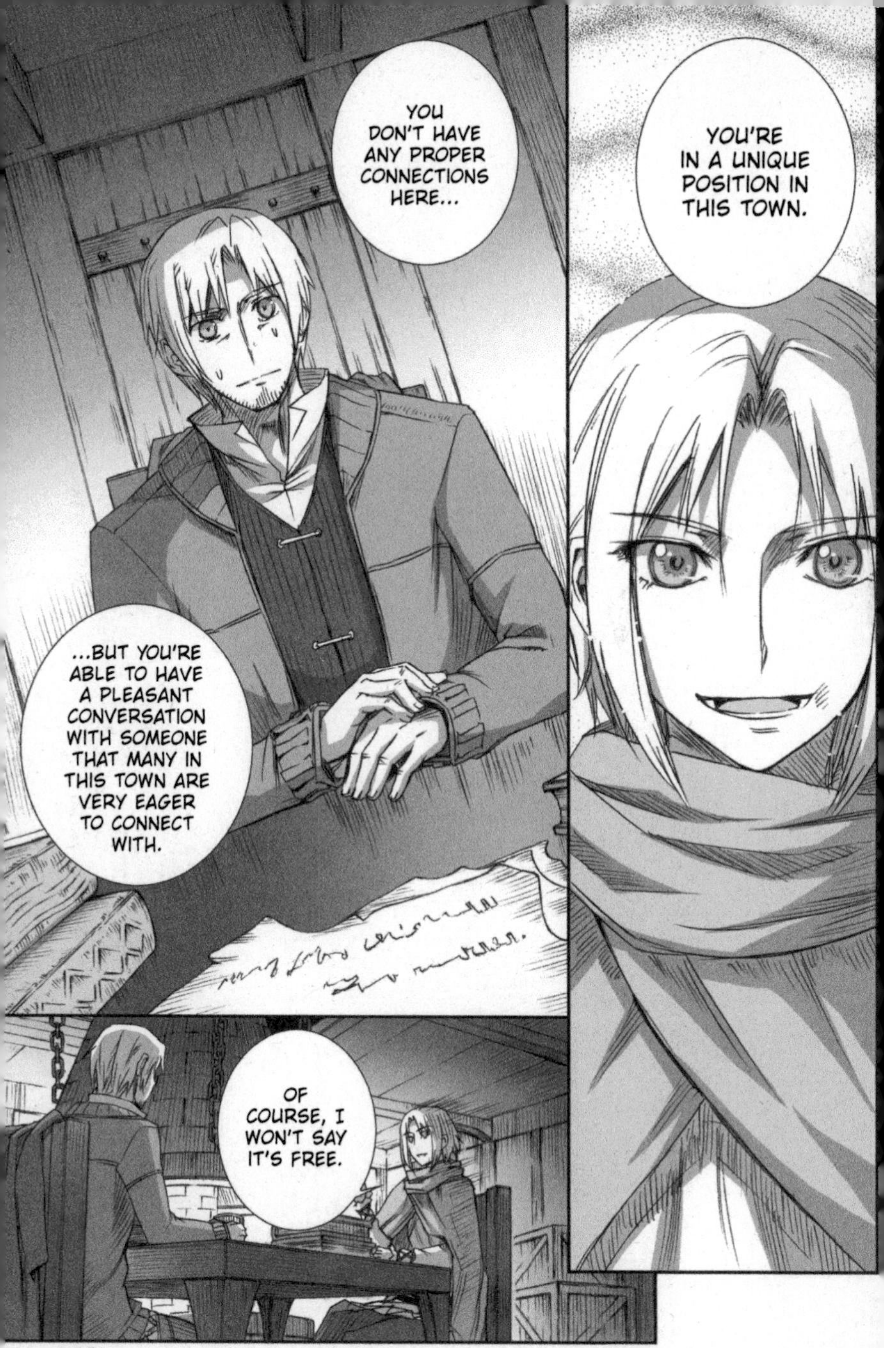
YOU'RE IN A UNIQUE POSITION IN THIS TOWN.
YOU DON'T HAVE ANY PROPER CONNECTIONS HERE...
...BUT YOU'RE ABLE TO HAVE A PLEASANT CONVERSATION WITH SOMEONE THAT MANY IN THIS TOWN ARE VERY EAGER TO CONNECT WITH.
OF COURSE, I WON'T SAY IT'S FREE.

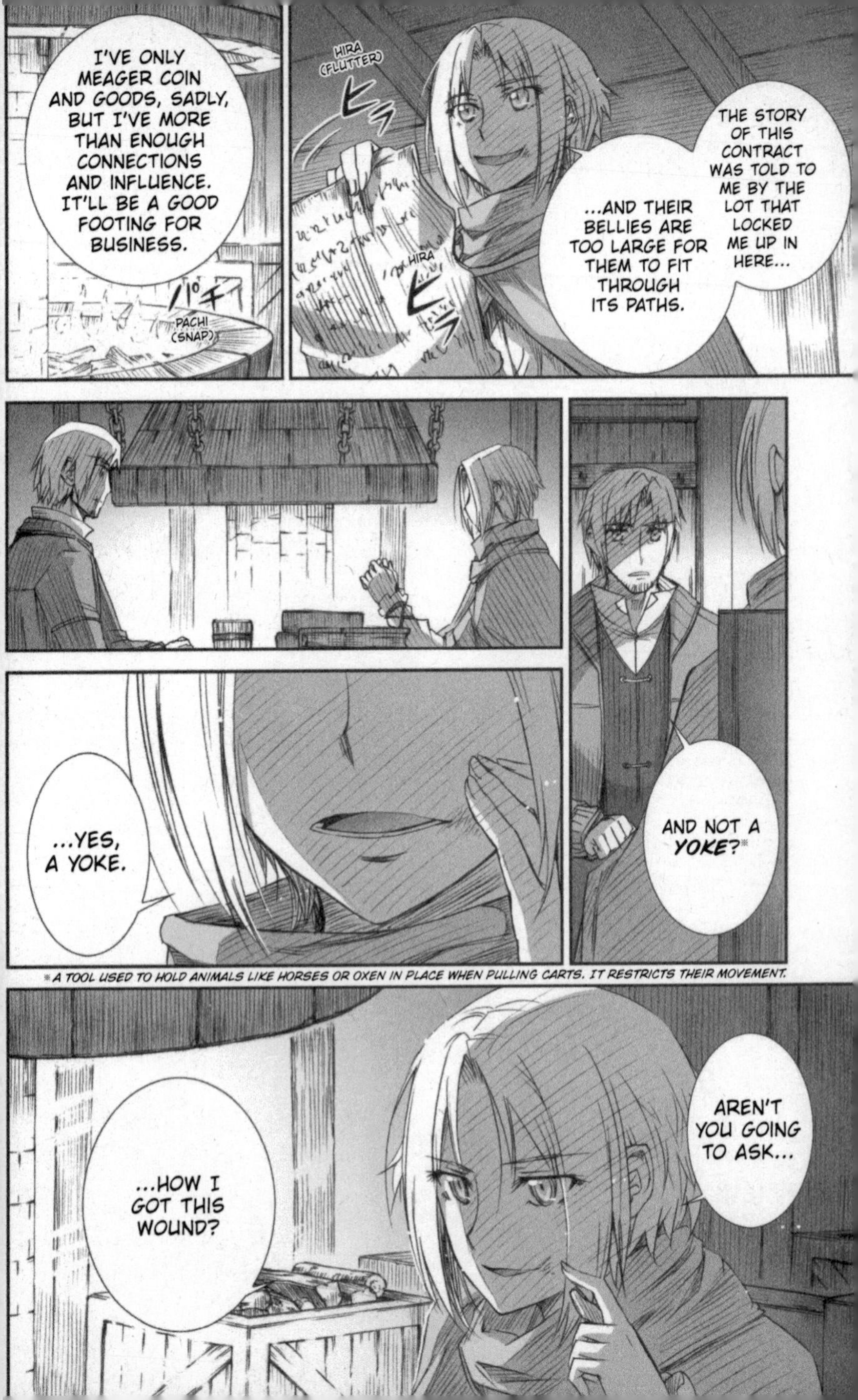
HIRA (FLUTTER)
THE STORY OF THIS CONTRACT WAS TOLD TO ME BY THE LOT THAT LOCKED ME UP IN HERE...
...AND THEIR BELLIES ARE TOO LARGE FOR THEM TO FIT THROUGH ITS PATHS.
HIRA
I'VE ONLY MEAGER COIN AND GOODS, SADLY, BUT I'VE MORE THAN ENOUGH CONNECTIONS AND INFLUENCE. IT'LL BE A GOOD FOOTING FOR BUSINESS.
PACHI (SNAP)
AND NOT A *YOKE*?*
...YES, A YOKE.
ARE'N'T YOU GOING TO ASK...
...HOW I GOT THIS WOUND?

*A TOOL USED TO HOLD ANIMALS LIKE HORSES OR OXEN IN PLACE WHEN PULLING CARTS. IT RESTRICTS THEIR MOVEMENT.

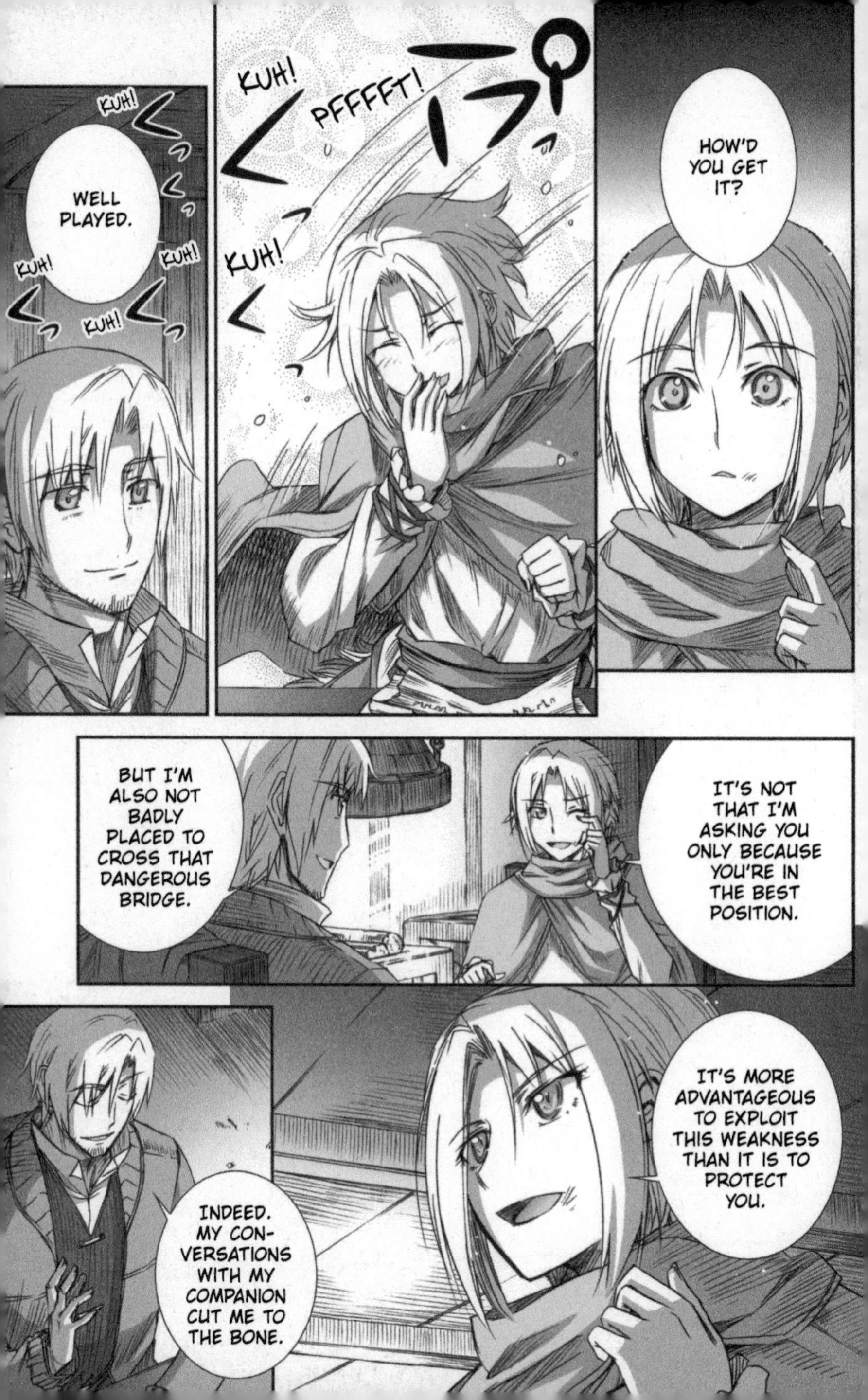
HOW'D YOU GET IT?
KUH!
PFFFFT!
KUH!
KUH!
WELL PLAYED.
KUH!
KUH!
KUH!
IT'S NOT THAT I'M ASKING YOU ONLY BECAUSE YOU'RE IN THE BEST POSITION.
BUT I'M ALSO NOT BADLY PLACED TO CROSS THAT DANGEROUS BRIDGE.
IT'S MORE ADVANTAGEOUS TO EXPLOIT THIS WEAKNESS THAN IT IS TO PROTECT YOU.
INDEED. MY CON-VERSATIONS WITH MY COMPANION CUT ME TO THE BONE.

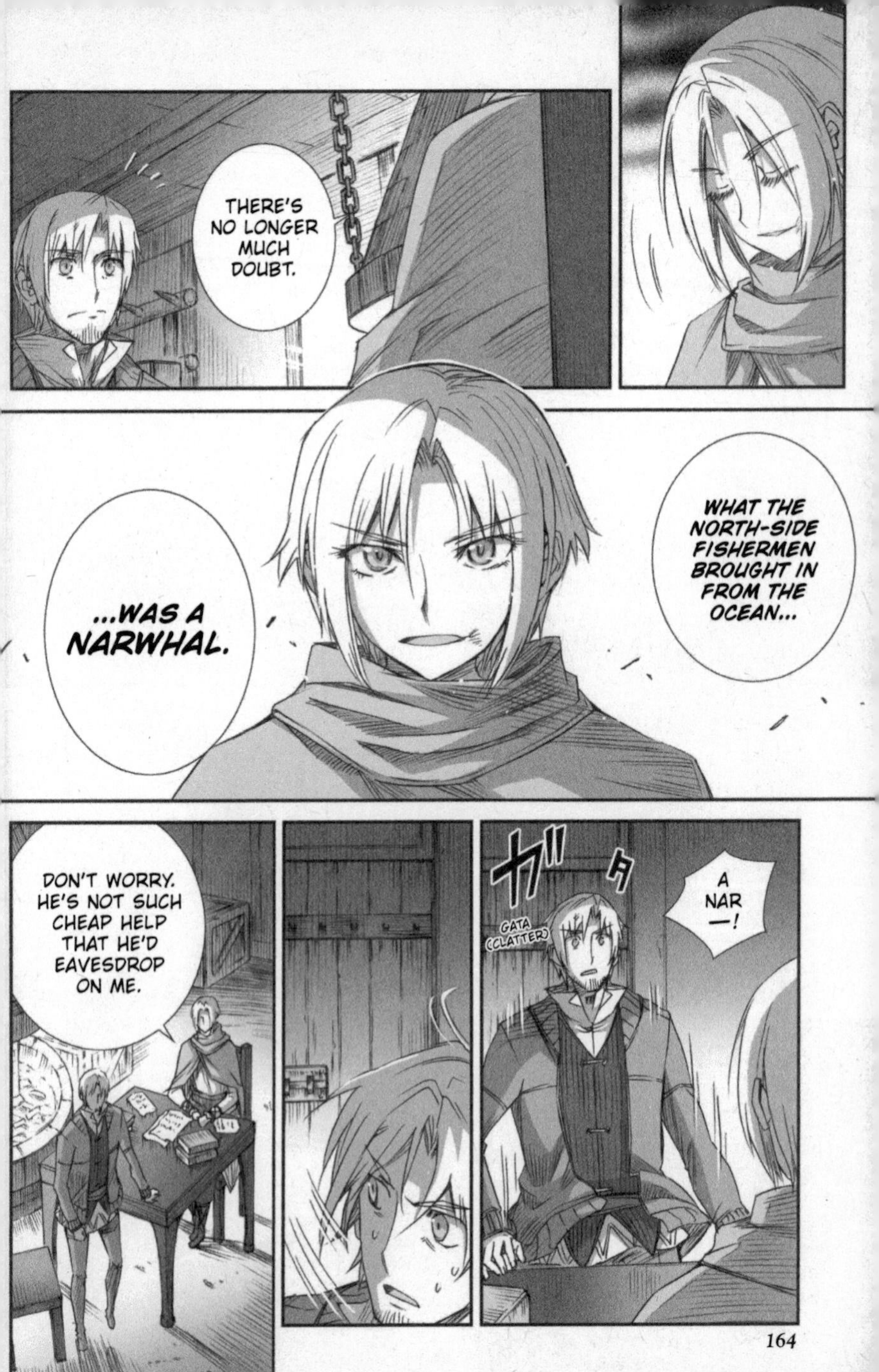
THERE'S NO LONGER MUCH DOUBT.
WHAT THE NORTH-SIDE FISHERMEN BROUGHT IN FROM THE OCEAN...
...WAS A NARWHAL.
ガタ
GATA (CLATTER)
A NAR—!
DON'T WORRY. HE'S NOT SUCH CHEAP HELP THAT HE'D EAVESDROP ON ME.

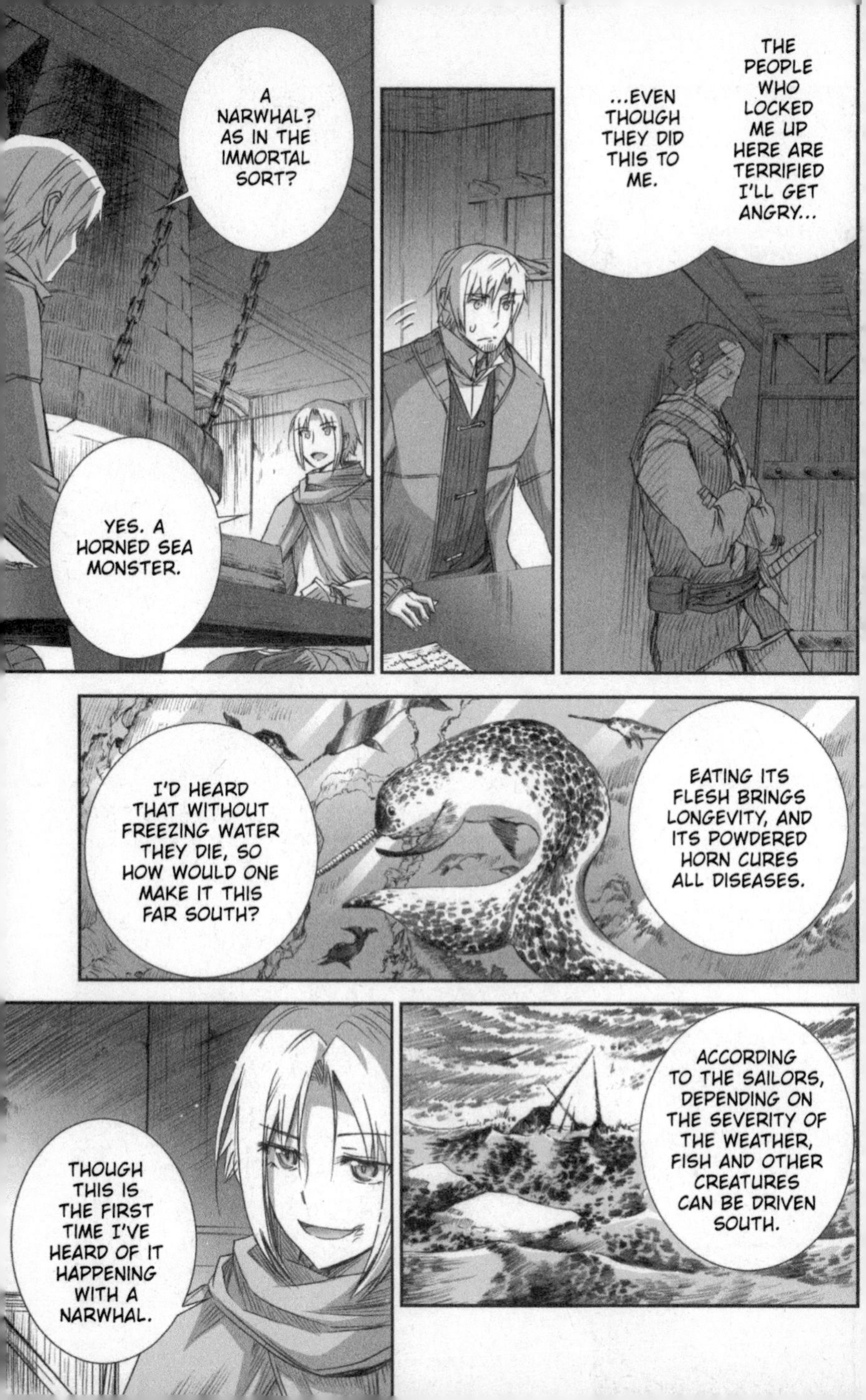
THE PEOPLE WHO LOCKED ME UP HERE ARE TERRIFIED I'LL GET ANGRY...
...EVEN THOUGH THEY DID THIS TO ME.
A NARWHAL? AS IN THE IMMORTAL SORT?
YES. A HORNED SEA MONSTER.
EATING ITS FLESH BRINGS LONGEVITY, AND ITS POWDERED HORN CURES ALL DISEASES.
I'D HEARD THAT WITHOUT FREEZING WATER THEY DIE, SO HOW WOULD ONE MAKE IT THIS FAR SOUTH?
ACCORDING TO THE SAILORS, DEPENDING ON THE SEVERITY OF THE WEATHER, FISH AND OTHER CREATURES CAN BE DRIVEN SOUTH.
THOUGH THIS IS THE FIRST TIME I'VE HEARD OF IT HAPPENING WITH A NARWHAL.

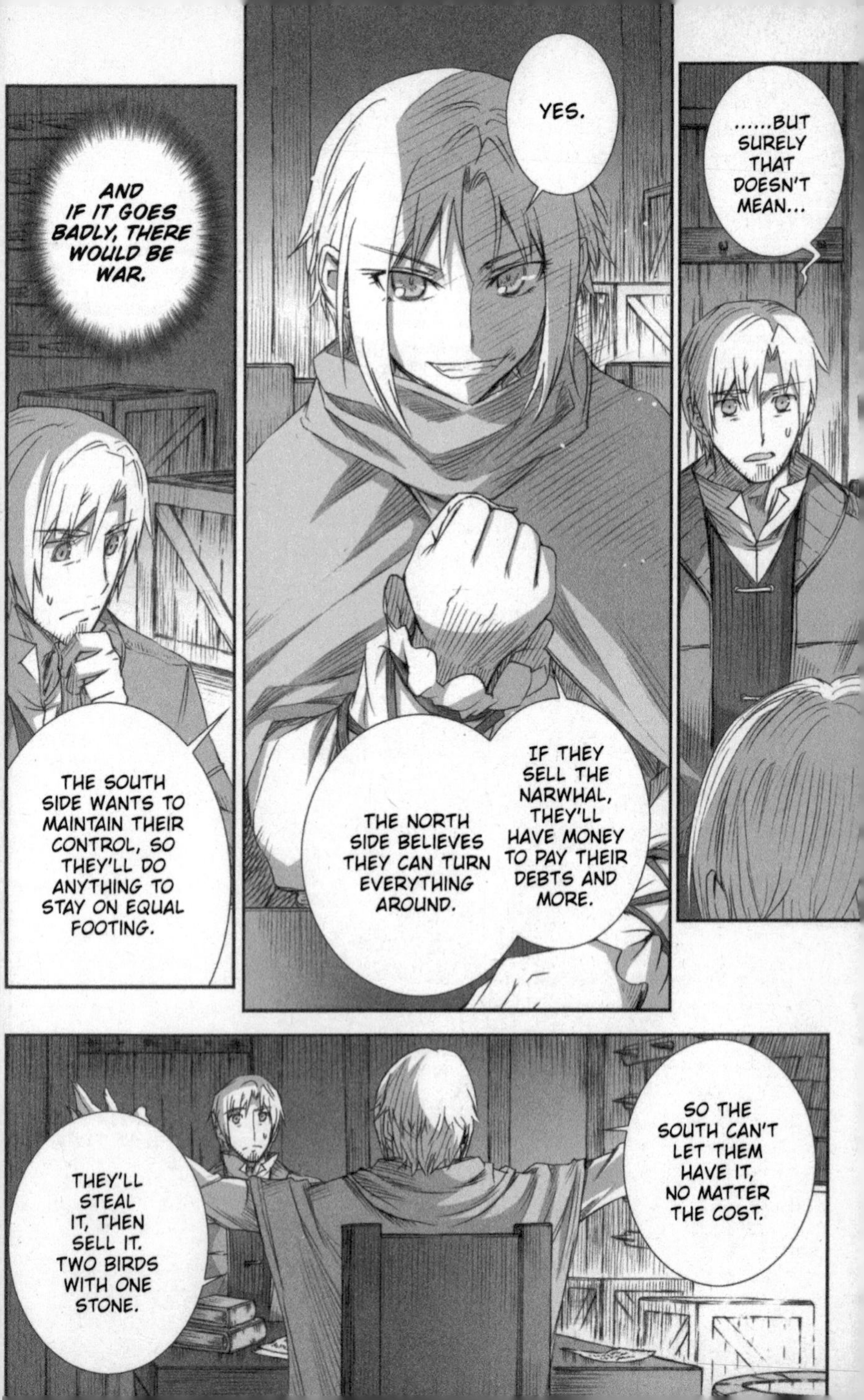
......BUT SURELY THAT DOESN'T MEAN...
YES.
IF THEY SELL THE NARWHAL, THEY'LL HAVE MONEY TO PAY THEIR DEBTS AND MORE.
THE NORTH SIDE BELIEVES THEY CAN TURN EVERYTHING AROUND.
AND IF IT GOES BADLY, THERE WOULD BE WAR.
THE SOUTH SIDE WANTS TO MAINTAIN THEIR CONTROL, SO THEY'LL DO ANYTHING TO STAY ON EQUAL FOOTING.
SO THE SOUTH CAN'T LET THEM HAVE IT, NO MATTER THE COST.
THEY'LL STEAL IT, THEN SELL IT. TWO BIRDS WITH ONE STONE.

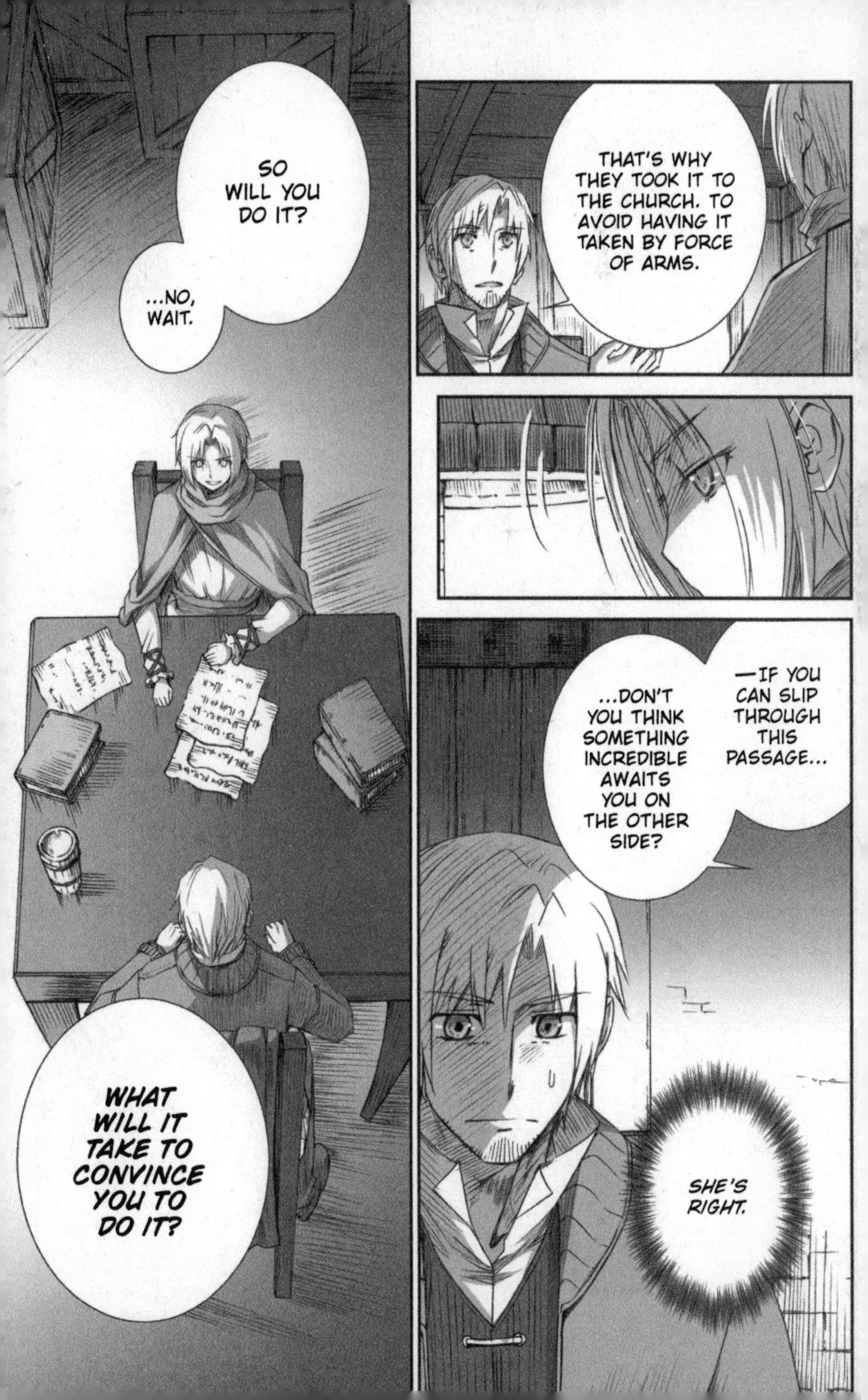
THAT'S WHY THEY TOOK IT TO THE CHURCH. TO AVOID HAVING IT TAKEN BY FORCE OF ARMS.
—IF YOU CAN SLIP THROUGH THIS PASSAGE...
...DON'T YOU THINK SOMETHING INCREDIBLE AWAITS YOU ON THE OTHER SIDE?
SHE'S RIGHT.
SO WILL YOU DO IT?
...NO, WAIT.
WHAT WILL IT TAKE TO CONVINCE YOU TO DO IT?

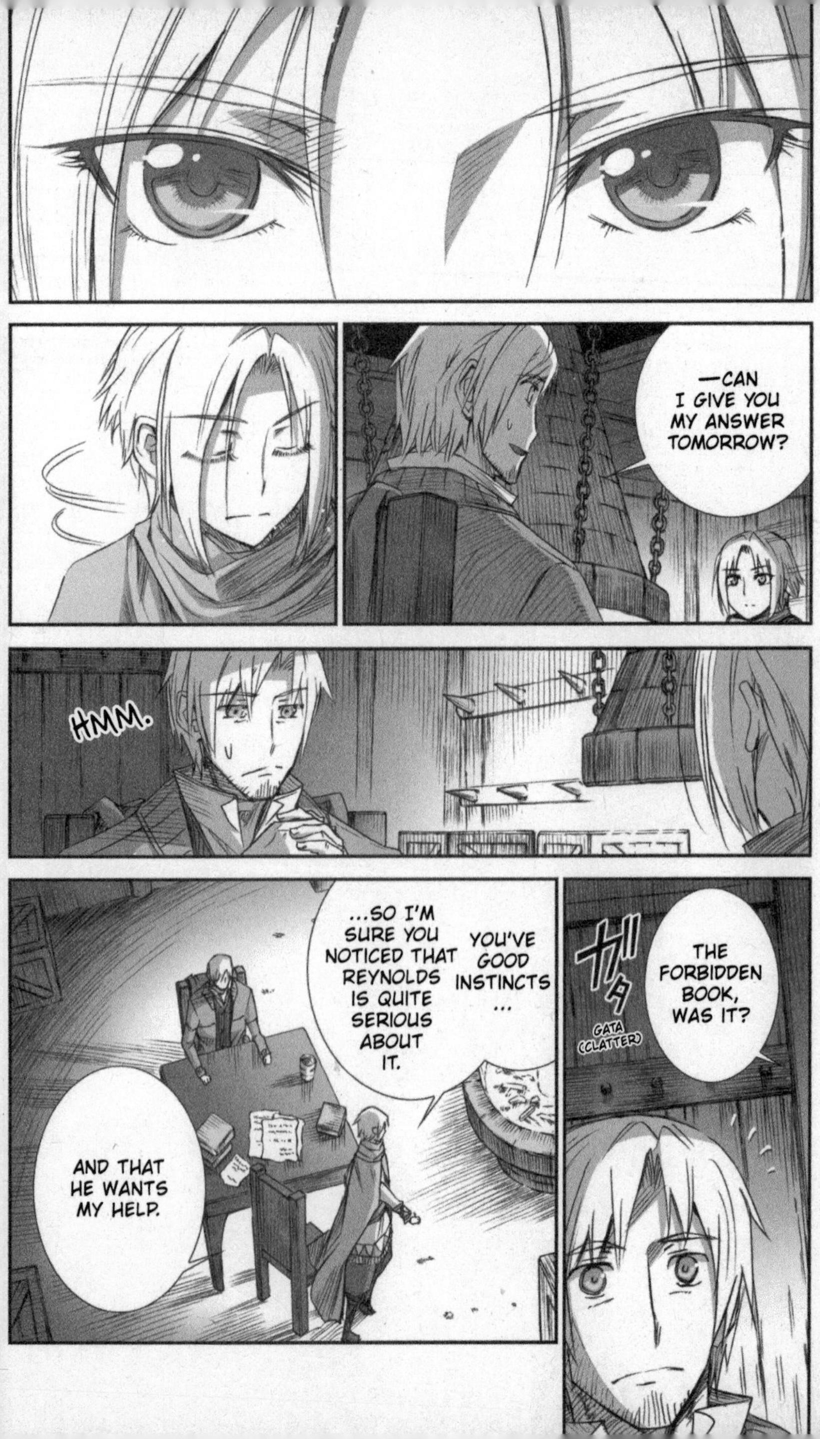
—CAN I GIVE YOU MY ANSWER TOMORROW?
HMM.
THE FORBIDDEN BOOK, WAS IT?
ガタ
GATA (CLATTER)
YOU'VE GOOD INSTINCTS...
...SO I'M SURE YOU NOTICED THAT REYNOLDS IS QUITE SERIOUS ABOUT IT.
AND THAT HE WANTS MY HELP.

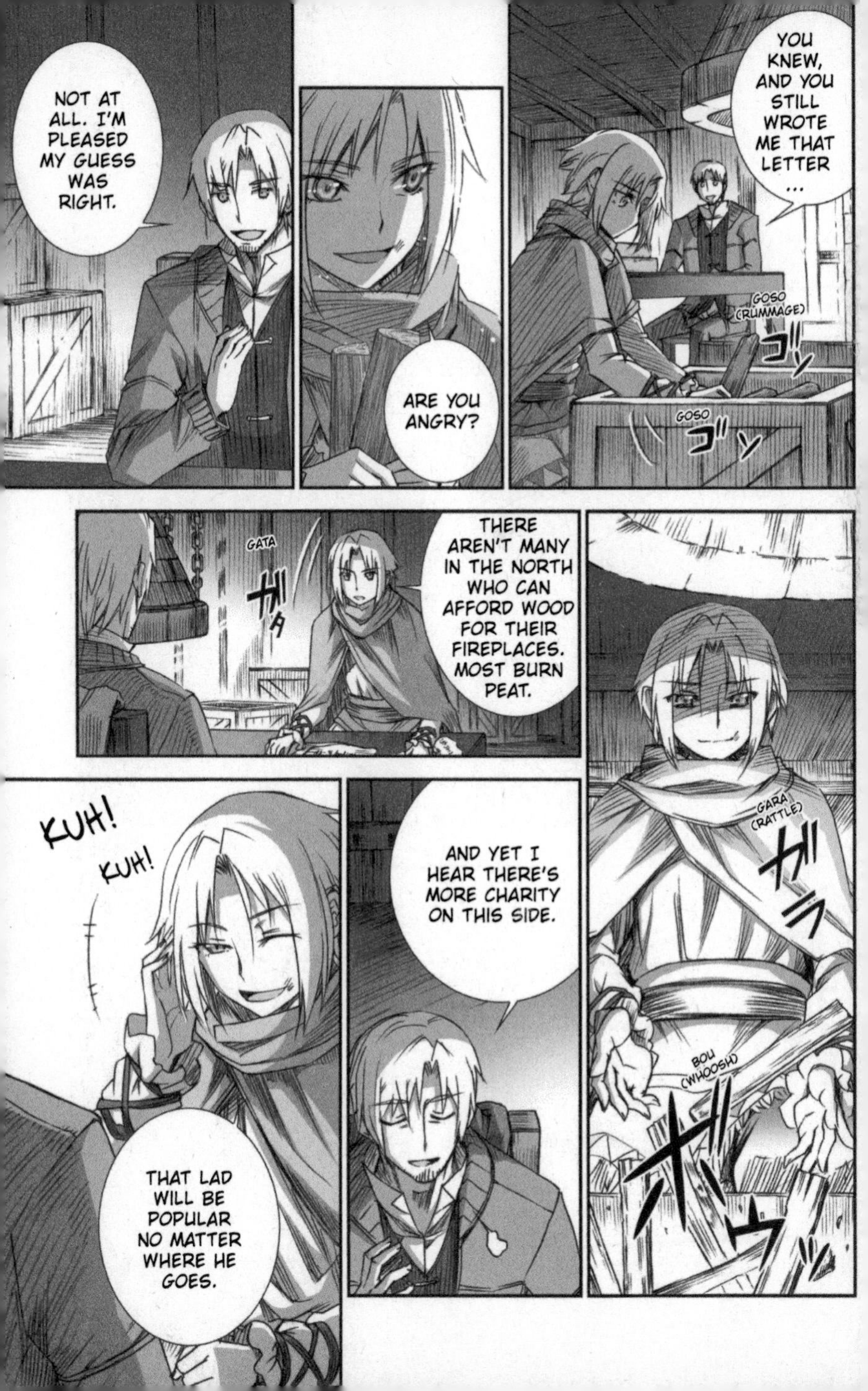
YOU KNEW, AND YOU STILL WROTE ME THAT LETTER...
GOSO (RUMMAGE)
GOSO
ARE YOU ANGRY?
NOT AT ALL. I'M PLEASED MY GUESS WAS RIGHT.
GARA (RATTLE)
BOU (WHOOSH)
GATA
THERE AREN'T MANY IN THE NORTH WHO CAN AFFORD WOOD FOR THEIR FIREPLACES. MOST BURN PEAT.
AND YET I HEAR THERE'S MORE CHARITY ON THIS SIDE.
KUH!
KUH!
THAT LAD WILL BE POPULAR NO MATTER WHERE HE GOES.

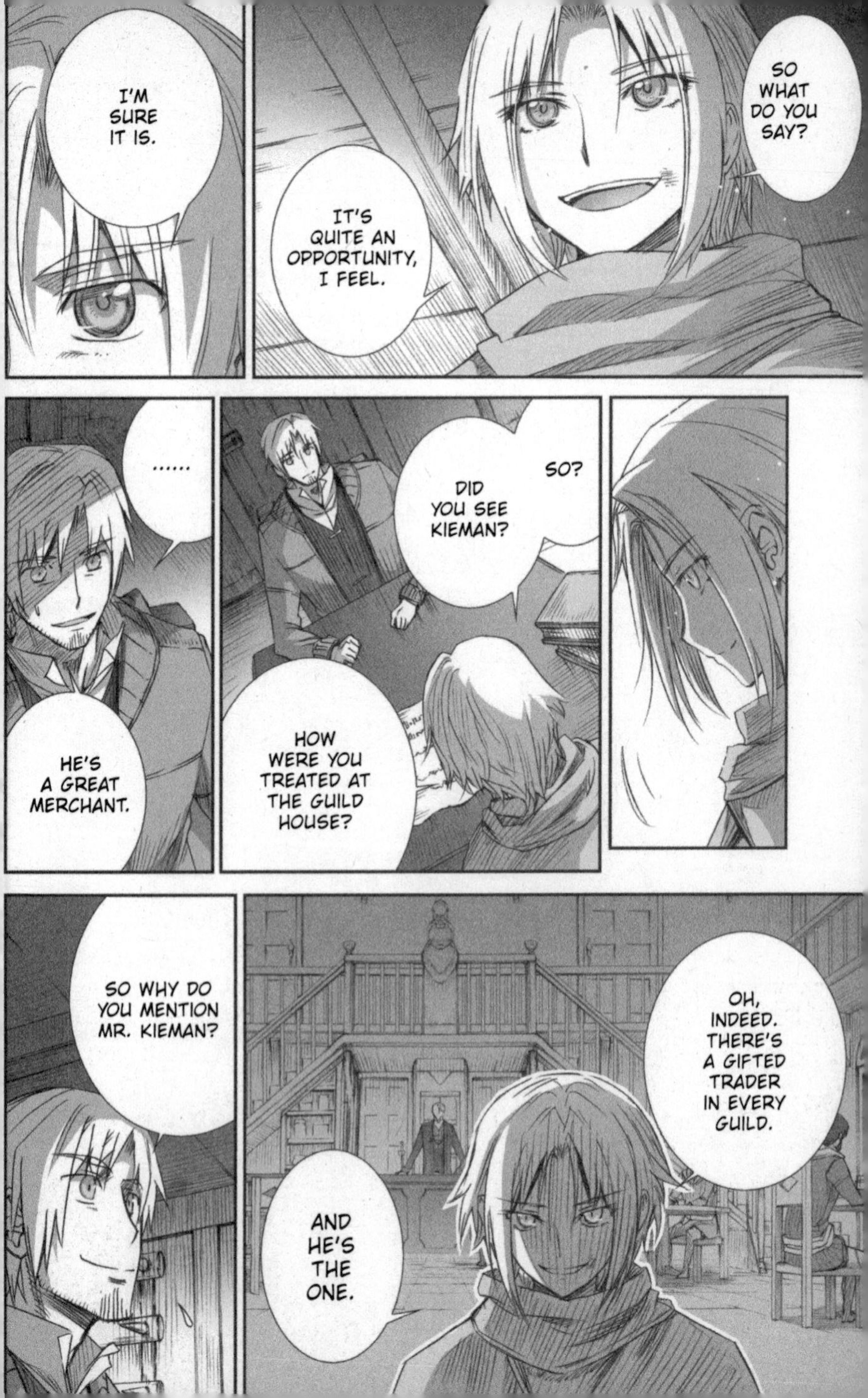
SO WHAT DO YOU SAY?
IT'S QUITE AN OPPORTUNITY, I FEEL.
I'M SURE IT IS.
SO?
DID YOU SEE KIEMAN?
HOW WERE YOU TREATED AT THE GUILD HOUSE?
......
HE'S A GREAT MERCHANT.
OH, INDEED. THERE'S A GIFTED TRADER IN EVERY GUILD.
AND HE'S THE ONE.
SO WHY DO YOU MENTION MR. KIEMAN?

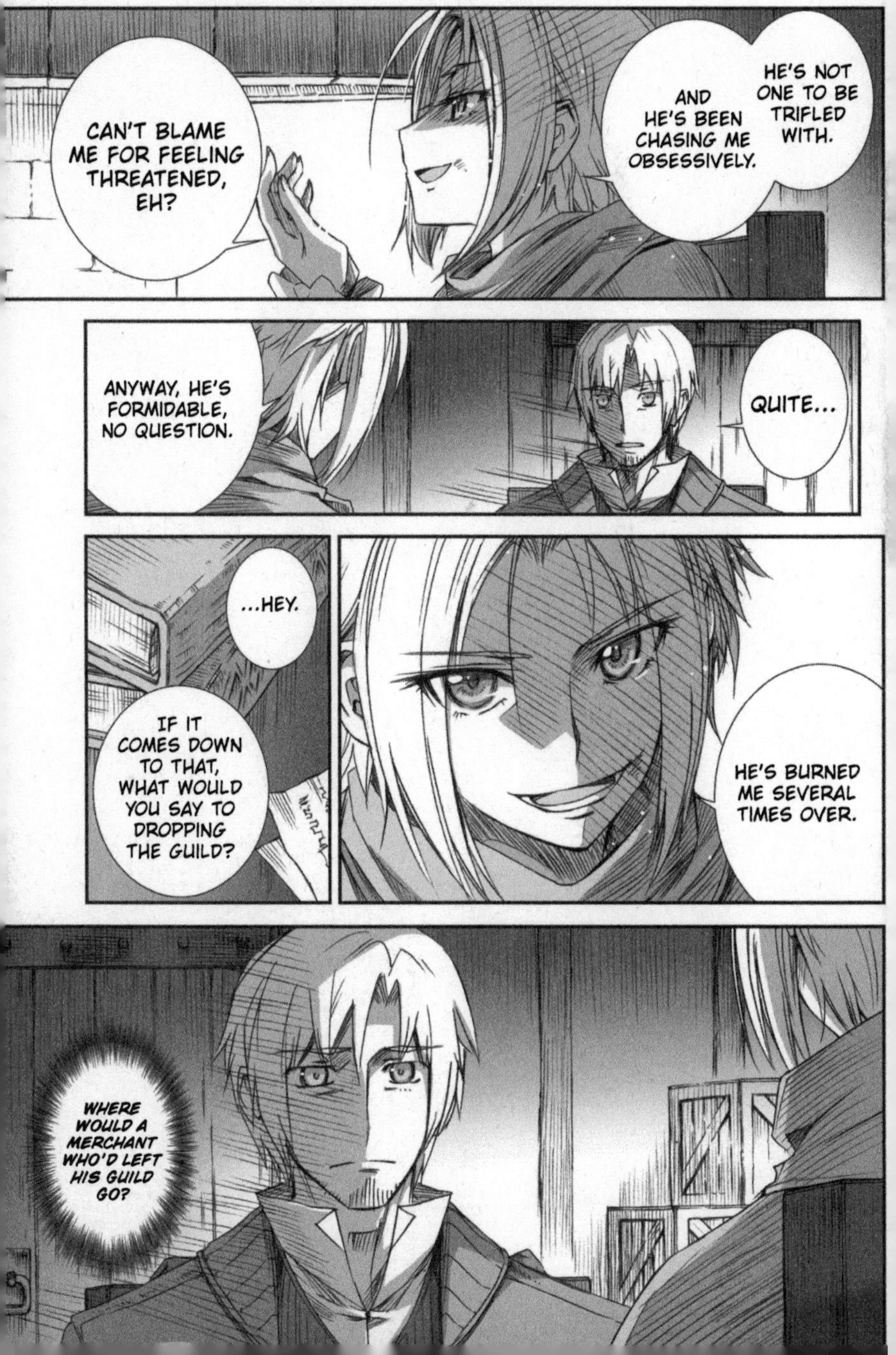
HE'S NOT ONE TO BE TRIFLED WITH.
AND HE'S BEEN CHASING ME OBSESSIVELY.
CAN'T BLAME ME FOR FEELING THREATENED, EH?
QUITE...
ANYWAY, HE'S FORMIDABLE, NO QUESTION.
HE'S BURNED ME SEVERAL TIMES OVER.
...HEY.
IF IT COMES DOWN TO THAT, WHAT WOULD YOU SAY TO DROPPING THE GUILD?
WHERE WOULD A MERCHANT WHO'D LEFT HIS GUILD GO?

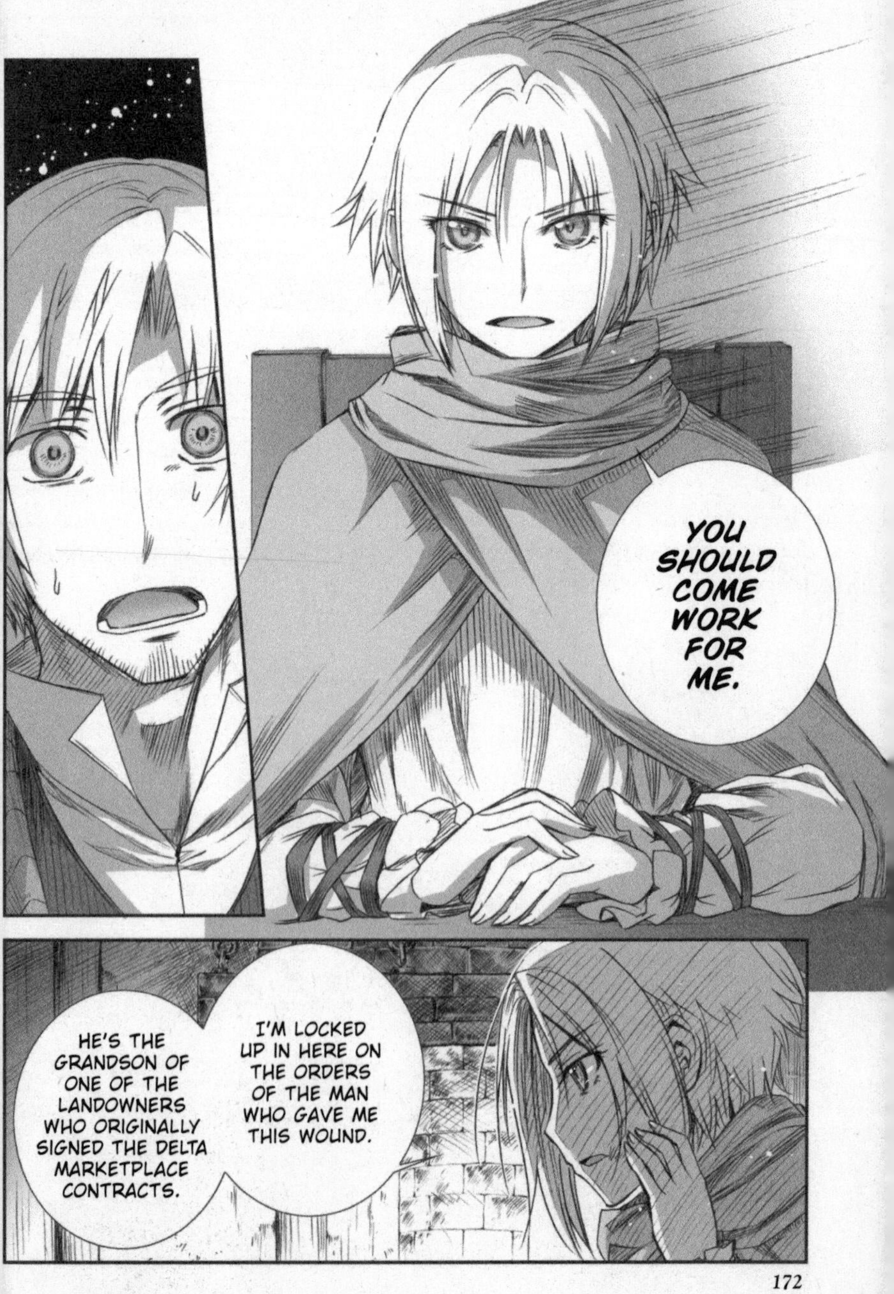
YOU SHOULD COME WORK FOR ME.
I'M LOCKED UP IN HERE ON THE ORDERS OF THE MAN WHO GAVE ME THIS WOUND.
HE'S THE GRANDSON OF ONE OF THE LANDOWNERS WHO ORIGINALLY SIGNED THE DELTA MARKETPLACE CONTRACTS.

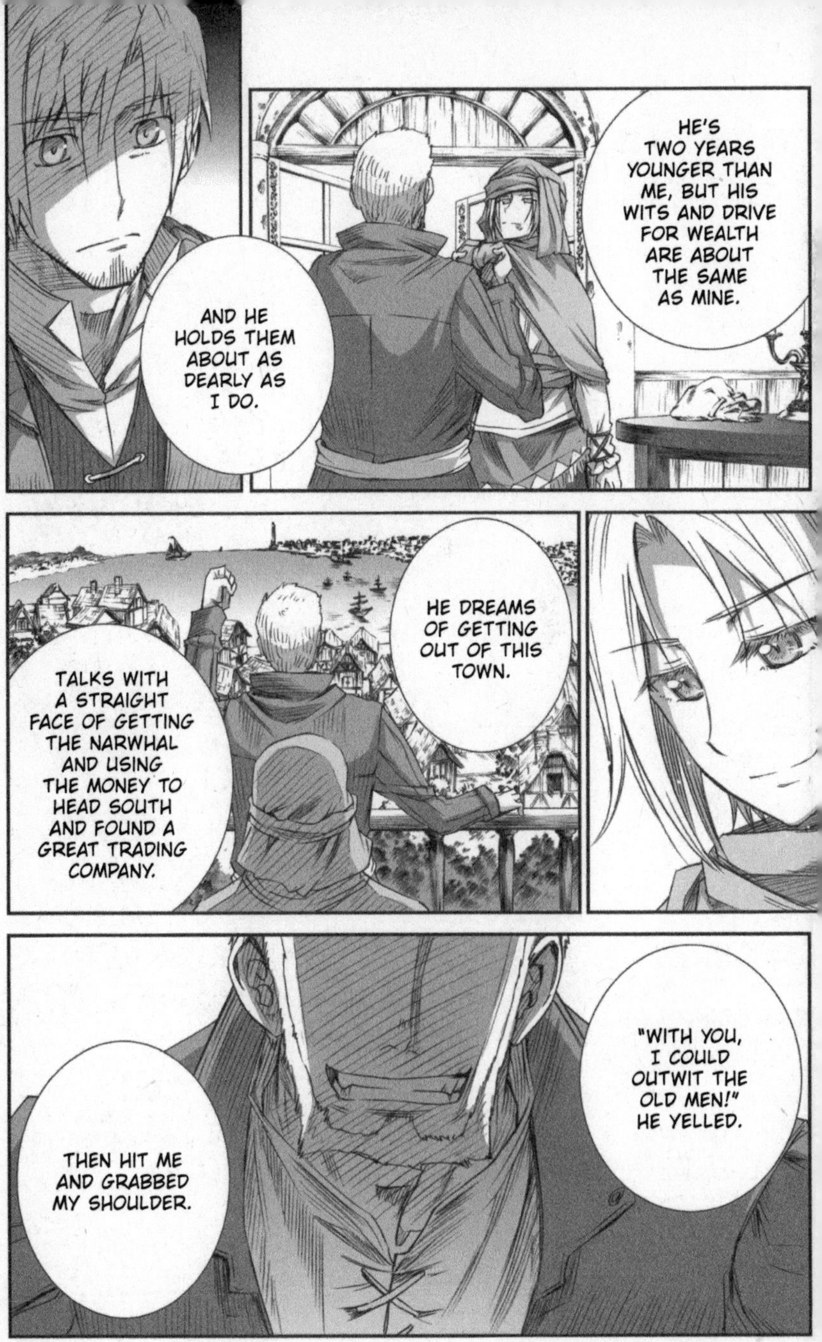
HE'S TWO YEARS YOUNGER THAN ME, BUT HIS WITS AND DRIVE FOR WEALTH ARE ABOUT THE SAME AS MINE.
AND HE HOLDS THEM ABOUT AS DEARLY AS I DO.
HE DREAMS OF GETTING OUT OF THIS TOWN.
TALKS WITH A STRAIGHT FACE OF GETTING THE NARWHAL AND USING THE MONEY TO HEAD SOUTH AND FOUND A GREAT TRADING COMPANY.
"WITH YOU, I COULD OUTWIT THE OLD MEN!" HE YELLED.
THEN HIT ME AND GRABBED MY SHOULDER.

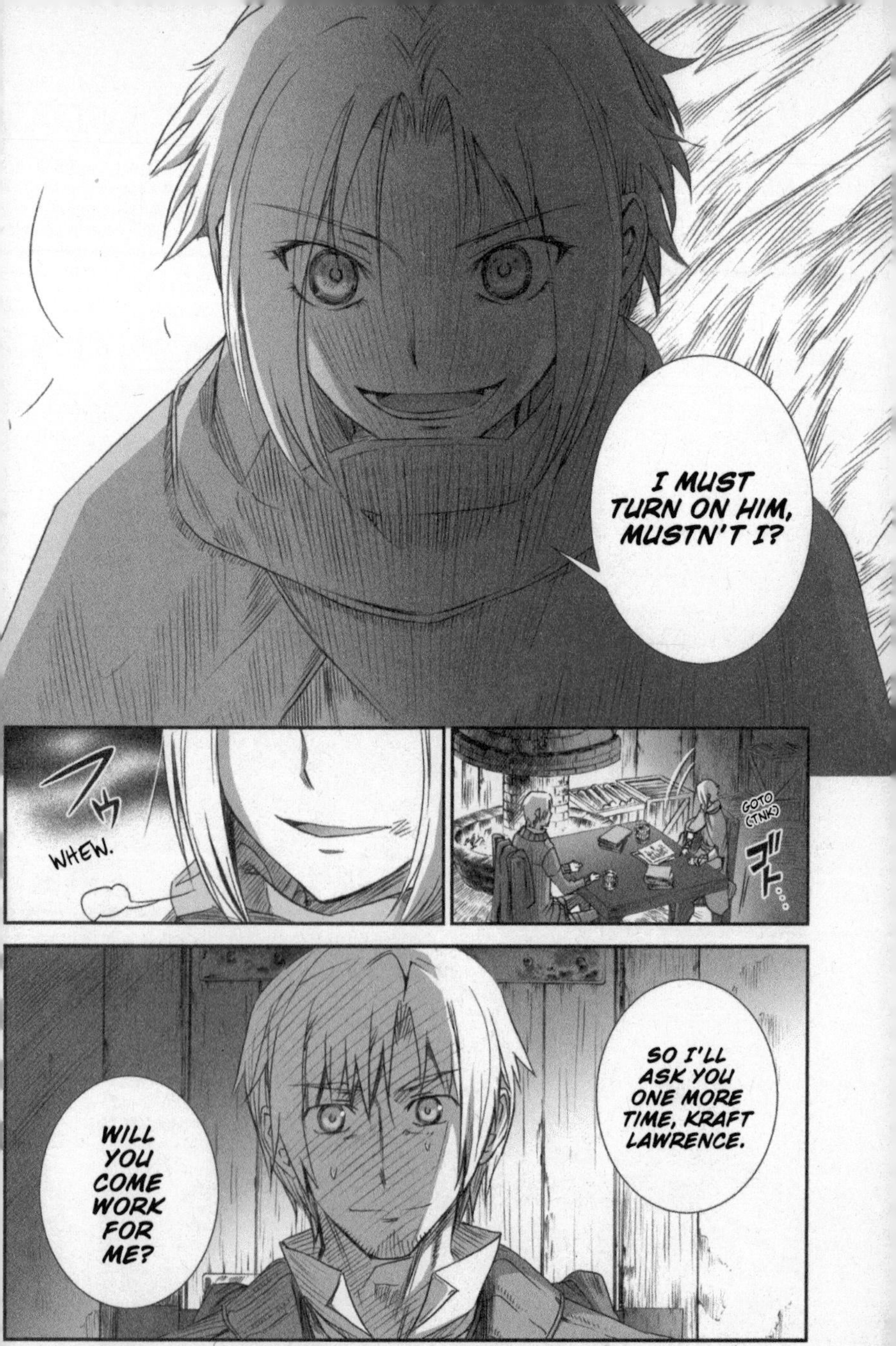
I MUST TURN ON HIM, MUSTN'T I?
ゴト...
GOTO (TNK)
フゥ
WHEW.
SO I'LL ASK YOU ONE MORE TIME, KRAFT LAWRENCE.
WILL YOU COME WORK FOR ME?

Special Thanks!!

MR. ITTOUHEI OKAMOTO, MR. TENTSU TOI, MR. YAKKUN, MR. N-TA, MR. A.

To be continued in Volume 10...

I turn around, and suddenly we're at Volume 9! Koume-san's Eve is so clever and surprisingly adorable that she makes my heart beat faster! I can't take my eyes off the story. Hang in there!

支倉凍砂

ISUNA HASEKURA

SPICE & WOLF

Congratulations on Volume 9 going on sale! Now that Eve's finally shown up, I'm more sucked into the story than ever before. I can't wait to see how the manga version of the story takes shape.

JYUU AYAKURA

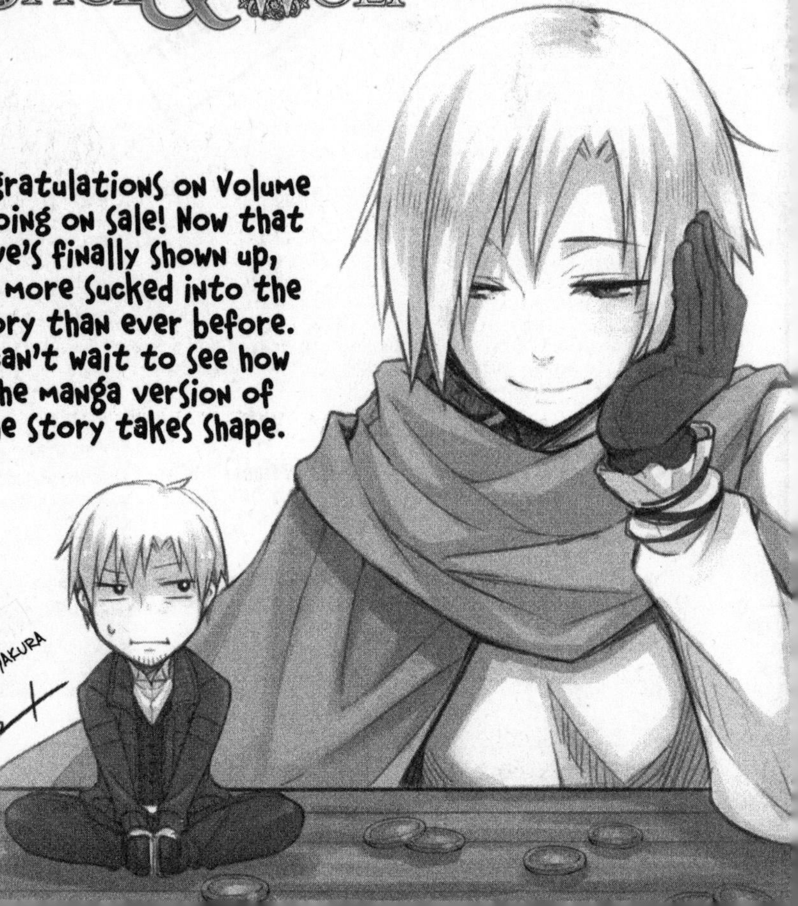

SPICE & WOLF ❾

ISUNA HASEKURA
KEITO KOUME
CHARACTER DESIGN:
JYUU AYAKURA

TRANSLATION: PAUL STARR

LETTERING: TERRI DELGADO

OOKAMI TO KOUSHINRYOU VOL. 9
©ISUNA HASEKURA/KEITO KOUME 2013
EDITED BY ASCII MEDIA WORKS
FIRST PUBLISHED IN JAPAN IN 2013 BY
KADOKAWA CORPORATION, TOKYO.
ENGLISH TRANSLATION RIGHTS ARRANGED WITH
KADOKAWA CORPORATION, TOKYO,
THROUGH TUTTLE-MORI AGENCY, INC., TOKYO.

TRANSLATION © 2014 BY HACHETTE BOOK GROUP

EN PRESS

ISBN: 978-0-316-29487-4

10 9 8 7 6 5 4 3 2

BVG

PRINTED IN THE UNITED STATES OF AMERICA